The first step is the last step.

—J. KRISHNAMURTI

K R I S H N A M U R T I

1 0 0 y e a r s

E V E L Y N E   B L A U

A   J O O S T   E L F F E R S   B O O K

S T E W A R T ,   T A B O R I   &   C H A N G ,   N E W   Y O R K

PHOTOGRAPHY CREDITS

Many of the earlier photographers whose
pictures appear in this book are unknown.
Their photographs are courtesy of the
Krishnamurti Foundation of America Archives.

Courtesy of The Academy of Motion Picture
Arts and Sciences and Cecil B. Demille Estate
    page 57
Cecil Beaton
    page 161
The Bettmann Archive, Inc.
    pages 58, 67, 78, 110, 111, 231
UPI/Bettmann Newsphotos
    pages 64, 105, 113
Evelyne Blau
    pages 4, 92, 127, 128, 138, 139, 141, 181,
    191, 199,216, 224, 225, 228, 231, 260, 262
Courtesy Linda Lee Cadwel
    page 222
Asit Chandmal
    page 221
Eloise Coyne
    page 170
Dale Duffy
    page 171
Mark Edwards
    pages 153, 154, 180, 268
Ralph T. Gardner
    page 90
D. M. Gawand
    page 133
M. A. Hamid
    pages 130, 200, 201, 209, 210, 252
Elijah David Herschler
    page 124, 157
Michael Mendizza
    cover, endleaves, and pages 9, 34, 35, 43,
    129,136, 137, 164, 166, 167,186, 187, 196,
    213, 234, 249, 251
Helen Nearing Collection
    pages 49, 55
Dawn Peterson
    page 65
Stanley Rogers
    pages 35, 38, 39
Fabrizio Ruspoli
    pages 8, 11, 12, 16, 24
Schell
    page 114
Earl Scott
    pages 240, 241, 248
Carey Smoot
    page 194
Timothy Teague
    pages 195, 197
Phillip van Pallandt
    page 46
D.R.D. Wadia
    title page
Beatrice Wood Collection
    page 97
Mary Zimbalist
    pages 177, 188, 217

A JOOST ELFFERS BOOK

TEXT COPYRIGHT © 1995 BY Evelyne Blau

KRISHNAMURTI QUOTATIONS COPYRIGHT © PRE-1968 BY
Krishnamurti Foundation of America

KRISHNAMURTI QUOTATIONS COPYRIGHT © POST-1968 BY
Krishnamurti Foundation Trust

DESIGNED BY Karen Davidson

PRODUCED BY Karen Davidson and Alice Wong

COPYEDITED BY Josh Gosciak and Bill Koehnlein

PUBLISHED BY Stewart, Tabori & Chang
575 Broadway, New York, New York 10012

DISTRIBUTED IN CANADA BY General Publishing Co. Ltd.
30 Lesmill Road, Don Mills, Ontario, Canada M3B 2T6

LIBRARY OF CONGRESS CATALOGING-IN-PUBLICATION DATA

Blau, Evelyne.
        Krishnamurti:100 years / by Evelyne Blau
        p.   cm.
Includes bibliographical references and index.
ISBN 1-55670-407-0: $29.95
1. Krishnamurti. J. (jiddu), 1895-1986. 1. Title
B5134.K754B57   1995
181' .4- - dc20
[B]   94-47595
                                                       CIP

PRINTED in Singapore

10 9 8 7 6 5 4 3 2 1

ACKNOWLEDGEMENTS

THIS BOOK IS THE WORK OF MANY PEOPLE. Their significant recollections and comments span the 100 years since Krishnamurti's birth and consist of writings of the past, as well as those of the middle period and contemporary times. Their contributions form the foundation of this work. Profound gratitude is due to everyone involved. Their names are listed in the table of contents and each is greatly and equally valued.

The Krishnamurti Foundation of America, the Krishnamurti Foundation Trust Ltd. of England, and the Krishnamurti Foundation India have kindly allowed the use of a wealth of writings by Krishnamurti as well as archival photographs ranging throughout his life. This book has been immeasurably supported by their generous cooperation. The Krishnamurti Foundation of America Archives and library have helped greatly in research. Thanks are due to Ivan Berkowitz, Douglas Evans, Tom Heggestad and Dawn Peterson. Chari Petrowski made special efforts. Professor Lloyd Williams is thanked for his contribution of needed material. I am especially indebted to Mark Lee for his invaluable help. Aaron Marking, Leslie Francis and Nandini Lee valiantly typed hours of transcripts. Curtis Wong secured a valuable article. Gabriele Blackburn contributed needed research. Special thanks are due to Michael Mendizza— many of the interviews published here are a result of our joint work: he as director and the author as producer of two documentaries on Krishnamurti. His photography is also seen in this book. Robin and Stephen Larsen are gratefully acknowledged for their contribution of the Joseph Campbell material. Earl Scott kindly allowed the use of his photographs of the Ojai Talks. Particular appreciation is due to Radha Burnier, president of the Theosophical Society for graciously making available needed early materials. Helen Hooker, as always, is the spirit of generosity. Thanks are due to Laura Huxley for permission to use the Aldous Huxley material. The scholarly contributions made by Mary Lutyens and Pupul Jayakar through their detailed biographies is significant. They form the foundation of much of the research for this work and I am greatly in their debt. Laurie Clewell has been an invaluable support. This book would not have been possible without the dedicated professionalism of Carole Koneff. She has tirelessly typed and retyped the manuscript. Her computer wizardry has kept every word in its marvelous memory and in perfect order. Thank you. A tribute to Joost Elffers who was the first to believe in this book, its vision and purpose. His associate, Karen Davidson, brings the gift of inspired design and tireless dedication to this work. Everything in its right place, as Krishnamurti would say. Alice Wong is thanked for her valuable suggestions. A special salute to Lena Tabori, who unfailingly saw the importance of a commemorative volume honoring the Krishnamurti centennial and guided it through its publication. Lastly, loving appreciation and thanks are due to my husband, Louis Blau, whose love, patience and support have made it all possible.

CONTENTS

PREFACE

1 PART I — THE FIRST STEP

4   Jiddu Narayaniah
5   Krishnamurti's diary
6   Helena Petrovna Blavatsky
7   Annie Besant
8   Charles Webster Leadbeater
10   Krishnamurti on the beach
11   Russell Balfour Clarke
13   Krishnamurti's diary
15   Krishnamurti's diary
17   The initiation; *At the Feet of the Master*
20   The brothers' first visit to England
21   Lady Emily Lutyens
27   James Montgomery Flagg
29   The brothers' second visit to England
29   Nitya's illness
32   Ojai and the pepper tree experience
37   The death of Nitya
44   Baron Phillip van Pallandt
48   Helen Knothe Nearing
57   Sidney Field
62   Krishnamurti's poetry
64   Joseph Campbell
66   Antoine Bourdelle
67   Leopold Stokowski
78   Dr. Hedda Bolgar
85   *Truth is a Pathless Land*; The Order of the Star dissolves

89 PART II — THE LAST STEP

91   Mary Lutyens
92   Theodore Besterman
94   Beatrice Wood
101   Harry Wolfe
104   George Bernard Shaw and the New Zealand radio ban
108   Vanda Scaravelli
109   Anita Loos
110   Aldous Huxley
111   Lex Muller
112   Baron Phillip van Pallandt
115   Sidney Field
116   William Quinn
124   Benjamin Weinniger
127   Ahalya Chari
130   Pupul Jayakar
139   Achyut Patwardhan
140   Sunanda Patwardhan, Ph.D.
144   Pama Patwardhan

146   Ingrahm Smith
148   Doris Pratt
149   Mary Cadogan
154   Dorothy Simmons
157   David Bohm, Ph.D.
169   Howard Fast
172   Asha Lee, M.D.
176   T. K. V. Desikachar
180   Alan Rowlands
181   Alan Hooker
184   Erna Lilliefelt; the formation of the contemporary Krishnamurti Foundations
189   Giddu Narayanan
191   David Shainberg, M.D.
193   Henry Miller
194   R.E. Mark Lee
198   Julie Desnick
199   Prof. P. Krishna
202   Angel Patrick Boyar
208   Michael Krohnen
212   Alan Kishbaugh
214   Jean Michel Maroger
216   Friedrich Grohe
218   Alan W. Anderson
221   Juan Colell
222   Robert Colet and Bruce Lee; The martial arts
224   Professor S. Rinpoche
226   Hillary Peter Rodrigues, Ph.D.
228   Michael Mendizza
230   Alasdair Coyne
233   Deepak Chopra, M.D.
        Lois M. Hobson
234   Sarjit Siddoo, M.D.
237   Van Morrison
238   Larry Dossey, M.D.
        Shigatoshi Takahashi
242   Mary Zimbalist
249   Mary Lutyens
253   Gary M. Deutsch, M.D.
255   Gary M. Deutsch, M.D. (continued)
256   Asit Chandmal
258   Evelyne Blau
259   Radhika Herzberger, Ph.D.
262   Evelyne Blau (continued)
264   Gary M. Deutsch, M.D. (continued)
269   Michael Krohnen

271   ENDNOTES

274   BIBLIOGRAPHY

276   INDEX

The mind that has put its house in order is silent. That silence has no cause and, therefore, has no end. Only that which has a cause can end. That silence—which has no ending —is absolutely necessary, because it is only in that silence that there is no movement of thought. It is only in that silence that that which is sacred, that which is nameless, and that which is not measurable by thought, is. And that which is, is the most sacred. That is meditation.

—PUBLIC TALK, MADRAS, NOVEMBER 29, 1981

OVER THE PAST CENTURY Krishnamurti has
touched our lives in profound, yet often hidden ways.
Although known to thousands upon thousands around the
world, to many he remains well below the level of instant recognition.
That he influenced many cannot be doubted as will be seen by the depth of
his impact on contributors to this book. Equally striking is the wide range
of people with whom he came in contact. They are authors, academics,
musicians, actors, scientists, business people—those from all walks of life.

Krishnamurti lived much of his life in an era of high technology and
instant communication, which clearly separates him from great teachers of
the past, whose sayings and teachings were often committed to memory or
were recorded hundreds of years after their death. Often those memories
were faulty, or the teachings not well understood and so strayed from the
original intent of the teacher. It is our good fortune that the words and
works of Krishnamurti have not been changed and are preserved in
Krishnamurti archives and libraries around the world.

During his lifetime, friends and Krishnamurti foundation members
were imbued with the need to plumb the depths of his teaching and incor-
porate their understanding into daily living. That was their main focus.
During his later days, the yearly round of his talks, in India, England,
Switzerland and the United States necessarily directed their attention to
needful things: preparation for the talks themselves and the thousands who
would flock to them, seeing to the schools, in addition to arranging for
publication of his works. For more than twenty years it seemed as if that
round would never stop. However, all things come to an end. A feeling for
history and the obligation to pass on to others not only Krishnamurti's
work itself but also a sense of the time and the impact on those fortunate
enough to have known him, as well as those who knew him through his
teachings, impelled the author to undertake a series of oral history interviews. These interviews were inspired by the example of close family
friend, Alex Haley, historian and author. Alex often told of the importance
of listening on the porch of a summer evening, to the stories told by the
elders. Their recollections of family history were told and retold by grand-
mothers, aunts and cousins. Those stories—to which were added travel
and research—became the book, *Roots*. It was during that period that the
importance of oral history became overwhelmingly apparent. It was history—alive, direct, and immediate. The "witnesses" to Krishnamurti's history have important stories to tell.

A series of informal conversations was begun and continues to this
day. The simple and unobtrusive technology of the tape recorder allowed
for recollections unaffectedly retold. Many who spoke, contemporaries of
Krishnamurti, are gone now, but their legacy lives on. Among those who
knew him from the earliest days was Russell Balfour Clarke, Krishnamurti's
first tutor, who was interviewed years ago in India when he was well in his
nineties. He was present at Adyar, Madras when Krishnamurti was "found"

on the beach at the Bay of Bengal in 1909. Baron Phillip van Pallandt, who many years ago generously gave his castle, Eerde, and thousands of acres of surrounding land for the young Indian's work, was also in his nineties when he was interviewed at DeWeezenladen Hospital, The Netherlands, in 1978. These, among others, are the "witnesses" whose priceless recollections form the basis of this book.

The oral history remembrances have been called "conversations". Others, who participated in the making of the documentary film *Krishnamurti: With A Silent Mind* are called "interviews". All have been conducted by the author except for the discussion between Krishnamurti and Leopold Stokowski in Part I.

Several contributors to this book have given their articles titles which are not included in the text: Alan W. Anderson, *On Krishnamurti's Teachings: An Ongoing Personal Response*; T.K.V. Desikachar, *Krishnaji—The Student and the Teacher*; Friedrich Grohe, from *The Beauty of the Mountain*; Michael Krohnen, *A Great Man who could Laugh at Himself*; Jean-Michel Maroger, *Krishnamurti, A Fundamental Discovery*.

In Kirshnamurti's early days, the young boy and man was called Krishna, as a shortening of his rather long name. Later he was called Krishnaji, which in India is an honorific appellation rather than a diminutive, as is often supposed. However, when referring to himself, (usually in the third person) he was simply "K" and that name and Krishnaji were freely interchanged by those around him.

It will be noted that there are fewer pictures of Krishnamurti from the middle period of his life. He had been extensively photographed during the early days and he retreated from having his picture taken during his middle years. His innate modesty even extended to experimenting with speaking from behind a screen or curtain at a certain time. Eventually that was seen, by him, as false and he came out from behind the screen.

It was also relatively late before he used amplification or the recording of his talks. They were taken down in shorthand and transcribed for publication as "Verbatim Reports" from 1933 to 1967. Later, his talks, dialogues and question and answer sessions were gathered into books, many of which are for sale in various languages in bookshops around the world.

Although Krishnamurti always gave his talks in English he was also fluent in French and Italian, and spoke some Spanish. His native tongue, Telugu was forgotten through lack of use, but he had a fondness for Sanskrit, and especially its chants.

Later in his life Krishnamurti accepted the impositions of video and film technology with good grace and was unendingly patient with its demands.

The impact on the 20th-century of a life as complex as that of Krishnamurti asks to be told from different points of view—through many voices. A single one cannot do it justice. This book, through its witnesses, speaks with many voices and although they may not totally convey the full flower of this remarkable man and his teaching, it is hoped that the reader might catch a fleeting scent of the perfume.

It has been difficult to eliminate or cut down what has been said by the witnesses, there is such a wealth of insight in the many articles, interviews and conversations they have contributed. For clarity writings and quotations by Krishnamurti in this book are printed in blue. The paring down of Krishnamurti's voluminous writings has been painful. One would like to include them all in their marvelous diversity. Fortunately, all of the writings of Krishnamurti are available in the libraries and archives of the Krishnamurti Foundations in India, England, Holland and the United States. Krishnamurti Committees which exist throughout Europe, Canada and South America also have extensive holdings.

Krishnamurti lived his life, for the most part, surrounded by people. Yet with all the attention focused on him, he remains essentially a mystery. Elusive, sometimes ambiguous about who he was, all of the scrutiny of the past one hundred years has not been able to probe the heart of that mystery. Perhaps it is best so. As he said, "It is the teachings which are important, not the teacher."

—EVELYNE BLAU, LOS ANGELES, 1995

PART ONE: *The first step...*

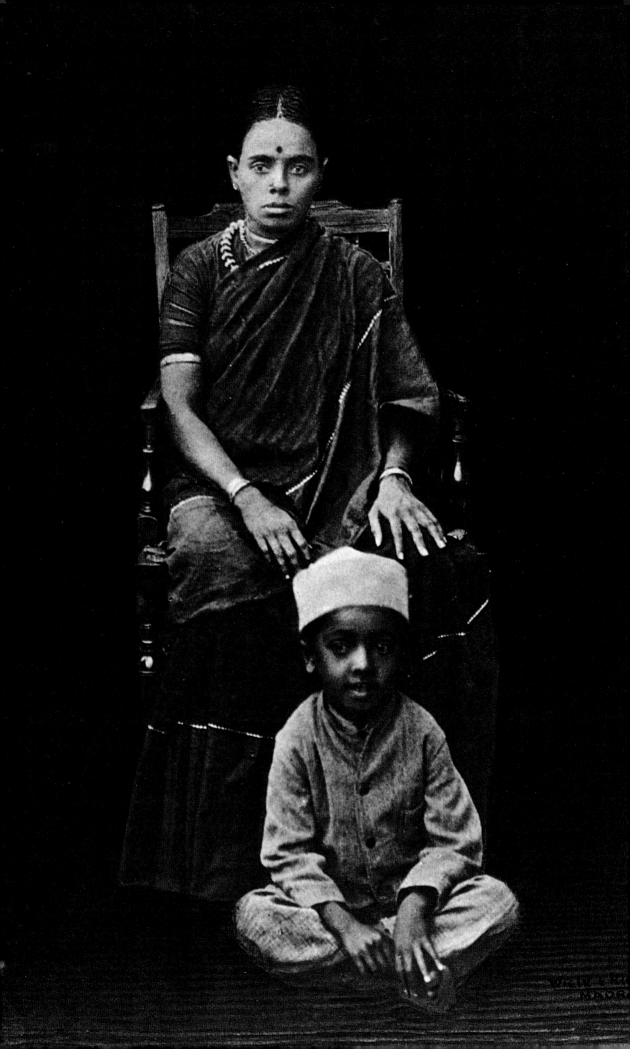

A guest am I

In this world of transient things,

Unfettered by the entanglements thereof.

I am of no country,

No boundaries hold me.

—*THE IMMORTAL FRIEND*, 1928

OUT OF THE MIST OF MYTH and memory the story of Krishnamurti emerges like a long-forgotten dream, the story of a slight boy, lost to the world, but found on the beach at the Bay of Bengal. The events that took place, beginning with his birth in 1895, do indeed have a mythic quality, each passing year adding a new layer of understanding, while retaining a central core of mystery.

The tale of the eighth child of an orthodox Brahmin family begins with his birth and six days later his naming. The cow-herd god Sri Krishna was himself an eighth child, and honoring that Hindu tradition the baby was named Krishnamurti (Krishna incarnate).

The mother, Sanjeevama, was a devoutly religious woman, said to be psychic, one who could see the color of peoples auras. This eighth child of hers, she intuited, was to be a rare and special human being. She insisted over the objections of her husband, Narayaniah, that the child be born in the puja room of their tiny house in the south of India, at Madanapalle. This was an extraordinary event. The puja room, the special sanctified heart of the home, was only to be entered for worship after a ritual bath and the wearing of clean clothes. For a birth to take place in that room would be considered a pollution, but Sanjeevama was adamant and shortly after midnight—at 12:30 a.m., May 12, 1895 (May 11 on the Indian calendar), the assisting midwife called to the waiting husband, "Sirsodayam!", meaning the head is visible.

According to Indian tradition, that is the precise moment of birth. In order to cast the child's horoscope, the exact time was necessary. So it was that into the world in that dark, cramped room came the infant, beloved of his mother, amid the flickering of tiny oil lamps.

The following day Kumara Shrowthulu, the noted astrologer of the area predicted that Krishnamurti would be a great teacher but only after contending with mountainous obstacles. As Krishnamurti grew to boyhood, that possibility seemed more and more remote as the empty, dreamy, and apparently dim-witted child seemed more like his retarded youngest brother Sadanand. It was his next younger brother, Nityananda, who was the lively and intelligent child who, for all their differences of character, was devoted to his older brother. It was he who gently led Krishnamurti home when he would be found standing by the roadside enfolded in dreams.

As the boy matured he was sickly and at age two barely survived a seri-

THE EARLIEST
KNOWN PICTURE
OF KRISHNAMURTI
WITH HIS MOTHER,
SANJEEVAMA,
CIRCA 1900.

ous attack of malaria. He clung to his mother and indicated a deeply religious bent, going often with her to the temple. Because of frequent fevers and bleeding of the nose and mouth he often missed school, once for as long as a year. An inauspicious beginning for his scholastic life.

At six the boy went through the "sacred thread ceremony," the Upanayanama. This ceremony, an induction into the rites of priesthood, is the first step in the life of a Brahmin boy—all of whom are born priests. The father, Jiddu Narayaniah, described it thus:

The boy was bathed and clothed in everything new—very rich clothes are used if the parents can afford them. Krishnamurti was brought in and placed upon my knee, while on my outstretched hand, I supported a silver tray strewn with grains of rice. His mother, sitting beside me took the index finger of the boy's right hand and with it traced the sacred word AUM. . . .[2]

The family had moved to nearby Cudappah when the unimaginable occurred in 1905. When Krishnamurti was ten years old, his mother died. Bereft, the boy clung closer than ever to his younger brother, the bright and loving Nitya. Narayaniah describes that following her death Krishnamurti frequently saw his mother:

We are in the habit of putting on a leaf a portion of the food prepared for the household, and placing it near the spot where the deceased was lying, and we did so accordingly in the case of my wife. Between 9 and 10 a.m. of the third day, Krishna was going to have his bath. He went into the bathroom, and had only poured a few lotas of water over his head, when he came running out, unclothed [though wearing a loincloth] and dripping wet. The house in which I lived at Cudappah was a long, narrow house, the rooms running one at the back of the other like the compartments of a train. As Krishna passed me running from the bathroom, I caught his hand and asked him what was the matter. The boy said his mother had been in the bathroom with him, and as she came out he accompanied her to see what she was going to do. I then said: "Don't you remember that your mother was carried to the burning ground?" "Yes," he said, "I remember, but I want to see where she is going now." I let him go and followed him. He went to the third room and stopped. Here was the place where my wife's saris used to be stretched for drying overnight. Krishna stood intently gazing at something, and I asked him what was going on. He said, "My mother is removing her wet clothes, and putting on dry ones." He then went into the next room, and sat down near the leaf on which the food was placed. I stood by him some minutes, and he said his mother was eating. By and by he arose and went towards the stairs, and still I followed him. He stopped half-way up, and said he couldn't see her any more.[3]

At eighteen years of age, when Krishnamurti was living at Varengeville in Normandy and was not too distant from the events of childhood, he began an account of his earliest remembered days. He entitled this, *Fifty Years of My Life*, apparently intending to continue with the succeeding years. He never did. However, the dozen and some pages contain his recollections of important events in his life.

KRISHNAMURTI'S BIRTHPLACE, MADANAPALLE, ANDHRA PRADESH, INDIA. (PHOTO WAS TAKEN IN 1988. THE BUILDING HAS SINCE BEEN PURCHASED BY THE KRISHNAMURTI FOUNDATION OF INDIA AND HAS BEEN RESTORED FOR USE AS A LIBRARY AND STUDY CENTER.)

Fifty years of my life.

Varengeville
July 10th 1913

The happiest memories of my childhood centre round my dear Mother, who gave us all the loving care for which Indian mothers are well-known. I cannot say that I was particularly happy at school, for the teachers were not very kind & gave me lessons, which were too hard for me. I enjoyed games as long as they were not too rough as I had very delicate health. My mother's death in 1905 deprived my brothers and myself of the one who loved & cared for us most, & my father was too much occupied with his business to pay much attention to us. I led the usual life as an ordinary Indian youth until I came to Adyar in 1908. Adyar was of special interest to me as my father used to attend the conventions of the Theosophical Society there. He also held meetings in our house at Madanapalle for the study of Theosophy & I learnt about Adyar from my mother & from him. My mother had a puja-room where she worshipped regularly; in the room were pictures of the Indian Deities & also a photograph of Mrs. Besant in Indian dress sitting cross-legged on a chowki or small platform on which was a tiger-skin. I was generally at home while my brothers were at school, for I suffered much from fever—in fact almost every day, & I often went into the puja-room about noon when she performed her daily ceremonies. She would then talk to me about Mrs. Besant & about Karma & Reincarnation, and also read to me from the Mahābharata & Rāmayana & from other Indian Scriptures. I was only about 7 or 8 years of age, so I could not understand much, but I think I felt much that I could not actually understand.

I T WAS TWO YEARS LATER, IN 1907, that Narayaniah was required to retire on a meager pension of Rupees 112 per month, just one half of his former salary. Although he was an orthodox Brahmin, Narayaniah joined the Theosophical Society in 1882, which welcomed all religions. He wrote to Annie Besant, president of the Theosophical Society, requesting permission to live on the compound grounds in exchange for his work as assistant to the recording secretary of the Esoteric Section of the Theosophical Society. After a series of refusals by Besant, on grounds that there was no school close enough for the boys to attend, she consented and the family moved to a small house just outside the compound walls.[4]

THE ROOTS OF THEOSOPHY are long and deep, going back centuries before the founding of the present Theosophical Society in 1875 in New York City. The Society's creators were Helena Petrovna Blavatsky and Colonel Henry Steel Olcott. Olcott, an imposing, bearded man who had seen service in the American Civil War and had been part of a three-man investigatory body looking into the assassination of Abraham Lincoln, was deeply interested in the passions of the period, clairvoyance and spiritualism. Overheated accounts were circulating of unusual occurrences, sightings of phantoms at the Eddy family farmhouse in Chittenden, Vermont, several hundred miles from New York City. Journalists from the area eagerly reported on "spooks and ghosts" to a breathless public. In part prompted by his own interest and in part functioning as a journalist, Olcott found his way to the Eddy homestead. It was there that he met Helena Petrovna Blavatsky for the first time.

She was dressed in a scarlet Garibaldi shirt, her "massive Calmuck face" with pale, hypnotic eyes surrounded by a thick, blonde mop of hair cut above the shoulders—"it stood out from her head silken soft and crinkled to the roots like the fleece of a Cotswald ewe." Not the usual picture of nineteenth-century femininity. Madame and her French-speaking companion stepped outside to roll a cigarette in the afternoon air. As she searched for matches Olcott stepped forward, "Permettez-moi Madame," and struck a match. As they strolled the grounds, he with his pipe, she with ever-present cigarette, they found much in common.

The larger-than-life, somewhat notorious Blavatsky, of the noble Dolgorukov and military Von Hahn families of Russia, was monumental in form and in powers of thought. She scandalized and intrigued all who knew her, with tales of riding Cossack horses bareback over the Steppes, traveling alone to Egypt and Tibet in search of highly evolved occult "Masters of Wisdom," and precipitating letters and objects seemingly out of the blue. Her travels were extraordinary for a woman unaccompanied in the nineteenth century, but Helena was an exceptional woman. She claimed to have contacted and studied with gurus, shamans, and supernatural masters in hidden mountain fastnessses. In Olcott she found a stabilizing center of gravity after years on the edge, living as best she could with questionable mediumistic demonstrations and shady "precipitations." This complex woman, in large part genuine seer and visionary but with the whiff of the charlatan, together with Olcott, founded the Theosophical Society. Its principals were in essence: To seek truth in the ancient religions of the East; to investigate the unexplained laws of nature; and to pro

HELENA PETROVNA BLAVATSKY FOUNDED THE THEOSOPHICAL SOCIETY IN 1875. THE LARGER THAN LIFE, SOMEWHAT NOTORIOUS BLAVATSKY WAS MONUMENTAL IN FORM AND IN POWERS OF THOUGHT.

mote the universal brotherhood of man without regard to race, creed, sex, or caste. Noble ideals at the flood tide of masculine Christian missionary zeal when religions other than Christianity were accorded little respect! The fulfillment of these principles Blavatsky stated "…will burst asunder the iron fetters of creeds and dogmas, of social and caste prejudices; break down racial and national antipathies and barriers, and open the way to the practical realization of the Brotherhood of all men."

With the establishment of the Theosophical Society, the newly centered Helena Petrovna Blavatsky—H.P.B., as she was called—embarked on her massive master works *Isis Unveiled* (1877) and *The Secret Doctrine* (1888). These scholarly and brilliant works remain today as the cornerstone of Theosophic thought.

The young Annie Besant was asked by W.T. Stead, journalist and editor of London's crusading *Review of Reviews* to write a critique of *The Secret Doctrine*. As she turned the pages she was "dazzled, blinded by a light in which all disjointed facts were seen as parts of a mighty whole.…" All her puzzles, riddles, and problems seemed to disappear.

The energetic Annie Besant already had a wide reputation in Victorian England. After a profound crisis of conscience she had lost her faith, refusing to take the sacraments or to attend the sermons of her husband, Reverend Frank Besant. There were long periods of depression. She was racked by headaches and refused to leave her darkened room. Breaking free at last, she left her husband in 1873 and embarked on a remarkable series of careers which saw her as a vibrant public speaker and pamphleteer on topics ranging from atheism to championing organized labor by supporting a strike by match girls at the Bryant and Mays Factory. She caused great controversy by publishing the "Knowlton Pamphlet" on birth control. She was an ardent suffragette at the dawn of feminism, and joined the Fabian Socialist Society, along with Sidney Webb and George Bernard Shaw. Shaw, who worked closely with Besant, was believed by some to be her lover.[5]

In 1888, a meeting was arranged between Blavatsky, who had by then moved to London, and Besant. The encounter struck a deep chord in both women and Besant promptly became her student. In 1907 after the deaths of Blavatsky and Olcott, Besant, with her superb organizational skills, was named president of the Theosophical Society. Shaw commented, "Mrs. Besant is a woman of swift decision. She always came into a movement with a bound and was preaching the new faith before the astonished spectators had the least suspicion that the old one was shaken."

She traveled tirelessly around the world, her innate religiosity finding at last its spiritual home in India. A dynamic and compelling speaker, she drew thousands on her tours. By 1909 she was voicing millennial expectations in proclaiming the coming of "the world teacher." She said:

I would ask you to consider if it seems so strange and so impossible that in our own days as aforetime, some mighty teacher should come into the world to uplift and to help. We are so apt, with all our pride of intellect, and of nationality, to deem ourselves too small to be blessed with the presence of a world teacher, and yet, if He has come before, under exactly similar conditions of a new type appearing on earth, why should this one be left out of the series and that which has been done before fail to our own generation? [6]

The synthesis of Hindu avatars who, according to legend, returned, again and again, to save humanity in time of need, mingled with Judeo-Christian messianic expectations and Buddhist thought, produced a growing interest in the coming world teacher.

The last figure in the Theosophical quartet was Charles Webster Leadbeater, a curate of the Church of England. He, too, was drawn into the Blavatsky orbit and in 1883 joined the Society. His interest in occultism and "The Hidden Side of Things" led him to leave the church and go with Blavatsky to India. There, his purported clairvoyance and psychic abilities blossomed in the warm Indian sun. After a stay of some five years he returned to England and formed a close association with Annie Besant, co-authoring many books with her. Both delved into psychic phenomena, the investigation of past lives, their own as well as those of close associates. It is believed that Annie relied more and more on C.W.L., as he was called. As she became immersed in social and political issues of India, founding the Central Hindu College, supporting women's rights, and working for home rule for India, she depended more and more on him for psychic guidance and his close contacts with the masters.

For centuries, in both Europe and the East, arcane teachings told of a "Secret Brotherhood," "a Great White Lodge," a complex hierarchy of occult masters who exerted their benign influence to help humanity. Above them, in staggering complexity, reigned hosts of invisible beings, ascending at last to the Lord of the World.

Despite Leadbeater's undeniable abilities as author, lecturer and clairvoyant, a cloud hung over him which, when lifted, revealed a pederastic interest in young boys. Charges of immorality were brought against him, and in 1906 he resigned from the Society. Although he vigorously denied the charges, nevertheless the shadow of suspicion and doubt was such that he could not remain in a society that laid great stress on mental, physical, and sexual purity. C.W.L. had many supporters who managed to keep him afloat until Annie Besant was elected president in 1907. After the initial shock on hearing of the charges, Annie became convinced of his innocence and rallied to his side. After much pressure she was able to secure his readmission. Leadbeater returned to Adyar, India in 1909. As a strong right arm he was greatly needed and their alliance remained firm until the end.

In the hothouse atmosphere of hidden masters, chelas, arhats and disciples, a distinct pattern of "spiritual becoming" arose. It was generally known who was an initiate, who was not, and who was enrolled in C.W.L.'s "past lives" research. A hierarchic pattern was well in place.

Into that milieu the constant refrain sung by Annie Besant of the coming world teacher enflamed and increased the sense of longing and hope so characteristic of millennial expectations. She claimed that Blavatsky had intimated that the T.S. (as the Theosophical Society was called) was founded for the purpose of preparing the world for the coming messiah and the highly evolved "root race" that was to be the prototype of a new humanity. Behind the visible world, she stated, is a great, guiding hierarchy, and over the millennia an avatar, or world teacher, was sent to help humanity in its time of need, each age and civilization requiring a teacher suited to the times—a Buddha, Mohammed, Christ, Moses or Sri Krishna.[7]

C.W.L. had been told by his Dutch friend Johann van Manen, then living at Adyar, that there were boys of Theosophical parents who might be of interest for special training. Narayaniah and his family had already

C.W. LEADBEATER (ABOVE) WAS DRAWN TO THE BLAVATSKY ORBIT AND JOINED THE THEOSOPHICAL SOCIETY IN 1883. HE RECOGNIZED SIGNS OF SPIRITUAL GREATNESS IN THE YOUNG KRISHNAMURTI (SHOWN BELOW) IN 1909 AT A BEACH ON THE BAY OF BENGAL.

OPPOSITE: THE GATE AT THE BEACH ON THE BAY OF BENGAL.

moved just outside the T. S. compound. As Leadbeater, Van Manen, and associate Ernest Wood walked down to the beach in the late afternoon, or early evening, of 1909, the voices of many boys could be heard playing by the water. It was there that he spotted two young Indian boys, Krishnamurti and Nityananda. He was profoundly struck by the size and purity of the older boy's "aura," a nimbus so radiant that he proclaimed it the most wonderful he had seen. It contained, he said, not a particle of selfishness. Surely it was not the boy's physical attractiveness that was so striking. At the time Krishnamurti was scrawny and undernourished. His teeth were crooked, not at all the dazzling young man he was to become.

Wood expressed surprise on hearing that Leadbeater should show an interest in Krishnamurti, as he had been helping both boys with their homework and considered him especially slow.

Later, it was decided that Krishnamurti and his brother Nityananda should be removed from the local school they were attending and tutored on the T. S. compound grounds. The young Krishnamurti who was thought to be vacant, stupid, and, even in Krishnamurti's own words, "moronic" had a difficult time in school. Vague and forgetful, he was frequently caned by his brutal teacher and sent from the classroom in tears. If no one remembered to call him back he would remain where he had been sent until dark, when his beloved younger brother, Nityananda, would come searching for him and lead him home.

It was in that context that the brothers entered into their new life at Theosophical headquarters. At first, only Krishnamurti was to be trained for the special part he was to play. However, he refused to come without Nityananda. "Either we both come or not at all," he said.[8] At the time they spoke only Telugu, the language of their part of southern India, and a young Englishman Russell Balfour Clarke, was called upon to teach them English and other Western skills.

Krishnamurti's family, known variously as Jiddu, Giddu, and Jeddu, was then living in a small house just outside of the T. S. compound walls.

At Adyar, in Madras India, in the winter of 1979, the opportunity to interview Captain Clarke, who was then well in his nineties, arose. "Dick," as he was called, had been Krishnamurti's tutor during his early days in 1909 when the boy was first found by the Theosophical Society.

Dick described how it was that he came to Adyar in 1909, the same year that Krishnamurti, then fourteen years old, was seen playing on the beach of the Bay of Bengal, where the Adyar River flows into the sea.

As a young man Clarke developed an interest in Theosophy through a meeting with Colonel Olcott in London. He had just completed his first engineering job in Nairobi, then British East Africa, and had an offer to erect power stations in West Africa. Should he pursue his interest in Theosophy or accept career advancement as an engineer? He felt he had reached a crossroads in his life.

RUSSELL BALFOUR CLARKE

FIRST TUTOR TO KRISHNAMURTI AND NITYANANDA

I wrote Annie Besant a letter and asked if I might meet her and she called me to her and I had a very, very wonderful interview. Now, during that interview I felt very shy and I felt that she was so much greater than I was. I wondered how I had managed to meet her at all. And then suddenly she looked at me and said "And so you want to throw yourself into the Theosophical stream." "Yes I do." And again she waited and I felt more embarrassed and then she said, "I did it myself, it's not for me to say no." And then she got up and said, "We must look into this matter. What are your circumstances?" "Well," I said, "I have a few hundred pounds from money I earned in Africa on this first job and I am free and I have stopped the university course and I finished an apprenticeship on the Metropolitan Railway and I had just completed a job in East Africa with Nairobi Power and Lighting Company." "We must see what can be done," she said.

Three weeks afterwards I met her at a Theosophical meeting and she called me to her and said, "I've been given two thousand pounds today to do what I like with and I thought perhaps if you would like, that I might invite you for a visit to India and a stay in Adyar, the headquarters of the Society." "Oh!" I said. "Oh no!" she said. "Don't decide now, think calmly about it for two or three days and decide whether you would like to go or not and let me know." I pondered this matter in my heart, but there was

> "AT SEVEN O'CLOCK EVERY MORNING WE SALLIED FORTH ON BICYCLES, OUR REVERED OLDER FRIEND C.W. L., USUALLY ACCOMPANYING US."
>
> —RUSSELL CLARKE

not much pondering to be done. I decided straight away that I would go. I wrote her a letter and then I had a little note, "Meet me at 10 o'clock outside the new headquarters." I arrived on the pavement exactly as Big Ben struck ten. A four-wheeler cab came alongside and a little silver head peeped through and she said, "So you've decided?" "Yes," I said, "I have." She handed me—very direct she was in her manner—she handed me an envelope, "Here is your passage money, Second Class British India would be quite suitable for a young man of your age. Ask them to give you a vegetarian diet and here is the letter of introduction to my agent in Adyar. So I sailed as early as possible and I arrived safely in Adyar."

From that time I never looked back. I spent the day, day after day, with C.W.L. in the octagonal bungalow, on the east side of headquarters on the banks of the river Adyar. And there one day I was introduced to two shy Indian boys, Krishnamurti and his young brother Nityananda. And after they had gone away, Leadbeater explained to me something about them. How his Dutch friend, Johann van Manen, who lived in the room next door, had suggested that C.W.L. might go down one day with him to the sea to swim, because there were some interesting young boys there, and you might notice amongst them, some boys of Theosophical parents. So they went down to the sea and they observed a group of some ten or fifteen young Telugu Brahmin and other boys frolicking in the sea. And Leadbeater suddenly noticed one of the boys, outwardly a rather skinny looking little boy with a shaved front to his head and a pigtail. He was about thirteen (actually fourteen but appeared much younger), and had a little brother

with him. He saw that around this boy was an aura of such brightness and glory as he said no one else in Adyar had, and that was so outstanding to him that he at once made friends with the two brothers. Then it was that his masters came along, the Master Kuthumi and the Master Djwal Kul, and they said to C.W.L., "So you found them! You are quite right in your surmise, they are special, and have been guided to Adyar with their worthy parent, who came to Adyar at Mrs. Besant's invitation. Here the boys are, and if they can be trained, the older boy has very important work that he may do in the future." Leadbeater himself knew nothing more than that at the time. Then subsequently he said to me, "You know you've been sent out here to help me with a very difficult piece of work, we shall receive a good deal of opposition from the orthodox Brahmins here. Caste is still very strong and the Brahmin is very severe about certain things." Without knowing, we were offending against these Brahminical rules. Some Brahmins adopted an attitude of hostility towards Narayaniah, the father of the boys, for allowing them to be so de-Brahminized, so contaminated. In my ninety-first year, I am trying to remember these things and it's not too difficult because much of it was so impressive and so beautiful.[9]

When we first went to Adyar we lived not in a house close to the new printing press. Every day we walked to the Mylapore high school. In the early mornings & in the evenings we prepared our home lessons. After some time we began to paddle in the sea with some other boys who lived near. On one of these occasions, in the year 1909, we met for the first time my dear friend & elder brother Mr. C. W. Leadbeater. The meeting was quite quite casual. As far as I remember he was going down to the sea with Mr. Van Manen & others to have a swim. I do not remember any particular conversation, especially as I did not know English at all well. After this we met very often & he sometimes invited us to his house or rather bungalow. He was living at the time of which I write in what is known as the river bungalow. When I first went over to his rooms I was much afraid, for most Indian boys are afraid of Europeans. I do not know how it is that such fear is created, but apart from the difference of colour which is no doubt one of the causes, there was when I was a boy much political agitation & our imaginations were much stirred by the gossip about us. I must also confess that the Europeans in India are by no means generally kind to us, & I used to see many acts of cruelty which made us still more bitter. I wish the English people in India could understand that Indian boys have as deep a love for India as the English have for their own country, & feel as deeply any insult however unintentional.

It was a surprise to us, therefore, to find how different was the Englishman who was also a Theosophist. We soon became very friendly with Mr. Leadbeater, & he helped us regularly with our lessons. Sometime later Mr. R. B. Clarke, a young engineer, arrived at Adyar & it was arranged with my father that my brother Nitya & I should leave school & be taught at Adyar by Mr. Leadbeater & Mr. Clarke. We soon began to make much better progress, than we had ever made before. Life became very regular. We came to Mr. Leadbeater's bungalow early in the morning, studied until what might be called breakfast, which we took at home, & then returned to him. In the afternoon we played tennis or went to the sea to learn swimming.

ABOVE: MRS. BESANT IS
GREETED ON HER RETURN TO
INDIA, NOVEMBER 27, 1909.
OPPOSITE: EXCERPT FROM
KRISHNAMURTI'S ACCOUNT OF
HIS EARLIEST REMEMBERED
DAYS, WRITTEN WHEN HE WAS
EIGHTEEN YEARS OLD.

Another event in Krishnaji's life during those early years is his meeting with Annie Besant. On November 27, 1909, quite a crowd had assembled on the railway platform in Madras to welcome the veteran president of the Theosophical Society upon her return from Europe. As she descended from the train, a little old lady with her wonderful head covered with crisp electric-white hair, she was garlanded by a slim and gracious Indian boy clad in spotless Indian silken clothes, and she gazed for the first time into his wondrous eyes with their preternaturally long silken lashes gently veiling them. He stood before her, a very embodiment of youthful South Indian aristocracy, greeting her with the reverent Hindu salutation of joined palms; after which he shook hands with her in the European fashion.

…Her unerring intuition enabled her to grasp the situation at once, and henceforward she drew Krishnaji and his brother into a sweet and motherly intimacy which continued ever since. As far as her very busy life permitted she also took vigorous part in the instruction of these, her two spiritual wards. She conceived the idea of taking over officially, as far as it could be done, the entire responsibility for their upbringing and education; so an agreement was drawn up and J. Narayaniah, father of the boys, signed it declaring that it was his wish that his two sons should become her wards.…It was my privilege and duty at this juncture to have the necessary interview with J. Narayaniah to promote this plan, to which, after some hesitancy at first, he assented. [Annie Besant was appointed guardian of the boys on March 6, 1910.]

All these changes took place amidst an atmosphere of increasing gossip and criticism on the part of many, of whom perhaps it might have been said that they should have known better.…From this time onwards Krishnaji began to change in his appearance to a remarkable degree. His hair, which fell to below his knees in a pigtail at the back, while close-shaven in the front, had been allowed to grow in front, and its length at the back had been reduced so that it hung just short of his shoulders; it was parted in the middle and brushed back from the face.[10]

Mrs. Besant was to arrive on the morning of the 27th of November, & a party of us — including Mr. Leadbeater, my father, the van Hooks, Mrs. Russak, the Kirbys & the Ruspolis — went down to the Madras Central railway station about eleven o'clock. There was a large gathering of Theosophists at the station, several of whom had garlands in their hands. I remember Mr. V. C. & Sesahchary giving me a garland of roses to throw over her. The sun was very hot, & we had to wait a very long time because while the first telegram which we received at Adyar informed us that she would arrive about mid-day, a second telegram to the station-master reported an accident to the train in which she was travelling. Some of us were bare-footed & that part of

the platform unprotected by the roof became very hot, especially as it was paved with slabs of stone. My feet grew so uncomfortable that, after dancing about for some time, I took refuge on Don Fabrizio Ruspoli's feet. In order to pass the time till four o'clock, at which hour she was expected, we took a long drive round Madras. At last she arrived & everybody pressed towards the railway carriage from which she stepped down. There was such a rush that I could hardly see anything of her at all & was only just able to get near enough to her to throw the garland over her & salute her in our Indian way.

After reaching Adyar we went back to Mr. Leadbeater's bungalow & waited there a long time while he was talking with Mrs. Besant in the main building. At last we heard the peculiar coo-ee by which Mr. Leadbeater often called us. He was standing on the shrine room verandah which looks down upon his bungalow, & he told my brother & myself that Mrs. Besant wished to see us. We both felt very nervous as we went upstairs for although we were very eager to meet her, we had heard how great she was. Mr. Leadbeater went into her room with us, & we found her standing in the middle of the room. Mr. Leadbeater said: "Here is Krishna with his brother". As is the custom with us towards those for whom we have great reverence, we both prostrated ourselves at her feet. She lifted us up & embraced us. I do not remember what she said to us, as I was still very nervous although full of a great happiness. He did not stop very long as there was to be a meeting of T. S. members as usual in the big drawing-room on the same floor. As we were going in we met my father & Mrs. Besant said to him: "I suppose this will be the first of these private T. S. meetings that your sons have attended. I hope you approve of their coming". He replied that he was very glad. I sat at her feet facing the people who were gathered there & I was very nervous.

Leadbeater took great interest in the brothers' earlier incarnations, and when Narayaniah brought them to his quarters at the Octagon bungalow he placed his hand on Krishnamurti's head and began to recount his past lives. It seemed that many in T.S. circles, including C.W.L. and Annie Besant had been clustered around the boy in previous incarnations. In order to identify the cast of characters each was given a name that would remain a constant in the ebb and flow of succeeding lives. The name Alcyone was given to Krishnamurti. Mizar was to be Nitya's name. Leadbeater was Sirius and Besant, Herakles. It became a question of some concern as to who was in and who was out of the *Lives of Alcyone*, two volumes by C.W.L. which supposedly recounted forty-eight of the incarnations of Alcyone. Many in the Theosophical group appeared again and again in the various contexts and relationships clustered around the central figure. This only increased the sense of spiritual snobbery that began to run rampant.

Important events followed rapidly. Shortly after Mrs. Besant left Adyar for Banares, now called Varanasi, she received word from Leadbeater that the young Krishnamurti was now prepared to undergo his first initiation on the night of January 11 and 12, 1910. Initiation rites and ceremonies have always played an important part in all sects and religions. So it was with the Theosophical Society. According to them, these rites take place in another dimension, unknown to the ordinary waking consciousness. Unlike First Communion, the Bar Mitzvah, or African initiation rites, the candidate is in direct communication with exalted beings, without the intermediaries of earthly priests, rabbis, or shamans. Quickly Besant gave orders that Leadbeater and the boy were to use her own rooms for this turning point in his life. As Nitya and Clarke kept guard outside the door, C.W.L. and Krishnamurti were said to be receiving spiritual instruction on the astral plane, and were out of their bodies for the best part of two nights and a day, coming back very occasionally and then only partially, though sufficiently to absorb nourishment (mostly warm milk) which was administered by Clarke at their bedsides. Krishnamurti lay on Mrs. Besant's bed and Leadbeater on the floor.[11]

In 1972 Krishnamurti, speaking about his early life, described what had happened:

So this boy was prepared, bathed, properly dressed and all the rest of it and taken to Dr. Besant's room and went to sleep or became unconscious—it is not clear, all this, for me, for twenty-four hours or more. And when he came out of this state, all of them—Ruspoli, Kirby, Cooper, Clarke—saw an astonishing change in the face of this boy and some of them fell on their knees and touched his feet.[12]

Krishnamurti wrote to Mrs. Besant telling of the wondrous events...

The Lord smiled at me, but He said to the master: 'Who is this that you thus bring before me?' And the master answered: 'This is a candidate who seeks admission to the Great Brotherhood.' Then the Lord asked: 'Do you vouch for him as worthy of admission?' The master replied: 'I do....'[13]

Memories of the instruction given him during that period came flooding back and the young boy struggled to put down his recollections. His English was still poor, but he was seen laboriously writing the instructions of his master.

KRISHNAMURTI FOLLOWING HIS INITIATION, WITH HIS BROTHER, NITYANANDA, 1910.

Krishnamurti, in his later years, denied any memory of writing the little book, *At the Feet of the Master*, which purports to be instructions given him by his master at the time of his initiation, and which was to become a spiritual classic. However, here are several accounts of that event:

The first notable event that happened was that I found Krishnaji writing every morning some notes in a schoolbook with a pencil and he would look up and say, "How do you spell so and so?" Leadbeater explained to me that he was trying to write from memory without saying much or being distracted in anyway, what he had learned from the master during the night. Well, I never liked to be rude or peer over the book or to be too inquisitive, but I do know that morning after morning he laboriously wrote something and he did tell Count Keyserling apparently some years afterwards, it's recorded somewhere, when he was asked, "Did you write that book At the Feet of the Master, *he said "I don't remember, but I do remember writing something very laboriously in English in my early days."* [14]

—RUSSELL BALFOUR CLARKE

The story of how this little book came to be written is comparatively simple. Every night I had to take this boy in his astral body to the house of the master, that instruction might be given him. The master devoted perhaps fifteen minutes each night to talking to him, but at the end of each talk he always gathered up the main points of what he had said into a single sentence, or a few sentences, thus making an easy little summary which was repeated to the boy, so that he learned it by heart. He remembered that summary in the morning and wrote it down. The book consists of these sentences, of the epitome of the master's teaching, made by himself, and in his words. The boy wrote them down somewhat laboriously, because his English was not then very good. He knew all these things by heart and did not trouble particularly about the notes that he had made. A little later he went up to Benares with Dr. Annie Besant. While there he wrote to me, I being down at Adyar, and asked me to collect and send to him all the notes that he had made of what the master had said. I arranged his notes as well as I could, and typed them all out....and in due course the book was published.

Numbers of people, literally thousands, have written to say how their whole lives have been changed by the book, how everything has become different to them because they have read it. It has been translated into twenty-seven languages. There have been some forty editions of it, or more, and over a hundred thousand copies have been printed. A wonderful work has been done by it. [15]

—C. W. LEADBEATER

The privilege is given to me, as an elder, to pen a word of introduction to this little book, the first written by a younger Brother, young in body verily, but not in Soul. The teachings contained in it were given to him by his master in preparing him for Initiation, and were written down by him from memory—slowly and laboriously, for his English last year was far less fluent than it is now. The greater part is a reproduction of the master's own words; that which is not such a verbal reproduction is the master's thought clothed in his pupil's words. Two omitted sentences were supplied by the master. In two other cases an omitted word has been added. Beyond this, it is entirely Alcyone's own, his first gift to the world. [16]

—ANNIE BESANT

GROUP PHOTOGRAPH
FOLLOWING THE PUBLICATION
OF *AT THE FEET OF THE
MASTER*, 1910. MRS. BESANT,
KRISHNAMURTI, AND C.W.
LEADBEATER IN CENTER.

ON THE FIRST ANNIVERSARY of Krishnamurti's initiation, the Order of the Star in the East was formed to pave the way for the coming world teacher. A magazine, *The Herald of the Star*, also appeared quarterly, with the first publication dated January 11, 1911. The membership at that time reached 50,000, with offices in over fifty countries. The magazine was to continue for many years, while the membership was devoted for the next eighteen years to preparing for the "Lord's coming."

The Order of the Star in the East has been established to gather into one body those who, within and without the Theosophical Society, look for the coming of the world teacher, and would fain share in the glorious privilege of preparing the Way of the Lord. Wherever one sees glittering the little Silver Star, one knows that it is shining above a heart that is beating with hope and joy. Every member of the Society who believes in that coming should wear the Silver Star, for we must not lag behind the less instructed world of non-Theosophists.

Work then, Brothers and Sisters, strenuously and well; study hard, in order that you may be able to teach the nonstudious; love, that your goodwill may spread abroad, and bless even the unthankful and the evil; cooperate with nature in her great work of evolution, and utilize her laws for the benefit of yourselves and all around you. And so may the peace of the masters be with you, and Their Wisdom guide your steps.

Your faithful servant,
Annie Besant, President
The Theosophical Society
Adyar, November, 1911 [17]

MRS. BESANT, KRISHNAMURTI,
AND NITYANANDA WERE MET
AT CHARING CROSS STATION
BY LADY EMILY LUTYENS AND
ADMIRERS, SPRING 1911.

Not everyone within the Society was as overjoyed with the promotion of Krishnamurti into a cult figure, a messiah-to-be. Some wrote angrily that Besant imposed her personal views on the membership at large. Rudolph Steiner, an eminent Theosophical colleague of Mrs. Besant in Germany felt that the T. S. was becoming "Orientalized" and refused to accept the boy Krishnamurti as having any kind of spiritual importance. He broke away and formed his own society, Anthroposophy, which flourishes to this day with an emphasis on education, the arts, and publication of books.

In refuting the charges, a spirited Mrs. Besant wrote in *The Adyar Bulletin* in June 1912:

...these members declare that I want to force my personal opinions on the Society....All my life long I have worked for freedom of thought and speech for others, and have taken it for myself, and I am too old to surrender my own freedom at the dictation of a few members of the T. S. That they are disturbed by it merely shows that they are not willing to allow to others the freedom they claim for themselves, and which they use, quite freely, to attack me, knowing that in this they in no way imperil their membership, and that I am the first to defend their freedom of thought and expression.[18]

Amid rising unease from several quarters, including Narayaniah, who was beginning to have serious doubts about the propriety of his sons' contacts with C. W. L., Mrs. Besant left with the brothers for England. The brothers continued their lessons on a broad range of subjects and were always surrounded by numerous teachers and tutors. An English education was thought to be of paramount importance.

In the spring of 1911 Mrs. Besant arrived in England and was greeted by immense crowds. It was known that she was bringing Alcyone with her, who they had read about in the *Lives*. And of course *The Herald of the Star* continued to bring news of Krishnamurti's activities. It was then that he met a woman to whom he was to be very close, Lady Emily Lutyens. The wife of eminent architect Edward Lutyens, daughter of the first Earl of Lytton, Viceroy of India, and granddaughter of Victorian novelist Bulwer Lytton. Lady Emily was a devoted and active Theosophist; she lectured and wrote articles, and was a confidante and supporter of Annie Besant. She recalled that first meeting:

I must now recount the memorable day when I first met Krishna. Mrs. Besant had left Adyar in March 1911, and sailed from Bombay in April, en route for England. She had the two boys, Krishna and Nitya, with her and also George Arundale, a large, dark, rather good-looking man, who was then thirty-three years old. Together with a crowd of other Theosophists I was at Charing Cross Station to meet Mrs. Besant and her wards. I had eyes for none but Krishna, an odd figure, with long black hair falling almost to his shoulders and enormous dark eyes which had a strange, vacant look in them. He was dressed in a Norfolk jacket. Mrs. Besant piloted him along the platform, anxious to keep the crowd from pressing on him. He was nearly fifteen, and Nitya was two years younger. As I left the station I found one of our members in an almost fainting condition. She was somewhat psychic and said that she had been overcome by the glory of Krishna's aura. [19]

The two young Indian boys shivered in the chilly English climate. Wearing Western clothes for the first time, and particularly wearing shoes, was a painful new experience and walking was agony. The public attention was frightening to Krishnamurti, who was still shy and retiring. Theosophical luminary George Arundale was brought along as tutor and the lessons and exercises continued. It was hoped that the brothers would attend Oxford. Although there was some resistance on the part of the university to admitting Indians at all, there was much hope that that would change.

After a stay of some months the party returned to India and the Theosophical convention at Banares. Speaking of himself in the third person as he often did, Krishnamurti recounted that:

He was literally worshipped—and he used to shrink from all that. There was a scene, I believe, when returning with Dr. Besant from Europe at a station in India, the train stopped and a huge mob came and wanted to see the boy. He had locked himself in the lavatory and wouldn't come out. Because he was shy he didn't want any of this. And Dr. Besant had to come and said: "Please come out." and only because she asked, he came out; otherwise he wouldn't have come. And the train was held up, I don't know for how many hours. Because they all hung on the rails, on the roof, and everywhere. And this boy, neither worship, nor flattery, nor crowds—nothing seemed to touch him. So—he was vague, moronic, perhaps that's not the word, but enough to describe a boy who was absolutely vacant. He would tell everybody: "I will do whatever you want." That used to be his favorite phrase. "I'll do what you want." Even now sometimes it happens. [20]

Then in 1911 an event of transcendent importance took place.

A good many members have joined the Order of the Star in the East during the convention, and somebody suggested (quite casually) that it would be a great pleasure to them if the head of the Order [Krishna] would himself hand them their certificates of membership. The idea was taken up with enthusiasm, and other older members also asked to be allowed to return their certificates in order to receive them again directly from the head. So a time was fixed (6 p.m. on December 28) and we went down to the Indian Section Hall. We thought of it merely as a formal little ceremony, and I even doubted whether the president would come, as she was tired after her lecture at four.

Only Star members were admitted, but the hall was full; I suppose there were about four-hundred people. Mostly they sat on the floor, but there was a line of benches round the walls, and a few chairs at the upper end. The president and I sat there, with Miss Arundale [George's aunt] and Nitya and a few others, and the benches were occupied chiefly by European ladies. The arrangement was that the head was to stand just in front of us, with Telang [the national representative for India] beside him. The members were to file past in a line, each handing his certificate to Telang, who read out his name, and then passed the paper to Krishna, who returned it to its owner...the first two or three members took their papers with a bow and a smile, and passed back to their places.

All at once the hall was filled with a tremendous power, which was so evidently flowing through Krishna that the next member fell at his feet, overwhelmed by this marvelous rush of force. I have never seen or felt anything in the least like it; it reminded one irresistibly of the rushing mighty wind, and the outpouring of the Holy Ghost at Pentecost. The tension was enormous, and everyone in the room was most powerfully affected. It was exactly the kind of thing that we read about in the old scriptures, and think exaggerated; but here it was before us in the twentieth-century.

After that each one prostrated himself as his turn came, many of them with tears pouring down their cheeks. The scene was indeed a memorable one, for the stream of devotees was remarkably representative in character. There were members from almost every country in Europe, from America and from all parts of India, and it was most striking and beautiful to see white and black alike, Brahmins and Buddhists, Parsis and Christians, haughty Rajput princes and gorgeously apparelled merchants, grey-haired men and young children, all prostrating themselves in rapt devotion at our Krishna's feet. The blessing poured forth was so obvious that everyone present yearned to share in it, and those who had no certificates with them tore off their Star badges and handed them in, so that they also might receive something at his hands.

He stood all the time with perfect grace and self-possession, smiling gently upon them, and holding out his hands in benediction over each prostrate form in turn. I think the culmination of the strangely affecting scene was when our dear Nitya threw himself at his brother's feet, and the whole congregation burst into enthusiastic applause. I hardly know why, but somehow it seemed at the moment not at all irreverent, but entirely appropriate and natural.

When the last of that great company had made his reverence, Krishna returned to his seat between us, and there were a few minutes of silent rapture, of strange hushed awe and expectancy.

Then the President whispered to Krishna to close the meeting, and he rose and held out his right hand over the heads of the audience, and said solemnly: "May the blessing of the great Lord rest upon you forever." And so we came down to the ordinary world again, and left the hall, feeling that we had passed through one of the greatest experiences of our lives...[21]

—C. W. LEADBEATER

True compassion is always full of power,

and those that are powerful in the true way

are full of tenderness. [22]

—*THE HERALD OF THE STAR*, OCTOBER 25, 1913,

FROM THAT DAY FORWARD, December 28, 1911 became a special, almost sacred day in the hearts of members of the Order of the Star in the East.

Narayaniah meanwhile was being greatly influenced by orthodox Hindus and enemies of Mrs. Besant who were anti-British extremists. They insisted that the boys were breaking caste and would leave Hinduism for inchoate Theosophical philosophies. They also brought up the earlier Leadbeater scandal.

Annie Besant was able to calm matters again by stressing how important an Oxford education would be for the future of the boys. Shortly after that, in February 1912, she spirited the boys out of India before Narayaniah could think twice about the matter, telling him that they would not return until their education was completed. This amounted in essence to a declaration of war. Narayaniah later responded by bringing a lawsuit against Besant to regain his children's custody. This protracted suit was eventually won by a determined Mrs. Besant in a case marked by charges and countercharges. Leadbeater's proximity to the boys was a constant point of dispute.

When Krishnamurti and his brother finally went to England [in 1912] I went a little while before and there I spent the first year in a very wonderful old house owned by Lady de la Warr, where we had a private dairy, wonderful milk, and cream and eggs and so on; and we lived in grand style with a butler and many servants in a very lovely house. We had a motorcycle, which engaged a great deal of our attention. And we used to take it to pieces and put it together again. He was a very clever mechanic and he liked that sort of thing very much.

At that time he was beginning to do the editorship of The Herald of the Star, *which of course George Arundale was helping with, but he was also beginning to feel a little revolt against being the head of the Order of the Star in the East. I used to comfort him, but his great comforter at that time was the Lady Emily Lutyens, who really filled the place of his dead mother. She was a very great solace to him in his passing through a very difficult stage of revolt against being made the head of something and talked about in such a manner that all kinds of people who he'd never met were calling him "our beloved head" and so on. One day he said to me "They call me their beloved head and they've never even met me." He said it to me with great pain one day and I tried to comfort him. Well, anyway, the war came, 1914 wasn't it? We split up, it was the end of our beautiful life together there, and I found myself in the army under training and ultimately I went to France. I went all through the war until 1918.* [23]

—RUSSELL BALFOUR CLARKE

KRISHNAMURTI IN INDIA, 1910
(C.W.L. IN BACKGROUND), AND A FEW
YEARS LATER IN CORNWALL (CIRCA 1914, BELOW)
WHERE EXCEPT FOR THE RETINUE OF TUTORS,
GUARDIANS AND DEVOTEES, THE BOYS HAD LITTLE
CONTACT WITH THE WORLD.

When I went to Europe for the first time I lived among people who were
wealthy and well-educated, who held positions of social authority; but
whatever their dignities or distinctions, they could not satisfy me. I was
in revolt also against Theosophists with all their jargon, their theories,
their meetings, and their explanations of life. When I went to a
meeting, the lecturers repeated the same ideas which did not satisfy me
or make me happy. I went to fewer and fewer meetings, I saw less and
less of the people who merely repeated the ideas of Theosophy. I
questioned everything because I wanted to find out for myself.

I walked about the streets, watching the faces of people who perhaps
watched me with even greater interest. I went to theaters, I saw how
people amused themselves trying to forget their unhappiness, thinking
that they were solving their problems by drugging their hearts and
minds with superficial excitement.

—*LIFE IN FREEDOM, 1928*

Krishnamurti and Nityananda were to remain in England and Europe for
almost ten years. During that period of study they lived in quiet isolation
in the English countryside. Except for the retinue of tutors, guardians, and devotees who surrounded them, they had little contact with the world at large.

While Krishnamurti and the little group were isolated in the countryside, the world was exploding outside. World War I raged in fierce battles
and nineteen-year-old Krishnamurti yearned to help. For a while he
scrubbed floors at a military hospital near London. In one of his weekly
letters to Annie Besant he wrote, "I do want to work, dreadfully, but
nobody wants me. It seems the real difficulty is that I am an Indian and that
seems to put off everybody." By the end of the year Mrs. Besant urged him
to give up all ideas of war service and continue quietly with his studies.
She reminded him, as she often did, that his happiness would lie only in the
work ahead.

He responded to her wishes by saying, "You don't know how sorry I
am if I have caused any anxiety...I know I have not taken my life seriously
so far and I am going to from now on. I'm beginning my studies Monday. I
will try to get into Oxford as soon as I can...."

During those years Annie Besant was far away in India, deeply
absorbed in politics and the struggle for home rule for her adopted country. In her public lectures, however, she continued to proclaim the coming
of the world teacher and warned of the dangers of rejecting his message, as
was done, two-thousand years ago.

THROUGHOUT 1916 the boys worked hard to pass their entrance examinations. Nitya had little difficulty, but Krishnamurti's hopes were dwindling. Both Oxford and Cambridge were out of the question. In addition to his academic weaknesses, it must have been diffi-cult for conservative universities to consider accepting an Indian boy who had been trumpeted around the world as the coming messiah! Krishnamurti recalled:

They were sent to a school, a carefully chosen school, where the younger brother did everything brilliantly. He got all the high marks, but the older boy found it awfully difficult to learn. For instance, he spoke French fairly well in those days, as he had stayed in France, but he couldn't pass an examination in French, though they had taught him for a year also in the school French, Latin, etc. He did fairly well in the school as long as he was left alone, but the moment he had to pass an examination, he couldn't put a thing on paper. He would go to the examination hall and look at the clock and blank. Nothing happened. They tried this at Sorbonne, London University, and so on and so on. Nothing. So Dr. Besant said, "That's enough!" The other brother liked law and he passed all the necessary examinations.[24]

The end of the war in 1918 brought increased activity among Theosophists. Annie Besant, as energetic as ever, was able to return to London. She resumed public lecturing and brought Krishnamurti into the forefront at meetings and as editor of Star publications. As he grew older, however, he felt increasingly estranged by what he saw as the limita-

tions and restrictions of any form that attempted to codify "the truth." He was restless and dissatisfied, but torn because of his loyalty to Mrs. Besant. "If I am to occupy a leading position in the Theosophical Society," he said, "it will be because of what I am, and not what other people think of me...."

Krishnamurti was in the painful position of genuinely and deeply car-ing for Mrs. Besant, who, in his frequent affectionate letters he continued to call "My Dearest Mother, Amma mine" and "My own beloved Mother."

But the burden of living up to the presumption of being the world teacher that she so ardently fostered was great. He had difficulty coping with the adoration of members of the Order of the Star. In addition it was now clear that he would not have the brilliant scholastic career that had been planned for him. For both Krishnamurti and Nityananda it was life under pressure—and then more pressure.

However, there was some respite during times of travel. In New York, Krishnamurti made the acquaintance of the noted and fashionable artist James Montgomery Flagg and sat for his portrait. Flagg wrote:

KRISHNAJI
JAMES MONTGOMERY FLAGG
JUNE · 5 · 1923

Mr. Krishnamurti—or Krishnaji, as his brother affectionately called him—sat for me for a pencil portrait, reproduced here, on an occasion of his lunching with my parents when he visited America a year or so ago.

He and his brother were happy youngsters and when you didn't look at them but listened you would swear two young Englishmen were talking. In spite of their brown skins I had no feeling of their being alien, as is usually the case between Occidental and Oriental. On the contrary I felt immediately as if I had met a much loved brother. To me it was an extraordinary episode. I did not know at the time that he had been actually selected to be the vehicle for the Christ, but this lad seemed to fill the studio to overflowing with a most unaccountable spiritual joy. I was with him perhaps an hour and a half but I was acutely sorry to say good-bye. Now that sort of thing doesn't happen—and I couldn't account for it. Krishnaji was simple in manner—boyish—and he had a sense of humor, bubbled over with smiles. He told us stories of his Brahmin upbringing in India—amusing episodes of his boyhood—of his father, priests, many things. He has an extraordinary face, huge eyes with long eyelashes, and he was well-dressed. I complimented him on his cravat. It seems that humor and being well-dressed are not incompatible with spirituality. But above all to me was my joy of being with him—I treasure that memory, that hour and a half. [25]

THROUGHOUT THE YEARS the Order of the Star continued to grow and by 1921 had gathered many members. Krishnamurti was becoming more assertive, but for Nitya, the future changed abruptly. He became ill, and was diagnosed as having tuberculosis. This was to be the first of a series of attacks that would plague and weaken him over the next years.

After a ten-year absence from his native country it was decided that Krishnamurti's mission would begin in Adyar. For Mrs. Besant the long-awaited day occurred early in December 1921. "The two brothers, who left as boys, have returned as men," she said. "One chapter was closing and the other opening."

Although Krishnamurti plunged into his work as head of the Order of the Star in the East, his internal struggles continued. "There is a rebellion within me, surging quietly, but surely… to what purpose I do not know. A continuous fight and then some more fighting."

Wherever Krishna went he was the object of curiosity. "As I go about the street they point me out…there goes that chap printed in the papers…the messiah, then they burst out laughing…oh, how I hate it all, and I shall have it all my life….Lord, what have I done to deserve all this."

Unfortunately, the many meetings and travels were a heavy strain on Nitya. He ran a high fever and was coughing badly. X-rays showed that both of his lungs were now diseased.

It was suggested by Mr. A. P. Warrington, general secretary of the Theosophical Society, that California was a healthful climate for tuberculosis patients. Travel arrangements were quickly made as a friend, Mrs. Mary Gray, offered two small cottages in the Ojai Valley some eighty miles north of Los Angeles—one for Warrington and one for the brothers.

They arrived in Ojai on July 6, 1922, and both young men delighted in the openness and freedom of the California atmosphere, so different from the class-, caste-, and race-conscious India and England.

For a short time Nitya seemed to be improving, but best of all, the brothers were alone. Privacy had been a luxury denied them since childhood. Now, they were in near-seclusion. Their only neighbors were Mr.

PHOTO-REMBRANDT

Warrington and a Mr. Walton, vicar general of the Liberal Catholic Church who lived nearby, and nineteen-year-old Rosalind Williams, sister of a friend of Mrs. Gray. Krishnamurti had an opportunity to be with himself.

He walked alone in the hills, climbing through orange groves and scrub brush to reach a mountain range that stretched high above the valley. A restlessness seized him and for several days he complained of suffocating heat. Nitya described the strange events in a letter to Mrs. Besant:

In a long and narrow valley of apricot orchards and orange groves is our house, and the hot sun shines down day after day to remind us of Adyar, but of an evening the cool air comes from the range of hills on either side. Far beyond the lower end of the valley runs the long, perfect road from Seattle in Washington down to San Diego in southern California, some two thousand miles, with a ceaseless flow of turbulent traffic, yet our valley lies happily, unknown and forgotten, for a road wanders in, but knows no way out. The American Indians called our valley the Ojai (pronounced, O-high), or the nest, and for centuries they must have sought it as a refuge.

Our cottage is on the upper end and no one else lives near except Mr. Warrington, who has a cottage all to himself a few hundred yards away; and Krishna, Mr. Warrington and I have been here for nearly eight weeks, taking a rest and getting well. We have an occasional visitor in Mr. Walton, the vicar general of the Liberal Catholic Church for America, who has a house in the valley, and Rosalind Williams, a young American girl, stays a week or two near by, spending her time with us. About two weeks ago happened this incident which I want to describe to you, when all five of us chanced to be here together.

On the evening of Thursday the seventeenth [August 1922] Krishna felt a little tired and restless and we noticed in the middle of the nape of his neck a painful lump of what seemed to be a contracted muscle, about the size of a large marble. The next morning he seemed all right, until after breakfast, when he lay down to rest...he was lying on the bed tossing about and moaning as if he were in great pain....He started again moaning and a fit of trembling and shivering came upon him, and he would clench his teeth and grip his hands tight to ward off the shivering; it was exactly the behavior of a malarial patient, except that Krishna complained of frightful heat....Some process was going on in Krishna's body, as a result of influences directed from planes other than physical....During the morning things got worse, and when I came and sat beside him he complained again of the awful heat, and said that all of us were full of nerves and made him tired; and every few minutes he would start up in bed and push us away; and again he would commence trembling. All this while he was only half conscious, for he would talk of Adyar and the people there as if they were present; then again he would lie quiet for a little while until the ruffle of a curtain or the rattling of a window, or the sound of a far-off plough in the field would rouse him again and he would moan for silence and quiet.

I sat near, but not too near. We tried our best to keep the house quiet and dark, but slight sounds which one scarcely notices are inevitable, yet Krishna had become so sensitive that the faintest tinkling would set his nerves on edge.

...(A) few minutes afterwards he was groaning again, and presently, poor fellow, he could not keep down the food he had eaten. And so it went on all the afternoon; shivering, groaning, restless, only half conscious, and all the time as if he were in pain.

...Krishna seemed much worse, he seemed to be suffering a great deal, the trembling and the heat seemed intensified and his consciousness became more

and more intermittent. When he seemed to be in control of his body he talked all the time of Adyar, and he imagined himself constantly in Adyar. Then he would say, "I want to go to India! Why have they brought me here? I don't know where I am," and again and again and again he would say, "I don't know where I am." Yet towards six o'clock when we had our evening meal, he quieted down until we had finished. Then suddenly the whole house seemed full of a terrific force and Krishna was as if possessed. In a voice full of pain said that he longed to go to the woods. Now he was sobbing aloud, we dared not touch him and knew not what to do; he had left his bed and sat in a dark corner of the room on the floor, sobbing aloud that he wanted to go into the woods in India. Suddenly he announced his intention of going for a walk alone, but from this we managed to dissuade him, for we did not think that he was in any fit condition for nocturnal ambulations. Then as he expressed a desire for solitude, we left him and gathered outside on the veranda, where in a few minutes he joined us, carrying a cushion in his hand and sitting as far away as possible from us. Enough strength and consciousness were vouchsafed him to come outside but once there again he vanished from us, and his body, murmuring incoherencies, was left sitting there on the porch.

Then Mr. Warrington had a heaven-sent inspiration. In front of the house a few yards away stands a young pepper tree, with delicate leaves of a tender green, now heavy with scented blossoms. . . .He gently urged Krishna to go out under that tree, and at first Krishna would not, then went of his own accord.

Now we were in a starlit darkness and Krishna sat under a roof of delicate leaves black against the sky. He was still murmuring unconsciously but presently there came a sigh of relief and he called out to us, "Oh, why didn't you send me out here before?" Then came a brief silence.

And now he began to chant. Nothing had passed his lips for nearly three days and his body was utterly exhausted with the intense strain, and it was a quiet weary voice we heard chanting the mantram sung every night at Adyar. Then silence.

. . .We sat with eyes fixed upon the tree, wondering if all was well, for now there was perfect silence, and as we looked I saw suddenly for a moment a great star shining above the tree, and I knew that Krishna's body was being prepared for the Great One. . . .The place seemed to be filled with a great presence and a great longing came upon me to go on my knees and adore, for I knew that the Great Lord of all our hearts had come Himself; and though we saw Him not, yet all felt the splendor of His presence.

. . .The radiance and the glory of the many beings present lasted nearly an half hour. . . .Then presently we heard Krishna's footsteps and saw his white figure coming up in the darkness, and all was over.

. . .The next day again there was a recurrence of the shuddering and half-waking consciousness in Krishna, though now it lasted but a few minutes and at long intervals. All day he lay under the tree in samadhi and in the evening, he sat in meditation as on the night before. . . .Since then and every evening he sits in meditation under the tree.

I have described what I saw and heard, but of the effect of the incident upon all of us I have not spoken, for I think it will take time, at least for me, to realize fully the glory that we were privileged to witness, though I feel now that life can only be spent in one way, in the service of the Lord.[26]

Following these extraordinary events Krishnamurti wrote his own account:

On the 17 of August, I felt acute pain at the nape of my neck and I had to cut down my meditation to fifteen minutes. The pain, instead of getting better as I had hoped, grew worse. The climax was reached on the nineteenth. I could not think, nor was I able to do anything, and I was forced by friends here to retire to bed. Then I became almost unconscious, though I was well aware of what was happening around me. I came to myself at about noon each day. On the first day while I was in that state and more conscious of the things around me, I had the first most extraordinary experience. There was a man mending the road; that man was myself; the pickax he held was myself; the very stone which he was breaking up was a part of me; the tender blade of grass was my very being, and the tree beside the man was myself. I almost could feel and think like the road-mender, and I could feel the wind passing through the tree, and the little ant on the blade of grass I could feel. The birds, the dust, and the very noise were a part of me. Just then there was a car passing by at some distance; I was the driver, the engine and the tires; as the car went further away from me, I was going away from myself. I was in everything, or rather everything was in me, inanimate and animate, the mountain, the worm, and all breathing things. All day long I remained in this happy condition.

...The morning of the next day [August 20] was almost the same as the previous day, and I could not tolerate too many people in the room.....eventually I wandered out on the veranda and sat a few moments exhausted and slightly calmer. I began to come to myself and finally Mr. Warrington asked me to go under the pepper tree, which is near the house. There I sat cross-legged in the meditation posture. When I had sat thus for some time, I felt myself going out of my body, I saw myself sitting down with the delicate tender leaves of the tree over me. I was facing the east. In front of me was my body and over my head I saw the star, bright and clear..... I could still see my body and I was hovering near it. There was such profound calmness both in the air and within myself, the calmness of the bottom of a deep unfathomable lake. Like the lake, I felt my physical body, with its mind and emotions, could be ruffled on the surface but nothing, nay nothing, could disturb the calmness of my soul. The presence of the mighty beings was with me for some time and then they were gone. I was supremely happy, for I had seen. Nothing could ever be the same. I have drunk at the clear and pure waters at the source of the fountain of life and my thirst was appeased. Never more could I be thirsty, never more could I be in utter darkness. I have seen the light. I have touched compassion which heals all sorrow and suffering; it is not for myself, but for the world....[27]

In the stillness of the night Krishnamurti had undergone a transforming experience that completely changed his life. In the months and years that were to follow Krishnamurti continued with the painful state of preparation that he was to call "the process." During this agonizing period no attempt was made to consult medical opinion, as Krishnamurti and others around him concurred that these events were a spiritual preparation of his body and, according to ancient Hindu texts, was "the awakening of Kundalini," the "fiery serpent" said to signify the awakened and liberated state.

Why this "awakening" should be accompanied by such excruciating pain was never answered in letters between the brothers and Besant and Leadbeater as they earnestly sought answers to unanswerable questions. In a very lengthy account Nitya wrote in part:

I think I've never prayed so fervently as on that night. It was a prayer, not that he might be spared the pain, for we were absolutely certain that They would not let him endure a second more than was necessary, but we all prayed that he should not remember any of it. It seemed impossible that he should not remember such positive infliction—such prolonged torture. We dreaded the frightful impression it would leave on his memory, if he were allowed to remember.

... he had felt a frightful burning in his spine and he wanted to find the stream which runs down the canyon and sink his body in it to relieve the burning. We felt thankful we had not let him go.

This was on the morning of the fifth [September 1922]. But the evening brought a climax in the preparation of the body, a definite portion, and perhaps the most difficult portion of the arduous work seemed to come to an end. Krishna's endurance and courage and the greatness of the occasion brought down a rare and wonderful benediction and all of us, Mr. Warrington, Rosalind, and I who were of the household, were fortunate enough to be present and to share the great privilege. The night, which was one of intense suffering, seemed to mark the success of the long period of work on the body.[28]

Krishnamurti's attitude toward his work underwent a profound transformation and with a new energy and intensity he embarked in 1923 on an intensive speaking tour of Theosophical centers across the United States, then went on to London, Holland, and Vienna. Over the year he continued to have agonizing bouts of "the process," although only those closest to him were aware of it.

Suffused with joy at his new found perceptions, and under the enlivened flame of his mission, Krishnamurti traveled the world. He spoke in Europe, India, Australia and the United States. These travels, with a full schedule of talks, meetings, and conventions, were a heavy strain on Nitya's delicate health. Some time earlier he had been diagnosed as having tuberculosis. As his condition worsened he wrote, "I've been in bed for four weeks and my bones are wearing through my skin....I walk to the precipice of death, look over and walk back again....it is becoming a habit with me."

THE JIDDU BROTHERS, AT
ARYA VIHARA, OJAI, 1922.

I N J U L Y 1 9 2 5 , ravaged by illness, Nityananda and his brother returned from a trip to Australia, to their beloved home in Ojai. With a high fever and near exhaustion Nitya was "fearfully thin and incredibly weak," but after some months stay in the dry climate of the valley and under the special Abrams Oscilloclast treatment he seemed to slowly improve.

Krishnamurti, desperately worried about his brother's condition, dreamed that he visited the Great Brotherhood and begged for Nitya's life saying that he would sacrifice his happiness in exchange. He would do anything that was required to let Nitya live, for "I felt his living was being decided." When he was told that he will be well, "It was such a relief that all my anxiety has completely disappeared and I am glad."

The reliance on esoteric masters, a cornerstone of Besant's and Leadbeater's teachings, had been an intrinsic part of Krishnamurti's youth. The dividing line between dream and wakefulness was blurred, visions and manifestations seemed part of ordinary existence to the sensitive youth. In later years he would say these states were projections of the mind.

In October, Mrs. Besant cabled Krishnamurti asking him to accompany her from England to India for the Jubilee Convention of the Theosophical Society. Madame de Manziarly, an old supporter from Paris days, was to come to Ojai to act as nurse for Nitya, along with Indian associate Rama Rao. Rosalind and Rajagopal, who had been in Ojai helping care for the invalid, were to go with Krishnamurti.

For years there had been unquestioning faith on the part of Star members that Nitya was chosen to stand at his brother's side in support of the work. It was part of a great plan. To fulfill his predestined role, Nitya's life would surely be spared. Still, it was with great reluctance that Krishnamurti left his ailing brother in Ojai.

On October 16, 1925, in a letter from the Gotham Hotel in New York, Krishnamurti wrote Nitya that his next letter would be from London, that his brother was always in his mind, and that he had not forgotten him, avowing that they loved each other more than anything in the world and would never be separated.

Adding to the turmoil was dismay that, in news from Huizen, the Netherlands, a startling series of events had taken place. Initiations were being handed out wholesale, and under seeming revelation George Arundale declared that twelve apostles to the world teacher had been named. Mrs. Besant, nearing eighty, confirmed in a lengthy speech at the August 1925 Star Camp at Ommen that "He will choose, as before, His twelve apostles....He has already chosen them."[29] Among them were Leadbeater, Besant, Arundale, Jinarajadasa, Lady Emily, and others.

"This apostles business is the limit." Krishnamurti said, "I don't believe in it at all. It makes me weep to see these sacred things dragged in the dirt." [30]

Those of you who are still hesitating, who are still groping, who are caught in this turmoil of sorrow and pain, anxiety and pettiness, may read books, attend schools where particular systems of philosophy are taught, where there are ceremonies, where there are limitations, but for those who have this one desire for liberation there is no school.

—THE STAR BULLETIN, 1924

When Krishnamurti and his party arrived in England on October 23, Lady Emily faithfully met them at Plymouth. She was subjected to an "avalanche of sarcasm." Krishnamurti repudiated all the pronouncements of initiations, arhats and apostles. Things of great solemnity had been made to look vulgar and ridiculous. Still, Krishnamurti's love for Mrs. Besant prevented him from speaking out publicly.

Krishnamurti wrote Nitya from London that he was once again made the focus of adulation, and he was so ill at ease with the people there, he said, with their pretentiousness and "high-sounding phrases."

Soon the enlarged party of fifteen, including Mrs. Besant, George Arundale and his wife, James Wedgewood, Lady Emily, Rosalind, Rajagopal, Shiva Rao, and others boarded the ship Ormuz bound for India and the Jubilee Convention. On November 9, at sea somewhere between Naples and Port Said, Krishnamurti again wrote his brother, wishing they were together. The past was like a nightmare but the future would be a "happy dream," and again he urged Nitya to get well quickly. He said he would post the letter the next day on reaching Port Said.

However, on reaching the port, a worrying telegram arrived saying that Nitya had influenza. A later cable ominously relayed "Flu little more serious. Pray for me."

But the implicit faith that the masters would guard Nitya's life seemed to preclude any disasters. Krishnamurti's mission, with his brother at his side, seemed immutable.

In 1909, when the gates of glory opened to the impoverished Indian boy, he refused to be trained, educated or prepared in any way for his new role unless Nitya could be with him. The childhood bond of brotherly love was strong and grew in depth over the years.

The young man, now thirty years old, had been stripped, over time, of all he held most dear. Beginning with his mother's death at ten, his removal from the background of his Indian heritage, being raised as an English gentleman, the breaking of caste rules, the estrangement from his father, and forgetting, through lack of use, his native tongue of Telugu—now the last living strand was to be broken. On the night of November 13, 1925, a great thunderstorm rocked the ship as it entered the Suez Canal. A telegram telling of Nitya's death was given to Mrs. Besant. All dreams shattered, she went to Krishnamurti's cabin to break the news. With the loss of his brother, Krishnamurti was now alone, cut off from the past, bereft of familial ties. Unbelieving and inconsolable he sobbed, at night moaning, calling aloud for Nitya in Telugu.

Shiva Rao, who shared the cabin with him, wrote that, "The news broke him completely; it did more—his entire philosophy of life—the implicit faith in the future as outlined by Mrs. Besant and Mr. Leadbeater, Nitya's vital part in it, all appeared shattered at that moment. During the next ten days he would sob and cry out for Nitya....Day after day we watched him, heartbroken, disillusioned." Then slowly, with immense effort, he changed, pulling himself together to face life without Nitya.

The pleasant dreams that my brother and I had of the physical life are over: the dream of being together, of seeing each other doing things, of traveling together, of amusing ourselves together, of talking and joking with each other and of all those little things that contribute so much to a life of pleasant enjoyment.

…Silence was of special delight to both of us; it was then so easy to understand one another's thoughts and feelings. Occasional irritation with each other was by no means forgotten, but we never went very far as it passed off in a few minutes. We used to sing comic songs or chant together as the occasion demanded. We both of us liked the same cloud, the same tree, and the same music. We had great fun in life although we were of different temperaments.

…An old dream is dead and a new one is being born, as a flower that pushes through the solid earth. A new vision is coming into being and a greater consciousness is being unfolded.

…A new strength, born of suffering, is pulsating in the veins and a new sympathy and understanding is being born of past suffering—a greater desire to see others suffer less, and, if they must suffer, to see that they bear it nobly and come out of it without too many scars. I have wept, but I do not want others to weep; but if they do, I now know what it means.

—THE HERALD OF THE STAR, JANUARY 1926

My brother died;
We were as two stars in a naked sky.
He was like me,
Burnt by the warm sun
In the land where [there] are soft breezes,
Swaying palms,
And cool rivers,
Where there are shadows numberless,
Bright-colored parrots and chattering birds.
Where green tree-tops
Dance in the brilliant sun;
Where there are golden sands
And blue-green seas:
Where the world lives in the burden of the sun,
And the earth is baked dull brown;
Where the green-sparkling rice fields
Are luscious in slimy waters,
And shining, brown, naked bodies
Are free in the dazzling light:
The land
Of the mother suckling her baby by the roadside;
Of the devout lover
Offering gay flowers;
Of the wayside shrine;
Of intense silence;
Of immense peace.
He died;
I wept in loneliness.
Where'er I went, I heard his voice
And his happy laughter.
I looked for his face
In every passer-by
And asked each if he had met with my brother;
But none could give me comfort.
I worshiped,
I prayed,
But the gods were silent.
I could weep no more;
I could dream no more.
I sought him in all things,
In every clime.
I heard the whispering of many trees
Calling me to his abode.
And then,
In my search,
I beheld Thee,
O Lord of my heart;
In Thee alone
I saw the face of my brother.
In Thee alone,
O my eternal Love,
Do I behold the faces
Of all the living and all the dead.

—*THE SONG OF LIFE*, 1931

Do not try to make amends to the dead,

but make amends to the living.

—THE STAR BULLETIN, 1931

A FTER THE LENGTHY SEA VOYAGE, those that met Krishnamurti and the Besant party, on arrival at Adyar, November 25, 1925, said that his face was clear, radiant, and untouched by the crushing loss he had experienced but ten short days earlier. Face to face with sorrow he came to comprehend its nature and moved through it. In moments of exhaustion he might still cry out for Nitya, but an understanding of suffering and the agony all human beings go through at the loss of loved ones resolved into quiet clarity. The bereavement was over.

But from that time forward Krishnamurti rarely spoke of occult hierarchies or the masters. He was now alone, leaning on no one.

In the few weeks leading up to the opening of the Jubilee Convention further strains erupted. Leadbeater and a party of seventy had arrived from Australia. He viewed the events at Huizen with great suspicion and coolness, and a rift occurred between Arundale, the architect of "Apostles," and the C.W.L. group. Annie Besant was at the center of these divisions, and even the devoted Lady Emily came to believe that Besant had been deceived.

The convention opened December 24 amid excited speculation that the masters themselves would appear for this event.

The New York Times and *New York Herald*, *The Times of India* and other papers, reported on the arrival of hundreds of delegates from around the world. Over three thousand people gathered in a fever of anticipation— but it was flat, nothing happened. Other than the regular routine of lectures and meetings there was no sign of the hoped for miraculous events many had been lead to believe would manifest for the fiftieth anniversary of the Theosophical Society.

The following day, December 28, under the great banyan tree, the Star Congress held its opening meeting. It was then that something did occur. Krishnamurti was speaking of the imminent coming of the world teacher. Some had a sense of expectation and spread their excitement to others in the group.

On December 28, 1925, a unique occurrence took place at which I was present. At a meeting of the Star Congress under the banyan tree in Adyar at 8 o'clock in the morning, with the amplifiers turned off, a dramatic event took place while Krishnaji was speaking. It came at the end of his talk. He had been speaking about the world teacher; suddenly his voice changed to an exquisitely sweet yet powerful tone and, through great waves of compassionate power, he continued: "He comes only to those who want, who desire, who long"—and then it became a different voice—calm, serene and with a ringing quality. He said: "I come for those who want sympathy, who want happiness, who are longing to be released, who are longing to find happiness in all things. I come to reform and not to tear down. I come not to destroy but to build."

I can testify that it was an unique spiritual experience, and of all those present, Annie Besant, C.W.L., and Raja were more deeply aware of its significance. Later, at the final meeting of the Star Congress, Annie Besant said: "...that event [of December 28] marked the definite consecration of the chosen vehicle...the final acceptance of the body chosen long before... The Coming has begun...." She wrote in the Theosophist: *"For the first time the Voice that spoke as never man spoke, has sounded again in our lower ways in the ears of the great crowd that sat beneath the banyan tree... and we know that the waiting period was over, and that the Morning Star had arisen above the horizon." [31] In the ninety-second year of my life my memory is probably defective, but I do recall this unforgettable experience with crystal clarity.*

—RUSSELL BALFOUR CLARKE

Once through the mouth of His vehicle, on the 28 December last, He spoke for the first time in our lower world for some two thousand years. Krishnamurti was speaking, and it was evident that he was under very strong influence at the moment before he was taken possession of entirely, and I will read what he was saying, because it shows the influence that was then playing upon him. He had been speaking about the world teacher: "We are all expecting Him, Who is the Example, Who is the embodiment of nobility. He will be with us soon, He is with us now. He comes to lead us all to that perfection where there is eternal happiness; He comes to lead us, and He comes to those who have not understood, who have suffered, who are unhappy, who are unenlightened. He comes to those who want, who desire, who long." The speaker started, stopped a moment, and then another voice rang out through his lips, a voice not heard on earth for two thousand years: "I come to those who want sympathy, who want happiness; who are longing to be released; who are longing to find happiness in all things; I come to reform, and not to tear down; not to destroy, but to build." [32]

—ANNIE BESANT, 1926

Krishnamurti's voice had increased in strength and power as he spoke. Then, as he changed to the first person and said in thrilling, compassionate tones, "I come," an electric current shivered through the audience.

Mrs. Besant was to say, "That event [December 28, 1925] marked the definite consecration of the chosen vehicle....the coming has begun."

From the flame you came forth,

to the flame you will return and

thus unite the beginning and the end.

—WHO BRINGS THE TRUTH?, 1926

S OME YEARS EARLIER Krishnamurti met the young Baron Phillip Van Pallandt of the Netherlands who was to give his ancestral home and estate, the Castle Eerde, to the Order of the Star.

Five thousand wooded acres surrounded the beautiful eighteenth-century buildings. Krishnamurti said it was one of the most beautiful places he knew. The Gobelin tapestries "were wonderful, they created an atmosphere of ancient dignity and beauty. Great trees, two or three hundred years old gathered around the castle...." For many years to come, Eerde was the chief European meeting place of the Order of the Star.

The castle itself became a center where small groups gathered. Nearby Ommen accommodated the thousands who came for the early camps.

CASTLE EERDE, THE
NETHERLANDS—ANCESTRAL
HOME OF BARON PHILLIP
VAN PALLANDT, GIVEN TO THE
ORDER OF THE STAR TO USE
AS THEIR EUROPEAN
HEADQUARTERS.

This is not the place to seek new labels, to satisfy personal vanities; this must be the place where each should live as dangerously as he can, as forcefully as he can, as adventurously as he can, according to this eternal Law. You must not make of this place a wilderness of false ideals, or yourselves into tame beings; you must not create little gods and worship at little shrines—this you can do elsewhere, this is not what is wanted here; this is the wrong kind of worship, the wrong kind of attitude, the wrong kind of devotion. When once you have drunk at this source, you do not want to drink anywhere else; when once you have worshipped here, you do not want to worship anything else in the world. Who wants to worship by the light of one candle, when he can have the sun?

—THE KINGDOM OF HAPPINESS, 1927

BARON PHILLIP VAN PALLANDT

EARLY SUPPORTER OF KRISHNAMURTI, ZWOLLE, HOLLAND

VP: There was a gathering in Ommen on one of my estates, of the Dutch Theosophical Society, and they invited a certain Wadia, a Parsi from the high mountains in India, to hold this meeting. Jack Burton who was a teacher at the Arundale school in England was also there. And he said, "Oh, you must ask Krishnaji to come." I'd seen him only once at a meeting in London, I never spoke to him.

EB: May I ask what year that was?

VP: 1921. Dates I always remember. And Jack Burton said, "You must directly ask Krishnaji to come from Paris because Wadia wants to set up secret centers and that might be dangerous." I said, "Jack, I don't know him. You ask him to come," which he did directly. Well, I think within 24 hours, Krishnaji was at Eerde. And the curious part of this gathering of the Theosophical Society of Wadia, was—oh yes! I mustn't forget to tell you, it was the *Secret Doctrine* morning, noon and night, now I don't know if you have ever looked into the *Secret Doctrine*? Well, have you ever understood anything? It is so deep, by Mrs. Blavatsky. Well, it's amusing to look into it because you don't understand a word, really not a word. And then Krishnaji came and what did he do? Well, Wadia had his talks morning, noon and night on the *Secret Doctrine*, and Krishnaji did nothing, he listened, but in the

meantime, he organized sports so as to prevent Wadia from making a secret center here. That was the object. And I'll tell you what kind of sports, it was awfully funny! One of the sports was to stand in the middle of a field with a rope and a stone, at the end of it, and swirl it round and he made all these old ladies jump over while it was swinging round. They had to jump over, all those old ladies of the Theosophical Society, it was very funny! He stayed at the castle, at Eerde with me. And from that moment we made great friends, really great friends.

EB: At that time were you aware that Krishnamurti was to be the so-called world teacher. What was your response to that?

VP: I was, of course, a lot younger than now, but I always viewed him as being the most extraordinary man that I have ever met. And also Dr. Annie Besant, who was the most wonderful woman I've ever met.

EB: In what way was Krishnamurti extraordinary?

VP: I'll tell you one really funny thing. When Wadia, who Krishnaji really opposed by organizing the sports, and Wadia must have felt it—when Wadia left in my little car, Krishnaji came along and twenty-seven kilometers from Ommen we had a puncture, a left-right puncture. I had driven cars for my father since 1900, since ten years old, I was far

and away the one who had driven longest, but I was frightfully unhandy and Krishnaji noticed that in changing the wheel. So within a fraction of a moment, Krishnaji took everything in hand and put on the new wheel with his slender hands, took off the dirty one—they were frightfully dusty roads, thick dust, and with his slender hands, took off the wheel and put the new wheel on and then we drove on. Every time that I pass that spot I have never forgotten the exact spot where we had that puncture. We raced on, although the train had started of course from Zwolle, so we had to drive very fast to catch the train. We arrived in Zwolle at the station. In those times you had to have a special ticket to come on the platform. Krishnaji didn't mind about that ticket, he jumped over all hurdles and arrived on the platform at the very spot, the moment that the train was moving away, with Wadia, without a bag, which he'd left at the station. Krishnaji, just after jumping over the hurdles went to the train and at that very spot, that moment, Wadia was looking out of the window, Krishnaji had nothing to do but just hand the bag—one of the most funniest moments I've ever witnessed in my life! And the train went on.

EB: To continue with those early days, can you tell us how the Star Camps came about and how the association with Castle Eerde came into being?

VP: I haven't thought about these things since tens of years, but still I remember quite a lot. I found something great in Krishnaji and I offered him the whole estate of 1,700 acres, Dutch acres, three times as much in English acres, and he said I don't accept anything! But we could form a foundation, and that's what happened, the Eerde Foundation.

EB: And he came every year to speak at Castle Eerde?

VP: Yes.

EB: Do you remember the content of his teaching? How did he express this teaching? In addition to his words, what did his presence mean to the gathering?

VP: Oh, a great deal. You must think that the Theosophists who were there, thought a lot about Krishnaji, because the Theosophical Society announced him as a coming world teacher—that you mustn't forget.

EB: Did he view himself as the world teacher?

VP: I expect perhaps in himself, but he never spoke about things like that. He was so frightfully simple. One of the special things about Krishnaji is that he is so awfully simple in everything. Even up to now.

EB: Is there anything else you can remember about him, what he did, what his activities were there?

VP: He was frightfully keen on motor cars. Once I was with Krishnaji, in Paris, at a big, automobile exhibition. Krishnaji jumped on one of the stands and got into a long conversation with a man. I think it was a Lancia car from Italy, and after that I heard the two men on the automobile stand talking to each other, "What an awful lot that man knows about motor cars." I who had driven motor cars from 1900, I knew nothing about mechanics, of machinery, absolutely nothing, but I only drove, I drove fast, never had an accident.

EB: Would you say that he is interested in any kind of mechanical thing? How things work?

VP: Very much so, very much.

EB: How would you say that Krishnamurti's teaching affected your life?

VP: Oh very much. But it is difficult to say how. I always felt and still feel that he is the greatest person I have ever met. But it was very, very difficult, for Dr. Annie Besant to follow him. At a big camp with 3,700 people in a tent at Eerde, Leadbeater went to sleep, I remember it so well, but Dr. Annie Besant, to the very very last second, listened intensely. But she couldn't follow him, that I can say.

EB: So, Leadbeater was not interested at all in what Krishnamurti had to say?

VP: Seemed not to be, he went to sleep and Annie Besant was listening very intensely before 3,700 people, and Leadbeater went to sleep.

EB: What was Krishnamurti's relationship with Leadbeater?

VP: Well, he said, "It was the most awful time of my life"—when he and Nitya were sent to Sydney to Leadbeater—"The most awful time of my life."

EB: Were there any other people there at the time that he felt particularly close to? He must have been very close to his brother. Do you remember Nitya?

"HE WAS FRIGHTFULLY KEEN ON MOTOR CARS." OPPOSITE: IN THE VAN PALLANDT CAR FROM LEFT TO RIGHT—HELEN KNOTHE, MARY LUTYENS, NITYANANDA, BETTY LUTYENS (STANDING), KRISHNAMURTI, AND LADY EMILY LUTYENS.

VP: Oh, very well. His death was something awful for him. Awful; he suffered so much. He heard it on board a ship between…Australia and India. There he got the message and it was something terrible. People who were there said that he suffered terrifically.

EB: Did you see him when he got back to India? When Krishnamurti returned from Australia to India after his brother's death, were you in India at the time?

VP: I was in India in 1925 at the fiftieth anniversary year of the Theosophical Society.

EB: After Nitya's death did Rajagopal help Krishnamurti in his work?

VP: He—I think after Nitya's death—Rajagopal put himself forward. Yes, he put himself forward after Nitya's death. I felt that Nitya was a most wonderful friend, quite different than Krishnaji. Nitya was most adorable, that's the word I can say. Nitya was a most adorable fellow, whom I liked awfully, and his death was something terrible to me.

EB: Baron Van Pallandt, is there anything else you would like to add?

VP: I wish I could remember more.

EB: Well, I think you've really recalled a great deal, it goes back over many, many years. Thank you very much.

VP: Not at all.[33]

I am always afraid of organizations and societies and orders, because there is in them all an inclination to regard their own particular form of words or jargon as the only truth; so that when the simple truth of reality is unfolded to them, they will misunderstand it, they will lose it, and even those people who are really looking and who have been really working and sacrificing may lose the thing for which they have sacrificed.

We must have truth in a specialized form, because we have been brought up in a particular group; we must have truth clothed in our own particular jargon, and as soon as it is not given in that fashion we do not understand it. That is why I often wish that there was no such thing as an organization, if you will not misunderstand me; I often wish that we were all free to think for ourselves, to feel the reality of things for ourselves, without having organizations, group leaders, national representatives, heads, and so on.[34]

—CHICAGO, 1927

During the same time period Krishnamurti met a young woman who was to be pivotal in his early life.

Helen Knothe was to open floodgates of romantic longing in the young man that had hitherto been firmly closed. She was a young American girl of seventeen, a violin student who was to study music in Amsterdam. Helen, who later married Scott Nearing, an important American social critic and back-to-the-land environmentalist (long before it was correct) lived a surprisingly free life for a young woman of the 1920s. Helen was taken to Holland by her Dutch mother to continue her violin studies there. She was seventeen at the time and Krishnamurti twenty-six.

H E L E N   K N O T H E   N E A R I N G

EARLY FRIEND OF KRISHNAMURTI

OPPOSITE: HELEN KNOTHE,
AN AMERICAN GIRL OF
SEVENTEEN, WAS PIVOTAL IN
KRISHNAMURTI'S EARLY LIFE.

HN: Before I started taking lessons in Amsterdam I went with my mother to Ommen, where Mr. Wadia, who was also a prominent Theosophist at the time, was holding courses, and my mother attended the courses. Krishna had been invited by Phillip Van Pallandt to come to Ommen because Phillip was interested in donating his large acreage there. Phillip heard of Krishnamurti—I think he must have been at this conference in Paris. He invited Krishnamurti and his brother to come to Ommen to see him with the thought of perhaps donating the land to Krishnamurti. Nitya was not well enough to come, so Krishna came alone. He had been a few days at Ommen, and Phillip took him around in his car, showing him that part of the country, and Krishna happened to see me racing with a Swedish girl—what we were doing out in the country I don't know, racing, I for America and my Swedish friend for Sweden—and I won the race. Krishna and Phillip Van Pallandt came up to me and spoke with me, and I asked Krishna for his autograph. Phillip Van Pallandt saw that he was intrigued or interested, and he said why don't you come to the castle for dinner or something. So I went to the castle and had lunch with him, and there was no other young person around at the time, and it was just coincidental that this somehow happened. That I was the young person, the young girl at the time, that Krishnamurti apparently fell for. I was about the right age.

EB: What were your initial impressions when you met this young man for the first time?

HN: There was not the atmosphere that later grew up around him. I had

no idea of his reputation and of what had been said about him, and he didn't seem to rely very much on that himself. He was unostentatious, he'd come with no entourage, he had come alone to see Phillip. Phillip was a very simple person, and treated him in a simple way. This was a young boy I met who was extraordinarily handsome and quite different from any I'd ever met, but I think he was more ready for the experience than I was at that time. He was so different from any boy that I had met before. He had only a week in Holland, I was staying longer, much longer, and he had a week there and he spent that time entirely with me—walking in the woods or bicycling, or in Phillip's car, Phillip's old Mercedes car I think it was—and finally at the end of about five days we were walking on the moors in the heather in Holland, and he avowed real love. He was so shy, he covered his face with a handkerchief. We were sitting on the heather and he admitted me into the trinity of his brother, whom he loved very much, Mrs. Besant, whom he called "Amma," and Lady Emily. He said, "These are my three greatest friends," and he admitted me into that category at the time. And it seemed to be something quite new for him. This was, of course, something extraordinary and out of the way.

EB: And he covered his face when he spoke to you?

HN: He was so shy. And his first letter as he left Ommen—he had to go back to London and then he had to go to India—and in his first letter he said: "Remember how staggeringly shy I was," and then he said also, "You don't feel the way I do about this." And I have kept, all these years, I've kept those letters. They are so pure, and so noble and so beautiful and so eloquent that they are part of his history.

EB: Did Krishnamurti express any views of marriage, his personal views on marriage?

HN: No, because I suppose we never thought of it. And I suppose that as close as we were during that time, I don't remember caresses, I don't remember hugs, I don't remember kisses, which is strange, I never thought, "Oh, we mustn't," or I don't think we thought, "We mustn't." It was another attraction, sort of a meeting of souls, and I had the sense at seventeen—and I was just a callow American girl, but I had the sense—to appreciate it for what it was.

EB: You are saying that there wasn't really a physical side to your friendship and your relationship?

HN: Not at all, not at all, and yet it was warm and deep, even passionate. Strange. It was a great outpouring of his love and spirit at the time, and he wanted me to be with him. He was desperate at going to India so soon after meeting me. We knew each other for a week in Holland, then he had to go back to England, and then he really fabricated a return trip to Holland to give a talk or so there, but it was really to see me again. And then we were together in Amsterdam, in the Dutch Theosophical headquarters for a few days, maybe a long weekend or part of a week, and then he had to go back to India.

EB: And during that period, did Krishnamurti talk about his work?

HN: Yes, and he was rather desperate about it. He wasn't ready for it yet, and he saw it ahead of him and he knew what he had to do. He had his very down moment which he wrote of.

EB: That was a period of great unrest in him and insecurity as to what his part should be?

HN: Yes, and fearful that people expected more of him than he had in him to give.

EB: I believe it was in 1923, when you were with Krishnamurti and the group at Ehrwald in the Austrian Tyrol. And there was a recurrence of the so-called "process"?

HN: That's right.

EB: Could you describe what happened?

HN: Well, I was with him every night of the month that we were in Ehrwald.

EB: That was the onset of these experiences?

HN: That was the start of it, yes. Nitya had written Lady Emily and me and some other people about what had been going on in Ojai but we didn't know if it would ever occur again.

EB: That was about a year after his so-called "pepper tree experience," the process leading up to the culmination of what happened in Ojai.

HN: It reactivated at Ehrwald and I was called on to help.

EB: Could you describe what happened?

HN: In the evening we used to sit out on the balcony overlooking the mountains, and Krishna and Nitya would chant, and we had songs and mantras, and it was obvious that Krishna was disturbed physically. So he left the group.

EB: How did that show itself?

HN: He was feverish and hot, disturbed and restless. He went into the house with Nitya, and after a while Nitya called me in, and I was to sit and hold his hand. And he was obviously in pain and distress, crying. And this was something hard for me to witness and go through, but I did what I could to help. That went on every evening, I kept a diary of all those days and the nights that I was with him. I think it was every night.

EB: It just occurred at night?

HN: Yes. Sometimes he would be particularly wild and gay and silly, and then he would relapse into this awayness and he would not be with us at all. He was a completely different person.

EB: There's discussion today of out-of-body experiences, is that how you would characterize those incidents?

HN: No. It was very much in the body, it was very intense. It was the body that was undergoing this experience. Although sometimes Krishna himself would seem not to be there, but a little boy, almost a child of three or four would be there, and this child, this "body elemental" would be enduring the pain and would even shriek at Krishna and say "Keep away, I can take care of this better than you can." It was like two strange personalities, and Krishna would come back and talk with this little "body elemental," and they would converse.

EB: There would be two different voices? The young child and the young man?

HN: That's right. And then the young man would sense beings coming and attending and helping, or even perhaps inflicting it on him. We didn't know, Nitya and I. Nitya sat off in a corner, and I was close to Krishna and holding the body and helping the body. Nitya and I were not clairvoyant but we would feel the benediction of this wonderful presence coming over the mountains and come into the room, and they would give messages to Nitya and to me and to Krishna.

EB: How were those messages delivered?

HN: Through Krishna's voice, and Nitya or I would scribble them down as well as we could in the dark. We were mainly in the dark. We took down these messages. Some were for Nitya. Some were for me, and some were for Krishna himself.

EB: What were those messages?

HN: They were what we should do and what we should be, and what the pain was about.

EB: What was the pain for?

HN: We thought it was the *Kundalini*. We thought it was the awakening of the *Kundalini*, and the clearing of the passages—we thought that the Lord would be coming through in these wonderful beneficent influences that we felt were to take over Krishna at that time. And then this little "body elemental" was so tender and so sweet and so dear, it was like I was in a room with Nitya and Krishna and some other little entity. Completely different. They talked together, they argued together.

EB: What did they argue about?

HN: The little one said, "I know how to take the pain better than you do, stay out." And Krishna would come back again and scream and fall....I'm sure that the peasants down below who ran the house in Ehrwald, they were only two floors down, they must have heard all of this, so I think John Cordes, who was attendant at the time, told them he had epileptic fits.

EB: Did you ever feel that it was anything like an epileptic fit?

HN: I didn't know anything about epilepsy at the time, so I was convinced that it was an esoteric endurance test.

EB: Do you still feel that today?

HN: I don't know. I can have no opinion of it now because I don't know how it develops or what it was.

EB: After these episodes, was there any change in the everyday Krishnamurti?

HN: He could be just perfectly normal, and we couldn't believe it was the same person.

It has been a struggle all the time to find the truth because I was not satisfied by the authority of another, or the imposition of another, or the enticement of another; I wanted to discover for myself, and naturally I had to go through sufferings to find out.

—*WHO BRINGS THE TRUTH?, 1927*

If you love truth intensely and yet absolutely for its own sake, you love all. If truth is the one comfort, and you have that comfort, your desire is to share it with others....

—*THE POOL OF WISDOM, 1927*

It is not a kingdom that lies far off, nor an abode for which we need make a voyage to the ends of the earth. You must find the key that opens all the gates of heaven, all the gardens of ecstasy; and that key is your intuition, and with that key you can enter and live everlastingly in that garden.

—*THE POOL OF WISDOM, 1927*

EB: Did he have a recollection of this upon awakening?

HN: No, not much.

EB: Did he have a sense of pain, or the release of pain?

HN: No, it was on or it was off. Sometimes Nitya would wake me in the middle of the night and say, "You'd better come in, Krishna needs you." And then I would go and be with him, and I don't know if it was Krishna then, or the little one, but naturally, I was there and happy to be with him. That went on for more than a month in Ehrwald, and then he persuaded me to come back to Australia with him and not stay and study the violin anymore. So I went back to Vienna to pick up my violin and my music and say good-bye to the people there, and to go home and persuade my parents that I wanted to go to Australia. I was with him a bit after that. He still suffered these things in the same way and on the boat going across from Southhampton to New York I was with him in the boat, but that heavy month of endurance and pain—I don't think that ever occurred again for that length of time when I was around.

EB: So it was approximately a month. That's a long time to endure something like that. Then it diminished, you say.

HN: But he needed and wanted me with him, and Nitya arranged that I had a connecting cabin, and I was with him.

EB: So there was an understanding that you had a special influence?

HN: Apparently a special role.

EB: Did he make other vows of love to you while you were there, while he was undergoing this process?

HN: Yes.

EB: So his affection and love for you throughout that whole period, wasn't damaged by this whole process?

HN: No, in fact, it was probably enhanced because I was close to him.

EB: Then you went with him on board ship. How long did your relationship last?

HN: He arranged for another young woman, Ruth Roberts and me, to go on to Sydney alone. He continued to write, hoping that I would do well. Krishna came to Sydney on the way to Ojai, because Nitya had to get out of India, he was not well. Krishna was not welcomed in Sydney by Leadbeater.

EB: Why was that?

HN: C.W. L. didn't understand this process that was going on. He said it had never happened to him, it had never happened to Mrs. Besant, and he turned rather cool to Krishna and kept him waiting in the hall in the manor in Sydney, and he was very worried about Nitya, and rightly too, because Nitya was going. We didn't know it, but Nitya was going.

EB: I'd like you to describe Krishnamurti's relationship with his brother.

HN: It was as close and as warm and as sweet and as dear as can be. I think

Nitya was the closest person to him in the world, then he also loved Mrs. Besant, and he also loved Lady Emily, and at that time he also loved me. Those were the ones that were closest to him, but Nitya was the closest of all, he was just a part of him, and Nitya's influence on him was very good, he helped him in so many ways.

EB: You never sensed that there was a jealousy, or so-called sibling rivalry?

HN: Never, they were just loving brothers, both appreciated the other tremendously, it was a lovely relationship.

EB: What was Krishnamurti's relationship with Annie Besant during that period.

HN: Very loving, very tender, very devoted.

EB: At that time, he was, in a sense, plunging into his work.

HN: That's right, and I had the sense to understand that.

EB: When did you first detect signs of estrangement between Krishnamurti and the Theosophical Society?

HN: Perhaps a bit in Australia when he came that second time with Nitya, but he was so engrossed in poor Nitya's health. It was beginning then because C. W. L. cut him off.

EB: There was a definite shift around that period, he became more and more open in what he wrote. He was becoming more independent, apparently in his personal relationships as well. Were you engaged to Krishnamurti at that time?

HN: No, we knew that nothing like that could occur. First, I seemed to have known of it myself, and he knew of it because of his mission. Mrs. Besant had said in so many words that we were very close and we would grow together, and would work together, but that there could be nothing like that.

EB: It was thought apparently that marriage would deflect him from his mission.

"KRISHNA MET ME IN SANTA
BARBARA AND DROVE ME TO
OJAI. HE WAS SWEET AND
AFFECTIONATE AS EVER, BUT
SOMETHING WAS CUT OFF...."
—HELEN KNOTHE

HN: Oh, certainly. But it did get into the papers, he was in Ojai at the time, and I thought perhaps wiser minds may have said to him, "This has gone pretty far." That may have started his detachment. I never knew. My family wanted me to come back from Australia at the time, and I left Australia reluctantly and came back and Krishna met me in Santa Barbara and drove me to Ojai. He was sweet and affectionate as ever, but something was cut off, or something was different, and I sensed that the period of our closeness was over. I stayed in Arya Vihara for maybe a week, and he drove me to the train. We were close friends and loving as ever as far as I knew, but that was the end.

EB: During this period, what was your sense of the teachings? Were you really interested in the teachings?

HN: I knew that he was teaching "live in the present." I think I imbibed all of that and reconstructed it into a philosophy for myself that has lasted to this day. I never disavowed anything which he said or wrote. I took it into myself and formulated my own mode of living and philosophy, which has lasted my whole life. I haven't thrown any of it away.[35]

Like everyone else Krishnamurti, in the past, searched, obeyed and worshipped, but as time grew, as suffering came, he wanted to discover the reality which hides behind the picture, behind the sunset, behind the image, behind all philosophies, behind all religions, all sects, all organizations, and to discover and to understand that, he had to hang on to a peg of unreality, of untruth, until, little by little, he was able to pass all those shrines that are limiting, that are binding, all the gods that insist on worship. In passing all those he was able to arrive where all religions, where all affections are consummated, where all worship ends, where all desire ceases, where the separate self is purified by being destroyed. It is because I have gone through those stages that I am able to speak with the authority of my own knowledge, and I would give to you of that knowledge, of that experience.

—WHO BRINGS THE TRUTH?, 1927

The swelling ranks of the Order of the Star impacted not only India, England, Europe, and the United State, but also Latin America. As Krishnamurti continued to travel tirelessly around the world, he gathered many lifelong friends along the way. Their regard for him never faded.

I N LOS ANGELES SOMETIME EARLIER he met a young man who was to become one of those lifelong friends. Sidney Field, diplomat and author of many Hollywood screenplays, was born in Costa Rica of an American father and Costa Rican mother. His parents were founders of the Order of the Star in Costa Rica and were good friends of both brothers.

SIDNEY FIELD

DIPLOMAT AND SCREENWRITER, LOS ANGELES, CALIFORNIA

SF: When we came to Los Angeles from Costa Rica in 1925 we bought a house at Crescent Heights Boulevard, and my father asked Krishnaji to come for tea. I was petrified because I thought, "He's going to see through me. I'm just an ordinary kid and I have done nothing at all to merit this meeting." We had meetings every Sunday in Costa Rica of the Order of the Star in the East, and we were supposed to prepare ourselves for the great coming. Finally I met him at home. He came with Nitya, and it was just the family and a newspaperman from New York, who had known about Krishnamurti and was very interested. I

KRISHNAMURTI VISITED THE SET OF THE CECIL B. DEMILLE OPUS OF THE LIFE OF CHRIST, *THE KING OF KINGS.* HE WAS INTRODUCED TO DEMILLE AND H.B. WARNER, WHO PLAYED CHRIST. "I LEFT SOON AFTERWARD," HE SAID, "I THOUGHT THREE SAVIORS ON THE SAME SET WAS PERHAPS A LITTLE TOO MUCH." KRISHNAMURTI IS SHOWN HERE BETWEEN VICTOR VARCONI, WHO PLAYED PONTIUS PILATE, AND DEMILLE.

mention this because after the meeting he said, "You know, Krishnaji is the more beautiful of the two, but Nitya has much more of the stuff that I would think a world teacher held." We spoke about all kinds of things, about leaders of the world and so on. It was truly an interesting conversation. Well, they left, because Nitya was not feeling well, but I asked Krishnaji when I could see him, and he said, "Call me and we'll arrange a date." From that point on, we started a very interesting friendship. I was just sixteen in May, and he was very much interested in what young people did and thought. That year when he came over I went to see him and I had an interesting situation. He had no car and asked me if I could drive him around. He told me to meet him at six at the Ambassador Hotel and that he was visiting a friend. And I was very curious about it, "What kind of meeting is this?" I didn't ask him who he was seeing. At six o'clock sharply, I knocked at the door of the room he had told me, and the door opened and there was John Barrymore, who looked at me very severely, and then Krishnaji heard my voice and came over and introduced me. That was a great surprise to me. I asked him "What do you and Barrymore talk about Krishnaji?" I didn't even know that he was interested in this sort of thing. He said, "Yes, he's very much interested, and he thinks that the renunciation of the Buddha was one of the great acts of history. And we talked a great deal about the Buddha, he knows quite a bit about Buddhist life." So Krishnaji asked Barrymore to visit him in Ojai. Of course you know that Barrymore was an alcoholic, and he promised Krishnaji that he would be strictly sober that day. Krishnaji told me the story afterwards. It seems that on his way to Ojai, he stopped in Ventura because he was very thirsty. He just wanted some water. Well, he ended up with a whole lot of beers. *And* drove to Ojai. He was an hour late, but Krishnaji had not started lunch, and he said, "Barrymore practically fell in my hands. He could hardly stand up. But he was very gentlemanly and very funny, a very witty man." And after a while, with gallons of coffee, he was sober and drove back home.

THROUGH JOHN BARRYMORE, KRISHNAMURTI MET MANY PEOPLE IN THE FILM INDUSTRY.

EB: Wasn't Barrymore supposed to have suggested that Krishnamurti play the Buddha in a film?

SF: Exactly. Barrymore was very much interested in making a film about Buddha. Krishnaji, by the way, said, "I tried to discourage him right away, I just told him it was a very difficult role, and so on…Though I thought that Ananda, Buddha's favorite pupil, was perhaps a more desirable thing to concentrate on." Anyhow, Barrymore got in touch with him later and said, "I think that you are very wise. I'm going to do the picture, and I will play Ananda." The Buddha was relegated to a practically unimportant role, and he wanted Krishnaji to play that role. Krishnaji refused it. Anyhow, Barrymore was never able to get the money for the picture.

EB: It would be a rather esoteric subject even for today. But in those days it would have been even more unknown.

SF: Right. So nothing was done, but they kept seeing each other. Through Barrymore he met many other people in the picture business. He got to know Norma Talmage well. I remember one time he came to dinner with us, and he had his hand held out when he came in and I thought he had injured himself. He went to the bathroom and said, "Let me wash my hand." When he came back, I said, "Excuse me, what did you do? Did you hurt yourself?" And he said, "No, it's Norma Talmage's perfume. I can't get it off my hand."

EB: To go back, could you tell us something about the Order of the

Star? You say in Costa Rica there was a group that carried out the mandates of the Order of the Star?

SF: Right. You see the Theosophical Society was founded in Costa Rica— and it was the first Theosophical Society in all of Latin America—by my grandfather, who was a famous painter in Spain, Tomás Povedano de Arcos, and my father and mother. They were the original three members who founded the Theosophical Society, and a year or two later—the Order of the Star in the East. And, as I say in my book *Krishnamurti: The Reluctant Messiah*, Krishnaji unwittingly became involved in Costa Rican politics, because one of our most prominent men, Federico Tinoco, was a great believer in Krishnamurti. He belonged to the Order of the Star in the East, and he finally took power in a coup d'état. He became president. And he announced that he would create a society that would reflect the ideas of Krishnamurti.

EB: Rather a brave thing to do, wasn't it?

SF: Extraordinarily brave thing to do, yes. My father was the president at that time, of the International Bank, which is now the National Bank and the country's biggest. They insisted they wanted his picture on the ten colon note, and on his lapel was the little Star of the East. Well, the Catholic Church was very much aroused by the whole thing, and made a tremendous campaign in the newspaper, saying that this was done expressly and with dishonest means to carry Krishnamurti's message throughout the whole country. People would ask, "What does that Star mean?" and then they would be told, and there was a big hullabaloo about it, ending in the burning of the Theosophical temple. For the first time the Theosophical Society had a really magnificent place that they built with some very wealthy members, and a priest then came out and said, "I burned it myself, I put a torch to it in the name of God." There was great excitement! There was also a column in the newspaper, *La Información*, the government controlled newspaper, in which were excerpts from *At The Feet of the Master*. All this went on in those days. So when Tinoco was up Krishnaji was very popular, and when Tinoco was down and finally kicked out of the country, Krishnaji was very unpopular. He got into all this political activity, and the man was totally innocent, and unknowing of it. He was very much amused when I told him. In Costa Rica, there had been a preparation that was unique in Latin America, because of Tinoco publishing excerpts of *At The Feet of the Master*. It became a fashionable thing to be a member of the Order of the Star, and people, even many of his cabinet members, were wearing a little star—which meant nothing, I think. It was just a question of pleasing the president.

EB: When Tinoco was removed from power, I'm sure that was the end of Krishnamurti?

SF: Oh, Krishnamurti's stock went way down. Now, another Theosophist and member of the Star by the name of Julio Acosta, who had been a professor, a charming person, I remember him very well, he was the one who started the revolution against Tinoco. When he came into Costa Rica with his troops, which were really a pathetic lot of peons, Tinoco was already on his way out. He knew that he had lost everything. Julio Acosta ran for president, and he became president.

So the whole thing started again—the publication of Krishnaji's writings or excerpts from *At The Feet of the Master*. So Krishnaji's stock went way up again.

EB: In Krishnamurti's private conversations with you did he speak along the lines of his teaching?

SF: Yes, he often would, but only generally—unless you pinned him down and asked him point blank, "What about this?" Then he would go into detail. The reason why it became a close friendship despite the great difference in age was that I never pushed him at all about any of his views. I was happy to be with him. I thought he was absolutely an enchanting person. I loved his sense of humor, and his laughter was so much like a child that I used to save jokes to tell him just to get him to laugh.

EB: But, as you say, you were so much younger, you were sixteen, seventeen years old. And he was relatively mature.

SF: Yes, he was around what, twenty-eight, thirty?

EB: Even though there was such an age difference, you still maintained a friendship?

SF: We still maintained a friendship, and a very close friendship. He felt very comfortable with me—and, after a while, I felt entirely comfortable with him.

EB: How would you describe his personality? You say he had a good sense of humor, but did you sense an underlying seriousness in him?

BOOK JACKET FOR *THE IMMORTAL FRIEND* PUBLISHED IN 1929 WITH A COVER ILLUSTRATION OF KRISHNAMURTI BY KAHLIL GIBRAN.

"WHEN HE ENTERED THE ROOM I SAID TO MYSELF, 'SURELY THE LORD OF LOVE HAS COME.'"

—KAHLIL GIBRAN

THE IMMORTAL FRIEND

by JIDDU KRISHNAMURTI

Author of The Kingdom of Happiness and The Search.

SF: Yes, very, very underlined definitely! Very serious, and very much interested in the person he was with as a human being. What you were going to do in this world, that sort of thing. I found in Krishnamurti an extraordinary selflessness; he seemed to be really interested in you and what was going on, and you felt that this was absolutely genuine, not just a put on.

EB: Over the years you heard Krishnamurti speak in the United States. Did you go to other countries to hear him speak?

SF: To Ommen, yes. He asked me to come to Ommen to the pre-camp. I spent a rather miserable ten days there, cooped up in my apartment, and Krishnaji was not to be seen anywhere. Then finally one day Lady Emily said, "Krishnaji will see you tomorrow at three o'clock." I was there the next day at three o'clock, I knocked at the door, Krishnaji said, "Come in." He looked absolutely magnificent in a golden robe. He had to ask me to come and sit down beside him, because I just stood there looking at him. I don't remember our conversation, but something was said. It was nothing, I think, too significant or important, but I suddenly got out of my body in a most extraordinary experience of joy that I've ever felt. It was something like having broken through into another world. It was all I could do to just keep from shouting with joy when Krishna was talking. I never told Krishnaji about this until many years later here in Malibu, and he told me, "What a pity, Sidney, that you didn't follow that because it could have been a breakthrough." Well, as it was I realized that I was just seventeen, and there are a great many interests in the life of a seventeen-year-old. I think that when an experience like that comes, you either give yourself up entirely to it and you don't know what's going to happen, or you hold back and the door begins to close. And that's what happened.

EB: Could you say what precipitated this experience?

SF: I don't know what precipitated it.

EB: Was it something that you incorporated into your everyday life?

SF: Well, it was incorporated in my everyday life in the sense that afterwards I felt a tremendous love and affection. Everything that my eyes touched, my heart went out to. It was a wonderful experience in that respect. Then it started to recede. And many times I would have this wonderful feeling, not with this strength, but much diminished.[36]

Do you need to be convinced of the beauty of the sunset, of the beauty of a rose, or of a single star in a naked sky, or of the cry of a bird in a still forest? It is there; and those who have the experience of sorrow and have the desire for immense knowledge, they will discover the beauty, they will recognize it, become one with that beauty.

—*THE HERALD OF THE STAR*, SEPTEMBER 1927

During the next several years a flood of poetry flowed from Krishnamurti's pen. Much of it was of an exalted, ecstatic nature. Krishnamurti speaks of "The Beloved" in much of the style of classics of mysticism both East and West. His slim books include *Come Away* (1927), *The Search* (1927), *The Immortal Friend* (1929), and *The Song of Life* (1931) among others. The year 1931 marked the end of these books, although poetry was to reappear later in his life in a quite different manner.

At this time a great longing also emerged to renounce all worldly life and live in ascetic retirement as a solitary sanyasi. This hope was never realized and except for brief interludes Krishnamurti lived most of his life surrounded by others.

As one beholds through a small window
A single green leaf, a small patch of the vast blue sky,
So I began to perceive Thee, in the beginning of
    All things.
As the leaf faded and withered, the patch covered as with
    Dark cloud,
So didst Thou fade and vanish,
But to be reborn again,
As the single green leaf, as the small patch of the blue sky.

For many lives have I seen the bleak winter and the
    Green spring.
Prisoned in my little room,
I could not behold the entire tree nor the whole sky.
I swore there was no tree nor the vast sky—
That was the truth.

Through time and destruction
My window grew large.
I beheld,
Now,
A branch with many leaves,
And a greater patch of the blue, with many clouds.
I forgot the single green leaf, the small patch of the vast blue.
I swore there was no tree, nor the immense sky—
That was the truth.

Weary of this prison,
This small cell,
I raged at my window.
With bleeding fingers
I tore away brick after brick, I beheld,
Now,
The entire tree, its great trunk,
Its many branches, and its thousand leaves,
And an immense part of the sky.
I swore there was no other tree, no other part to the sky—
That was the truth.

This prison no longer holds me,
I flew away through the window,
O friend,
I behold every tree and the vast expanse of the limitless sky.
Though I live in every single leaf and in every small
    patch of the vast blue sky,
Though I live in every prison, looking out through every
    small casement,
Liberated am I.
Lo! not a thing shall bind me—
This is the truth.

—THE SEARCH, 1927

I walked on a path through the jungle
Which an elephant had made,
And about me lay a tangle of wilderness.
The voice of desolation fills the distant plain.
And the city is noisy with the bells of a tall temple.
Beyond the jungle are the great mountains,
Calm and clear.

In the fear of Life
The temptation of sorrow is created.

Cut down the jungle—not one mere tree,
For truth is attained
By putting aside all that you have sown.

And now I walk with the elephant.

—*THE STAR BULLETIN*, DECEMBER 1930

Doubt is as a precious ointment;
Though it burns, it shall heal greatly.

I tell thee, invite doubt
When in the fullness of thy desire.
Call to doubt
At the time when thine ambition
Is outrunning others in thought.
Awaken doubt
When thy heart is rejoicing in great love.

I tell thee,
Doubt brings forth eternal love;
Doubt cleanses the mind of its corruption.
So the strength of thy days
Shall be established in understanding.

For the fullness of thy heart,
And for the flight of thy mind,
Let doubt tear away thine entanglements.

As the fresh winds from the mountains
That awaken the shadows in the valley,
So let doubt call to dance
The decaying love of a contented mind.

Let not doubt enter darkly thy heart.

I tell thee,
Doubt is as a precious ointment;
Though it burns, it shall heal greatly.

—*THE SONG OF LIFE*, 1931

I N THE SUMMER OF 1924, Krishnamurti, Nityananda, Helen Knothe, Rajagopal, and Rosalind, (who were to marry several years later), went by steamship to England. On board they met a young man with whom Krishnamurti would have a friendship that lasted over many years, the mythologist Joseph Campbell.

The friendship continued during a visit to Paris. Then, as Krishnamurti returned to London and on to India, they parted until some time later.

According to the Joseph Campbell biography by Stephen and Robin Larsen, Campbell had stayed on in Paris and became friends with Angela Gregory, a young student studying sculpture under the renowned Antoine Bourdelle. She wrote of her meeting with Campbell:

I was very interested when I found out that he [Campbell] knows Krishnamurti, the young Hindu messiah—intimately. It is he who posed for Bourdelle last fall and swept him off his feet with his wonderful personality. Campbell was so thrilled to find that I was interested in Krishna—having been boosted by his book The Kingdom of Happiness...

...Bourdelle had invited Krishnamurti for lunch with him and Madame Bourdelle.

Madame Bourdelle said, "My husband has an American student who knows a young American who knows you—Joseph Campbell."

Krishna was enthusiastic. "Oh, Joseph Campbell—I would love to see him. Tell him to meet me after my lecture tonight at the Theosophical Club."

That Tuesday would be an historic occasion, for though the two young men had been friends for three years, and corresponded as well as spoken on philosophical subjects, it would be the first time Campbell heard Krishnamurti give one of his spellbinding public lectures.

As usual, the hall was packed, but after Krishnamurti came in, passing through the audience, "he grasped Joe's hand as he went down the aisle [he hadn't seen him for two years]." ...After the lecture, they talked for a long while and arranged to see one another again in Paris, in June [1928], when Krishna would return from America.

...The simplicity and force of his message was effective on Campbell, bringing him back many times over the next year and half to his friend Krishna's inspired talks.

Campbell later recalled themes from some of Krishnamurti's lectures: "What he said had to do with the problem of integrating all the faculties and bringing them to center. He used the image of the chariot drawn by the three horses of mind, body and soul. This was exactly in my line; and though I didn't feel that it could be classified as a New World Teaching, I was led to think of my problem now in terms of psychological centering."

Campbell was now under the influence of both Krishnamurti and Antoine Bourdelle in a merging of the artistic with the spiritual, which was to become the hallmark of his life's work.

In 1928 Campbell visited Castle Eerde with Krishnamurti and wrote:

After a delightful visit to Krishnamurti's castle in Holland, I can scarcely think of anything but the wisdom and beauty of my friend. I walked with him in the woodlands which are all about his home. He answered me my questions, and

JOSEPH CAMPBELL (ABOVE) WAS INFLUENCED BY KRISHNAMURTI AND ANTOINE BOURDELLE TO MERGE THE ARTISTIC WITH THE SPIRITUAL. THIS BECAME THE HALLMARK OF HIS LIFE'S WORK. ANTOINE BOURDELLE (OPPOSITE) SCULPTED THE HEAD OF KRISHNAMURTI IN 1928. THE SCULPTURE IS NOW IN THE LIBRARY OF THE KRISHNAMURTI FOUNDATION OF AMERICA IN OJAI, CALIFORNIA.

thrilled to the beauty of trees. He gave me a great deal to think about, and set me off on a quest for something which I scarcely understand...

...About two miles from the castle there is a huge camp [Ommen]. During the first week in August three thousand people were there to hear Krishna. They came from fifty-odd countries—Iceland, Java, Brazil...

I spent most of my time strolling with people under great trees, and arguing to beat the band. Every morning at eleven Krishna would give us all a little talk, and we'd say what we had to say about things, if we happened to have something to say. After supper we'd sit around the fireplace and discuss things. There were some delightful people there, and the talk was pretty lively.[37]

⌐

There were people from all over the world at Eerde that summer, and Campbell was so excited by the cross-cultural richness that he began to make plans to go around the world and visit all his new friends. It would be India first, he thought, with its grand sacred sites, perhaps to Adyar, on the east coast, where Helen Knothe had gone a few years before, and where there was a permanent center: the world headquarters, in its graceful park....there was much turmoil present at Eerde during the summer of 1928. Krishnamurti, the man who had been declared "perfect," not only would not say the things he was supposed to say but would commend the souls of his listeners to a deep personal introspection and an imperative to confront the inevitable turbulence they would find within. To Krishnamurti's followers, and the dismayed Theosophists, the impact of this was like that of Jesus when he said, "I come not to bring peace but a sword," or when he overthrew the tables of the money-changers in the Temple. There was war in the heaven that brooded above Eerde.

An article in *L'Intransigeant* that appeared March 1928 in Paris, described Bourdelle and Krishnamurti as "Two Messengers."

The Great Sculptor Talks of One Who is Called the Messiah.

Imagine quite a young man not yet thirty, a Hindu of noble birth, radiant in face and gentle of movement, in other words a man to whom all the allurements of life might legitimately appeal and who says to you, "I come to bring back to the world the message of peace and love." This young man leaves his country and, in spite of Brahmanical opposition, betakes himself to Western countries. Many are against him, and many are the smiles. But laughter and enthusiasm mean little to this Hindu of wondrous calm; he has within himself centuries of wisdom. Indifferent to riches, to the excessive tokens of admiration, he pursues but one end, that of impressing upon the world its misery and the way out. They talk of a messiah; the skeptics scoff, the brilliant minds harangue, but he goes on, in no way posing as a god, confident in his mission. That is Krishnamurti.

And now we see a man who wrestles with one of the densest forms of matter—stone—he cuts it, hammers it, changes it, wresting away its inertia. His two hands, which are not large, suffice to breathe life and spirit into this matter which he masters. A man of short stature, broad shoulders, an astonishing face framed in a beard which is nearly white, of apostolic aspect, he has brought and still brings to the world a message—that of art. As an artist, and a great artist, he has great dreams and great anxieties. That is Bourdelle.

Bourdelle and Krishnamurti have come together. The master was asked to make a bust of the young sage. He has done so and has been conquered. Should one be astonished thereat? One can easily imagine the conversations exchanged during sittings. The keen study of the artist seeking to fix in stone the actual mystery and depth of the bronze-colored and immobile face. But I called on Bourdelle especially to talk to him of Krishnaji and it was with a gentle kindliness that he said to me: "When one hears Krishnaji speak one is so astonished. So much wisdom and so young a man! One expresses this astonishment to him, he replies by referring to his various lives. Do not smile: this refers to a belief which in India is a certainty. There is no one in existence who is more impersonal than he, whose life is more dedicated to that of others than his. As I said to him one day: 'And who knows, Krishnaji, if some day men may receive you with stones?' He answered me that his life was of no account. He has written very beautiful poems, yet he is neither a poet nor a writer. He is the man who comes to tell us to kill out our pride, our love of the transitory; the eternal things are the only things which matter. Well, yes, the Christ came and spoke the same language, but do we remember it? And is the renewal of these words of peace superfluous? Krishnamurti is a great sage and were I fifteen years of age I would follow him." As I listen with eyes wide open, Bourdelle rises and fetches a copybook. He reads me some stirring pages, all replete with the force which characterizes him and devoted to Krishnamurti. It is a magnificent tribute which is to appear in a review in which the maître takes a personal interest and which is placed under the mysterious sign of the five-pointed star. Thus has the handsome young Indian passed beneath our skies. And he has charmed those among us who in days gone by would have molded the cathedrals of the time.[38]

As the 1920s moved toward their close Krishnamurti came in contact with yet another in a group of artists and intellectuals. Leopold Stokowski, the internationally known conductor, visited the Castle Eerde to speak with Krishnamurti on music and art.

LEOPOLD STOKOWSKI

CONDUCTOR

LEOPOLD STOKOWSKI AND KRISHNAMURTI MET AT CASTLE EERDE IN THE 1920S FOR A LONG, REFLECTIVE DIALOGUE ON INTUITION, MUSIC AND INTELLIGENCE.

LS: Every art has its medium of expression. The dramatist—stage, actors, lights, costumes, decoration in color and form; the sculptor—stone or wood; the poet—words; the painter—canvas and pigment; the musician—air vibration. It seems to me that music is the least material of the arts, and perhaps we could even conceive of an art still subtler than that. It occurred to me that there are aspects of music that are extremely immaterial, that are almost pure spirit—and that some day an art might develop that would be immaterial, pure spirit....

K: Don't you think that it is not so much a question of comparing one art with another as of the evolution of the individual who produces that art? With regard to the possibility of evolving an art still more subtle than music, isn't it the question of inspiration? Inspiration, according to my idea, is keeping intelligence enthusiastically awakened.

LS: I feel that inspiration is almost like a melody or a rhythm, like music that I hear deep, deep inside of me, as if it were a long way off.

K: Because you are a musician you will hear that intelligence to which you are awake all the time, and will interpret it through music. A sculptor would express that intelligence in stone. You see my point? What matters is the inspiration.

LS: But do you think inspiration has much "rapport" with intelligence?

K: In the sense in which I am using it, yes. After all, sir, that is the whole point. If you are not intelligent, you are not a great creator. Therefore, intelligence, if fanned and kept alive, will always act as a medium for inspiration. That is what I call inspiration. You get a new idea because you are keeping your intelligence awakened.

LS: That is not the sensation I have inside at all. I can describe it this way: when I have an inspiration, it is as if I remember, become conscious of something which five minutes or ten minutes ago somehow came into my brain. It was there before but had not come into my consciousness. I have the feeling that it has been there in the background a long time—I do not know how long—and that it has just come forward.

K: I should say that is intelligence which is working to get this idea. After all, sir, please let us take it concretely: a being without intelligence would not be inspired in the highest sense of the word. I feel inspired when I see a beautiful thing, beautiful scenery, hear beautiful music, or someone recite poetry, because my intelligence is all the time seeking. And if there is beauty, I want to translate that vision into something which people will understand. Isn't that it?

LS: That is one form of expression.

K: And there are hundreds of forms. I am only one form, in the sense that we are discussing, and there may be the form of a poet, a sculptor, musician and so on.

LS: I have the feeling inside of me that inspiration comes from a higher level than intelligence.

K: No, I say intelligence is the highest level. Sir, intelligence, to me, is the accumulation of experience, it is the residue of experience.

LS: What is the relation between "intelligence" in your sense of the word and "intuition"?

K: You can't divide intuition from intelligence in the highest sense. A clever man is not an intelligent man. Or, I should rather say, that a clever man need not necessarily be an intelligent man.

LS: No, but often there is a great distance between an intelligent man and an intuitive man.

K: Yes, because, again, it is on a very different scale. Intuition is the highest point of intelligence.

LS: Ah, now I feel entirely with you.

K: Intuition is the highest point of intelligence and, to me, keeping alive that intelligence is inspiration. Now you can only keep alive that intelligence, of which intuition is the highest expression, by experience, by being all the time like a questioning child. Intuition is the apotheosis, the culmination, the accumulation of intelligence.

LS: Yes, that is true. May I ask you another question? If, as you say, liberation and happiness are the aim of our individual lives, what is the final goal of all life collectively? Or, in other words—how does the truth, as you enunciate it, answer the question as to why we are on this earth and toward what goal we are evolving?

K: Therefore the question is: If the goal for the individual is freedom and happiness, what is it collectively? I say, it is exactly the same. What divides individuals? Form. Your form is different from mine, but that life behind you and behind me is the same. So life is unity; therefore your life and my life must likewise culminate in that which is eternal, that which is freedom and happiness.

LS: In the whole design of life do you not find any farther-on goal than freedom and happiness, any farther-on design or function for all of life?

K: Now, sir, isn't it like a child who says: Teach me the higher mathematics? My reply would be: It would be useless to teach you higher mathematics unless you have first learned algebra. If we understand this particular thing, the divinity of that life which lies before us, it is not important to discuss what lies beyond, because we are discussing a thing which is unconditioned with a conditioned mind.

LS: That is perfectly answered, clear and brief. People remember better what is brief. It has always seemed to me that art words should be anonymous. The question in my mind is: Is a poem, or drama, or picture, or symphony the expression of its creator, or is he the medium through which creative forces flow?

K: Sir, that is a point in which I am really interested.

LS: Now, you are a poet and I am a musician. What I am interested in is to compare our sensations when we are creating in our respective mediums. Do you ever feel a total stranger to what you have written?

K: Oh, surely.

LS: I do… and I wake up the next day and say, did I write that? That is not like me at all!

K: Now I say that is inspiration. That is your intuition, the highest point of your intelligence acting suddenly. And that is my whole point. If you keep your mind, your emotions, your body in harmony, pure and strong, then that is the highest point of intelligence, out of which the intuition acts. That is the only guide. Now take, for instance, poets, dramatists, musicians, all artists: they should be anonymous, detached from all that they create. I think that is the greatest truth. To be, to give, and be detached from what you give. After all, the greatest artists of the world, the greatest teachers of the world say: "Look here, I have got something which, if you really understand it, would forever unfold your intelligence, would act as your intuition. But don't worship me as an individual—I am not concerned, after all." But most artists want their names put under the picture, they want to be admired. They want their degrees and titles.

LS: Here is an old old question. Is the truth relative or absolute? Is it the same for all of us, or different for each one?

K: It is neither, sir.

LS: Then what is it?

K: You cannot describe it. You cannot describe that which gives you inspiration to write music, can you? If you were asked: Is it absolute or is it relative, you would answer, "What are you asking me? It is neither." You see, you cannot say it is the absolute or the relative. It is far beyond matter, time and space. Take, for example, the water in that river out there. It is limited by its banks. Then you might say, looking at the water: "Water is always limited," because you see the narrow banks enclosing it. But if you were in the midst of the ocean where you see nothing but water, you could say: "Water is limitless."

LS: That is a perfect answer…you do not need to say any more—that is complete.

Is there a standard or criterion of beauty in art, or does each person find his own beauty to which he responds? The question is related to

Intuition is the highest point of intelligence and, to me, keeping alive that intelligence is inspiration.

—FROM CONVERSATION WITH LEOPOLD STOKOWSKI

69

the question of taste. People are always saying, this is good taste, that is bad taste. By what authority do they say that?

K: I should say by their own experience.

LS: That is a personal response. Then can any authority say what is good or bad in art?

K: No; yet I hold that beauty exists in itself beyond all forms and all appreciations.

LS: Ah, then that is an everlasting thing?

K: Like the eternal perfume of the rose. Sir, you hear music and I hear music; you hear a whole vast plane of vibrations, I only hear that much—but that much fits in with all your vast plane.

LS: Yes. It is a question of personal absorption, experience. So the answer is like that to the other question: In itself it is both relative and absolute, but for us it is relative.

K: Must be!

LS: We see design in life, in the arts, in our body, in machines and everything, and the design of an automobile is made always with idea of its function. What is the function of life, of all life?

K: To express itself.

LS: How does order come from your doctrine of freedom?

K: Because, sir, freedom is the common goal for all—you admit that. If each man realizes that freedom is the common goal, each one then in shaping, in adapting himself to this common goal can only create order.

LS: Do you mean that, in living up to the ideal of freedom, the ideal of beauty, we must all finally come to the same goal?

K: Of course; is that not so?

LS: …and so order will come?

K: At present there are you and I and half-a-dozen others who have all got different ideas as to what is the final goal. But if we all sat down and asked, "What is the ultimate aim for each of us?" We should say freedom and happiness for one and all. Then even if you work in one way and I in another we still work along our own lines towards the same goal. Then there must be order.[39]

It has been a struggle all the time to find the truth because I was not satisfied by the authority of another, or the imposition of another, or the enticement of another; I wanted to discover for myself, and naturally I had to go through sufferings to find out.

—WHO BRINGS THE TRUTH?, 1927

In spite of the stimulating and broadening friendship of the many around Krishnamurti, a sense of disquiet remained as a constant in his life, and as the single-pointed probing and acid dissent of Krishnamurti became more and more apparent to the thousands who thronged to hear his talks, unease and confusion roiled through the Order of the Star. What was happening to the beautiful young man whose speeches in the past seemed but a calming continuation of what was already known? Where were the words of comfort to soothe the troubled? Were the golden platitudes for a world weary of war, lost and disillusioned in peace? At public talks he was questioned sharply by his audiences.

QUESTION: THE IMPRESSION OF A WORLD TEACHER AS GENERALLY CONCEIVED CONVEYS ABOVE ALL THE IDEA OF COMPASSION. SOME PEOPLE FIND IN YOUR TEACHING THE LACK OF THAT QUALITY. COULD YOU DEFINE YOUR CONCEPTION OF COMPASSION?

A surgeon who sees a disease that is eating up a man, says: In order to cure him, I must operate. Another less experienced doctor comes, feeds him and lulls him to sleep. Which would you call the more compassionate? You want comfort, that comfort which is born of decay and which you imagine is compassion, affection, true love. The shadow of that comfort you would have, but if I gave it to you, that would not be the world of a real teacher.

—*THE STAR BULLETIN*, SEPTEMBER/OCTOBER, 1928

QUESTION: ARE YOU THE CHRIST COME BACK?

Friend, who do you think I am? If I say I am the Christ, you will create another authority. If I say I am not, you will also create another authority. Do you think that truth has anything to do with what you think I am? You are not concerned with the truth, but you are concerned with the vessel that contains the truth. You do not want to drink the waters, but you want to find out who fashioned the vessel which contains the waters. Friend, if I say to you that I am, and another says to you that I am not, the Christ—where will you be? Put aside the label, for that has no value. Drink the water, if the water is clean.

—*LET UNDERSTANDING BE THE LAW*, 1928

QUESTION: IF WE ARE ASKED BY PEOPLE ON WHAT GROUND WE BELIEVE THAT YOU, KRISHNAJI, ARE THE WORLD TEACHER, WHAT ANSWER WOULD YOU LIKE US TO GIVE?

I know the questioner is very serious, but his seriousness is misleading. If you merely repeat words which you have learned from me, they will have no value to anyone. How do you know that I am the world teacher? Some of you know neither Krishnamurti nor the world teacher. It is amusing and yet, in a sense tragic, that you should pay such importance to words. I have been saying over and over again that it does not matter out of what well you draw the waters so long as the waters are pure, so long as the waters shall quench the thirst of men. You are concerned about the construction of the well and not with the waters.[40]

—OMMEN, HOLLAND, 1928

MRS. BESANT AND KRISHNAMURTI
DURING THEIR SPEAKING TOUR OF
1926: AT ONE OF MANY PRESS
CONFERENCES ABOARD THE S.S.
MARICOPA WHICH HAD JUST
RETURNED FROM AUSTRALIA (ABOVE)
AND UPON THEIR ARRIVAL IN
CHICAGO ON AUGUST 30, 1926, TO
ATTEND A THEOSOPHICAL SOCIETY
CONVENTION (OPPOSITE).

shnamurti Is 28th in Long

Hopes of 100,000 Cente

LD TEACHER" DUE

30-Year-Old Hindu, Coming
erica as Leader of Theosophists

Aug. 22. (Exclusive)—A remarkable young man lands
next Tuesday. He is Jeddu Krishnamurti, 30-year-old Hindu of
s speeding hither on the White Star liner Majestic. No sea
spirit, communer with the occult or teacher for him as Krish
to America with the way so well paved for him as Krish
... of the universe is merely using
... the body of Krishnamurti as a ve-
... hicle through which to deliver his
000 of the 100,000 mem-
message to mankind.
Order of The Star of
According to Mrs. Besant, the
roughout the world, who
world teacher so Used the body of
to prepare mankind for
Jesus and before Jesus, the body of
America. They
Prince Siddhartha, or the Buddha of

Christ, and many other lesser ones.
Further, the study of history shows us
that these appearances have not been
sporadic, but have formed quite a definite series, connected — be physical and intell— of the
hum— e under

the cult to
to in all
before
is to

he spoke
... the
... er, the
... he
... world
... piece
... will b

AGO WELCOMES HINDU

Theosophist "Messiah"
To-morrow, Shunning

City Theosoph
How Messiah

urti Employs Parables in Explaini
Religion to R—

16
Aug. 28. (P)—A
heosophy awaits
o Chicago today
welcome of his f

throngs of the
uged him with a
whence and confronted
and women eager
evidences of his inv—
vine gifts, he had litt
or meditation even :
bungalow where h

who asked, as other
like's shores 2000 year
" he spoke in parables
his theosophical tenets
pret his position as the
of the God whom theos-
e world teacher.
urti is about 30 years of
ge has been computed by
pe, for the date of his
known and he may be a
older. A slight man, he
cal facial cast of the
the same coffee-colored
with a thatch of thick
The occidental clothes
England and America are
ween the star in the
all these ideals are
with the coming of

the Messianic tradi-
Oesterley, of Cam-
England, said that
of in a savior of the
the inborn desire of
from his life and to
peace and justice

Krishnamurti and His Chief Apo
to Make Only Brief Stop on
Old World to Chicago and

Flippant paragraphs in New York
newspapers respecting J. Krishnamurti,
theosophist messiah to America, have
modified plans for the reception to the
Indian holy man when he arrived tomorrow on the White Star liner Majestic.

Krishnamurti and his mentor and
chief apostle, Mrs. Annie Besant, in recent newspaper characterizations of the visitor, as a
"tea hound messiah." They feel their
representatives in New York said was
terdas that the irreverent tone adopted
by a section of the press may injure
Krishnamurti's message in this country.

Instead, therefore, of taking Krishnamurti from the Majesti on a private
tug and extending to him the honors
of the port, his advent in New York
will be inconspicuous and studiedly
simple. He will make no public appearances in New York, will be rushed
o Chicago for the convention of American theosophists and depart at once
for California to remain in seclusion
for three months.

Only three persons, L. W. Rogers,
f Chicago, president of the American
Theosophists; A. P. Warrington, of
New York one time pre-dent, and
Ned B Pond, insure bureau exam-
will go down the bay to meet Krishnamurti and Mrs. Besant. A demonstration at the White Star docks in Chel-
being discouraged by theosophist

On Frid
Krishnaamurti, vate recei
America, to the spiritual
Chicago Limited.
occupy a
to the t.
"it is
plained
itual
from
indeed
much
pres

"Bo
sant
by
we
they
full-
mer
eigh
Land of
to three short
Win which to
needed Him so
ing the intuition
greatness, persecuted
the body after three
work. He was there
to teach His disciple
planes, which He dld
eighty years.

By Rebecca L. Finch

MY attention has been directed to a
very misleading article in the
Times purporting to come from a
theosophist, concerning the belief of
theosophists about the near coming of
the Christ, which is most vital at this
particular time.

Having been a theosophist for many
years and being closely in touch with
the movement in all of its differen
ses, I believe that the statement
h I am ready and anxious
should command attention
t.

our theosophical literature
is made clear to us that whe
ist came two thousand year
He chose for His vehicle in whi
manifested Himself, the pure
the disciple Jesus who had c
prepared himself for this gre
spending many years with
enes in Egypt and in th
al forest, what its
Land of Shamballa in T
born a new world
strike kindred flam
and minds of Theos
here from all parts of

Patiently, hopefully,
wants ministered to
tion of modern scien
women await what they
reincarnation
teacher in the body of a
min, J. Krishnamurti
Only their eyes f
almost fanaticall
religious denominations. He
come in a cloud of glory blinding
vision, but is born first in our hearts

land
give
and
of
ve
i

Krishn
min, Pr
Cong

From World
Special Ca
OMMEN. He
While airplanes d
l forest, what its
Prove a new wor
born among the

Most theosophists
near coming again, a

In his
wrote an
as Service
acknowled;
who also v
Both boo
of the faith
many langua

...ine of Expected Messiahs

...a Young Hindu

ere, defied the power of Rome in Palestine for three years of war. Down even to the seventeenth century there were those professing to being Messiahs, such as Shabbathai Sebi, a youth of wondrous physical beauty, whose ideals succumbed at last to the great prosperity which proved his temporal ruin.

The same idea of the coming of a deliverer appears in the Mahometan faith. When days of adversity come the faithful think of the coming of the Mahdi, who shall wield the sword of Allah and save them from their foes. The Mahdi, who in the '80s gave the British such a struggle in the Sudan, asserted that he was the twelfth Imam, and that he had a divine mission to make "holy war" upon those who had blasted the hopes of Islam. The Mahdis, whose name is translated "the divinely guided" conceived themselves to be Messiahs, a race, however, not ...

...Tells ...ll Come

...age, where he was ...vantage of schooling ...and now at 30 years' ... 1926, when the ... marvelous ...

anie B eighty, ess of

passing cenes, his isited by he have don their leav, the light

... new history, i ... as one wi ... h

YOUNG HINDU TO BE WORSHIPPED AS REDEEMER

Manifestations Are Expected In Christmas Season; New 'Root Race' Reported.

LOS ANGELES, Dec. 11.—... The ... Theosophical Order of the Star in East, organized fourteen years ... prepare for the second visita... ...st on earth, is making ...he Savior in the body ... young Hindu, at ... Madras, India ...

was made here ... out Stone inter ... reasurer of the ...

...ions are looked for ... ing Christmas season ...urti, who now is in ... o hailed as the human ... ing the manifestation of ... a mission on earth as ... er.

...ew Race Appearing

...h root" race, the Theosophid ... making its appearance on the ... ...rn slopes of this hemisphere and ...n Australia.

...octor Stone cited statistics given ... by the government theological ... ...epartment that new physical char- ...teristics have been perceived ...children of the last generation, in sup- ...ort of his contention that a new ... "root" people is about to take its ...place on earth.

The "new Christ," he said, would ...near as a teacher for this new race ... ... rise from the ...

... which the ...

Herald Tribune photo—Acme
Jeddu Krishnamurti, who arrived yesterday on the Rotterdam

Mrs. Besant's '2d Messiah' Renounces Her Support

Hindu Student Says He Was Misled by His Early Training

Jeddu K...shnamurti, Hindu student, who was ...ralded upon his arrival here ...eral years ago by Mrs. Annie Besant ... the ...hor of "Deva," "Second ...sion" and "Voice of the Great ...eacher," it is well yesterday that he ...as renounced Theosophy and the ...represe...tions Mrs. Besant had made ...upon spent his ...rival here on the Holland-American Lines Ro... ...

...st passenger on the Rotterdam was a boy ... s said how he had been ...osen by ...rs. Besant to ...fill the beneficent... role as the "Voice of the Great Teach...

He was ... by a friend of ...s, a fellow Hindu student, Mrs. Besang ...ried of ... conversion told about ...nnes Bes...t. In gesture after and ...his father, he said, they obviousl... ...ved in all sincerity that his grasp ... theosophy at that age and his re... ...s warranted their assumption that ... ...had at last discovered the "Am... ...of Truth."

...recalled how he had been raised ...s Besant in the belief that he ... ...he at first thought was his voca... ...But later when his mental facul... ...matured he saw the error into ...he had been led, possibly by ... ...of ardor. He said that gradu... ...ifted away from the beliefs ... ...Mrs. Besant and, in fact, from ... ...altogether.

...led that each of us must do ...hinking," he continued. "The ... ...better life—lies within each ...

...ophist Hosts Gather ...ail New World Teacher

...Young Brah-
...d in Mystic
...Holland

...espondent ...orld ...uly 28.— ...a mediae- ...hope will ... is being ... which ... hearts ...thered

...material ...ica- ...and ...be ...

QUESTION: HAVE YOU ONE TEACHING FOR THE MASSES AND ANOTHER FOR YOUR CHOSEN DISCIPLES?

I have no chosen disciples. Who are the masses? Yourselves. It is in your minds that the distinctions exist between the masses and the chosen ones, between the outside world and the inner world. It is in your minds that you corrupt, step down the truth. O friend! if you are in love with life, you will include all things, transient or permanent, in that love. You want to have a special teaching for the chosen few, because in your heart there is segregation, separation; and you wish to confine the pure waters of life and keep them for yourselves. Can you ask the sun if it shines for the masses or for the chosen few? Can you ask the rains whether they are meant for the plains or for the mountains? If you do not understand you will, as has always been done, make this teaching for the few, and so step down the truth and betray it. Because there is limitation in your heart, you divide the water of life which is meant for kings and for beggars alike. Whether it comes out of a golden well or out of a running stream the water is the same and quenches the thirst of all without separation into colors, castes, creeds, and the specially chosen. It is because for so many years, for so many centuries, for so many eons, truth has been limited and stepped down that you wish to do it again, and you are already doing it when you ask, "Is truth meant for the masses or for the chosen few?" You say that the masses do not understand; that it is too difficult for them to grasp; that it is only the few who can climb high. Do you think I have not as much affection and love as anyone of you? But because I have been through all your stages I say: Do not go through those stages but avoid them, put them aside, and gather your strength as men who climb high.

—*LET UNDERSTANDING BE THE LAW, 1928*

Then, in a statement that was to foreshadow dramatic events to come in 1929 Krishnamurti wrote:

Because you have placed beliefs before life, creeds before life, dogmas before life, religions before life, there is stagnation. Can you bind the waters of the sea or gather the winds in your fist? Religion, as I understand it, is the frozen thought of men out of which they have built temples and churches. The moment you attribute to external authority a spiritual and divine law and order, you are limiting, you are suffocating that very life that you wish to fulfill, to which you would give freedom. If there is limitation, there is bondage and hence suffering. The world at present is the expression of life in bondage. So, according to my point of view, beliefs, religions, dogmas, and creeds, have nothing to do with life, and hence have nothing to do with truth.

—*LIFE THE GOAL, 1928*

OPPOSITE: KRISHNAMURTI AND MRS. BESANT AT THE OPENING OF THE OMMEN CAMP.

There was to be no turning back, no compromise. Knowing how deeply Annie Besant cared for him, Krishnamurti still had to walk the only road he knew. Loving her, yet unable to bring her along with him, he moved on. Lady Emily too, almost a mother to him for so many years, was also left behind, although they still maintained a caring and friendly relationship. Both were unable to fathom the diamond clarity of his perception, unable to give up cherished masters and ceremonies.

A worried Mrs. Besant had earlier asked "What is going to happen to you? Where will you get money? Who will listen to you?" This to the young man who in former years showed an interest only in clothes and cars and spoke beautiful, expected words.

I N 1929 a young Austrian girl whose family were leading Theosophists in Vienna, who organized many of the lectures and gatherings held there, became herself involved in the Star work. She attended many of the Ommen Camps, and over sixty years later recalled the special camp of August 3, 1929. Doctor Hedda Bolgar was on the faculty of the University of Chicago for many years. She is a member of the International Psychoanalytic Association and is the founding director of the Wright Institute, Los Angeles, and a cofounder of the Psychoanalytic Institute in Los Angeles, where she is currently training and supervising analyst.

DR. HEDDA BOLGAR

PSYCHOANALYST, LOS ANGELES, CALIFORNIA

EB: Dr. Bolgar, can you describe the expectations that were built up around the Ommen talks of 1929?

HB: I think I have to backtrack a little bit. We are talking, essentially, about the end of a decade which was trying to cope with the devastation of World War I. During that time, both the defeated and the victors, had to come to terms with the incredible destruction of the war, with the untold deaths of young people, the general economic upheaval, the restructuring of all of Europe. It was an extremely difficult, also a very interesting, decade. People were stirred up in a lot of different ways and, as always after wars, people are looking for answers to a lot of questions; they are looking for explanations, how could it happen? How could we avoid it? Where did we go wrong? There was a great deal of despair and, therefore, some hope for

something better, for somebody to help them, for somebody to guide them. I think those are the times when people always look for saviors of some kind. Indeed, that decade, I think, was really very ripe in new ideas, new philosophies, new political movements, new art forms and a great deal of interest in the occult and a great deal of interest in new answers; not necessarily philosophical answers, religious answers, ethical answers. There were many, many forms of inquiry and searching. And in that atmosphere, one of the things that emerged was a great deal of talk about the coming of a so-called world teacher. It originated with Mrs. Annie Besant, who was well known to some people, certainly in the United Kingdom and to some labor leaders on the Continent, to some feminists on the Continent. Mrs. Besant had been very active in the Fabian Society, had been active in the women's movement, had been active in the fight for social justice and equality,

THE OMMEN CAMP OF 1929 OCCURRED AS THE WORLD WAS TRYING TO COPE WITH THE INCREDIBLE DESTRUCTION OF WWI, THE GENERAL ECONOMIC UPHEAVAL, AND THE RESTRUC- TURING OF ALL OF EUROPE.

OPPOSITE: KRISHNAMURTI WAITING TO SPEAK AT THE CAMP, SEATED NEXT TO MRS. BESANT.

in that context, many people knew her. However, she was also a Theosophist and she was also involved in questions of India and also, I believe, of the Indian liberation movement so that she was a well-known person; and she was one of the major spokespeople for this belief, that the time had come for a world teacher. "World teacher" was the word that, I think, she and Leadbeater chose to characterize this new savior and because the movement at that time was very international and certainly interdenominational, there was an attempt to make it something that wouldn't offend any one religion and would bring together people who were looking for answers along spiritual lines. The world teacher was going to be this young Hindu, who had been brought over from India by Mrs. Besant, with his brother, to be educated in the West and to fulfill the mission that she saw for him. He was supposed to be the next messiah, Buddha, prophet, whatever; and as far as most people knew, he was a shy, young, very beautiful Indian who occasionally spoke gently and mildly and said reasonably acceptable things about man's path to a better life, a better inner life. That was the general expectation. There was going to be this second, third coming, whichever context people saw it in.

EB: Why do people look for a savior or a messiah?

HB: Well, the assumption being that here are all these unresolved questions, here is the struggle, here are the doubts, here is the wish to believe, to have somebody who is better, wiser, more knowledgeable, to whom one can look up, who has answers, who will deliver us from the pain of not knowing, of having to cope with so many of the human conflicts and difficulties of the time; the need to be saved, the need to be guided, the need to be told how to achieve salvation, ultimately. But in the meantime just a state of spiritual well-being. And in those critical times I think it was even more urgent. Everybody was looking for somebody who would help.

EB: What was the reaction to Krishnamurti's statement regarding the dissolution of the Order of the Star?

HB: It was a very complex reaction. There were many aspects to it. The first one was absolute shock; something that you'd been building up to and been expecting for years and years, and here was the person who was going to be it and you were all geared to follow and to be led and to admire and to worship, and suddenly the person who is supposed to be all that says, "No, I won't do it. I am not it. That's not the way. Don't look to me as the person who will answer all your questions." In effect, "Go and find your own answers." That's a very big thing to take.

EB: You have suggested that—this in a sense, proved the greatness of the man—that he was, if not the world teacher, at least something along those lines, a great teacher.

THE BON FIRE AT THE
OMMEN TALKS.

HB: Well, anybody who could stand up to the incredible pressure of expectations and being groomed by somebody who really was a second mother to him and who, I am sure, he loved and respected a great deal and who had made the announcement to the world that he was going to be the world teacher, and all the people who were sitting around that campfire in Ommen expecting to hear the acceptance speech, and instead were told that he was dissolving the organization, that he did not believe that anybody could be anybody else's guide in these ways—I think it took tremendous strength and tremendous capacity to withstand pressures of all kinds—and the idea that there was no one person who could guide you, that you have to be your own person, in today's vernacular, was a real revelation; it was really new, it was so totally different from anything anybody expected, that it really came like an incredible pronouncement.

EB: Is there a correlation between the analytic method, if you will, and what Krishnamurti was saying, particularly in reference to his nonauthoritarian statements?

HB: Some of us think of the psychoanalytic process, or the psychotherapeutic process as following human development. We all start out as babies, depending on our mothers first and then on our father, and gradually we become somewhat less dependent and we learn things—we learn to do things for ourselves. In the beginning there is a great deal of need and our well-being depends on having those needs understood. Gradually we learn that mother isn't there only to take care of us, that she has a life of her own and that manifests itself in lots of ways, and so, gradually, the urge, and I think the built-in need, in human beings to become independent, to become autonomous, to know their own will and their own ideas, grows stronger. And if a child is lucky enough to have parents who respect that, there will be a normal development in the direction of greater and greater independence,. In action independence, in thought independence, in feelings, which doesn't mean that one lives as an isolate, but it means that one begins to really have a fairly integrated self that knows its own value. Now it seems to me that the end point of this development is very much the sort of thing that Krishnaji was talking about when he implied that you have to find your own way, you have to find your own answers. You cannot look for organizations and for hierarchies and heads of hierarchies and for designated people to tell you what to think, what to feel, how to live. I think this emphasis on the importance, on the individuality, the own-self, and the search within one's self, rather than the taking of ready-made ideas and beliefs, is the real relationship there.

EB: What is the real role of a religious figure?

HB: I think all great religious figures, religious leaders, are trying to change people's minds, to change people's points of view, their habitual ways of living and thinking. All great religious leaders also were basically political activists and they were really, in some way or another, attacking the establishment, trying to reduce the power of the establishment. Jesus, I think, more so than some of the others, perhaps because he was alive in our culture, more or less Western culture, and because we understand the social environment a little better than we do some of the more distant religious figures, like Mohammed or Buddha. I think Krishnamurti's real contribution in 1929, when he dissolved the Order of the Star, when he made his statement about how organizations are not going to do it, what he really did was dismantle a rather carefully erected hierarchy, a carefully structured power elite within a group of people who were all looking forward to the fulfillment of the prophesy.

EB: How do you think Krishnamurti viewed his actions in 1929?

HB: In 1929 when Krishnaji made his famous statement, when he dismantled the Order of the Star, when in the face of everything Mrs. Besant and everybody else had been saying for years, he essentially denied the fact that he was anybody in particular; certainly he was not the world teacher. He said that he would go on lecturing and talking and writing but, that he by no means was somebody whose word was scripture. And in the atmosphere of the expectation and the extremely organized and hierarchic setting of the Theosophical Society and of the entourage of Krishnamurti in those days, this was an incredibly revolutionary statement; this was very much the equivalent of driving the Philistines out of the Temple. This was a political action, a psychological and spiritual declaration of independence. From that day on, Krishnaji was his own man. He would say what he believed and what he wanted to say. He would withstand any attempt to trap him into the old position, and there were many such attempts, and to witness the incredible strength and integrity and wholeness of this man, in itself, seemed to belie the fact that he was just somebody who was on a search of his own. He came through with incredible power and it was, I think, very difficult not to say, "You don't want to be the world teacher, but actually look at what you are doing. It's not because Mrs. Besant says you are the world teacher but just because of this act of becoming totally independent of any kind of power structure." That, I think, made it very difficult not to think that he was somebody very special.

EB: What did you do after the dramatic events of the Ommen Camp?

HB: In reality, I dropped out of the entire—I don't know what to call it at this point since it wasn't an organization anymore. I really needed to get back to my studies and my friends and traveling to places other than Ommen. So, for a long time, there really was no connection at all. I went my own way and eventually became a psychologist and a psychoanalyst, and I have often wondered how those early years affected my work and my choice of profession. I have never consciously made the connection but as I think about it now, it seems to me there must have been the residue of an impact because I responded so easily and so readily to the idea of abolishing spiritual authorities and to fighting orthodoxy. I have done that in my own field where, God knows, there is plenty of orthodoxy. You constantly have to fight it. I have found that very easy to do and without the kind of guilt that I see in some of my colleagues who question Freud, with great conflict. There is a tremendous reluctance to give up the hierarchy and the worship of the established leader.

EB: What is the real problem that human beings face on the road to independence and sanity?

HB: I think the real difficulty that every human being experiences is the fear of being alone. It's so hard to grow up, to leave home in the real sense, to take on responsibility for one's own life and one's own belief and one's own thoughts, without looking somewhere for somebody who at least will approve or encourage or say you are on the right track. But when it comes to looking for what some people call "the truth," ah... then I think you have to search within yourself and you are alone on that journey and you have to be alone on it because otherwise it becomes somebody else's truth.

EB: What is your strongest memory of that period?

HB: I always remember the feeling, back there in 1929 in Ommen, of this slight figure of a beautiful person and how incredibly alone he was at that moment, when he had really given up perhaps the last tie, the last attachment that he had a minute before he made the announcement, and then I thought how much he had actually lost. I remembered the stories I had heard about his childhood and how Mrs. Besant took him, essentially, away from his family and brought him to England; and I was thinking how different the climate must have been, how cold and grey it must have been after India, and how he had lost his family and all the familiar smells and sounds and foods and the only link he had was Nitya, his brother, and then Nitya died, so he lost even that; and here he was, really, in a very strange land and the major support was Mrs. Besant, his second mother, who he certainly loved a lot and how incredibly difficult it must have been to stand up to her, to say 'No' to her, to disavow her in public and how much courage it took and how much strength and how by that time he must have been able to be alone and how alone he has been ever since. Now, I don't think that we expect ourselves, ordinary people, to be able to tolerate that kind of aloneness, but I know that is the fear in this process of developing some kind of independence or interdependence but certainly the giving up of childhood dependence. I remember so many patients, when I have asked them what is so frightening about growing up, and they all say, "It feels so alone." So aloneness is a very frightening thing for most people, and yet it's very difficult to develop answers to your own questions unless you can stand alone.[41]

To stand alone was to be a major theme for Krishnamurti. Throughout the days and years of his teaching he questioned all assumptions, even his own, especially his own. Everything was scrutinized rigorously and afresh with no lag over of previous thought. The chrysalis ever becoming the butterfly. Alone and unblinking Krishnamurti looked at the questions of life. Major themes never resolved themselves into dogmas, there were no pat answers and easy assurances for the searching, sometimes desperate, questions that were put to him.

Other elements, other aspects of the teachings emerged over the years, but they rested on the bedrock of standing alone. "Be a light to yourself," he said. He questioned, allowing the imposition of the psychological or spiritual imperative of another, however exalted, on our lives. Their truth was only our second hand opinion. Those nesting in the comfort of ready-made beliefs would never fly.

AT THE OMMEN CAMP ON AUGUST 3, 1929 KRISHNAMURTI ISSUED HIS MANIFESTO:

TRUTH IS A PATHLESS LAND

THE DISSOLUTION OF THE ORDER OF THE STAR

We are going to discuss this morning the dissolution of the Order of the Star. Many people will be delighted, and others will be rather sad. It is a question neither for rejoicing nor for sadness, because it is inevitable, as I am going to explain.

You may remember the story of how the devil and a friend of his were walking down the street, when they saw ahead of them a man stoop down and pick up something from the ground, look at it, and put it away in his pocket. The friend said to the devil, "What did that man pick up?" "He picked up a piece of truth," said the devil. "That is a very bad business for you, then," said his friend. "Oh, not at all," the devil replied, "I am going to let him organize it."

I maintain that truth is a pathless land, and you cannot approach it by any path whatsoever, by any religion, by any sect. That is my point of view, and I adhere to that absolutely and unconditionally. Truth, being limitless, unconditioned, unapproachable by any path whatsoever, cannot be organized; nor should any organization be formed to lead or to coerce people along any particular path. If you first understand that, then you will see how impossible it is to organize a belief. A belief is purely an individual matter, and you cannot and must not organize it. If you do, it becomes dead, crystallized; it becomes a creed, a sect, a religion, to be imposed on others. This is what everyone throughout the world is attempting to do. Truth is narrowed down and made a plaything for those who are weak, for those who are only momentarily discontented. Truth cannot be brought down, rather the individual must make the effort to ascend to it. You cannot bring the mountaintop to the valley. If you would attain to the mountaintop you must pass through the valley, climb the steeps, unafraid of the dangerous precipices. You must climb towards the truth, it cannot be "stepped down" or organized for you. Interest in ideas is mainly sustained by organizations, but organizations only awaken interest from without. Interest, which is not born out of love of truth for its own sake, but aroused by an organization, is of no value. The organization becomes a framework into which its members can conveniently fit. They no longer strive after truth or the mountaintop, but rather carve for themselves a convenient niche in which they put themselves, or let the organization place them, and consider that the organization will thereby lead them to truth....I maintain that no organization can lead man to spirituality.

If an organization be created for this purpose, it becomes a crutch, a weakness, a bondage, and must cripple the individual, and prevent him from growing, from establishing his uniqueness, which lies in the discovery for himself of that absolute, unconditioned truth. So that is another reason why I have decided, as I happen to be the head of the Order, to dissolve it. No one has persuaded me to this decision.

This is no magnificent deed, because I do not want followers, and I mean this. The moment you follow someone you cease to follow truth. I am not concerned whether you pay attention to what I say or not. I want to do a certain thing in the world and I am going to do it with unwavering concentration. I am concerning myself with only one essential thing: to set man free. I desire to free him from all cages, from all fears, and not to found religions, new sects, nor to establish new theories and new philosophies. Then you will naturally ask me why I go the world over, continually speaking. I will tell you for what reason I do this; not because I desire a following, not because I desire a special group of special disciples. (How men love to be different from their fellowmen, however ridiculous, absurd, and trivial their distinctions may be! I do not want to encourage that absurdity.) I have no disciples, no apostles, either on earth or in the realm of spirituality.

...If there are only five people who will listen, who will live, who have their faces turned towards eternity, it will be sufficient. Of what use is it to have thousands who do not understand, who are fully embalmed in prejudice, who do not want the new, but would rather translate the new to suit their own sterile, stagnant selves? If I speak strongly, please do not misunderstand me, it is not through lack of compassion. If you go to a surgeon for an operation, is it not kindness on his part to operate even if he causes you pain? So, in like manner, if I speak straightly, it is not through lack of real affection—on the contrary.

...For eighteen years you have been preparing for this event, for the Coming of the world teacher. For eighteen years you have organized, you have looked for someone who would give a new delight to your hearts and minds, who would transform your whole life, who would give you a new understanding; for someone who would raise you to a new plane of life, who would give you a new encouragement, who would set you free—and now look what is happening! Consider, reason with yourselves, and discover in what way that belief has made you different—not with the superficial difference of the wearing of a badge, which is trivial, absurd. In what manner has such a belief swept away all the unessential things of life? That is the only way to judge: in what way are you freer, greater, more dangerous to every society which is based on the false and unessential? In what way have the members of this organization of the Star become different?

...You are all depending for your spirituality on someone else, for your happiness on someone else, for your enlightenment on someone else; and although you have been preparing for me for

eighteen years, when I say all these things are unnecessary, when I say that you must put them all away and look within yourselves for the enlightenment, for the glory, for the purification, and for the incorruptibility of the self, not one of you is willing to do it. There may be a few, but very, very few.

So why have an organization?

...I said last year that I would not compromise. Very few listened to me then. This year I have made it absolutely clear. I do not know how many thousands throughout the world—members of the Order—have been preparing for me for eighteen years, and yet now they are not willing to listen unconditionally, wholly, to what I say.

So why have an organization?

...You will see how absurd is the whole structure that you have built, looking for external help, depending on others for your comfort, for your happiness, for your strength. These can only be found within yourselves.

So why have an organization?

You are accustomed to being told how far you have advanced, what is your spiritual status. How childish! Who but yourself can tell you if you are incorruptible? You are not serious in these things.

So why have an organization?

But those who really desire to understand, who are looking to find that which is eternal, without beginning and without an end, will walk together with a greater intensity, will be a danger to everything that is unessential, to unrealities, to shadows. And they will concentrate, they will become the flame, because they understand. Such a body we must create, and that is my purpose. Because of that real understanding there will be true friendship. Because of that true friendship—which you do not seem to know—there will be real cooperation on the part of each one. And this not because of authority, not because of salvation, not because of immolation for a cause, but because you really understand, and hence are capable of living in the eternal. This is a greater thing than all pleasure, than all sacrifice.

So these are some of the reasons why, after careful consideration for two years, I have made this decision. It is not from a momentary impulse. I have not been persuaded to it by anyone. I am not persuaded in such things. For two years I have been thinking about this, slowly, carefully, patiently, and I have now decided to disband the Order, as I happen to be its head. You can form other organizations and expect someone else. With that I am not concerned, nor with creating new cages, new decorations for those cages. My only concern is to set men absolutely, unconditionally free.

PART TWO: *The last step...*

Gods, masters, apparitions may exist, but they are

of no value to the man who is seeking truth,

for they are still in the world of phenomena.

—*THE STAR BULLETIN*, SEPTEMBER/OCTOBER 1932

The Theosophical leaders were forever saying, "When the Lord comes you must be prepared for him to say things [which are] utterly different from what you expect, things that will rock the very foundations of your existence. Be warned. Be warned. Be prepared."

When in 1927 Mrs. Besant, president of the Theosophical Society announced that the Coming had taken place, and Krishnamurti began to speak for himself, it was they, the leaders, who could not accept the unexpected things he said, they whose lives were rocked to their foundations. They repudiated him and so, in a strange way, their prophecy was fulfilled. This is really an extraordinary thing to consider, and to consider what he was and what he will remain. His teaching is unique....[42]

—MARY LUTYENS

KRISHNAMURTI IN
HOLLYWOOD

I N 1929 Krishnamurti left the dream world of Arcadia behind and walked into a new life. He was on his own. In some ways it was not too different from his earlier one in that the frantic pace of travel continued as before. In Budapest, Krishnamurti was undeterred by threats against his life by angry Catholic students, threatened by his stance against nationalism. A plain-clothes guard had to follow him everywhere. His talks continued in Yugoslavia, Frankfurt and Vienna.

1931 also saw the construction of Vasanta Vihar in Madras which was built by the Star Publishing Trust, the new entity headquartered at Ommen which now printed *Verbatim Reports* of all of the talks. They were sold through Madras, London and Hollywood, translated into eighteen languages and had agencies and representatives in as many countries.

Although many of the older followers from his "messiah" days dropped away in despair, some remained steadfastly at his side. By that time Krishnamurti was *persona non grata* at Adyar and so he stayed at Vasanta Vihar. It remains today as the headquarters of the Krishnamurti Foundation of India.

The Theosophical Society, riven by conflict over his departure, regrouped as best it could, but without the strong central figures of earlier times. Annie Besant, now 86 years old and with her great energy and intellect failing, lived until 1933. Krishnamurti remained devoted to her until the end, but with increasing intervals in their affectionate, long-time correspondence. He saw her several months before her death and although she held his hand and showed affection Krishna felt that perhaps she really did not recognize him. Charles Webster Leadbeater lived only a few months after Besant's death, and with his passing the two dominant figures of the Theosophical Society faded into history. Helena Blavatsky and Henry Steel Olcott were already memories. The ambitious George Arundale at last became president of the Theosophical Society. Another powerful figure in

the movement was James Ingall Wedgewood of the family of the great potter Josiah Wedgewood. C. Jinarajadasa too, continued on as a tiller of the fields, but without Besant the galvanizing force was gone.

Krishnamurti, over the next several years, spoke with increasing clarity and force, without the constraint of having to hew to an acceptable line. His language gradually moved from a florid Victorian/Theosophical style to the concise, pared-down language of his later years. An inveterate dictionary hunter, he frequently consulted a favorite one for meanings and derivations. There was no elliptical jargon to be learned in order for anyone to come to his teaching. The words were limpid and ordinary as water, words that most could understand. Although frequently suffused with poetic content they nevertheless were accessible to all. Indeed, his entire teaching was for everyone. It went directly to his listeners—without any intermediaries. One need not be an initiate or belong to an esoteric group to come to the heart of his teaching. There was no dogma that was a precondition to understanding, no beliefs in masters, saviors, commandments, or scriptures of any kind. Neither reincarnation nor belief in a heavenly afterlife was necessary. The Upanishads, Bible, Torah, Sutras or Koran need not be read, for when you quote, Krishnamurti said, you are merely repeating, and what you are repeating is not the truth. Truth cannot be repeated. Labels such as Christian, Muslim, Hindu, Jew or Buddhist were meaningless and divisive. One need not believe in any hierarchic order or struggle to attain spiritual goals. There were no steps on the road to enlightenment. Indeed, there was no road, path or goal.

One might ask then, what was left?

When the mind is swept clean of image, or ritual, of belief, of symbol, of all words, mantrams and repetitions, and of all fear, then what you see will be the real, the timeless, the everlasting, which may be called God; but this requires enormous insight, understanding, patience, and it is only for those who really inquire into what is religion and pursue it day after day to the end. Only such people will know what is true religion. The rest are merely mouthing words, and all their ornaments and bodily decorations, their pujas and ringing of bells—all that is just superstition without any significance. It is only when the mind is in revolt against all so-called religion that it finds the real.

—*THINK ON THESE THINGS*, 1964

Krishnamurti had transformed himself from a beautiful, if vague young man—some said, an Edwardian dandy—into a modern man, free of the bonds of past conditioning.

For Mr. Krishnamurti to have burst in so clear and uncompromising a manner the swaddling-clothes in which he had been wrapped for eighteen years, to have in a sense rejected his high destiny, to have thrown away great wealth, to have risked the loss of all his friends and disciples, boldly, in short, to have taken his life into his own hands, this was an action which must have called for quite exceptional courage and force of character. When one considers the sort of life Mr. Krishnamurti had been compelled to lead since childhood, its demoralizing and tempting nature, it is impossible to withhold a tribute of admiration for the [43] *spectacle of so rare and even magnificent a gesture.*

—THEODORE BESTERMAN

The story now takes a different turn. The intensely dramatic elements leading up to Krishnamurti's renunciation of the world that had been offered him, smoothed into a far simpler life, freed from the tensions of conflicting loyalties.

Rajagopal traveled everywhere with him, taking the place—but never filling it—that was once held by the beloved Nitya. As a coordinating manager, confidante and secretary, he was focused on detail and by nature very exacting. He was a superb organizer, and records were always meticulously kept. The very opposite of Krishnamurti who remained indifferent to business matters and whose retiring and gentle nature was at variance with that of his friend. Just how much at variance was not seen until many years later.

Over the next several years at question and answer sessions, which were part of the format of his talks, Krishnamurti continued to face intense questioning regarding his earlier background.

QUESTION: WHAT MEANING AND VALUE DO YOU ATTACH TO THE TERM "WORLD TEACHER"? IS EVERYONE WHO REACHES LIBERATION A "WORLD TEACHER"?

Do not trouble yourself with terms, labels and phrases. I look upon the "world teacher" as one who has realized truth. The ocean cannot be brought to the river, so the river must seek the ocean. Likewise, in order to attain this state of liberation, which may be likened to the sea, the individual must go towards that sea; it cannot come into him because it cannot be conditioned. To me the reality of the "world teacher" is not in the name, but in the fact of attaining this liberation, this enlightenment. To me the reality is that an individual can attain to that freedom of self-consciousness, to that purification, to that liberation of the self which gives to him immense calmness, serenity, pliability, strength and affectionate detachment from all things.

QUESTION: DO YOU DENY THE IMPORTANCE OF RELIGIONS AND RELIGIOUS ORGANIZATIONS, AND HUMANITARIAN SERVICE?

I do not deny anything. I assert that religions are the frozen thoughts of men out of which they build temples and churches. Religions are systematized forms of thought, but as thought itself is life, you cannot bind it. Because you are binding life by codes, by sets of belief, by creeds, by religions, there is confusion, conflict and sorrow. life is free, and if you try to bind life by religion, which is a systematized form of thought, you will kill life.

I desire to free man from fear, to make him rely on himself, to show that he can be master of himself, that he is responsible for his own actions, for his own happiness. But because he loves to deceive himself, to shelter himself in the comfortable shadows of the temples of religions, there is no understanding; and hence there is sorrow and continual strife.

—*THE STAR BULLETIN*, MAY/JUNE 1932

Krishnamurti spent part of each year in New York, home to many artists. It was also, at the time, the home of the then aspiring and now noted artist, Beatrice Wood.

BEATRICE WOOD

CERAMICIST AND ARTIST, OJAI, CALIFORNIA

BEATRICE WOOD, 100 YEARS OLD IN 1993. "WHAT I'VE REALIZED FROM KRISHNAMURTI IS, IF I WILL FACE THE ACTIVITY OF MY MIND, IT'S DISTRACTIONS, IT'S JEALOUSY, IF YOU WISH— AND JUST LET GO—I DO TOUCH, WHAT IS FOR ME, A STILLNESS."

BW: I imagine that I met Krishnamurti the first time in 1923. A friend, Reginald Pole, brought him to my little walk-up apartment in New York. Then we went to the Metropolitan Museum and looked at Indian art. I had lunch with him and his brother Nityananda, Rajagopal, and Mima Porter, whom he'd known when he was young. We all had lunch at the Gotham Hotel, and I was very shy and very much in awe of him.

EB: What was your impression when you saw him for the first time?

BW: Well, I think I put in my diary, "One of the most beautiful people I've ever seen." I actually didn't hear him speak until several years later. I was at his first camp in Ojai in 1928. The camp lasted a week. I'd had lunch with him several times because we had so many friends in common. I was not a close close friend, I was a good friend. Because the camp lasted a week, it was decided there should be some entertainment, and he put me in charge of arranging plays. We put on three one-act plays, one by Tolstoy, one by George Bernard Shaw, and I think one by Barry. And people in the camp who were interested took part in it. I had the job of rehearsing them, and then we put on *The Light of Asia* as one of the plays. It was very wonderful, those first talks, sitting under the oaks on the ground. There was never any talk of money, nothing. And there was a wonderful atmosphere, and I listened. I was reading another philosopher, and then I read Krishnamurti, and I found him the most profound speaker, though I have no idea how much I have absorbed of what he said. There was a great silence at those early talks, and I remember the same thing in India many years later, the great silence of the audience.

EB: Do you think that was because people felt that he was a messiah-to-come, because there had been those proclamations?

BW: Well, I think that must have had a great deal to do with it. During those first years he gave interviews very easily. I had five with him and one has been with me and helped me especially. Do you want me to say?

EB: Yes, please.

BW: It had to do with jealousy. I am generally not jealous of other people doing art, but once I saw a glaze that I'd been trying to make. I went up to Claremont, and here was this glaze I'd struggled to get and hadn't. It was like a physical impact of jealousy, and I was horrified with myself. So I went and had a talk with Krishnamurti. These are not his exact words, but it's the impact of what he made me perceive. He said something like this—All right, we're all jealous. Don't try not to be jealous. Drop it, and go on to another thought—and that has helped me in ever so many ways. I was not jealous about art, but jealous, I'd say, about people. This thing of trying not to be jealous, but instead to touch the stillness of the mind.

EB: Do you think that the fact that he spoke so often about observing your own reactions and your own responses made you more aware? Previously, jealousy might have arisen in you, but now you were aware of it.

BW: Well, that is in his teachings so much, and every great religious teacher through the ages has said, "Know thyself." And what I've realized from Krishnamurti is, if I will face the activity of my mind, it's distractions, it's jealousy, if you wish—and just let go—I do touch what is for me a stillness. The thing is, as he said, to watch from moment to moment. Of course I don't do that. I can only say he's had a great impact on me and I'm different than if I hadn't heard him.

In 1930 he invited me and a good friend of mine to go to Holland, to the pre-camp, for one week before the official talks opened, and there were many discussions. We went to Holland and Ommen, and it was very cold. Most of the people were in little huts, and Krishnamurti then was staying in the castle—and he invited us with others to stay in the castle. But he was mobbed by people and he refused to put them out. So instead we stayed with the manager of the camp.

EB: Were those pre-camp discussions different from the regular talks?

BW: The pre-camp? Well, in Holland that was the only pre-camp that I went to. We were a smaller group of people, and here in America he had pre-camps, he had groups of twenty, and I went to at least four of them, as I remember, but I think that was in the thirties, not the twenties. And questions were answered, and I remember he said to one woman, "None of you listen, there's no real exchange between you." I enjoyed them because there was a closeness in which we could ask any questions we wished.

EB: What was your next contact?

BW: Well, my next was when I'd come up to Arya Vihara to spend a night or two.

EB: Were you living in Ojai at that time?

BW: I was living in Ojai, and then in 1948 I moved to a house just opposite his so I saw him very continually. For a while I worked for Rajagopal, but my eyes weren't good. I just wasn't quick and accurate enough to continue working for him. We were young people then. All intertwined, knowing each other.

EB: And what was it that brought you to Ojai in the first place?

BW: Oh, I came on account of Krishnamurti without any question. I'd met him in New York, and I'd met Rajagopal and Rosalind. My heart had been broken in a love affair, and I had to have something to survive. And I knew Krishnamurti, and that's how I came to the first Star Camp. I've functioned wonderfully as an artist since I've been here. I never gave moving to Ojai a thought. What I was concerned with was that I was lost. My heart actually was broken, and I wanted something to help me understand life. I took my last hundred dollars to get on the train, so I came out.

EB: And there was a community of interested people around Krishnamurti?

BW: Oh yes, always. Huxley of course, and Robert and Sarah Logan were what was called aristocracy. I hate that word, but there's a word, up something.

EB: Upper-class?

BW: Upper-class Philadelphians. They gave up society after they met Dr. Besant and Krishnamurti. He used to speak at their home in Sarobia, Pennsylvania, and then, Robert Logan bought a house right in back of Arya Vihara, and he and I were good friends. We were all seeing each other continually.

EB: I'd like to go back a little bit in time. Were you aware of what happened when Krishnamurti had his so called "pepper tree" experience?

BW: I was told about it. But otherwise not aware.

EB: Were you able to see any difference, a new awakening or some other understanding?

BW: No. I can't say that I did because whenever I saw Krishnamurti he was just a human being, like all of us. He wasn't up on a tree speaking high things. He would help when he was at Arya Vihara, with the raising of the animals, I think he milked the cow for a while. He brought up Radha, that little daughter of Rosalind and Rajagopal, he practically brought her up. he did the things that anybody would do. But he also taught me, taught is the wrong word, but listening to him I began to realize the importance of what ever I did in the present, to do it perfectly. Because I'm very slovenly, very careless, and I'm trying to watch that. That's his impact upon me. When I was in my forties, I delivered pottery to one of the big stores—my agent had gone away—and the manager said, "Where's your invoice," and I said, "Invoice, what's an invoice?" She said, "It's a list." I said, "Madam, I'm an artist, I don't think lists." She said, "How do you expect to get paid?" And that was a great revolution in my life. So the practical power of his exactness made me aware of order. He made me see the importance of being inwardly truthful. He made me aware of the conditioning of the mind.

EB: One of the significant things that he pointed out, was what is actually going on in the mind. It's rather unusual, this emphasis on the mind, on thinking itself as an obstacle.

BW: Oh, yes, as I've said, I was reading another philosopher, very highly thought of, and then I picked up one of Krishnamurti's books, and Krishnamurti seemed to me so far beyond in profound thought.

EB: What was your feeling when Krishnamurti dissolved the Order of the Star?

BW: Well, I'm against organization. I don't see how a person with his breadth can work through any organization. Because the moment you

BEATRICE WOOD WITH
KRISHNAMURTI AND RADHA
RAJAGOPAL, DAUGHTER OF
ROSALIND AND RAJAGOPAL.

have an organization, you're caught up with tightness and rules. That never bothered me at all. You see, I think life's very mysterious and let's face it, just the subject of sex, which is such a problem for seemingly, everybody in some way or another…I say we don't know their different customs, we don't know, and the thing is it's strange we put such emphasis on it instead of bothering about being inwardly honest. To me that is the first thing, and I'm conscious of the conditioning of my mind, and I struggle more to be straight than I struggle to make pottery or anything, but I don't succeed. But I struggle, and that's really important. I think for all of us, it is important to go towards that which is honest and compassionate, and we don't need an Order of the Star.

EB: Do you think Krishnamurti's physical beauty had an impact? Do you think it helped or hurt his role as a teacher?

BW: I have no idea, I should think if anything, it would help because it makes us feel good to see a beautiful person. I will listen to a beautiful person much more quickly than a plain person, and I have to learn to be nice to people who are not attractive looking.

EB: Do you think that might have put people on the wrong track? We are attracted to powerful people, beautiful people, but what he had to say was overwhelming in its impact. Do you think that people were not paying so much attention to what he was saying because they fell in love with this beautiful man?

BW: I wasn't conscious of that, but I was conscious that some women felt personally closer to him than I did, though I may have seen him many more times. Probably because I was in awe of him. I lost a little bit of it when I met him in India in the sixties. I know he objected…that's the wrong word, he pointed out all my jewelry and I said, I like jewelry, and I'd even have a diamond in my nose if it didn't hurt me, and he raised his hands in horror and I said, "Krishnaji, you're just not the same as women, you're not coquettish the way we are." He

The transformation

of the world is

brought about by

the transformation

of oneself.

—BANGALORE, 1948

pointed to all the bracelets on my arm. One Indian woman said, laughingly, "We met you when we were in America, and saw the jewelry that you were wearing and we laughed together saying, 'what will it be like when she comes to India.'" Now, the Indian woman wears a lot of jewelry. I've always loved jewelry, so I wore even more. I've loved jewelry since I was sixteen. It's supposed to be vulgar, and in bad taste. I don't care, I like jewelry, so I wear it. I'm happy when I see it on other women. Now, I would be lacking in understanding, it seems to me, if I stopped wearing jewelry just because Krishnamurti may not have

liked it. He said, "You look like a prisoner with these." I had more on my arms. I just laughed at him. "You don't know, you're not a woman," but he was very careful of the way he dressed,

much more so than I am. He was always very beautifully groomed, spotless and neat, so he had no right to say a word to me! I was at one meeting in India and I realized, because I was very unhappy, that aloneness was probably the basic problem. That next day I went to hear him and there was a big crowd of Indians in the open air, and I thought he was quite wonderful the way he brought around the fact of the mischief of man's aloneness. It was wonderful the way he did it.

EB: People still have that sense of isolation, they feel that they're isolated and alone, and really yearn for someone to talk to about important matters.

BW: But man is principally alone, in spite of being part of the human race, and he made me realize that most of our distraction and activity is to escape that aloneness, but if we face it, the activity of life goes on like a song. It's entirely different if one can face it.

EB: What is the most significant thing, that you have learned from hearing K speak? You mentioned earlier order, a sense of order…

BW: I don't know exactly how to answer that because I think trying to be free of the conditioning of my mind is what I struggle with most. Now that doesn't mean one shouldn't laugh, say silly things…that's entirely different.

EB: Do you think that there were ways in which Krishnamurti could have been more clear in expounding his teaching?

BW: I don't know. You see, he's talking about the formless. We cannot hold thought in a form, and he goes into such depth, I don't see how it could be clearer, but I have no idea how much I have absorbed. How can I tell? I just know that as far as I'm concerned, I struggle in the direction of being a more honest human being than if I hadn't met him. There it stops.

EB: Did you continue to hear Krishnamurti over the many years?

BW: For many years, until about fifteen years ago when I began to become deaf. The last years when I returned from India, I began getting deaf, so I didn't go, but I read him constantly. Not every night, but often, because I don't want to be fanatical. In fact, every night when I go to bed I read something of a philosophic nature—except when I want to cheat, and I cheat every now and then when I have a detective story and cannot wait to hear the end.

EB: I don't think you'd be blamed for that. As a matter of fact, it's well-known that Krishnamurti liked to read detective stories.

BW: Maybe he cheated too. I think what we all have to watch is fanaticism. I think we have to watch that very carefully.

EB: Krishnamurti himself constantly questioned everything. He questioned his own thoughts, his own teaching in a sense, so he could never have become a fanatic himself. He never laid down any laws for anyone to follow. I think he was a good example of freedom from fanaticism.

Thank you so much for your contribution. I have to compliment you on your magnificent memory.

DURING THIS PERIOD KRISHNAMURTI SPOKE FREQUENTLY AT ROBERT AND SARAH LOGAN'S HOME IN SAROBIA, PENNSYLVANIA (BELOW). THE INFORMALITY WAS IN CONTRAST TO MORE STRUCTURED GATHERINGS SUCH AS THE ONE HELD IN ARNHEM, HOLLAND IN 1925, WHERE A MASSIVE CROWD CLUSTERED AROUND KRISHNAMURTI AND MRS. BESANT (OPPOSITE).

BW: I don't think it's so good.

EB: Well at one hundred years, I think we can't complain.

BW: I'm thirty-two to me, only a hundred to the rest of you.

Because you are the world, your actions will affect the world you live in, which is the world of your relationships. But the difficulty is to recognize the importance of individual transformation. We demand transformation, the transformation of society about us, but we are blind, unwilling to transform ourselves.

—BANGALORE TALK II, 1948

In the thirties during the annual Ojai Star Camps in California Krishnamurti made many new friends, not all of them artists or intellectuals. Among them was Harry Wolfe.

HARRY WOLFE

BUSINESSMAN, LOS ANGELES, CALIFORNIA

EB: Mr. Wolfe, you said that your wife introduced you to Krishnamurti, brought you to hear him. Could you describe that?

HW: When I came home from a long business trip, Mrs. Wolfe suggested that we go to Ojai to listen to a very fine human being. And I said, "Well Laura, I prefer to play golf than to go out and listen to a lot of conversation," you know most of these teachers or talks are based on religion or something, and I'm not interested in religion. After convincing me that I should go and we could play golf after he finished his talk, I decided to go along. I listened very intensely because I wanted to get the full significance of what he was talking about. He had me in a corner where I couldn't dispute a thing that he had to say, so, after listening to him, instead of wanting to play golf, I really wasn't in the mood for golf, I thought, "We'll come back tomorrow because I want to hear him again." So we did come back the next day and I again listened very intensely and couldn't dispute a thing that he said. And I wanted to come back the following weekend. He had my interest so that I just wanted to listen, and after the third weekend I wanted an interview—which he was giving at the time—fifteen minutes at a time. I think this was in 1930. Fifteen minutes was up and I said, "Well I guess I better go." He said, "No wait a minute, I want to ask you something, talk to you some more." I told him about my business and I explained how corrupt the diamond industry was, and how the wholesalers were cheating on the retailers, and there was no real integrity in the business. My own business as well as the jewelry business. I was exclusively in the diamond business, and jewelers are the same way. And, I explained many things like that to him, and he was interested in what I had to say so he let me stay—he put his hand on my knee and he said, "Wait a minute, it's all right." So we continued talking, I don't remember exactly what I had to say after that, but he realized that I was taking inventory of what was going on in the way of corruption...

OPPOSITE: THE FIRST OJAI CAMP IN 1928 LASTED A WEEK.

EB: Did that seem something new to him?

HW: Well he was surprised that I was taking such an interest in finding out what the situation was in business. I told him the diamonds, more that 95 percent of the diamonds that are cut for the world market are cut improperly—what we call in the trade swindled. Because the lead weight on the stone, on the piece of rock, should be ground away—because they want a two carat stone instead of a carat and a half. You see every diamond has fifty-eight facets, and those little facets are just like tiny mirrors, and if the geometrical angles of those little mirrors are at the right angle it's impossible to shoot the light rays back to the surface. That's what gives it it's own light and beauty.

EB: Was Krishnamurti surprised to hear that the business was so corrupt?

HW: Yes, he was.

EB: You had heard him speak several times, what was your response on meeting him for the first time?

HW: Oh, he was so friendly and so easy to be with that I had no trouble in talking to him. I just told him exactly what I thought. And we got along very well. And after that I had—I don't know how many talks, I went to Ojai at least a half a dozen times. On one trip I asked him, "Krishnaji, what do you think is going to happen to India when they're freed from the domination of Britain?" And he said, "Well, they'll be exploited by the Indians instead of by the British. Same thing." He realized that people are people, and people are only interested in gaining advantage for themselves at the expense of somebody else.

EB: How would you compare the talks in those days to what he says today?

HW: Well, it's hard to explain. It varied a little bit, but the principle is the same. The main core of his teaching is pretty much the same now as it was then. Different words, different presentation. In fact, I offered him five hundred dollars—in those days that was a lot of money—as a token of appreciation for what he had done for me. He said, "I can't do anything for anybody, you have to do it." Well, I realized that I began to think differently, act differently, and feel differently towards human beings, realizing that they're all conditioned, and they are not responsible for what they do or say because how can you blame a tape recorder for being conditioned to play a tune. So I began to be a little more tolerant of people who want to take advantage of me, I didn't blame them because that's the order of the day. That goes in business, that goes in law, every department in human relations is corrupt.

EB: Krishnamurti must have had quite an impact on your life?

HW: Oh, he has, absolutely. He changed my life completely. I quit my business—I quit my business because I realized that I was the same kind of a human being that everybody else was. I was corrupt. I was taking advantage of the confidence that people placed in me by selling them more than they needed, by using salesmanship, and I realized what I was doing. So I quit it. You see, I handled the kind of diamonds that the average jeweler doesn't even see, the diamond that isn't swindled, that has maximum beauty. And I decided that I don't have to sell them, they'll buy if I explained what it is. So I had to manufacture my customers by showing them the difference between a stone that isn't cut right and a stone that is cut right. I made a lot less money, but I enjoyed doing business that didn't misrepresent perfect blue white. There's no such thing as perfect or blue white. It's either blue or it's white, or it's yellow or it's pink. There's no double colors, because the color of a diamond is determined only by the body color, not by the brilliance of the stone. We used to grade our stones for exactly what they were—the color, the degree of clarity, and the cutting. Cutting is the most important thing because that's what gives you the light.

"HE CHANGED MY LIFE
COMPLETELY. I QUIT MY
BUSINESS—I QUIT MY
BUSINESS BECAUSE I
REALIZED THAT I WAS THE
SAME KIND OF A HUMAN
BEING THAT EVERYBODY
ELSE WAS. I WAS CORRUPT."
—HARRY WOLFE

EB: Did you find that your business declined?

HW: Oh yes, it declined a lot. I made less money, but I enjoyed it because I didn't have to press or sell—people bought. There's a big difference.

EB: Do you think that if you hadn't met Krishnamurti, that you would have come to these, let's say, ethical feelings, independently? Or would you have gone on as you were before?

HW: I don't think so. He awakened me to the fact that I was no different than anybody else. I was just as corrupt as anybody else. And I had to see that in myself—actually see it, in order to be free from it.

EB: And you did see that instantaneously?

HW: Oh, yes. Yes sure, it wasn't hard to do.

EB: Very often people say that it takes time, and Krishnamurti always says that it can be instantaneous.

HW: It's instantly. You either see it or you don't see it. If you see it there's no use going any further. You see it and that's it. The truth is instant.

EB: So it was simply your intelligence in operation. You saw it and you acted upon it.

THE TALKS AND GATHERINGS CONTINUED AROUND THE WORLD. THE STAR CAMP CANTEEN AND SHOP, OMMEN, HOLLAND (ABOVE).

HW: You know the minute you see something that's a fact, you don't go any further, that's it. My thinking is entirely different, because I don't make comparisons. I just look at the facts as they are, you don't have to go any further than that. Awareness, I think, is the most important factor, because you're only partly living if you're not aware. If you walk into a room and you don't pay any attention to what's there, you're not aware. Most people are not aware, they only want to see what they want to see and that's it. But, awareness has been my teacher you might say, because I couldn't speak English when I came to this country as a boy of twelve, of course my vocabulary is quite limited.

EB: I think you express yourself quite well.

HW: I do the best that I can with what I have.[45]

N THE FOLLOWING YEARS extensive speaking tours brought Krishnamurti and Rajagopal around the world. In 1933 they traveled to Cairo, Alexandria, Athens, Oslo, Paris, and Rome. There was another camp at Ommen, Holland, and then on to India for a one-month tour.

In 1934, in Australia, Krishnamurti met with large and enthusiastic crowds; however, as he moved on to New Zealand, again to a receptive audience, something surprising happened to him—and to George Bernard Shaw!

NEW ZEALAND RADIO BAN

NEW ZEALAND. The Krishnamurti radio ban in New Zealand caused considerable agitation. The matter has since been brought up in parliament and Krishnamurti's name appears frequently in the press and is much mentioned in political speeches. This has given his recent visit much unsought publicity and increased public interest in his ideas. Friends in New Zealand say they may have quite a problem in securing a hall large enough to hold those anxious to hear Krishnamurti when he next visits their country.

NEW ZEALAND. The *Verbatim Report* mentioned in Mr. Rajagopal's foregoing letter contains Krishnamurti's talks in the Town Hall, Auckland, where he addressed a full house of 3000 people on two occasions; three morning talks in the Vasanta School Gardens; one talk to business men in Auckland and a talk to Theosophists in New Zealand. The New Zealand press gave much space to Krishnamurti's visit and activities, and many of the newspapers deplored the action of the Government authorities in refusing to allow him to broadcast on the grounds that his talk contained controversial matter. Mr. George Bernard Shaw happened to be in New Zealand at the same time and the epilogue of his play *Androcles and the Lion* was also banned. The following extracts from the newspapers may convey some idea of the excitement caused.

KRISHNAMURTI'S BROADCAST BAN

THE AUCKLAND STAR. Thousands of listeners who were looking forward to hearing Jiddu Krishnamurti, the Indian philosopher, through the medium of IYA broadcasting station will be disappointed, as he will not be allowed to use the microphone from that station. The information was contained in a letter from the manager of the New Zealand Broadcasting Board.

The Board was notified of Krishnamurti's visit some weeks ago, and a request was made that he should be allowed to broadcast from Auckland station an address on the lines of one broadcast from the Town Hall, Sydney. A copy of the address was forwarded with the request. The reply received was to the effect that the matter was controversial, and therefore could not be permitted to go on the air in New Zealand.

Unfavorable criticism of the Board was heard in many quarters this morning when it was made known that Krishnamurti's public addresses were radio banned.

KRISHNAMURTI'S ATTITUDE

THE DOMINION, WELLINGTON. Mr. Krishnamurti said today that it was a unique experience for him. He was on the air in Australia four or five times, and had been relayed all over Europe and America. "Of course I can do nothing about it," he said. "If the Government does not wish me to speak through its microphone, that is the Government's business. It is like somebody asking you not to go into his private house. You do not go, and that is an end of it. It certainly seems absurd." He said that in his opinion if any subject was not controversial it was useless and meant nothing.

MR. G. B. SHAW'S COMMENT

EVENING POST, AUCKLAND. Mr. George Bernard Shaw is not seriously disturbed over the banning of the broadcast of the epilogue of his play *Androcles and the Lion* at Christchurch. He considers, however, that the refusal to allow the well-known Indian religious teacher Krishnamurti to broadcast is a much more serious mistake. "A far less excusable case is the refusal to allow Mr. Krishnamurti to broadcast. He is a religious teacher of the greatest distinction, who is listened to with profit and assent by members of all churches and sects, and the prohibition is an ignorant mistake.

"The excuse as to broadcasting being controversial is nonsense. Everything that comes over the wireless is controversial except the time signal and the weather report...The authorities are evidently ignorant of Krishnamurti's standing, and his admirably catholic doctrine, and class him just as an Indian heathen. When he becomes known in New Zealand they will be sorry for it." [46]

IN THE 1880S, THE YOUNG GEORGE BERNARD SHAW WORKED CLOSELY WITH ANNIE BESANT AS A MEMBER OF THE FABIAN SOCIALIST SOCIETY, AND WAS BELIEVED BY SOME TO BE HER LOVER. IN THE 1930S, HE CONSIDERED THE REFUSAL TO ALLOW KRISHNAMURTI TO BROADCAST A MUCH MORE SERIOUS MISTAKE THAN THE CENSORSHIP OF HIS PLAY.

The tiring years of travel left Krishnamurti in a depleted state and after a short stay in Hollywood with long-time friend John Ingleman, he went on to Ojai for a brief period. The trio of Krishnamurti, Rajagopal, and Rosalind and their baby daughter, Radha, went on to Carmel in northern California for a few months' rest.

During that stay in 1934, Krishnamurti made the acquaintance of the great American poet, Robinson Jeffers. The two walked often together and although the laconic Jeffers spoke very little, he did write a poem entitled "Credo" which many feel refers to Krishnamurti.

> *My friend from Asia has powers and magic,*
> *He plucks a blue leaf from the young blue-gum*
> *And gazing upon it, gathering and quieting*
> *The God in his mind, creates an ocean more real than the*
> *Ocean, the salt, the actual*
> *Appalling presence, the power of the waters.*

Jeffers was especially struck by the force of Krishnamurti's person which, he felt, was more eloquent than his words. Mrs. Jeffers said that "light seems to enter the room when Krishnamurti comes in." [47]

Another visitor to Carmel was author Rom Landau, who had met Krishnamurti earlier in England and had been deeply impressed with him. Landau came to Carmel expressly to interview Krishnamurti for his book, *God Is My Adventure*. After lengthy daily walks and talks together his visit was drawing to a close. He expressed amazement that:

Neither in the records of Western mystics nor in the books of Eastern yogis and saints do we find the story of a "saint" who after twenty-five years of preparation for a divine destiny decided to become an ordinary human being, who renounces not only his worldly goods but also all his religious claims.

It was quite dark and the first stars were beginning to appear. The attention was not distracted by the lights and colors and shapes of the day. The mysterious pattern of Krishnamurti's remarkable fate was becoming clearer, and I began to understand what he had meant when he said that until a few years ago life had been a dream to him and that he had scarcely been conscious of the external existence around him. Were not those the years of preparation? Were they not the years in which the man Krishnamurti was trying to find himself, to replace that former self through whom Mrs. Besant and Charles Leadbeater, Theosophy and a strange credulity, acted for over twenty years?

Indeed, was not Krishnamurti's a supreme story? The teacher who renounces his throne at the moment of his awakening, at the moment when the god in him has to make way for the man, at the moment when the man can begin to find God within himself? Have not even the years in which his spirit lingered in dreams been full of a truth that as yet is too mysterious to be comprehended by us? [48]

In 1935 Krishnamurti embarked on an eight-month tour of South America, traveling to Brazil, Uruguay, Argentina, Chile and at the end of the trip, Mexico. Many who saw his photograph in newspaper articles followed him in the streets for a look at the young Indian. However, in Buenos Aires, the Church took a negative stand and one of its priests flooded the streets with pamphlets "Contra Krishnamurti."

Although an effort was made to study Spanish before embarking on the trip, Krishnamurti, in his twenty-five talks in Latin America, spoke only English. How much was really understood was a question.

QUESTION: HOW CAN WE BEST HELP HUMANITY TO UNDERSTAND AND LIVE YOUR TEACHINGS?

It is very simple: by living them yourself. What is it that I am teaching? I am not giving you a new system, or a new set of beliefs; but I say, look to the cause that has created this exploitation, lack of love, fear, continual wars, hatred, class distinctions, division of man against man. The cause is, fundamentally, the desire on the part of each one to protect himself through acquisitiveness, through power. We all desire to help the world, but we never begin with ourselves. We want to reform the world, but the fundamental change must first take place within ourselves. So, begin to free the mind and heart from this sense of possessiveness. This demands, not mere renunciation, but discernment, intelligence. [49]

—RIO DE JANEIRO, BRAZIL, APRIL 17, 1935

...In the world of the spiritual, the search for security is expressed through the desire for immortality. In each one there is the desire to remain permanent, eternal. This is what all religions promise, an immortality in the hereafter, which is but a subtle form of egotistic security. Now, anyone that promises this selfish continuance, which you call immortality, consciously or unconsciously becomes your authority. Look at the various religions in the world and you will see that out of your own desire for security, for salvation, for continuance, you have created a subtle and cruel authority to which you have become utterly enslaved, which is constantly crippling your thought, your love.

Now, to interpret this authority, you must have mediators whom you call priests, who become in fact your exploiters. (Applause) Perhaps you applaud rather too quickly—because you are the creators of these exploiters. (Laughter, applause) Some of you may not consciously create these spiritual authorities, but subtly, unknowingly, you are creating other kinds of exploiters. You may not got to a priest, but this does not mean that you are not exploiting or exploited.

Where there is the desire for security, certainty, there must be authority, and you give yourself over entirely to those people who promise to guide you, to help you to realize that security. So religions have become throughout the world the receptacle of vested interest, and of organized, closed belief. (Applause) Sirs, may I suggest something? Please don't bother to applaud, as it is a waste of time.[50]

—MONTEVIDEO, URUGUAY, JUNE 21, 1935

QUESTION: DO YOU BELIEVE IN GOD?

Either you put this question out of curiosity to find out what I think, or you want to discover if there is God. If you are merely curious, naturally there is no answer; but if you want to find out for yourself if there is God, then you must approach this inquiry without prejudice; you must come to it with a fresh mind, neither believing nor disbelieving. If I said there is, you would accept it as a belief, and you would add that belief to the already existing dead beliefs. Or, if I said no, it would merely become a convenient support to the unbeliever.

If a man is truly desirous to know, let him not seek reality, life, God, which will only be an escape from sorrow, from conflict; but let him understand the very cause of sorrow, conflict and when the mind is liberated from it, he shall know. When the mind is vulnerable, when it has lost all support, explanations, when it is naked, then it shall know the bliss of truth.[51]

—SANTIAGO, CHILE, SEPTEMBER 7, 1935

The South American tour had been arduous, and after a period of rest and an attempt to regain the weight lost during the trip, the round of talks began again. First Ojai, then Sarobia, at the Logan estate, and on to Ommen and at the beginning of 1937 back to India again for another series of talks.

Conditions in India were, as always, a shock, as poverty and degradation remained entrenched and the corrosive rise of nationalism further threatened the dying British Raj.

India was not the only country experiencing unrest. The lowering menace of events in Europe moved inexorably toward world conflict. Hitler was consolidating his power and watched events in Spain closely. There the civil war raged, and with the fall of Madrid in 1939 Franco locked his grasp on the soul of his country.

Spanish-speaking peoples had long had an interest in Krishnamurti, but as Madrid burned, so did the entire stock of Krishnamurti books, translated into Spanish. It was a tremendous loss and one that took years to rectify.

Before the return to Ojai, Krishnamurti stopped again in Rome. The Mussolini ban on public talks allowed for only intimate gatherings at private homes and the circle of friends there made continued contact with Italy possible. It was there he met the young Vanda Scaravelli, née Passigli. Over the years he frequently stayed at the Scaravelli home in Florence. In later years it was Vanda who made his stays in Switzerland at Chalet Tannegg possible, when he began his important European gatherings in the sixties.

Why are Krishnamurti's teachings—the result of deep compassion and love—so important? An attentive mind is an intelligent mind. With the simplicity of his language, the clarity of his thought and the passion with which he expresses himself, he is able to awaken our intelligence. This is the miracle!

—VANDA SCARAVELLI

BACK IN OJAI IN 1938, Krishnamurti made new friends. Gerald Heard and Aldous Huxley, both authors and credentialed intellectuals, had left England in the face of darkening threats of war. Coming to the mecca of southern California they were drawn into the Krishnamurti orbit. Huxley, his wife Maria, and Krishnamurti soon became fast friends. Long serious discussions were interrupted by light-hearted picnics. Anita Loos, a well-known dramatist and screenwriter, describes one such picnic:

ANITA LOOS

DRAMATIST AND SCREENWRITER, HOLLYWOOD, CALIFORNIA

Both Aldous and Maria loved picnics; the thought of one made them happy as little children. I recall one particular outing with dramatis personae so fantastic that they might have come out of Alice in Wonderland. There were several Theosophists from India, the most prominent being Krishnamurti. The Indian ladies were dressed in saris which were elegant enough, but the rest of us wore the most casual old sports outfits. Aldous might have been the giant from some circus sideshow; Maria and I could have served as dwarfs, but with our tacky clothes the circus would have been pretty second-rate....

Greta [Garbo] was disguised in a pair of men's trousers and a battered hat with a floppy brim that almost covered her face; Paulette [Goddard] wore a native Mexican outfit with colored yarn braided into her hair. Bertrand Russell, visiting Hollywood at the time, Charlie Chaplin, and Christopher Isherwood all looked like naughty pixies out on a spree. Matthew Huxley was the only one of the group who was a mere normally disheveled teenager.

The picnic gear was as unusual as the cast of characters. Krishnamurti and his Indian friends, forbidden to cook their food or eat from vessels that had been contaminated by animal food, were weighed down with crockery and an assortment of clattering pots and pans. Greta, then strictly a vegetarian, was on a special diet of raw carrots which hung at her side in bunches. The others could and did eat ordinary picnic fare, but Paulette, to whom no occasion is festive without champagne and caviar, had augmented the equipment with a wine cooler and Thermos cases.

We had started out in several motor cars, with no definite objective except to find a spot where a fire could safely be built....Krishnamurti and the Indian delegation set about cooking their rice. And while the remainder of us were unpacking sandwiches, Greta's raw carrots, and Paulette's caviar, we were shocked by a gruff male voice ringing out with, "What the hell's going on here?"

Stunned into silence, we turned around to face a Sheriff, or some reasonable facsimile, with a gun in his hand.

"Don't anybody in this gang know how to read?" he demanded of Aldous.

Aldous meekly allowed that he could read, but still no one got the man's implication until he pointed out the [No Trespassing] sign....Then Aldous played his trump card. He indicated the presence of Miss Garbo, Miss Goddard, and Mr. Chaplin. The Sheriff's measly little eyes squinted only briefly at the group.

"Is that so?" he asked. "Well, I've seen every movie they ever made," said he, "and none of them stars belong in this outfit. So you get out of here, you tramps,

or I'll arrest the whole slew of you."

We folded our tents like the Arabs, and guiltily stole away. It was not until we were in the garden at the Huxley house where the picnic was resumed that we began to think about the titillating headlines...." Mass Arrest in Hollywood. Greta Garbo, Paulette Goddard, Charlie Chaplin, Aldous Huxley, Lord Bertrand Russell, Krishnamurti, and Christopher Isherwood Taken into Custody." [52]

The friendship with Huxley bore fruit. He urged Krishnamurti to publish after seeing examples of his writings. Some years later, Huxley wrote the introduction for Krishnamurti's book *The First and Last Freedom.*

ALDOUS HUXLEY

AUTHOR, NOVELIST AND PHILOSOPHER

"KNOWLEDGE IS AN AFFAIR
OF SYMBOLS AND IS, ALL
TOO OFTEN, A HINDRANCE
TO WISDOM, TO THE
UNCOVERING OF THE SELF
FROM MOMENT TO MOMENT."

—ALDOUS HUXLEY

There is a transcendent spontaneity of life, a "creative reality," as Krishnamurti calls it, which reveals itself as immanent only when the perceiver's mind is in a state of "alert passivity," of "choiceless awareness." Judgement and comparison commit us irrevocably to duality. Only choiceless awareness can lead to non-duality, to the reconciliation of opposites in a total understanding and a total love. Ama et fac quod vis. If you love, you may do what you will. But if you start by doing what you will, or by doing what you don't will in obedience to some traditional system or notions, ideals and prohibitions, you will never love. The liberating process must begin with the choiceless awareness of what you will and of your reactions to the symbol-system which tells you that you ought, or ought not, to will it. Through this choiceless awareness, as it penetrates the successive layers of the ego and its associated sub-conscious, will come love and understanding, but of another order than that with which we are ordinarily familiar. This choiceless awareness—at every moment and in all the circumstances of life—is the only effective meditation. All other forms of yoga lead either to the blind thinking which results from self-discipline, or to some kind of self-induced rapture, some form of false samadhi. The true liberation is "an inner freedom of creative reality." This "is not a gift; it is to be discovered and experienced. It is not an acquisition to be gathered to yourself to glorify yourself. It is a state of being, as silence, in which there is no becoming, in which there is completeness. This creativeness may not necessarily seek expression; it is not a talent that demands outward manifestation. You need not be a great artist or have an audience; if you seek these, you will miss the inward reality. It is neither a gift, nor is it the outcome of talent; it is to be found, this imperishable treasure, where thought frees itself from lust, ill-will and ignorance, where thought frees itself from worldliness and personal craving to be. It is to be experienced through right thinking and meditation." Choiceless self-awareness will bring us to the creative reality which underlies all our destructive make-believes, to the tranquil wisdom which is always there, in spite of ignorance, in spite of the knowledge which is merely ignorance in another form. Knowledge is an affair of symbols and is, all too often, a hindrance to wisdom, to the uncovering of the self from moment to moment. A mind that has come to the stillness of wisdom "shall know being, shall know what it is to love. Love is neither personal nor impersonal. Love is love, not to be defined or described by the mind as exclusive or inclusive. Love is its own eternity; it is the real, the supreme, the immeasurable." [53]

THE SITUATION IN EUROPE under Hitler's implacable threat grew more and more desperate. Fear clouded people's lives and the Camp that year was to be the last. World War II erupted and lives were in turmoil. Lex Muller who has long been associated with Krishnamurti's work in Holland was a young student at the time. He was one who was caught in Hitler's dragnet:

LEX MULLER

PROFESSOR OF ENGINEERING

LM: It happened just before the War, when I was interned in the old Star camp during the War. I suddenly discovered that I was eating from plates which had the name Star camp Ommen on them.

EB: Could you describe how you came to the Ommen camp?

LM: During the War the German Occupation had troubles with the students. At a given moment they decided they wanted the students to sign an act of loyalty to the German Occupation Forces, but there was quite a reaction among the students! A lot of people didn't sign it and I didn't. I stayed at home for a while and did not go back to my job and then after some time, I think it was May 1943 or so, the Germans said the students had to assemble in a few gathering centers in the country. For myself it was in Utrecht and I had to stay there until later.

EB: Was this in retaliation for refusing to sign the loyalty act?

LM: Yes. So, I had to decide on what to do, either go underground, and my mother felt she couldn't quite deal with me underground, so I decided to go. We assembled there in Utrecht and the next day we were moved on by train to Ommen and we stayed there a few days and then we were sent into Germany.

EB: But you hadn't realized that it was the Star camp until you saw the Star plates?

LM: Yes.

EB: I understand that the camp at Ommen was used, during a portion of the War, as a concentration camp.

LM: Yes, all the time I think.

EB: Would it have been used against any kind of dissident, or was it directed against Jews or any person that was non-conforming?

LM: They assembled the Jews there before transporting them to Germany and Poland.[54]

Baron van Pallandt, who was the generous donor some years earlier of the Castle Eerde and Ommen estate to the young Krishnamurti, wrote in a letter to friends of the terrible situation in Holland during WWII and, in particular, of events at Eerde:

BARON PHILLIP VAN PALLANDT

EARLY SUPPORTER OF KRISHNAMURTI

It is quite impossible to give you in words an adequate idea of Holland during the period May 1940—April 1945 and I am not attempting to do so. These are only a few thoughts which come to my mind, chiefly about Eerde, as I wake up this Sunday morning of June 10, 1945 and I am writing them down for you on paper. As it is not possible for me to write a long letter to all my friends individually, I am having this letter copied.

After four years and eleven months, we at Eerde were freed by the Canadian armored cars of the Manitoba Dragoons on the morning of April 6. Five days later Ommen was freed by the Black Watch (Royal Highland Regiment) of Canada. While looking at the building of a pontoon bridge over the Regge, we met there Major Robert Macduff D.S.O. of this regiment, who eventually became a very good friend. That feeling of liberation, after so much persecution, can hardly be expressed. No one who has not been persecuted by a ruthless enemy for five years, can understand what it means to be free again.

Practically everyone in Holland, except the very young and the very old, was hunted down by the Germans. About 370,000 workmen, 120,000 Jews and 20,000 political prisoners were taken to Germany. Of the 150,000 Jews in Holland about 30,000 managed to hide: under floors, between double walls, underground; 120,000 were taken to Poland and Germany and of the latter between two and three-thousand are believed to be still alive. Of a group of 700 Amsterdam Jewish boys, I saw arrive at Buchenwald in February 1941, only one is still alive. Now the enormous work of repatriation of the Dutch forced laborers and the political prisoners in Germany has started, nearly half a million men and some women. Eerde is being used as a hospital for these political prisoners, men and women, who are too weak and ill to go straight home. Many of them are just skeletons and weigh less than half their normal weight although they have been liberated seven or eight weeks. Their stories are terrible and they all think it a marvel that just they have escaped being gassed or tortured to death.

…Perhaps in no country in the world did the underground movement work so efficiently and on such a large scale as in Holland and I read a few days ago that Mr. Churchill had at the time decided not to mention any of the great results of this work so as not to endanger it. For you must understand that nowhere in West Europe was the Gestapo, the Sicherheitsdienst and the Green Police more ruthless than in Holland, which from 1940 they considered part of Greater Germany.

The V.1-weapons passed Eerde to the South in great numbers. They were too far off to be seen but they made a noise like extremely heavy airplane engines. But the V.II brought the suffering of England still closer to our minds. They used to be filled at Archem on the opposite side of the river Regge and let up at Hellendoorn. It was a fantastic sight to see these rockets go up into the stratosphere against a clear sky in daytime or at night.

…As it was, Eerde itself escaped marvelously. None of the oak paneling

suffered in the least, but after the Russian prisoners, who followed the German units fleeing from Belgium, had camped on straw in all the large rooms of the castle and done their own cooking there, it was in a filthy state.

The old family silver, which at the time of Napoleon had been hidden at the bottom on the inner moat at Eerde, we buried in our garden on May 10 when the Germans entered Holland.

When the old church bells were taken to Germany to be melted, the two huge bells of 1517 of the early Gothic church of Ommen were also taken. I went to hear the noon pealing for the last time.

The Star Camp was used as a concentration camp for several years by the Germans and it was the underground movement in Holland which saved us by getting hold of it when the Canadians were approaching just before the order could be carried out for it to be burned down.

…On the morning of October 11, 1940 I was taken off with others to Buchenwald concentration Camp. We were put in a sort of enclosure inside the large camp so that we could not mingle with the rest of the prisoners. Although we, as reprisals for the German prisoners taken in the Dutch East Indies, were not put to work and not beaten, many of the group died. But the terrible thing was to see and to know, what was going on around us. Nothing that has been said about Buchenwald has at all been exaggerated. The Poles and the Jews had even a shorter life than the political prisoners and nearly all were starved,

NAZI PARATROOPERS MANNING A LIGHT MACHINE-GUN POST IN THE NETHERLANDS DURING WORLD WAR II.

beaten or frozen to death while they had always to work twelve hours or more a day, for seven days a week on a few slices of bread and not enough of the watery cabbage soup.

But the one amazing thing about the tortured men and women, who have been able to get out of these Hells alive, and I have spoken to many of them, is that I have not come across a man or woman who regrets the experience. There is an inward strength developed which one misses when back again and one longs, as I felt myself, to be among one's comrades and it takes a long time to feel at home again in a world without the inner intensity of the concentration camp. This inward intensity is a very real thing. I remember well when I arrived at Buchenwald and thought that we might be put up against a wall and shot, that I said to myself: "If they do this then I will stand there with a smile on my face." And I have always felt that it was worth while to have been in Buchenwald to have gone through this experience of being free from one's physical self if only for that brief moment.[55]

DURING THE FIRST YEARS OF THE WAR IN EUROPE, America remained uncommitted, and full engagement did not take place until the attack on Pearl Harbor on December 7, 1942. Travel was practically at a stand-still and Ojai seemed far removed from the turbulence of the times, although young men and women were called to military service from every part of the country.

The talks and discussions then were far fewer and were centered in Ojai and Hollywood, with one trip to the Logan home, Sarobia, near Philadelphia. Krishnamurti made no secret of the fact that he was a pacifist, as was his friend Aldous Huxley.

Krishnamurti saw few people in those years of retreat. The Rajagopals and their daughter lived in close proximity, Krishnamurti at "Pine Cottage" and the Rajagopals at "Arya Vihara," although Rajagopal spent much of his time in Hollywood seeing to business and publishing matters.

Old friend, Sidney Field, was able to see Krishnamurti fairly often—when gas rationing permitted—and was concerned about his friend's anti-war statements:

I saw quite a good deal of Krishnamurti during the War years, he was here for several years without traveling any place. I had a contact with the FBI, a man by the name of McFarlane, he told me that there were Secret Service men at some of the talks—Krishnaji's talks in Ojai—and they were very much concerned because he was anti-war in the things he was saying. When I told this to Krishnaji, he laughed. During the next meeting, this was the first meeting after the War, he went after war in the strongest way, he just never softened his words for a second, I knew two or three of the men there who were Secret Servicemen. They would take notes. People who were for war interrupted him and insulted him, and those who were against the war went for the "war love" people, and there was almost a general brawl under the oak trees. Krishnaji remained perfectly calm, and it was at that time that he wrote me that he needed an extension on his passport, and they were having difficulties getting it, and was there anything I could do. So I wrote the Chief of Immigration, and it seemed to me so ridiculous that I couldn't help but laugh at it, my giving Krishnaji a recommendation that he was a man of high moral standing, and that we all consider ourselves very fortunate to have been there for his talks in Ojai. Well, finally, he did get his extension, but he was told that it was difficult because of what he had said. As I said, he never changed his approach to war at all. As I say, there was almost a fist fight. In every talk there were people who rudely interrupted him, and he would just stop and very gently say "The war that you should be concerned about is within you not outside." [56]

When a man is not in strife within himself, then he does not create strife outwardly. The inward strife, projected outwardly, becomes the world chaos. After all, war is a spectacular result of our everyday living; and without transformation in our daily existence, there is bound to be the multiplication of soldiers, drills, the saluting of flags and all the rubbish that goes with it.

—BOMBAY TALK 9, 1948

The very word science means knowledge, and man hopes through science he will be transformed into a sane and happy human being. And so man is pursuing eagerly knowledge of all the things of the earth and of himself. Knowledge is not compassion and without compassion knowledge breeds mischief and untold misery and chaos. Knowledge cannot make man love; it can create war and the instruments of destruction but cannot bring love to the heart or peace to the mind. To perceive all this is to act, not an action based on memory or patterns. Love is not memory, a remembrance of pleasures.

—*KRISHNAMURTI'S JOURNAL*, 1982

Another friend of those early days, and one who continued to be close until Krishnamurti's death, was William Quinn. A thoughtful, introspective man, who has probed the depths of Krishnamurti's teaching. He later became one of the three founding directors of the influential Esalen Institute at Big Sur, California.

WILLIAM QUINN

CO-FOUNDER, ESALEN INSTITUTE, BIG SUR, CALIFORNIA

WQ: I first met Krishnaji in November of 1944. I was twenty-one. I arrived at Arya Vihara with two other young men, and we waited for him in a little room. He arrived breathless, having run down from his house, and as he threw open the door and entered, radiant and youthful with a brilliant smile, his flashing eyes taking us in, I had an instant and naive response. I was physically swept through and through by some soaring violin music of Prokovief, intensely lyrical and joyous.

> "KRISHNAMURTI FELT THAT A LARGE PART OF OUR CONFUSION IS FROM REPETITIVE THOUGHTS, AND THEY ARE REPETITIVE BECAUSE NOT COMPLETED."
>
> —WILLIAM QUINN

I questioned him about the meaning of awareness, and he said: "If you look into your minds, you will see it's like thousands of butterflies whirling about! You can hardly trace a single idea in this complexity. A way to bring clarity to the mind is to write down your immediate thoughts and feelings in response to the events of the day, and then ponder them. If you emphasize one particular problem in this writing, it will gradually lead to all others." Krishnamurti felt that a large part of our confusion is from repetitive thoughts, and they are repetitive because not completed. By thinking these through to the end they would no longer clamor in us, and the mind would be freer and more spacious, more "aware." Krishnamurti worked enormously hard for many years to clarify his own mind, and this work was part of the background that enabled him to be a teacher. Krishnamurti was immensely conscious in the late twenties and early thirties of the tidal movement toward another great war. This became a central theme in his public talks all over the world.

EB: You've told me that the impact of the Second World War on you was substantial. Were you a conscientious objector?

WQ: The war started in 1939 when I was sixteen. Prior to that time I was preparing myself for a life in the physical sciences. But from the moment the war began I saw with incredulity how scientists were lending themselves unconscionably to the general conflagration.

Perhaps it was simplistic, but I concluded that if I became a scientist my talents would be used in the war, which I found unacceptable. Therefore, I felt I should give up science. I also concluded that I could not be a soldier, and expected to be sent to prison, because I had no religious basis for this stand, as was required by the government's definition of a conscientious objector.

EB: Was it youthful idealism which had made you feel science could cure the world's problems?

WQ: No doubt. But there were also several scientists of world stature in the twenties and thirties who were immensely idealistic about the amelioration of life through science, and as a boy I was greatly affected by their high-minded vision.

EB: Although you were willing to go to prison, that did not happen?

WQ: No. I was lucky, and I was free, as few young men were at that time. But the questions raised by the fact of the war and my relation to it became a complete preoccupation, and formed the core of my consciousness. What was I to do with my life? How could science be so complicit in this evil? This led me to question the nature of knowledge itself.

EB: Did you come to Krishnamurti in that frame of mind? You had read him, and then you wanted to speak with him personally.

WQ: Through friendship with an eminent physicist, I came to see clearly, by the time I was twenty, the tentative and provisional character of scientific formulation and theory. This was an immense relief for me, but my consciousness of the war continued to burn, as it did in many other hundreds of millions.

In the summer of 1944 I worked as a firewatcher on a tower in the Bitterroot Mountains in northern Idaho. It was a wilderness then, with vast tracts of virgin forest. Right away I experimented with meditation, and the first time I did so, something remarkable happened. Without having even conceived of such a possibility, my mind stopped spontaneously and I was awakened to the glory of life. I instantly saw that this new dimension of perception was the "answer" to the war then raging to its climax, and the answer to "What am I to do with my life?" This extraordinary state lasted for months.

When the fire season ended, I hitchhiked to Los Angeles. En route I felt as if I was being carried along by some current of destiny, toward what I did not know. On the day of my arrival I met by chance another young man of my age who told me within an hour about Krishnamurti. I immediately said to myself, "I'm going to live with that man!" I talked with my new friend for a couple of days about Krishnamurti, and read a little of his talks given in the thirties. Then it all seemed to come together, some glimpse of the unitary nature of fear and desire. For a week I roamed the city in a state of awe, astonished and not comprehending. Shortly after this, the two of us with a third young man visited Krishnamurti. In our talks I didn't emphasize the war, since we seemed to think along parallel lines on that matter.

EB: What would have happened if Hitler had won? If one is faced with implacable evil, what is the right response?

WQ: I'm sure Krishnamurti was aware of how monstrous Hitler was, perhaps more acutely than the rest of us. His view was that if you resist evil, you become evil. Then evil escalates in a blind conflict which has no end but ruin and exhaustion. Prior to the war he said publicly that he was himself a pacifist, unconditionally. Later he was leery of that term, and of "nonviolence" as an ideology, because he thought that if one's position were merely ideological, and not of the heart, it had little meaning.

In his Ojai talks of 1944 and 1945, while the Second World War was still raging, the meaning of the War is a central theme. Someone asked during the 1945 talks, "Can I find God in a foxhole?" Krishnamurti answered, *"A man seeking God will not be in a foxhole...You and the soldier have created a culture which forces you to murder and to be murdered, and in the midst of this cruelty you desire to find love."*

By the way, the candor with which Krishnamurti spoke against the war in the forties was almost unique in this country at the time. The position of young conscientious objectors was very difficult, for we were supported by virtually no one in our parents' generation and the social pressure was enormous.

The way of peace is simple. It is the way of truth and love. It starts with the individual himself. Where the individual accepts his responsibility for war and violence there peace finds a foothold. To go far one must begin near and the first actions are within. The sources of peace are not outside us and the heart of man is in his own keeping. To have peace we must be peaceful. To put an end to violence each one must voluntarily free himself from the causes of violence. Diligently one must put himself to the task of self-transformation. Our minds and hearts must be simple, creatively empty and watchful. Then only can Love come into being. Love alone can bring peace to the world and then only the world will know the bliss of the real. The way of peace.

—ALL-INDIA RADIO BROADCAST, BOMBAY, APRIL 3, 1948

EB: Did he suggest any resolution to those conflicts which found their expression in war?

WQ: Well, in 1945 people were already worried about a Third World War. He was saying then that we were each individually responsible for the present war's mass carnage; that we were all in it, as if one family, all part of one stream, our individualities like little whirlpools in it. The only "answer" was for us each to recognize his own responsibility and to permit his own life to be changed.

I think he had a sophisticated understanding of the world's political structures. In early days he and his brother Nityananda talked about these things intensively. Krishnamurti's circumstances brought him in close touch with prominent Socialists, as well as the aristocracy and

OPPOSITE: ARYA VIHARA IN OJAI, CALIFORNIA.

people in the inner circles of power throughout the world.

In the 1920s K and many other creative people felt that there was still hope for mankind, and perhaps that we'd learned something from the First World War. Writing and speaking during those years K had a kind of lyrical optimism, which seems naive to our disillusioned eyes today.

EB: Did your personal talks with Krishnamurti in the forties address individual problems rather than the social scene or the war?

WO: I think I was trying to get at the center of his thinking, mainly, what is the nature of awareness. That was his key word in those days. He spoke very little in public about meditation then, but spoke instead of choiceless awareness, awareness-in-action, and meditative awareness as a constant sate of being.

EB: He apparently dropped the word "awareness" later, because he felt it was being overly used.

WO: He used the term constantly, and everyone who was interested in his teachings used it so incessantly that it was entirely burnt out. So he abandoned the word, and attempted to come at its substance in other ways.

But I like the word nowadays. It's cognate with "awake," and suggests a primal, inbuilt capacity, like sight, but comprising all the senses and emanating from something beyond the senses.

However, he personally "meditated," that is, he would set aside a time and place and, as I understood it, then sat, receptive and available if something should happen, but not in a state of expectation.

EB: As you know, in his later years he rather derided the idea of meditating at fixed times, and said one can meditate on a bus.

WO: I questioned him closely as to what he meant by meditation. Did it have the same intensity all the time? He said, "Oh no! For me it is like a stream, in which there are deep pools. Now the last three days I couldn't meditate in the mornings because I had a bad cold, but this morning the cold was better, and meditation became extremely intense." He conveyed this by gestures suggesting an immense expansion. "But," he said, "I let it go only so far, lest it burn out the organism!" He went on to say that the quality of meditation would come upon him unexpectedly at odd moments, for example while walking, and that this was the best kind of meditation.

EB: When Krishnamurti said he let meditation go only so far, did he mean it could be too intense for the organism?

WO: Perhaps, to make an analogy, you might say it's like getting out of the sun. I don't control the sun's heat and light, but I can control the amount of my exposure to it.

EB: Did he say what was necessary for this kind of meditation? Was a cleansing or purity necessary. Or, was it a gift?

WO: He felt that "purity" was very important, and through all the years I knew him he brought it up many times. He also felt that the writing he suggested would make meditation possible.

EB: What did he mean by purity?

Truth is a danger

to society.

—THE STAR
BULLETIN, 1932

WQ: He once said to me, "You must be simple, like the raindrop." I think purity meant for him a crystal-clear perception, uncontaminated by images and projections.

EB: Would you say that Krishnamurti was a mystic?

WQ: I believe he was, although he avoided the word. The word in Greek implies "hidden," and in the old Christian tradition it meant specifically hidden to the mind of image and concept. In other words, direct perception. St. John of the Cross had a wonderful metaphor for this: *"If I hold my hand before my eyes, I cannot see the sun; if I have an image of God, I cannot see God."*

EB: Can you say what it was like being with Krishnamurti?

WQ: In our talks and in working together, as in the garden, or tending the bees, I never felt a hair's weight of manipulation or pressure to be other than I was. I would have been sensitive to any hidden motives, but he was crystal clear. This permitted intimacy, and conversation which was profound and tender, like cello music.

He never "talked shop" except at times we set aside for careful discussion. He was never in daily life the man who presided at the talks. The public persona was utterly absent. It was distinctly as if the mind we know through his writings were put aside completely, like a tool when it's not needed.

In our ordinary daily life he talked on simple levels, as if abstraction and analysis were unknown to him. Much of the time he made me think of an exceedingly alert and courteous child, most often silent, but wholly present. He was utterly modest and self-abnegating. Since he never emphasized himself, we could relate to him in the simplest way, completely unselfconscious ourselves.

EB: Would you say that Krishnamurti was innocent?

WQ: I think so! And even ingenuous and naive, in many ways, and susceptible to manipulation by his friends. He had a very childlike quality. But this had its limits, and in fundamental matters he was immovable. What I think was central was that he questioned his role as world teacher, and rejected that role. In the late twenties he radically denied the need for spiritual authority, and said that truth is a pathless land.

You could say that the idea that he was to be the world teacher was an extraordinary manipulation. He was force-fed in his youth with Theosophical doctrine, like those geese who generate *pâté de fois gras*. The miracle is that he came out of it, and paradoxically became the world teacher.

EB: Did Krishnamurti indicate that questions about personal love had been troubling for him?

WQ: He told me that he had worked out three major problems as a young man, pondering them for many years. One of them was sex. Was asceticism the right way? Or, since it is apparently natural and given to us, should we use sex?

EB: If one thinks purity means chastity, then it would be difficult for a person to have a natural relationship with the opposite sex.

WQ: I asked him specifically about that, and he said there was no general answer to this question. He talked about it tenderly. He said it was an issue everyone had to work out for themselves, and you couldn't say that you must be chaste, or that personal love and sexuality would be inimical to the spiritual life.

As for friendship, I think he felt that the experience of our commonplace personal love was the very flame, and perhaps the only flame, that could awaken us, although we hedge it around with possessiveness and so on. After all, it was certainly his brother's death which fully awakened him. After that event, everyone sensed the new man.

Throughout his life he had any number of intimate and long-lasting friendships, among them many women.

EB: Did he feel that personal love could take one beyond oneself, and was that a sort of liberation?

WQ: Well, yes, with qualifications. He enormously emphasized the importance of common ordinary life, which of course includes our private affections. Obviously we can be trapped in personal love. But if we understand its selfishness, I think he implies we can go beyond it, and yet the love remains. But this love is not then anchored in its object, nor dependant on it, but it frees the object as well as oneself. And this doesn't mean that the object is discarded; to the contrary it's enhanced.

EB: Was there a sense that he could be turned away from his spiritual mission in life by having personal friendships and affections? That's part of the traditional view of abstinence and sexual chastity.

WQ: He said once, "liberation is not out of manifestation, but into manifestation." What he meant, I think, is that it's not through the avoidance of life that we can find what he then called liberation. Detachment does not mean dissociation! It's the end of the separation between me and thee.

EB: How do you think he defined the term "liberation"?

WQ: It meant freedom from the bondage of a narrow conditioning, and from the conflicts that maim most of us. Essentially it meant freedom from ourselves, not some licentious freedom from social constraints.

EB: During those wartime years, what was daily life at Arya Vihara like? It must have been quite simple.

WQ: There were only the four of us, Krishnaji, Rosalind, her daughter Radha and myself, who were in daily contact. Mr. Rajagopal was seldom around. Because of wartime rationing, we lived almost completely off the land. We had orchards, vegetable gardens, eighty chickens, a cow, and bees. Krishnaji took care of the chickens, and I milked the cow. We both worked in the garden and tended the bees. Rosalind, always cheerfully industrious, made cottage cheese and butter, and baked a wonderful whole wheat bread. She cooked our meals. Krishnaji and I would wash the dishes, and I often felt an astonishing bliss in this humble activity.

Ojai was a village then, and seemed remote from the world. We had few visitors because of gas rationing, and public transport was co-opted by the military. It was incredibly difficult to get to Ojai even from Los Angeles.

EB: Do you think that K felt trapped in Ojai during the war years and during his illness, and did this create a tension in him?

WQ: I don't know about that, but I've thought those years may have been deeply valuable to him. Before the war he had been exceedingly active, talking all over the world and involved with great numbers of people. So, in the forties, for several years, there was an enforced quiet and solitude, and he lived in a very lovely place which had the most creative associations. It was there, under the pepper tree, that he began to find himself in the early twenties. That event also had been possible because for the first time since boyhood he was alone and outside the turbulence of public life. I think this time in the forties was one of almost continuous meditation and "recollection," a word he liked, and that out of this emerged the wonderful clarity of his public utterance in subsequent years.

EB: Do you think Krishnamurti's going to India was a step in his liberation, in a sense?

WQ: Not really, because I think the fundamental event occurred in the late twenties, following his brother's death. But what he called "the process" apparently continued throughout his life. And it was no doubt intensified in response to the extraordinary challenge of India. I conceive the process to be that stream of meditative awareness he told me about, in which there were deep pools. And I think that this stream was his life, or rather the life that flowed through his organism, contracting and expanding with its own extraordinary rhythms. He didn't think of it as "his" life, but as life.

The world had changed during the years of his retirement. Europe was in ruins, and the network centered in Ommen irreparably rent. When he went to India, he got away from the sterility and spiritual paralysis of the United States, which persisted for many years more into the McCarthy era and beyond. The United States didn't begin to awaken until the young people of the Korean War generation began to dissociate themselves from the establishment in the fifties, as seen in the so-called Beatniks, precursors of the sixties' youth movement.

He arrived in India in late 1947, at an extraordinary time, and when he was inwardly ripe, in the full flowering of his maturity. The whole of Asia was in ferment. India had freed itself from the British tyranny a few weeks before.

I've fancied that intelligent people in India were awakened, in ways people in the United States couldn't have been, to profound questions about the nature of society and the individual in society, what form of government would be right for India, and so on, with a life-and-death intensity. India meant the renewal of his public life, and he talked all over the country. He immediately came in touch with a remarkable group of people, some of whom had been in the front lines of those enormous events. A circle of friends, including Pupul Jayakar, Ahalya Chari, and so many others, began the dialogues with him which

"HE WAS INITIALLY FASCINATED BY THE YOUTH MOVEMENT... AND INTRIGUED BY [THE YOUNG PEOPLE'S] OPENNESS AND AFFECTION, THEIR ANTI-WAR STANCE AND GENERAL REJECTION OF AUTHORITY AND THE CORPORATE CULTURE, BUT HE CAME TO BE HORRIFIED BY THEIR WIDESPREAD USE OF DRUGS."

—WILLIAM QUINN

continued for the rest of his life.

EB: Do you think that Krishnamurti was fundamentally different than other human beings, from birth as it were?

WO: I don't, and there, to me, lies his chief beauty and significance. He apparently was an exceptionally selfless child, but he came to his maturity through exceedingly hard work. It was precisely his sense of kinship with the rest of us which impelled him to speak.

One could say that in his maturity there was a fundamental change, in the sense that self-centeredness was smashed, and that he then functioned from a different dimension of life. But his whole message was that this transformation is for all of us.

As for how the spiritual energies should unfold in us, I like the New Testament image: *The wind bloweth where it listeth, and thou hearest the sound thereof, but canst not tell whence it cometh, and whither it goeth: so is every one that is born of the Spirit*—John 3:8.

EB: How did Krishnamurti feel about young people and their use of drugs in the sixties?

WO: I think he was initially fascinated by the youth movement, and the young people of that milieu whom he met. He was intrigued by their openness and affection, their anti-war stance and general rejection of authority and the corporate culture. But he came to be horrified by their widespread use of drugs. We talked about this many times. It came to the point that I couldn't mention young people without his thinking about drugs, and being carried away into tirades. I had been a close observer of the development of the drug culture myself, and we had similar perceptions. We felt that Aldous Huxley and Alan Watts in particular bore a primary responsibility for that plague. Like Pied Pipers they had used their prestige to convert the young to their belief in this magical short cut to religious reality. K felt that a religious mind has to flower in a humble, unconscious, organic way, and that drugs were an illusory short cut, smashing through complex and delicate psycho-physical structures. He said the use of drugs by would-be holy men had been observed for centuries in India, and was known there to be a complete dead end.

In the seventies and early eighties I met many young people of a different breed, who had come for the Ojai talks. A typical story was that a boy of sixteen or so would come upon one of Krishnamurti's books and immediately begin a quiet revolution in his life. Then, years later, he would show up in Ojai. These young people were typically modest and thoughtful, and I met so many of them that I told Krishnamurti about them, since he was unlikely to meet them in the orbit in which he moved. He urged me to give him a sort of lecture on the whole background of the U.S. culture from which they emerged, and what their prospects were. I said that our culture had no place for such young people, and they would have to find their own way. He became extraordinarily excited, almost beside himself, as I talked. I still feel this to be immensely important, because there is no way of knowing how many such young people all over the world have likewise been touched by Krishnamurti.[57]

The emphasis that was placed on the psychology of the human condition and the nature of the mind, with its labyrinth complexities inevitably drew mental health professionals to Krishnamurti and his work. There has been a long-standing relationship with people in this field. One of those drawn to him was Benjamin Weinniger, former head of the Baltimore-Washington School of Psychiatry.

BENJAMIN WEINNIGER, M.D.

PSYCHIATRIST, SANTA BARBARA, CALIFORNIA

"KRISHNAMURTI'S PERCEPTIONS OF THE HUMAN MIND WERE CLEARER THAN ANYBODY'S THAT I HAD ENCOUNTERED."

—BENJAMIN WEINNIGER

BW: In 1946, I introduced Krishnamurti to all of the psychoanalysts in the Washington Psychoanalytic Society. He was at my house for a week and he talked every day. The ones that were there were very much impressed with him. Harry Stack Sullivan, Eric Fromm, David Rioch and Margaret Rioch. During that period Karen Horney asked me to come to New York. I spent two hours with her discussing the teaching of Krishnamurti and she was not only impressed with him, but she saw the similarity between his teaching and her whole school, the Karen Horney group of psychoanalysts. They became interested and began to write about Krishnamurti's teaching. Later, David Shainberg and his whole psychoanalytic group from the Karen Horney circle became absorbed in Krishnamurti's teaching. K used to go there every year for several talks, to those analysts. They are still involved in one way or the other. one of the people dropped out of psychoanalysis altogether and became an artist. So that was one of the important effects.

EB: Was Krishnamurti able to clearly lay out his view of the human mind to the psychoanalysts?

BW: Krishnamurti's perceptions of the human mind, were clearer than anybody that I had encountered. It was obvious to me, that he had a better understanding and when I brought him to Washington D.C., and he talked to the psychoanalysts, they asked me, "How did you know we would be interested in Krishnamurti?" I told them it was obvious to me that it would be the case. They became very much interested and it had an effect on their practice and their lives too.

EB: Krishnamurti must have looked forward to these meetings.

BW: Well, I have seen Krishnamurti fearful and I think it's an important thing to describe the circumstances under which it happened. When he was talking to the psychiatrists and psychoanalysts for the first time in Washington, D.C., he came to me and he was shaking with fear. He said, "I'm scared." And I tried to reassure him that it would be alright, and then when he went in to the talk, I realized that he was able to drop the fear. He allowed himself to experience the fear fully and then let it go. Most of us don't do that, we stay with the fears instead of letting it go. This is what he means when he says, I have no fear. I also asked him, "Would you be afraid if you were dying?" and he said, "I don't know. I would have to see, I would have to be aware to see whether I was afraid."

In love there is

neither "you" nor "I".

—*THE STAR BULLETIN,*
MARCH/APRIL 1933

EB: Was there a particular area that was of special interest to the group?

BW: There's been a considerable interest among psychoanalysts and psychiatrists recently in self-centered activity and actually, self-centered activity is something that Krishnamurti has talked about all his life and maybe the psychiatrists are beginning to catch on to it. It is a very important point, most of us, if we are hurt strongly in childhood have a more difficult time interrupting self-centered activity. Another way of saying it is excessive self-involvement. It's easier to do that to the degree that one has had a pleasant or good childhood. Then it is easier to drop the self-centered activity; other-wise it is more difficult. Some people never break away from it.

EB: Is there any special focus in mental health today?

BW: Psychoanalysts today are emphasizing the importance of love, even Freud emphasized the importance of work and love. But today they even more emphasize the importance of love. Most psychoanalysts and psychiatrists have a more limited view of love and I feel, that they don't go far enough. They stop short of the goal. If a person doesn't get into a spiritual awakening and understanding of the whole person, then it's incomplete. Most psychiatrists/psychoanalysts work, in my opinion, is incomplete and the influence of Krishnamurti was able to help me go further in my own life than I would have done without him.

EB: What do you think Krishnamurti was actually talking about?

BW: When I had my private talks with Krishnamurti he told me what he thinks he is talking about. Psychology, philosophy and religion, that's the subject he is talking about—all three. It's not just one thing, they are all related, interrelated. You can't separate them. Psychoanalysts, modern psychoanalysts, think that without philosophy there is no psychoanalysis. That's the beginning, the philosophical orientation.

EB: Has there been a change in your practice because of your interest in Krishnamurti?

BW: In the first five years of my training, I was practicing regular Freudian psychoanalysis, but after I finished the training I found myself drifting back to my interest in Krishnamurti's way of teaching. The change was partly that I was having more of a relationship with the person, the patient. I was not so impersonal and I didn't hesitate to talk about my philosophy and share it with the patients. I often gave them Krishnamurti's pamphlets to read and I think I had a lot of impact through that, and many of them became very much interested and they followed the teaching. My psychoanalytic practice was criticized for being so involved with Krishnamurti but I kept on teaching. A lot of the things that happened to me and my patients are really non-verbal. The feeling between us is what gets through. There's one element as far as the practice is concerned and this is a point that I learned from Krishnamurti. The condemning quality that I have is very strong and I learned through the course of the years to be aware of my condemnation. It came across as impatience because they felt that when they came into my office and the world at large, they were being condemned every day. Later, when they came to my office they had a sense that somebody here is not condemning and they left the office feeling, virtually as I used to do when leaving Krishnamurti.

EB: Throughout his life Krishnamurti stressed freedom, psychological freedom. What is your view of this emphasis?

BW: Many psychologists don't believe there is such a thing as psychological freedom—they think that you are conditioned and you are a victim of your past and nobody is psychologically free. Non-psychologists sometimes say, if there is only one other person in the world besides yourself, you are not free to do as you please; the other person won't let you. But Krishnamurti is not talking about that kind of freedom, he is talking about psychological freedom and this is often very confusing. We are a part of our total past, but psychologically we can be free. We have a hard time in understanding Krishnamurti because he is often talking about psychological freedom, psychological death, psychological ending and he doesn't mean technically ending. Psychologically free means being free of past conditioning.

EB: Most religions and philosophies see the importance of self knowledge. What is the key to self-understanding?

BW: The key to self-understanding in psychoanalysis is based on the revealing of past history and Krishnamurti makes a very important point—a slightly different point. The key, as he sees it, is to be aware of your reactions. Usually your images of the way things should be are constantly being threatened, and when your image is threatened in any area, you react and sometimes you react with anger or hurt and those reactions are always from your past. So you can get at your past by understanding your reactions rather than digging into the past history.

EB: Can you give a description of Krishnamurti, both the man and the teaching?

BW: In my experience, there is no way of describing Krishnamurti in words. You can say he was a world teacher or you can say he was a great psychologist, philosopher and a great religious teacher and that wouldn't convey anything to the other person. There is no way, in my limited vocabulary, of describing Krishnamurti other than by reading his teachings. You get some feeling of it through the films and the video tapes, then you can get a feeling of Krishnamurti without reading him. But, I don't think I could convey it to anybody—not in words. His presence was very powerful, what he transmitted, to me was really the kind of person he is, so that when I saw him in 1945 for a series of talks, he was late for the appointment—five minutes—and he came out to tell me he was late and he shook hands with me and left quickly. The impact of his shaking hands, his presence was so vibrant, that after he left, I felt I was ready to go home, it was such a strong impact. His presence is what is communicated and many people who hear the talks don't even remember what he said. Some of them do remember and are able to talk about it, but many are not because what is communicated from Krishnamurti is non-verbal, the sacred part, the silent part is communicated and that is mostly non-verbal, and this is what people respond to, even though they may not understand anything he said.[58]

K RISHNAMURTI HAD A LONG-TIME INTEREST IN EDUCATION.
It was considered to be a three-fold endeavor involving students,
teachers and parents. All were to be learning together. In 1928,
the first school had opened at the beautiful Rishi Valley site near his birthplace of Madanapalle in India. A second one, the Rajghat School was on the
banks of the sacred Ganges near the ancient city of Banares, or Varanasi, as it is
now called. The school was inaugurated in 1934, although the land had been
purchased years earlier. Ahalya Chari was one who had a long-standing
bond with Krishnamurti's work. In her book *Krishnamurti at Rajghat*, she
describes the serious intent with which Krishnamurti viewed education.

A H A L Y A   C H A R I

AUTHOR AND EDUCATOR, RAJGHAT SCHOOL, VARANASI, INDIA

AHALYA CHARI, AUTHOR AND
EDUCATOR AT THE RAJGHAT
SCHOOL ON THE BANKS OF
THE GANGES RIVER, 1989.

*In 1928 Krishnamurti was inspired by the great university at Berkeley,
California, to set up educational institutions in his own right. In looking for
land, from the very beginning, Krishnamurti seemed to know that he wanted:
"Four hundred acres of land on the banks of the river at Banaras (Varanasi)." The
task was entrusted to Sanjeeva Rao, a young man close to Dr. Besant, who was
also a member of the Indian Educational Service. Sanjeeva Rao set out on this
"mad adventure" to buy the land, even though it was to him "a staggering
proposition." After locating a hundred-and-fifty acres of land on the banks of the
Ganga (Ganges) which belonged to the British Military Cantonment Board, with
single-minded devotion and tenacity he managed to persuade the authorities to
sell the land. Money was found and, then, in due course, Sanjeeva Rao
negotiated the purchase of the two-hundred and twenty-five acres that lies across
the Varaná river, near the village of Sarai Mohana.*

*Between 1928 and 1948, Sanjeeva Rao built a co-educational, residential
school at Rajghat, calling it The Rajghat Besant School. Later, the Vasanta College
for women students and Vasantashrama, a women's dormitory, were located there.*

*When Krishnamurti returned to Varanasi in 1948 after an extended
absence, he stayed at Rajghat in a house overlooking the Ganga. And during the
next thirty-eight years he returned to this house again and again, talking to
students, scholars, and visitors from all over the world.*

*The Ganga rises in the Himalayas and flows across the great plains of
northern India into the Bay of Bengal. Except along one stretch lying between
the ghats of Varanasi where the river suddenly turns and flows northward
towards its source, it follows a south-easterly course. For the ancient geographers,
the river turned back on itself, like the meditating mind of the sage, was
symbolic of the river's sacredness.*

*In Krishnamurti's writing, the river Ganga as an image for the meditating
mind is a recurrent metaphor. Writing at Rajghat in his notebook, he says:
"Meditation was like that river, only it had no beginning and no ending; it
began and its ending was its beginning."*

*The metaphor is carried forward, for the life-giving waters of the Ganga
share with the meditating mind the power to end:*

The river curves majestically as it flows east past the villages, town and deep woods, but here, just below the town and the bridge, the river and its opposite bank is the essence of all river banks; every river has its own song, its own delight and mischief, but here, out of the very silence, it contains the earth and the heavens. It is a sacred river, as all rivers are, but again here, a part of the long, winding river, there is a gentleness of immense depth and destruction.

"Life is like a river," he told the children of the Rajghat School. "Never still, always moving, always alive and rich...we all have to prepare for it...A place like [Rajghat] should provide an atmosphere where you are given every opportunity to grow, uninfluenced, unconditioned, untaught, so that when you go out of [this place] you can meet life intelligently, without fear."

Education was central to Krishnamurti's declared aim "of setting man unconditionally free," and learning about life was essential to this process. the challenge posed by him, of creating a new generation of young capable of asking fundamental questions, of freeing themselves from the actions of fear, anger and envy, of setting aside the past, the burdens of tradition, dogma and belief, was unique. It included both the educator and the educated. And it contained within itself the seeds for the regeneration of humankind and of society.

The very manner in which Krishnamurti posed the challenge was unsettling. He allowed the educator no space for settling down into the working out of pedagogical theories. Sensing the hold that millennia of tradition had upon the minds of the teachers, he was passionate, impatient, unrelenting in his discussions with them, demanding their highest attention. "Is there a group of people working together to bring about a radical change in themselves and in the students?" he would ask, over and over again. And over the years many teachers came to Rajghat and tried in their own way to keep the intention alive. But the task has always been overwhelmingly difficult, for here in these places set up by Krishnamurti, you are not dealing with systems or methods, but with the world of the within that is living, moving, changing and ever eluding your grasp. Walking with Krishnamurti was like walking with fire; if you kept the flame within you alive you came upon the joy of discovery suddenly, in an instant, otherwise not.

With the students Krishnamurti was gentle and affectionate. He talked about fear and unravelled with immense patience the many ways in which parents, teachers, the society at large and religion use fear to mould their minds. He pointed out in different ways how habit, imitation and conformity destroys minds and hearts. And he shocked the elders who were present by awakening students to "the violence of obedience." Krishnamurti was impressed by the children of Rajghat, by their ability to sit quietly and to listen, by their sense of wonder. "Where in the world would you find such innocence?" he once remarked. And students felt free in his presence to ask all kinds of questions.

The plight of women in India was a matter of deep concern to Krishnamurti. He reached out to the young women of the college patiently and with immense affection. The girls too listened and wondered if they could ever lead independent lives of their own, free of superstition and free of the domination that men had over them.

Krishnamurti's compassion for the poor of the land was profound. He wanted the K.F.I. (Krishnamurti Foundation of India) Schools to learn to care for their neighbors. Again and again he would prod the children and ask if in any way

they felt related to the poor. In one of his public talks he spoke pointedly to his audience: "You know one of the strange things is that though India is a very sad country, there is always a smile. The poor smile. They are starving, downtrodden, they have no happiness, they are perpetually working and, yet, as you go by the street, especially in the countryside, they smile at you. This happens nowhere else in the world. This is the miracle of this country." [59]

Krishnamurti had long wanted to start a school in Ojai. Years earlier, in 1926 and 1927, Annie Besant had appealed for funds to purchase land. When $200,000 was raised the Happy Valley Association was formed and 450 acres in the upper Ojai and 240 acres in the lower Ojai/Meiners Oaks area was purchased. This lower tract included the Oak Grove where Krishnamurti held his talks for so many years. The three original trustees were Krishnamurti, Rosalind Rajagopal and Aldous Huxley. It was a small beginning, but the passion for education in all of its forms, for children as well as adults, impelled Krishnamurti to establish a center in the "New World" where his educational ideas could be put into practice. With Rosalind as its director, he felt the fledgling school was in good hands. The plan was then to leave for Australia and India but yet another in a series of illnesses prevented that trip until 1947.

In India there had been growing pressure earlier for the British Government to "Quit India," as the movement was called. Spearheaded by the visionary M.K. Gandhi and his followers, not only was this movement a political action aimed at removing India from the colonial fold and thus truncating the British Empire, it was at the same time a movement of social reform within India. These idealistic young Socialists saw their country not only free of foreign rule, but at the same time, demonstrating a compassionate equality for all its citizens.

It was in August 1947 that India won its independence from Britain and in that heady atmosphere of freedom, Krishnamurti returned alone to his homeland after an absence of nine years. However, it was not only freedom from Colonial rule that was exhilarating but an expansive sense of freedom from the smothering and somewhat dictatorial impulses of the Rajagopals that was liberating for him. For many years, Krishnamurti had lived in close daily contact with them, the only respite was long solitary walks. Now, at last, he plunged into contact with a vital and serious group of people with an ancient spiritual heritage. Discourse was a daily part of life and Krishnamurti flowered in its ambiance.

A group formed around him, including the brightest young minds of the day. On fire with their new found political freedom, yet saturated with thousands of years of a tradition of searching dialogue, the group coalesced into a long-lasting association. From 1947 until the present time the bond has continued, enriched and enlivened by an ongoing influx of newcomers. They came from many walks of life, political and literary, artistic and academic. Many were freedom fighters who had spent the requisite time in jail in the struggle for independence from British rule.

...Then I came to India and I saw that the people there were deluding themselves equally, carrying on the same old traditions, treating women cruelly. At the same time they called themselves very religious and painted their faces with ashes. In India they may have the most sacred books in the world, they may have the greatest philosophies, they may have constructed wonderful temples in the past, but none of these was able to give me what I wanted. Neither in Europe nor in India could I find happiness.

—*LIFE IN FREEDOM, 1928*

One of these young people was Pupul Jayakar, who was at the time one of the anti-colonialist fighters and was an ardent social worker intent on lightening the burden of India's depressed classes. Today she is a distinguished author and biographer of Krishnamurti and Indira Gandhi, with whom she worked closely. She is a recognized cultural leader and one of India's outstanding intellectuals.

PUPUL JAYAKAR

AUTHOR AND BIOGRAPHER, BOMBAY, INDIA

PUPUL JAYAKAR AND
KRISHNAMURTI, 1979.

PJ: Krishnaji returned to India in 1947, after the war and an absence of several years. In January of 1948, I had gone to see my mother. I was a social worker, who had an interest and was involved in politics. I had at this time, no interest in anything at all connected with a religious life. My father had died a few years earlier and my mother had never got over the shock. There was an old friend of my father's, Sanjeeva Rao, who had been connected with Dr. Besant for many years, who at the time was responsible for organizing Krishnaji's visit to India. He had come to see my mother, and when I went there he told me that he was taking my mother to see Krishnaji. As a child I had been in the Theosophical girls school in Benares. I remember seeing Krishnaji for a minute and being overwhelmed by the extraordinary beauty of Krishnaji as a person. As I had nothing else to do, I thought I would go with my mother to see this very beautiful person. We went to Carmichael Road where he was staying and after a little while Krishnaji walked in. If you had seen him at the time...it was like a sudden explosion of a presence, the sudden entrance of a presence unlike anything that had ever been seen before. He had great beauty, which he still has, but seeing it for the first time, the impact was total. He was dressed in Indian clothes. I remember he used to laugh a lot in those days, and he was laughing when he came in. Sanjeeva Rao introduced us and Krishnaji sat down and my mother started telling him all about my father. After a little while he turned to her and said, "Amma, you've come to the wrong person. I have no sympathy to give you." This came as a blow, I didn't know what he meant. He said, "Which husband do you miss? the husband you married, the husband who was the father of your children, or the man he would have been if he had been alive. Do you miss the memory of the man?" It was all very confusing. I felt a little disturbed and distressed and a little angry, that he couldn't give my mother the solace she needed. Then he turned to me and asked, "And what do you do?" I said, "I do social work." He started laughing. I was again very disturbed as to why he should laugh at this. He said, it's like a person who takes a bucket to the well, the bucket has a hole, and the more water you put in the more water flows out. He talked in this way for a little while. We were there for about one hour. When we came home I swore to myself that I'd never go again, but I couldn't keep away and when I heard he was giving some public talks I went to hear him again. I couldn't understand a word of what he said, but went again. Then Sanjeeva Rao came and said to me that Krishnaji wanted me to come to his smaller talks. I started going and after that there was no turning back.

EB: What was said at that time that was decisive in your thinking?

PJ: Right from the beginning he had very small group discussions in India, where twelve, fifteen people used to gather round him. In those days he used to sit every morning and evening and people would walk in, sit round him, and ask him questions. There was a tremendous openness, and a tremendous compassion which flowed from him. It deeply moved me. I remember he used to speak to individuals, relentlessly challenge them, question them, till listening to him, there arrived a point when one could see. This instant of seeing, which itself is impossible to describe, transforms the whole nature of the self. It happened to me and I think that instant of seeing, listening was for me the most significant thing which took place, I actually saw myself as I was in that instant.

EB: That must have been an overwhelming experience, and that was what you felt you could not turn back from?

PJ: Yes, and from there the teaching started unfolding. He was quiet…there was this tremendous outpouring of energy. He gave a lot of time, he met people in groups mornings and evenings, had small and large discussions, gave public talks, and a number of private interviews. Krishnaji is totally different in each of these areas, and when he used to give private interviews it was as if he literally became a mirror which he held up to you. The individual Krishnaji was not, it was just a mirror in which the very presence of Krishnaji made you look at yourself for what you were. He refused to allow you to move away from the seeing of what you were. In the discussions, one of the most interesting things for me, was to see this man start at the same level as all the people who sit around him. As he questions, he questions himself as much as another. He's prepared to withdraw and look at what he says. I think another very vital element was the quality of listening which was manifest in Krishnaji. One was not used to that type of listening. I don't think it exists in the world. A listening, in which there is no movement of the self. A listening which takes in, in a sense, the totality. You felt it. It is something that is tangible.

EB: During those years were you able to see him in another context, other than as a teacher, in a more informal way?

PJ: Yes. He used to go for drives with us. He often came for dinner at our house. Two or three things I remember very vividly. It's difficult to say that Krishnaji has personal relationships. Each individual feels a sense of uniqueness in his or her relationship to Krishnaji. He responds to each individual by supplying that which each individual lacks. He laughed a lot and my mother, who was a very good cook, used to specially cook for him. He enjoyed good food. He enjoyed excellence. Whether it was the way a house was arranged, or the way a meal was prepared or served. He would participate in situations in a very human way.

EB: You mentioned his relationships, and said that there is a line or perhaps something where people are not capable of being in total relationship with him.

PJ: No, I say that when he is the teacher, sitting on the platform, giving his talks, you cannot imagine yourself having a relationship to him, because there is a totality; he is an empty vessel, and yet there is total fullness in him. There is no personal element in him at all. When he gives an interview, even though you feel the warmth and compassion, gentleness, and love of the man, there is nothing personal. When you meet him at a dinner table, or you drive with him he would tell and listen to jokes, ask all about India, all about our children, our families and our problems. He was also concerned about the position of women in India. You could see this concern reflected in many of the talks he gave.

EB: Would you say that his understanding of the position of women in India was allied to an understanding of the extreme poverty there?

PJ: No, it had nothing to do with the poverty of India. It was the social position and the economic position which the Indian woman had at the time, where she was dependent on the husband. Inheritance laws had not made her a sharer in the inheritance of the father. Krishnaji's talks were full of sections where he expressed his distress at the plight of women in India.

EB: You mentioned that he likened social work to carrying a bucket with a hole. Does he still view it in that light? Is there no other action worthy of complete attention in the social sphere?

PJ: He used to often tell me, "Why are you wasting your time, Pupul?" Yet he was greatly interested in the weaver and crafts, I was concerned with. It was very strange, after I gave it all up, which was last year, he said, "You know, you have created this over the years, are you going to abandon it?" I said, "Why do you ask? It's over now." He said, "But are you going to abandon it?" I think, to him, the creative moment is very important. Out of that creative moment things happen.

EB: Would you say that Krishnamurti has had close friendships in his life?

PJ: Yes. I would say so. He in fact said a very strange thing to me very soon after I met him. He said, "People usually adore me, treat me like their divinity, or they hate me. To be a friend is difficult."

EB: Krishnaji has shown a great interest in a variety of things over his lifetime, in automobiles, in clothes, would those be areas where he might be more playful?

PJ: He would be playful. There's a side of him which relaxes, laughs, is

"A TREMENDOUS COMPASSION FLOWED FROM HIM. IT DEEPLY MOVED ME."

—PUPUL JAYAKAR

human. Sometimes an individual who doesn't know Krishnaji can misunderstand his capacity to relax. It is growing less than it was. I don't think that side of Krishnaji is as spontaneous as it was. He has become much graver.

EB: You said previously that you and your sister were with Krishnamurti at Ootacamund in 1948. Could you tell us about that?

PJ: Well, I had known Krishnaji for just five months. I was beginning to know him but, he was still very much the unknown stranger, if I may put it. He asked us to come to Ooty. We had no intention of going to Ooty.

EB: Could you tell us first where Ooty is?

PJ: Ootacamund, or Ooty, is a hill-station in the south, in the Nilgeris, at a height of about eight thousand feet. It is very heavily wooded. It has great avenues and forests of pines and trees, meadows, it is very green. Krishnaji agreed to stay with a friend there for six weeks or so. I suddenly got a letter from him asking my sister Nandini and me to go to Ooty. We went. Nandini had many domestic problems, she had a whole family, but we went. After about a fortnight he suddenly asked us if we would mind staying on in the evening. He asked us to come to his room. We went to his room. He said, "Whatever happens, don't be afraid. Under no circumstances be afraid. If I faint and my mouth remains open, close my mouth. Just sit at a distance of about four feet from me. Just keep on watching me."

EB: Just you and your sister were present?

PJ: Yes, just the two of us. He first started complaining of tremendous pain in his tooth. We thought he had a toothache but, he said, "No, no no, you don't understand. No no, sit quietly." So we sat. Then he complained of a tremendous pain in his head and in his spine. There was a stream of poetic language that came from him. He used to keep on moaning and then this stream of marvelous language would flow.

EB: Was that language part of his teaching?

PJ: He used to talk of nature and leaves and stones, and then he would say. "They're having a great time with me. Do you know what they're doing? They're completely emptying my mind." I've got it written out, I don't remember the exact words today. He implied there were some forces that were working inside his brain, cleaning up the brain, making it totally empty so that it could receive. This used to go on for hours, it went on for sometimes four hours, five hours, sometimes six hours.

EB: Over a period of successive nights?

PJ: Fifteen or sixteen nights at a stretch. There was a tremendous sense of sacredness in the whole place. We were quite new to it, but we couldn't help feeling this tremendous sense of being in a temple. Not an ordinary temple, but a great presence. There was another very strange thing. He kept on shouting his own name. "Krishna has gone away, he's left me. Oh no, no, he's told me not to call him. I mustn't call him, he'll be very angry. I mustn't call him." Then one day he said, "They're back, don't you see them? Washed by raindrops, spotless." After this went on for some time he would faint. Then he would come to and he would be completely Krishnaji again for a little while. Then again he would start this…and the three things were the tremendous pain, the tremendous sense of presence in the room, and the great flow of language.

EB: When he spoke in that way was he speaking in his own voice?

PJ: When he spoke about nature it was his own voice, but when he used to call out for Krishna it was a different voice. It was a voice which was an empty voice. Totally empty as if it were…how shall I put it? It was an empty bubble who was calling him. There used to be times when the body would suddenly grow. You felt a tremendous fullness.

EB: It appeared physically larger?

PJ: When you say that it sounds so stupid that it's difficult to say, but it was as if suddenly a light would come.

EB: Would he be unconscious then?

PJ: He would be unconscious then. Once I remember very well, it was the end, he fainted. As he fainted his face was worn with pain, but suddenly it changed. It became totally quiet. Every vestige of pain disappeared. It became a deeply meditative face, with a beauty that cannot be contained in any words. We just kept on watching, we got a strange feeling of wanting to fold our hands. Then, it was as if he came out of his faint. He lay there and then turned to us. He said, "Did you see that face?" We said "yes." He said, "The Buddha was here." I don't know how we remained quite balanced and sane through it because we didn't know where we were. Here we were like two babes in the wood, suddenly thrust into a situation which was incomprehensible, completely beyond anything we could ever have conceived. Then one day it didn't happen.

Another incident I remember very well, in the middle of this period. We went for a walk. He said he wanted to walk in the woods. It started to rain, so we took the car as we thought he would get wet and we could bring him back. We went along that road but couldn't find him, so we came back. Within two minutes he entered the room. He was completely dry. We said, "Krishnaji where did you walk?" He said, "Along that road." I said, "You were not there, we went on that road and you were not there." Suddenly he switched off, lay down on the bed, and started speaking. He said, "They covered me with leaves, I was covered with all the leaves that fall from the trees. I nearly didn't come back." To this day I don't know where he went for a walk. He said he went for a walk on that road but he was not on that road. It was a strange, strange experience for us.

EB: During this time did he carry on his regular activities?

PJ: Oh yes. The moment he came through with this he was perfectly well. He'd grown a beard at that time. He used to go for walks. I remember he used to have a great stride in those days.

EB: He still does.

PJ: He used to walk down the hill and we used to sometimes watch him come down. I remember a group of women carrying wood on their heads who on seeing this figure walking past removed the loads from their heads, and prostrated themselves on the ground as he walked by.

EB: Did the thought ever occur that a doctor should be called at these times?

PJ: Right at the beginning, yes. We said, "Shall we call a dentist?" Then he said, "no, no, no, just sit. Don't be afraid. Whatever happens don't be afraid." He was very concerned that there should be no fear. That incident which took place in Ojai, when he said that inside the house he felt everything dirty. He couldn't bear the touch of anything, and therefore he had to go under the tree and take a mat and lie down. There was nothing like that here. He never spoke of any kind of pollution. If there's one feeling which I came away with, it was a sense of sacredness. Great sacredness.[60]

EB: Do you think this is something that is happening to this day? Is this process still continuing?

PJ: Not in that way. The presences which were there in that room, the throbbing presence, happens sometimes.

EB: Those things that he's written about in *Krishnamurti's Notebook*...

PJ: Yes. It's not a continuous thing that takes place.

EB: During that period did he ever talk about the masters or any such thing?

PJ: Except that one time; "They are here, they are here. Spotless," I think he used that phrase, like dewdrops or raindrops, but he never spoke of the masters. He used to say they are having fun with me. They won't leave me. He felt that his brain was being completely emptied.

EB: In the *Notebook* he speaks of his brain being carved out.

PJ: Well it was that kind of a thing going on, but it was an intense physical thing. What else it was one doesn't know.

EB: What would you say was the relationship between the physical, the pain of that, and the other...

PJ: When the pain became too great he used to faint.

EB: I'm trying to understand the role of that pain.

PJ: I really couldn't tell you. It was not possible to say. I remember asking him, "You speak of Krishna as if he were some outside person? Are there two entities?" He said, "No no Pupul it's not quite like that, it's not quite like that." He implied that there is only one entity.

EB: Could you observe any change in his teaching after these experiences?

PJ: I think 1948 was a period when his teaching was, in my view, different from the teachings which took place previously. Whether it was due to this or something else I don't know. I have noticed that whenever he has gone through this kind of an experience it has had an effect. It has not had an effect on the teaching but the teachings have shown a new dimension. I would say that as far as teaching, I would consider the main phases to have been 1948, 1960-1961, and 1972-1973. These are the three main periods. In 1948, he used to take you literally by the hand into self-knowledge. He would lead you from thought to thought, till there was an ending of thought. He would do this, for example, with the thought of greed. He would do this with a rising of fear. He would keep on saying, "And then what arises? And then what arises?" so that you started observing, "what is," as it arose.

You also observed, "what should be" as it arose in thought. So that one was awake in that instant of "what is." In 1961 that phase was over. In 1961 he said, step by step is the process of analysis. He wiped out all that, and he said, self-knowledge is necessary, it is essential. But he concerned himself with the whole not the fragment, with the total seeing of a thing. It has become, as I've often told Krishnaji, far more abstract. It was most personal in 1948. In 1972 there is no personal relationship in his teaching. It is a teaching which is absolute, which has no relationship to the personal me. While in 1948 there was a relationship to the personal me. There has been a deepening and maturing and a widening of the teaching. It has become universal. For the first time now he is talking about a life of correctness, which is a life which is completely free of self-centered activity. He said that is essential before anything else can be. He never said that in 1948.

EB: So that there has been constant change actually.

PJ: I say there is a constant change, there was a time when he told the members of the foundation that "I have nothing to do with the foundations. I have nothing to do with institutions. Don't use my name in the institutions or use me in any sense as an authority. It's not my wishes which are in the picture. I'm only concerned with the individual and awakening self-knowing in the individual. I'm not concerned with anything else." He said once, "My real *dharma* is that."[61]

Many years before meeting Pupul Jayakar, Krishnamurti addressed an issue of great concern in India and one that continues to be a problem in all countries of the world, east and west, more than sixty years later. In 1928 Krishnamurti addressed the Women's Indian Association.

Life is one, whether in men or in women. Because there is sorrow, in woman as in man, suffering is in woman as in man; so to divide human beings into men and women, from the very start, is wrong. Because they have different bodies, we think—men think—that they must be treated in a different fashion and educated in a different way. But do not women suffer in the same way as men do? Have they not the same doubts, the same troubles, the same sufferings as men? So if you look from the bigger point of view, sex disappears, as it should. With that disappearance of the compartments of humanity—men and women—life will become much simpler; and we can solve the problems that each must face.

...Women are keepers of tradition much more than men. If women made up their minds to alter anything in the world, they could alter it tomorrow. They are capable of much more self-sacrifice than men, and so have greater strength. But the woman who is a keeper of tradition, if she is to understand life, must change her attitude of mind. She must no longer be a slave. I use this word expressly, because women allow themselves to be dominated. I know that many women agree with me, when they are far away from their husbands, but when they return to their homes, the trouble begins. Then the men begin to dominate. Why should you yield? You are as good as men; you have greater strength! In America, in certain schools, there have been strikes among students, because the professors treated the students in a cruel manner. So you should form a Women's Union, and strike over things that matter.[62]

—MADRAS, INDIA, 1928

She was carrying a large basket on her head, holding it in place with one hand, it must have been quite heavy, but the swing of her walk was not altered by the weight. She was beautifully poised, her walk easy and rhythmical. On her arm were large metal bangles which made a slight tinkling sound, and on her feet were old, worn-out sandals. Her sari was torn and dirty with long use. She generally had several companions with her, all of them carrying baskets, but that morning she was alone on the rough road. The sun wasn't too hot yet, and high up in the blue sky some vultures were moving in wide circles without a flutter of their wings. The river ran silently by the road. It was a very peaceful morning, and that solitary woman with the large basket on her head seemed to be the focus of beauty and grace; all things seemed to be pointing to her and accepting her as part of their own being. She was not a separate entity, but part of you and me, and of that tamarind tree. She wasn't walking in front of me, but I was walking with the basket on my head. It wasn't an illusion, a thought-out, wished-for, and cultivated identification, which would be ugly beyond measure, but an experience that was natural and immediate. the few steps that separated us had vanished, time, memory, and the wide distance that thought breeds, had totally disappeared. There was only that woman, not I looking at her. And it was a long way to the town, where she would sell the contents of her basket. Towards evening she would come back along that road and cross the little bamboo bridge on her way to her village, only to appear again the next morning with her basket full.[63]

—*COMMENTARIES ON LIVING*, THIRD SERIES, 1960

Another of the group around Krishnamurti was the daring Achyut Patwardhan. Aflame with revolutionary zeal, he was a leader of the people. Living for long periods underground, he disguised himself in order to hide from government authorities. In 1947 he came, desolate, to Krishnamurti, as he clearly saw that the struggle for assertion and power, held in check as long as the enemy was the British, reasserted itself as soon as they were gone, among the Indians themselves. In addition, the assassination of Gandhi in January of 1948 threw the country into a frenzy of factionalism and despair. These sobering realizations prompted Patwardhan to give up the political life and turn to more contemplative issues.

ACHYUT PATWARDHAN

ANTI-COLONIALIST FIGHTER AND PHILOSOPHER, MADRAS, INDIA

"KRISHNAMURTI WAS QUITE DIFFERENT BECAUSE HE SAID THAT THE DUALITY BETWEEN THE TEACHER AND THE TAUGHT HAS TO DISAPPEAR BEFORE YOU CAN UNDERSTAND ANYTHING."

—ACHYUT PATWARDHAN

EB: Krishnamurti seemingly functioned like a great guru. In what way do you think he was different?

AP: This is a very interesting question. Particularly for a man like me, who began by looking upon him as a guru. In what sense did Krishnaji explain that he was not a guru? Our whole relationship is in terms of getting knowledge from another, getting inspiration from another, getting guidance from another. What Krishnamurti has been insisting on is that, if we depend on another, howsoever elevated his position may be, then we remain second-hand human beings. So we have first to say that there are things which others cannot do for you. Of course, there are psychologists and there are philosophers who give us some very important guidelines; a yoga teacher will tell you how to sit straight and how to organize your day. All these things may be useful but Krishnaji wanted you to understand that there is one important function which you have to do for yourself and that is to understand what nobody else can do for you: that is to look at your own ego-process. To look at your ego-process is something which nobody else can do for you and therefore, he was helping us to understand exactly how thought operates, how desire operates and how this entire mechanism of acquisitiveness operates. In this he was following the great tradition of the Buddha. And he called this, "The self-sustaining process of ignorance which has no beginning but which has only an end." These words are reminiscent of the Buddha's. Krishnamurti was insistent that man must understand that there is part of his development which is achieved through knowledge, memory, reason, thought and reflection. And there is also a point at which he sees the limit of thought, sees that thought creates the problem and cannot solve all the problems that it creates.

What is the intrinsic limitation of thought? He thought that this was something a man has to probe for himself and the answer must be sought within oneself. The capacity and desire to seek a problem and seek an answer by yourself meant that you cannot afford to depend on another for the source of your inspiration or for your enlightenment. What you needed above all was to understand the ego-process. Now the ego-process is different. When you say, "I," it is a self-centered point, but when you say, "the ego process," it is the "I" of everybody; it includes everybody. Therefore, you use the "I," you use your own brain and your own thought processes to understand the ego-process. This is an important impersonal factor. In this way Krishnamurti was quite different because he said that the duality between the teacher and the taught has to disappear before you can understand anything and understanding consists in ending this duality.

AN ANECDOTE: I remember we were sitting, a few of us together, and someone said, "What is your teaching, Krishnaji?" And Krishnaji looked a little stern and said, "There is no teaching." To those of us who were listening to him, this response created no problems because we knew that what he was trying to communicate is, that if he said anything it immediately becomes knowledge and is stored up in memory and brought to use whenever we need it and in that sense he was not going to offer something to make second-hand human beings of us. So, we felt chastised and we kept quiet. And, after a few moments, he turned again and said, "It's very simple. Where you are, the other is not," and he turned away.[64]

Revolution, this psychological, creative revolution in which the "me" is not, comes only when the thinker and the thought are one, when there is no duality such as the thinker controlling thought; and I suggest it is this experience alone that releases the creative energy which in turn brings about a fundamental revolution, the breaking up of the psychological me.

—*THE FIRST AND LAST FREEDOM, 1954*

The beautiful and brilliant Sunanda Patwardhan, sister-in-law of Achyut was one of the core group around Krishnamurti at that time. She continues to be actively involved in the work of Krishnamurti, and with her husband Pama, is working toward the establishment of another Krishnamurti school in Poona.

SUNANDA PATWARDHAN, PH. D.

SOCIOLOGIST, POONA, INDIA

SP: Krishnaji is one of the greatest teachers of humanity. It's not as though other teachers have not talked about the ending of suffering, the ending of the ego-process and the nature of transcendence; but to me, and I am sure to the thousands of people who have listened to him, Krishnaji's teaching bring out certain unique features.

First of all, he points out the fact that the destiny of humanity is one undivided whole. It is not just a matter of your personal salvation, that you go and meditate and then you end the source of conflict for yourself. On the contrary, to the extent to which you change yourself, you transform the world and so it is your responsibility to change yourself. Therefore, his primary statement or sutra, that "you are the world and the world is you," I think, is very important. Each one of us is responsible for changing this world of hate, of conflict, of antagonisms, of division as different groups of people, as Hindus, as Muslims, as Indians. That is, I think the uniqueness of this teaching.

E B: Could you talk about the physical dimension of Krishnamurti's teaching?

S P: Krishnaji shows the importance of the role of the senses in bringing about a quietness of the mind and in awakening a new sensitivity. It is not by suppressing the senses; it's not by denying or sublimating the senses, but rather by awakening your eyes, your ears, your touch, sense of smell, everything. Generally we use or are aware of only one or two senses at a time whereas he talks of all the senses operating simultaneously. Then there can be a ground of a deep non-verbal state. This awakening of the senses has in it vibrancy and vitality without a center.

E B: You said earlier that a teacher like Krishnamurti only comes along once in a thousand years. Can you explain what you mean by that?

S P: You see, the Buddha belonged to the great break-away traditions of India. That was more than 2500 years ago. He repudiated everything traditional, ritual, rites, orthodoxy, etc. Like the Buddha, Krishnaji has broken away from the mainstream of Indian tradition. He was brought up, denying his mother tongue and was taught English and French. In a way he was brought up to speak to the whole of humanity in the English language which is understood in many countries of the world. I think this is a very significant thing so that whatever he says can be understood directly by many persons in many parts of the world.

E B: There are hundreds of gurus and Krishnamurti, in some sense, has functioned as a guru. In what way was he different?

"KRISHNAJI WAS QUITE DIFFERENT AND UNIQUE BECAUSE HE WAS VERY EMPHATIC IN SAYING THAT THERE IS NO SPIRITUAL AUTHORITY."

—SUNANDA PATWARDHAN

S P: I think Krishnaji was quite different and unique because he was very emphatic in saying that there is no spiritual authority; that there is no authority whatsoever in spiritual matters. Many people may have looked upon him as a guru; he was known as the guru who was a non-guru. He asked each one of us to be responsible for ourselves in this journey of inquiry; there is no authority in spiritual life. Therefore, he never gave answers. He said; "Look at the problem. The problem will reveal itself, you have to inquire, you have to observe *what is* and in that very observation *what is* will reveal itself and a transformation can take place. For this to happen, no guru can guide you. If you are suffering, if you are in a state of agitation, no guru can help you. You have to observe it, and that awakens a capacity to be independent and inquire in freedom from the very beginning."

E B: Did affection have any place in Krishnamurti's teachings?

S P: I would say, emotion had no place in his teachings. Sentiment had no place in his teachings. The mere response from the intellect too, is limited; it has no basis of affection and sensitivity in relationship between human beings. It is only when we human beings come together in affection that there can be a new quality in our daily living. He certainly has given tremendous importance to affection and love. If we have that, relationships pose no problem.

"KRISHNAJI IS ADDRESSING
HUMANITY, WHICH HAS
ALREADY BECOME CLOSER
TOGETHER AS A GLOBAL
VILLAGE. HE IS ADDRESSING
HUMANITY AS ONE UNIT."
   —SUNANDA
      PATWARDHAN

I am reminded of a conversation with him. A friend of mind told me, "You know, in Krishnaji's teachings there is place only for compassion. There is no place for ordinary human affection, pleasure or fondness. How does one live then?" Later when I met Krishnaji, I talked to him about this. He said, "Compassion is a very vast thing, it can be quite abstract. Many people cannot understand or comprehend what compassion is. It is very difficult. But that compassion can touch a person. It can relate itself to an individual and when that happens you will understand it." Compassion can remain a concept, but affection one can feel where there is no prejudice, no demands of reciprocity. Then it is possible to have effortless understanding and empathy for each other.

EB: Did the presence of the teacher in any way prevent an understanding of what he was talking about?

SP: What does the presence of a person who is a so-called "realized person," a witness to that supreme intelligence and compassion do? We have descriptions in scriptures, in books, of those states of "otherness," of transcendence. But when a person actually lives in the presence of such a person, he experiences a different quality because there is a communication in silence of that which is sacred, not just through word, symbol or thought. The living presence of an individual who is a witness and a holder of that extraordinary sacred dimension and pure energy, has a significance which is beyond all measure.

EB: In what way did Krishnamurti change as he grew older and did that change reflect in the talks?

SP: I think Krishnaji changed over the years a great deal. I first met him in Madras when he came to India in 1947. Of course, personally speaking, I absolutely fell in love with the teachings, with him, and it meant a whole lot of change in the direction of my life. He was a delight to be with; he would walk with you, he would talk with you, such fun it was, being with him apart from the seriousness of the teaching itself. I would say, perhaps by the end of the fifties this personal factor gradually started diminishing. Personally, I observed that he became more severe, very serious, and from then onwards, there was very little of the personal in him. I could see that he was deeply concerned with the state of humanity. For fifty years he had taught, spoken and travelled all over the world. Why was not a single person transformed? He was certainly concerned with this problem. Therefore, there was hardly any place for the personal factor.

EB: Do you think that Krishnamurti's teaching may create the foundation for a new civilization?

SP: I feel so, though I may not be able to substantiate it; it is only a gut feeling about this direction. Today, Krishnaji is addressing humanity, which has already become closer together as a global village. He is addressing humanity as one unit. Therefore, human consciousness is being spoken to, being touched through word and through non-word by his presence, and therefore the whole stream of human consciousness is being affected in depth. This awakening of the collective consciousness of humanity, could be the ground for the release of a new creative process. New energies in perception, in

relationships, can be released. One can be related to other human beings without images; a new creative process is set in motion, in dialogue with oneself, in dialogue with nature, in dialogue with people.

EB: Are there aspects of Krishnamurti's teachings that can only be understood non-verbally?

SP: We all know that the word is very limited and thought is limited. Our relationship to each other is based on mutual pleasure, pain, dependence, insecurity . We have observed all this—and the word is not the thing. Not only because Krishnaji has said it, but we have also comprehended it. One of the great things which he said was that images in relationship prevent you from being really related to another. It is only when there is sensitivity, a listening, a sharing without wanting anything, that there is real relatedness. One of the grounds of the non-verbal quality is to be sensitive and be related in affection to each other. If human beings can love each other, have affection for each other, perhaps we may find a way out of all the extraordinary chaos in this world.[65]

...I saw people who desired to serve going into those quarters where the poor and the degraded live. They desired to help but were themselves helpless. How can you cure another of disease if you are yourself a victim of that disease?

—*LIFE IN FREEDOM, 1928*

Pama Patwardhan, like his brother Achyut and his wife Sunanda, has had a long-standing association with Krishnamurti. One of the group raised in revolutionary fervor, he too, had come to see life in terms other than those that socialism provided. Answers were not to be found only by tinkering with the outer social structure, but rather by looking at the changes that each can effect within.

PAMA PATWARDHAN

PUBLISHER AND SECRETARY OF THE KRISHNAMURTI FOUNDATION OF INDIA

EB: Krishnamurti was asked if the ordinary person could understand him. What did he reply?

PP: I think the way he was unfolding his teachings, he intended that any person, without any special knowledge or learning, should be able to take in and work with his teachings. He felt that those persons who had specialized in philosophy or in any specific field had become scholarly, and for them it was difficult to understand and to take in his teachings. Denying their knowledge and really listening to Krishnamurti was something which a learned man found difficult. Because of his learning he will compare, contrast, he will assess. He was really not listening. I think that a common man would be able to understand what Krishnaji was saying better than a person who was learned.

EB: What was Krishnamurti's position on social action?

PP: It has been very difficult in India for people to understand his position on social action. There is so much inequality, so much squalor, so much hardship, so much deprivation that any sensitive person, any person with a world view, would consider that social action is the right thing to do. This issue came up especially during the "back to the land" Bhoodan movement of Vinoba Bhave. He had started his walking tour in India for the donation of land, declaring that "land like water, could not be a property of anyone," that people with excess land should donate it. He was drawing a large following. Krishnaji felt very strongly that this kind of social action was futile, it would not produce the basic changes that the social activists had in mind. It would always be a kind of a cosmetic, peripheral change. Those who turn to social action, he also felt, were different as they had great potential, great feeling for the common man, for their suffering. Instead of turning to action, if they turned to a fundamental change in the human psyche, they would be able to really go to the root of the problem. We found that what he said was so true.

My family and I were greatly involved with political action for the freedom movement and social action for the land revolution. We couldn't understand why Krishnaji was so much against all this and between ourselves we used to say, "Well, there is something which Krishnaji is talking about which we don't understand." But after twenty-five years, all those movements failed—nothing came out of it. We saw it with our own eyes, the truth of what he was talking about. We were far away from our goal. The movement didn't produce any of the results that we had thought. It would have been far better if we had turned to the basic problem of human misery, which is turning inward, which is going to the root of the problem in oneself rather than trying to reform society. But when there is poverty around you, you can't just say you are working on yourself and do nothing. But Krishnaji had always said that you must keep your room clean, you have a certain duty; you owe it to yourself and to society to do whatever is possible to correct the inequality, the squalor of people around you. But you cannot make it the focus of your action and your life, knowing that the focus is inside you. Unless that center is quiet, unless you understand the various causes of misery, merely acting on the outside is futile.

EB: What was the impact of Krishnamurti's teaching on your life?

PP: The impact has been so tremendous, so deep. Even though I was listening to Krishnaji from 1948, I came into much closer contact with him when I became the Secretary of the Foundation in 1976. I think after that the impact was so great that I am not the same person. I used to be competitive when I was in business. I wasn't aware of many problems of life in general or of my own life. I shut myself off by becoming insensitive, which I didn't know at that time. Now, as I look back, I see how enclosed I had become, how self-centered. But when I came into closer contact with Krishnaji he used to point out things and as I geared myself completely to understanding the teachings, I now see that I am not the same man. I am not claiming that I am transformed or any such thing, but I think I am much more sensitive. I am out of a lot of confusion, conflict, misery, that generally men get involved with. I think the teachings have affected me profoundly. It has been a tremendous thing to me. I think that if a person can give attention to what Krishnaji is talking about, the whole quality of his life will be different, he will be a better human being.[66]

We want to bring about changes in the world—economic changes, social changes, but it seems to me, that one cannot really bring about a significant outward change, unless there is a radical psychological revolution, transformation.

—LONDON TALK 5, 1949

We want transformation through legislation, through outward revolution, through systems, but yet we are inwardly untransformed. Inwardly we are disturbed, we are confused; and without bringing order, peace and happiness inwardly, we cannot have peace and happiness outwardly in the world.

—BOMBAY TALK III, 1948

Ingram Smith first met Krishnamurti in 1938, but it was in 1949, when he was controller of programs for Radio Sri Lanka that more extensive opportunities arose to walk and talk with Krishnamurti. He continued his fruitful work for many years. His anecdotes and recollections are many and varied. This is just one of the many.

It touches on a meeting with the master. During Krishnamurti's adolescent association with the Theosophical Society, belief in the masters was a fundamental tenet of the organization, as was said earlier. Blavatsky, Besant, Leadbeater and others all told of receiving significant messages through masters visible and invisible.

Krishnamurti himself had purportedly written the little book *At the Feet of the Master* following his initiation. At that event, his supposed Master Kuthumi (or Koothumi or KH) had given him certain instructions which when written down, became that well-known book.

Perhaps the most significant of Krishnamurti's personal experiences was told to me in December 1949.

It was during Krishnamurti's visit to Colombo, as we were driving out of the city for our brisk evening walk. Gordon Pearce, who had known Krishnamurti since his childhood, and who was to become the principle of the Rishi Valley School later that year, was sitting in the front seat, and Krishnaji and I in the back. Gordon enjoyed talking about old times, and this evening he was questioning Krishnaji about those early days.

"It is true," he asked, "that you used to talk with the Master Kuthumi?"
"Did you actually see him and talk with him?"

It came as great surprise to me, when Krishnaji answered, "Yes." After a pause, he repeated, "Yes, I did."

Then he went on to explain what took place. He told us that he had talked with Kuthumi on a number of occasions, usually in the early morning while he was meditating. One morning, just after sunrise, Kuthumi appeared in the doorway of Krishnamurti's room. They talked for a while, until Krishnaji, who had participated in similar discussions before, decided that he wanted more than verbal communication, not just words. He needed some tactile contact, to actually meet and touch Kuthumi. So he stood up, and walked to the sunlit door.

Then came the telling words.

"I walked right on through the figure. I turned around. There was no one there. I never saw the Master Kuthumi again."

There were no more questions. We rode on in silence.[67]

—INGRAM SMITH, COLOMBO, SRI LANKA, 1949

To go very far you must begin very near, and the near is you, the "you" that you must understand. And as you begin to understand, you will see that there is a dissolution of knowledge, so that the mind becomes totally alert, aware, empty, without a center, and only such a mind is capable of receiving that which is truth.

—BOMBAY, 1957

DURING THE EARLY FIFTIES there had been an especially heavy load of travels and talks. In August 1950, Krishnamurti felt the need for a complete withdrawal—a retreat—which was to last for a year, but actually lasted until January of 1952. Although he did some traveling, he did not speak publicly. At the end of this period he gave a series of twelve talks at Vasanta Vihar, Madras and continued with his regular speaking schedule in London, Holland, Ojai, etc.

1953 saw the publication of his first important book, *Education and the Significance of Life*, leaving aside the questionable early work *At the Feet of The Master*. This was followed in 1954 by *The First and Last Freedom* with a foreword by Aldous Huxley, a part of which appeared earlier in this book. These works were the beginning of a steady stream of some fifty books which came out over his lifetime and has continued after his death.

Ill health plagued him over the years and he came down with frequent fevers, some more serious than others. Krishnamurti was a frail man, his inherent constitution weakened by childhood illnesses. It was only through the extreme care that he took of his body that he was able to survive into old age. He was meticulous about his diet (he was a lifelong vegetarian) and exercised regularly. The daily practice of yoga kept him supple and lithe—he maintained that for him yoga did not pertain to anything but physical strength and flexibility, and was not a "spiritual exercise." Daily walks were a constant in his life. Not only were they a part of his physical regimen, but also gave the sustenance of communion with nature.

During those years another school was founded in Bombay by Nandini Mehta, sister of Pupul Jayakar. She was one of the early group that formed around Krishnamurti when he first returned to India in 1947. She and Pupul had been at "Ooty" as a continuation of the strange "process" unfolded.

The school, named Bal Anand, is an after-school center where poor and street children gather to participate in arts and crafts and in yoga. It provides an oasis for deprived children through a caring environment enriched with cultural activities. The school has since become part of the Krishnamurti Foundation India.

Several years later during the continued travels that were the very fabric of Krishnamurti's life, events drastically changed their course. He again had become seriously ill while in India. A planned speaking tour of Helsinki, London, Biarritz, Ojai and Sydney had to be cancelled. During a period of recuperation in Switzerland with Rajagopal, the fragile relationship between the two men reached the breaking point and never really recovered. Among other things, Rajagopal said that he had tired of being Krishnamurti's "travel agent." He left leaving only just enough money to cover the hotel bill.

During that time of turmoil however, a new thought had been germinating. Rather than the incessant travel, why not a center in Europe where yearly gatherings could be held? Travel would then be restricted to only three or four locations per year. That was the birth of the Saanen gatherings which lasted for twenty-five years afterwards.

Three English women were largely responsible for the enlivened work in England and later Europe. They were Doris Pratt, Mary Cadogan and Dorothy Simmons.

Doris Pratt had for some years organized the work in England. She acted, in a sense, as a deputy to Rajagopal reporting to him and turning over all finances with a strict accounting of monies spent. Doris remained a friend and worker until her death.

DORIS PRATT

ORGANIZER OF KRISHNAMURTI TALKS, LONDON

I remember an interview once with Krishnaji, when I told him I wanted to discuss my problem. The problem was that I wanted to give up smoking. And he said to me, "Miss Pratt, you've been talking to me about your problem, but really, there are four things: there's one, the fact is that you smoke. Then there comes the myth that you smoke and like it. The second is the myth that you wish you didn't smoke, and then comes the ideal, you wish you could be the ideal, somebody who had never smoked; and fourthly, there is the inner emptiness that makes one either smoke, or go in for sex or anything else. So that you had a struggle between the fact, and the emptiness and in the middle was the myth, and then he said, "By Jove, I had a myth once." He said, "I had the myth that I was to be the world teacher when I really was an ordinary young man. At that time—and I wanted to do everything that a young man wants to do: fall in love, get on a motor bike, race around—I was just a young man. I had a struggle between the myth and the fact."

Doris had the early opportunity to have long thoughtful discussions with Krishnamurti. In one of them he discussed the nature of thought and its relationship with love:

Thought destroys love, doesn't it? Because while the mind is occupied with thinking, it is a useless mind; it's occupied; it's going round and round in its own occupations, it's own interests, and there can only be love when there is a background of emptiness, silence, that love can fill. Love can't come in while thought is there, can it? I don't think it can. We may say that we love, but the love we know is possessive. It includes jealousy and it includes envy and fear, the fear of losing it, but the love that he was talking about and that he exemplified and lived so magnificently, is a love that knows no such restrictions and comes from a deep silence.

Krishnamurti's equivocal avowal of his role is revealed in this early statement made to Doris Pratt:

"The tears of all the world have produced the world teacher." [68]

QUESTION: IN WHAT MANNER SHOULD ONE LIVE ONE'S DAILY LIFE?

If you had only one hour to die what would you do? Would you not arrange your worldly affairs and so on?...ask family and friends for forgiveness?...and forgive them? Would you not die completely to the things of the mind, to desires and to the world? And if it can be done for one hour, then it can also be done for the days and years that may remain.

—*COMMENTARIES ON LIVING, 1956, 1959, 1960*

The war had stirred and changed lives around the world, bringing up for questioning old values and ways of thinking. One of those who was searching for new answers at the time was Mary Cadogan. She tells the story of how the search began and what its consequences were to be. For some thirty years Mary Cadogan has worked for the Krishnamurti Foundation Trust. She has been especially active in coordinating the work of the various European Committees and in seeing to the publication of Krishnamurti's books. She is herself a noted author.

MARY CADOGAN

AUTHOR, LONDON, ENGLAND

"I FOUND HIM MORE AUSTERE THAN I HAD ANTICIPATED.... IN FACT HE WAS URGENT, PASSIONATE, INTENSE—IN SOME WAYS EXTREMELY STERN WITH HIS AUDIENCE."

—MARY CADOGAN

EB: Mary, how did you initially come in contact with Krishnamurti, and what did his teachings mean to you?

MC: It's interesting to discuss this, because I am of a generation that came to Krishnamurti in a new way in the late 1940s, soon after the ending of the Second World War. Before then his audience had been a largely Theosophical one. People who had once been in The Order of the Star, especially. After the war Krishnamurti suddenly began to appeal to many young people who had none of that background and who saw him in an entirely new context. This was the slow beginning of what was to become an explosion of interest by the early 1960s.

He was in America throughout the war and out of contact with European audiences and readers. In the mid-1940s, I was a young woman and, like others who had survived the war, was extremely aware of life as something infinitely precious. We really wanted to find out how to use it, and not again get caught up in the dreadful conflicts of nationalism. I felt that what I was looking for was to be found in the realm of the religions, but I couldn't say exactly what it was. I considered the religion with which I had grown up, which was Christianity, and found that, for me, it didn't provide all the answers. It was simply my conditioning.

During the war years I had realized that religious and political conditioning was apparently an accident of birth, and that there must be something over and above the limited orthodoxies and received opinions. If, for example, I'd been born only a few hundred miles to the east, I would have been a German, and "on the other side" during the conflict. And I was strongly conscious of Jewish people's cultural backgrounds because a great number of them had come to southern England as refugees from Naziism; I'd gone to school with girls from several different countries whom I would never have met if it had not been for the war.

So, in the mid-1940s, I was looking into other religious approaches—into yoga, Ramakrishna Vedanta, and then Theosophy. Theosophy was appealing in its internationalism but as far as I was concerned it seemed too glib in some of its mystical explanations. But it introduced me to books by Krishnamurti, and, as soon as I began to read these, I realized that here was something different from what I had known, written by someone who had a way of using words which was unique. I felt this even in his early writings because they pointed to that which was beyond words; immeasurable. Of course I read his later books too and responded to them. Not only did Krishnamurti use language in an extraordinarily sensitive way but, even at the level of logic, what he said was inexorable and impossible to deny. However, at first I resisted it somewhat. I said to myself "This man takes away our crutches before he shows us how to walk." Which of course he does! It is a revolution that he talked about, a personal, individual revolution: a fundamental change of every value that one had ever held including all those subtle and very deep images of oneself. Until then my religious quest had been of a rather reassuring nature, but suddenly through Krishnamurti I saw the transparency of the complicated clothing I had wrapped around the ego.

EB: Could you describe what your response was when you met Krishnamurti for the first time?

MC: Yes. I met him for the first time in the early 1950s when he was giving talks in London. I was then living in the country, fifty miles away. When my husband and I heard that he was coming to London it was a tremendous thrill, but I was rather bewildered by the actuality of seeing Krishnamurti. I had expected him to be beautiful and charismatic, which he was, but I found him more austere than I had anticipated. I must have had an image of someone from whom there would be a tremendous outflow of warmth and serenity. In fact he was urgent, passionate, intense—but in some ways extremely stern with his audience.

Over the years that I've known him, more tenderness has come across. Also more sense of really individual communication, so that even when he's talking to several hundred or several thousand people, he still managed to talk as if he actually was speaking with a friend. In those early days I don't think he could quite do that.

I was very fortunate that Doris Pratt, the person who was organizing these London talks, asked if we would like to meet Krishnamurti after his talk, and of course I said, "Yes." We met him in a small room and I then had quite a different impression of him, because there was all the warmth of being in the presence of someone who gave you his total attention. To be on the receiving end of this was a deeply satisfying experience. All the nuances of exploitation of one human being by another fell away to absolute ashes in his presence. Although there was vital attention, there was not even remotely any emotional usage. This intrigued me; I realized, even at this first short meeting—and I've since felt it many times—how extraordinarily open he was. In a sense, although he was a male, he had transcended maleness or femininity. He was neither a man nor a woman, neither of the East nor the West, neither young nor old. There was true universality.

EB: A human being without being divided into any kind of category.

MC: That's right. I suppose that could make him sound rather dull and featureless, but it wasn't like that at all. There was immense vitality which I've never met in the same way in anyone else.

EB: You spoke of a different quality about him, an otherness somehow. How did that manifest itself?

MC: There are many anecdotes I could give, but perhaps for me it was best expressed in his extraordinary repose and inwardness, and that beauty which was not of externalization but something coming from within.

EB: After this initial meeting, what was your next contact?

MC: I went on reading his books—we had no records, tapes or videos then, and when Krishnamurti came to London I was often invited to small group discussions with him. I asked if I could have an interview with him (in those days he gave a lot of time to meeting people individually). My question was that some part of me—of the conscious, intellectual mind—refused to be quiet, and I felt that, without the quietness and gaps between thoughts which he had described, I was unable to go further in understanding. So my question to him was, "Why can't I be quiet?" Before I had the interview I thought this was a valued question. I went into the room and he was sitting there very still and very quiet almost overpoweringly quiet. I felt I shouldn't even open my mouth to put a question! In a way he was already providing elements in which were the "answers" to my question. When I did ask it, he received it in total silence. Then, rather nervously, because one doesn't always like to sit in silence with another human being, I found myself going on, and trying to phrase other questions. Again he made little response—then I just stopped. I felt "This is a terrible disappointment, a total waste of time. I should never have asked to see him. I'm not ready: I should just walk out of the room and not come back."

Then he turned to me and asked, "Now, what did you really want to discuss?" He started to talk a little bit about quietness but soon moved away from this. What he did—and I realize that this was his supreme value—was simply to hold a mirror up to me. In ways that I couldn't have done before, I saw myself. And the question that I'd come with just didn't apply any more. In fact, it wasn't a question; and there wasn't an answer. I realized that I'd been going about things in a way that was not productive, and this was remarkable because he said very little.

EB: In what way did he hold a mirror up? He must have said something that made you see yourself?

MC: I think it was his total stillness. That was the mirror—and his creative listening. Previously I had been reaching out for supposed quietness in an artificial way.

Then he asked several questions which I thought were irrelevant, although probably they weren't. Or maybe they were to relax me. I think he was all the time saying "Wake up and look. You really have not looked at yourself at the deeper levels." He was pointing out that what I was really doing was to look through the screen of images.

All I can say is that I came out of the room a different person from when I went in. It was as if I'd looked in a kind of x-ray mirror which showed all the layers.

After that I felt that my relationship with what he was saying became absolutely real. In 1958, after talking with Krishnamurti and Rajagopal (who took overall responsibility for the offices of Krishnamurti Writings, Inc. in America, India and Britain),

Doris Pratt asked if I would take over the London office, which covered the work in Europe, the Commonwealth and many other parts of the world. Of course I said that I would like to do so, but I would work mainly from my home because I had a small baby to look after. The office was not then nearly as busy as it was to become soon afterwards.

I asked him whether the interest in his work which began to flower in the 1960s could have happened earlier. He implied that the "revolution" happened then because that was the time when it had to come. All over the world things were changing. Many of the old traditions and restrictions were breaking down—the way people dressed, talked, thought: the transcending of the restraints of social class, or racial and nationalistic distinctions. The change was partly triggered by the first international publication of a Krishnamurti book *Education and the Significance of Life*—in 1953, followed by *The First and Last Freedom*. These and subsequent books reached an enormous public. Many of those who came to the talks said they had first heard of Krishnamurti through reading *The First and Last Freedom*.

Krishnamurti took a decisive step in 1961, when he started the international gatherings at Saanen in Switzerland. At that time the management decisions (if I can call them that) were not discussed with Krishnamurti. I believe it was about this time that he resigned from the Board of Krishnamurti Writings, Inc. but he hadn't been active on that board for some time.

EB: He was there as a figurehead?

MC: He felt it was right that he should be involved because, after all, much money and effort had been given in his name. He had trusted others to do the work but was probably realizing more acutely that he had to take a serious and active interest. Because the work was not flowering as one might have expected it to do.

I remember saying to him in the fairly early 1960s "I wish you would take more interest in the way the work is done" and he made it clear that he intended to do so. I must say that he always honored that, even in occasionally very difficult situations.

Going back to 1961, he suggested having the international gathering in Switzerland because it had traditionally been a neutral place. Also he knew and loved the mountainous terrain of the Bernese Oberland. Saanen was settled on, and he formed some of us into the Saanen gatherings committee which was not directly connected with the Krishnamurti Writings, Inc. or other organizations. The several-week long annual gathering gave a whole new impetus to the work. It originated in Europe because, at that time, not too much seemed to be happening in California which had, some years earlier, been the center of the work. Things were going well in India, however, where there were schools of the Foundation for New Education, which was inspired by Krishnamurti.

AT SAANEN (SHOWN ABOVE),
GATHERINGS CONTINUED FOR
TWENTY-FIVE YEARS. THEY
WERE A TREMENDOUS FOCAL
POINT OF KRISHNAMURTI'S
WORK IN EUROPE.

The Saanen gatherings continued for twenty-five years, growing larger all the time. Saanen was a tremendous focal point; the decision to start a school in Europe (eventually, of course, this was at Brockwood Park in England) might never have been taken without the vitality and stimulus of so many seriously motivated people.

The large marquis in which the meetings were held which could be physically and psychologically "folded away" at the end of each gathering—seemed particularly appropriate for Krishnamurti's talks in Switzerland. Many young people came from all over the world during those so-called "flower-periods" but there has been no lessening of the numbers of young or old who came to hear Krishnamurti in Saanen and elsewhere over the decades. If one looks at any of his meetings I suppose one could say that there was always present a total cross-section of humanity.

Krishnamurti spoke with some urgency about how we would carry on the work after his death. Then—apparently "out of the blue"—I found myself asking "When Krishnamurti dies, what happens to all the energy and understanding that he is? Does it continue in some way—does it go on through all of us?" His answer was clear and uncompromising; he grasped my hand and said with the intensity that characterized his most serious moments "Yes, of course—so long as you make the right foundation." His response to my deeply felt question seemed at the time and in retrospect awesome, profound, expansive and positive. Krishnamurti always responded to questions according to their context: there was for him no such thing as a static, isolated question or problem. And there were no rigid answers. Part of his great legacy is that he has left us with questions and explorations rather than with answers and reassurances. [69]

The last of the trio of English women is Dorothy Simmons. Vibrant and passionate in the depth of her concern for Krishnamurti's work, she was the founding director of Brockwood Park Education Center and the mainstay during its beginnings. Again, the emphasis on education was to be partially academic excellence, but also concern and affection for the student, not only filling them with information in order to pass examinations.

The other aspect of Brockwood Park concerns learning to live together, as students and staff live in close proximity in a boarding school setting. That, perhaps, is the most challenging aspect of living and one that has caused adjustments to be made on all sides.

DOROTHY SIMMONS

FOUNDING DIRECTOR, BROCKWOOD PARK EDUCATION CENTER, BRAMDEAN-NEAR-ARLESFORD, ENGLAND

AERIAL VIEW OF BROCKWOOD PARK EDUCATIONAL CENTER, HAMPSHIRE, ENGLAND.

DS: I consider it an immense privilege to have worked with Krishnaji and even to have lived in the same time. It opened up everything. He was an artist in living and that was the beauty of him. He gave generously; it was the generosity of his life and the joyousness of his life and he looked happy with life, even though he was aware of all the suffering and difficulties. What he wanted to do, I feel, was to reveal how you, yourself, could end these miseries by understanding yourself. That is what I feel he really wanted to share with us.

Krishnaji educated himself and he didn't do it by a reference to what had gone before, not through history. He took a glance at history and said we're the outcome of it. He approached it in a different way, not in an academic way at all; he approached it through his senses, not accumulating knowledge and reference to what had gone before but how it could be met this day that had never happened before. That is a very fundamental difference. It's not through knowledge, it was through perception and sensibility to all that was not him.

EB: What do you mean by "perception and sensibility to all that was not him?"

DS: You have your life. You're unique, in a way, but you are also identical, you are similar to everybody else; but out there is the whole world that is being born, that is new and is a miracle and that is speaking of its own life and energy. Krishnaji received that. All that is not you, is out there. The not you, is what comprises life.

Really, life is energy and Krishnaji paid great attention to his own energy: he nurtured it, he cared for it, he went into great detail as to what he ate; everything mattered. And then, having done that, and made his body as sensitive as it could be, he then went on to see what else was in the world; he related to it, and therefore he received communication about what energy was in life. It's all interconnected and nourished by this approach of being concerned about yourself but also concerned about everything, receiving it, the communication that life is making all the time.

Affection is the beginning of how you approach anything. You can't see anything or perceive anything without affection, but I think it needs to go deeper. It has to generate an energy, really amounting to passion, if you're going to share with anybody and everybody, whatever it is you've perceived. It's the passion with which Krishnaji received and gave to life, that gave the quality that he bestowed on the world. It was great affection—it was love—which I think is the vital quality of his whole approach. It's the most wonderful thing—you can do nothing without it, you can do nothing at all.

EB: What relationship did Krishnamurti's presence have with the teaching?

DS: Well, he *was* the teachings, although I hesitate to use the word "teachings." It makes it finite and I think it was an ongoing quest, adventure and, in this, he personified...he was the teachings. He lived it, by the care and attention that he gave to everything and the depth of his passion and his affection and love for mankind—yes, I think it did have an impact. You felt leavened by his presence. He carried a quality with him that was rare and strong and people drew themselves together and tried to receive the seriousness and passion that he brought to life and gave to life.

As Einstein was to Newton, so Krishnaji was to us. He broke fresh ground. He saw that our behavior was childish. That we were destroying ourselves because we weren't able to see, we weren't in control of our emotions. We were children with terrific facilities to destroy and hurt and damage and he said, "I will give you the tools to help you grow up to be responsible for your actions and your way of living," and that is exactly what he did. He said, "Your greed, your fears, your selfishness, your angers and aggression, all of these are stopping you from receiving all this incredible world. So take a journey inside and find out about yourself and grow up. Stop being juvenile." Which is really what we are.

He saw that the world had stayed still for a long time; it was still adolescent, and he heightened our consciousness, and saw that our behavior was what was blocking any deepening, any responsibility for the state of the world.

EB: What were Krishnamurti's intentions for Brockwood and all the schools?

DS: Really, if you look at it, all you can do in a school and what Krishnaji was probably doing, was to show that there was a different way of living. That's really all you can convey, it's all behavior and that is the essence of what Krishnaji was revealing. I don't think you can teach it; you just make it known by how you live, by how he lived. There are some things you can do and some things you can't do and that has to be conveyed to young people. One has to be educated to the way to behave in life, towards everything and everybody.

EB: What is it that prevents right behavior and understanding of Krishnamurti's teachings?

DS: Why don't we live the teachings? Because our attention is so slight. We don't give our total attention to it. We think about it but that's not enough; that's to intellectualize it, to put it at a distance. But we don't passionately feel it. If we did, it would simply fall away, all these silly things that are holding us. The thing is, we feel we'll do that later on, because we enjoy the things we enjoy, and they're easy, and they're familiar.

EB: How does learning take place at Brockwood? Krishnamurti described how you didn't teach a baby to walk, and to talk, etc.

DS: There's a lovely little story that I was told right at the beginning of Brockwood, which impressed me very much. There was a little girl, trying to thread a needle and not being able to do it and her mother came along and she just took the needle and she said, "There you are, my dear." And the child said, "Mommy, I didn't want the needle threaded. I wanted to thread the needle." And I felt that was the way to begin teaching. You really couldn't teach anything at all; all you could do was to remove the barriers and make it possible for a child to learn themselves.[70]

"IT'S THE PASSION WITH WHICH KRISHNAJI RECEIVED AND GAVE TO LIFE, THAT GAVE THE QUALITY THAT HE BESTOWED ON THE WORLD. IT WAS GREAT AFFECTION—IT WAS LOVE— WHICH I THINK IS THE VITAL QUALITY OF HIS WHOLE APPROACH."

—DOROTHY SIMMONS

The first demand then, the first challenge is to observe what is, which is to know yourself as you really are, not as you should be, that is a childish game, an immature struggle that has no meaning—but to look at violence and observe it. Can one look and how does one look? This is an extraordinarily difficult problem because there are certain factors which we must understand very clearly. Firstly, we must observe without identification, without the word, without the space between the observer and the thing observed; we must look without any image, without the thought, so that we are seeing things as they actually are. This is very important, because if we do not know how to look, how to observe what we are, then we will inevitably create conflict between what we see and the entity who sees.

—*TALKS WITH AMERICAN STUDENTS, 1970*

As the fire of interest and enthusiasm for Krishnamurti's work took hold in England, a new relationship was formed, one which was of the greatest importance to physicist David Bohm as well as Krishnamurti himself.

Bohm was a man of vast intellect, capable of exploring questions in depth, yet with a scientist's tentativeness.

During the war years he worked on the "scattering of nuclear particles" under the supervision of J. Robert Oppenheimer. He became assistant professor at Princeton University in 1946, where he began discussions with Einstein. However, the pervasive climate of fear during the McCarthy era brought many artists, scientists, and intellectuals to account for views which did not necessarily conform to those of a committee of the U.S. House of Representatives. Allegations were brought against Bohm by the House Un-American Activities Committee. Because he refused to testify, on principle, he was found to be in contempt of Congress. His work in the United States thus damaged, he left to work in Brazil, at Technion in Israel, and later settled in London as professor of theoretical physics at Birkbeck College. He was cleared of contempt charges and was eventually allowed to travel in the United States.[71]

The meetings with Krishnamurti became legendary and gave renewed urgency to the term "dialogue" as a fundamental of Krishnamurtian teaching. "Exploring together, like two friends sitting under a tree," or "thinking together" is the way this process has been described. However one would characterize it, dialogue is an old yet new way at looking at and questioning the human condition.

DAVID BOHM, PH.D

PHYSICIST, LONDON, ENGLAND

EB: Dr. Bohm, could you say how you first came into contact with Krishnamurti or his teaching?

DB: Well, the background is that in my work in physics I was always interested in the general philosophical questions as they related to physics, and more generally, universally as it might relate to the whole constitution of nature and of man. One of the points arising in physics which is somewhat related to what Krishnaji is doing, is in quantum theory, where you have the fact that energy is found to be existent as discrete units which are not divisible.

EB: Could you clarify the word discrete in that context?

DAVID AND SAREL BOHM, LONDON, 1987.

DB: One view is that matter is continuous, flowing, and the other view is it's made of atoms, which are discrete, but there are so many atoms that it appears to be continuous. Like grains in an hourglass, they flow as if they were water. But obviously they are made of discrete units. So the notion of the atomicity or discreteness of matter had already been common for many centuries, but in the early 20th-century there arose a discovery that energy is discrete as well. Energy comes in units, though they're very tiny; therefore, we don't easily see them, and the number is so great that they appear to be continuous. Now this has important consequences because it means that things cannot be

There is no method.

There is only attention,

observation.

—NEW DELHI, 1966

divided from each other. If two things interact by means of an energy that cannot be divided, that link is indivisible. Therefore, fundamentally, the entire universe is indivisible, and in particular, it means that the thing observed and the apparatus which observes it cannot be really separated. Now, we already had this point that the observer cannot be separated from the observed. In fact, whenever you observe, the thing observed is changed because it cannot by this interaction be reduced below a certain level. Therefore, you have the transformation of the object observed in the act of observation. I had already noted the similarity to consciousness: that if you try to observe your thought in any detail, the whole train of thought changes. That's clear isn't it? So therefore, you cannot have the separation of the observer and the observed in consciousness. The observer changes the observed, and the observed changes the observer, therefore, there was a mysterious quality which was not really understood in physics.

EB: Was this part of your observation, scientifically, as well as philosophically, when you first came in contact with Krishnamurti?

DB: That's right, let me add one more point. My interest in physics…I had always had a tendency to say that what I was thinking about in physics should be taking place within me. I felt that there was a parallel between what is in consciousness, and what is in matter in general, and I felt movement was also a question, that the movement that you see outside, you feel inside. In general therefore, I felt that we directly apprehended the nature of reality in our own being.

EB: Had you pursued this through contacts with other teachers, or philosophers, or was this a purely scientific matter and your own self-observation?

DB: At that point, it was probably mostly my own. The question of the observer and the observed was obviously looked at in quantum mechanics as to its implications, especially by Nils Bohr, who in fact was influenced by the philosopher William James, an American. He had developed an idea of the stream of consciousness, along the lines I have been saying. But as a matter of fact, that idea occurred to me independently as soon as I read about quantum theory. There was an analogy between this stream of consciousness and the behavior of matter. That was the background of my interest in science. I was also trying to understand the universal nature of matter. Questions like causality and time and space, and totality, to grasp it all.

EB: Is this something that is shared by other scientists, are there similar observations?

DB: Those who are inclined that way do, but most do not. Most scientists are very pragmatically oriented, and mainly want to get results. They would like to make a theory that would predict matter accurately and control it, but a few are interested in this question. Say Einstein. I should say that I had some discussions with Einstein on the quantum theory when I was in Princeton. Most physicists know the quantum theory cannot be understood, they take it as a calculus, as a way of getting results, predicting. They say "That's all that really matters, and that a deeper understanding might be nice, but it is not really essential."

EB: So with the background of this kind of interest, you came to reading a book by Krishnamurti?

DB: Yes. As I said, scientists have an interest in cosmology, many of them are trying to get a grasp of the totality of the cosmos. Einstein particularly wanted to understand it as one whole. What happened in regard to Krishnamurti was that my wife and I were in Bristol. We used to go to the public library where I got interested in philosophical or even mystic or religious books, such as those of Ouspensky and Gurdjief because I was somewhat dissatisfied with what could be done in the ordinary sphere. My wife Sarel and I came across *The First and Last Freedom*. She saw a phrase there, "The observer and the observed," so she thought it might have something to do with quantum theory, and she pointed it out to me. When I read the book, I was very interested in it. I felt it was a very significant one, and it had a tremendous effect on me. That the questions of the observer and the observed were brought to the psychological level of existence, and I had the hope that one could tie up physics and psychological matters. I also read the *Commentaries on Living*. They were the only other books in the library. I wrote to the publisher in America, and asked whether one could get more books, or whether Krishnamurti was around. Somebody sent me a letter suggesting that I get in touch with the people here in England. I wrote to them and they sent me a list of books.

EB: Do you remember what year that was?

DB: It could have been about 1958, or 1959. Then somewhere around 1960, he came back to England and gave talks. It could have been 1960. In my letter ordering books, I asked if Krishnamurti ever came to England, and they said, in fact he was coming and there would be a limited number of people who could come to hear him. I came with Sarel and, while I was here, I wrote a letter to Doris Pratt, asking if I could talk with Krishnamurti, and then I got a phone call from her arranging to make an appointment. They were renting a house in Wimbledon, and I waited for him with Sarel. Then he came in, and there was a long silence, but then we began discussing. I told him all about my ideas in physics, which he probably couldn't have understood in detail, but he got the spirit of it. I used words like totality, and when I used this word totality, he grabbed me by the arm, and said, "That's it, that's it!"

EB: What was your initial impression? You had read books by Krishnamurti. What was your impression as you first met this man?

DB: Well, you see, I don't usually form those impressions, I usually just go ahead. But the impression I got was that when we...you see we remained silent, which was not usual, but it didn't seem odd to me at the time, and there was no tension in it. Then we began to talk. Now in talking I got the feeling of close communication, instant communication, of a kind which I sometimes get in science with people who are vividly interested in the same thing. He had this intense energy and openness, and clarity, and a sense of no tension.

I can't remember the details, but he couldn't understand very much of what I said, except the general drift of it.

OPPOSITE: KRISHNAMURTI
PHOTOGRAPHED BY CECIL
BEATON IN LONDON DURING
THE 1960S.

EB: You were speaking on a more scientific level?

DB: I was speaking about the questions I was talking of earlier, like quantum theory, and relativity, and then raising the question of whether the totality can be grasped. I should also say that my interests had turned toward understanding thought, which I've forgotten to mention. I gradually began to see that it was necessary to understand our thought. In going into philosophy, and going into causality, and questions like that, it was a matter of how we are thinking. I had earlier been influenced by people who were interested in dialectical materialism and when I went to Brazil, I talked to a man who had read a lot of Hegel, and raised the question of the very nature of our thought. Not merely what we are thinking about, but the structure of how our thought works, and that it works through opposites. Our thought inevitably unites the two opposite characteristics of necessity and contingency. When I got to Israel, I met another man who was very interested in Hegel. What he said was, "You should pay attention to your thought, how it's actually working." So I had become very interested in how thought proceeds. Considering thought as a process in itself, not it's content, but it's actual nature and structure.

EB: So you found similarities between what Krishnamurti was saying, and someone like Hegel.

DB: There is some similarity, yes. I found a relationship, and that was the reason I was fascinated by Krishnamurti. He was going very deeply into thought, much deeper than Hegel, in the sense that he also went into feeling, and into your whole life. He didn't stop at abstract thought.

Truth or God is something totally unknown. You may imagine, you may speculate about it, but it is still the unknown. The mind must come to it completely stripped of the past, free of all the things it has known, and the known is the accumulated memories and problems of everyday existence. So if there is really to be a radical change, a fundamental transformation, the mind must move away from the known. For love is not something which you experienced yesterday and are able to recapture at will tomorrow; it is totally new, unknown.

—ATHENS TALK, 1956

EB: So over a period of years you became deeply acquainted with Krishnamurti's thought. In the course of that how did you look at the source of Krishnamurti's teaching?

DB: Well, I didn't raise the question for a while. What happened was that we began to meet every time he came to London and had one or two discussions. In the first year I wanted to discuss the question of the universal and the particular with him, and we raised the question "Is mind universal?" and he said, "Yes." We used the word individual, is intelligence individual, and he said, "Yes" at the time. We had quite a good discussion on that. When we left I had the feeling that the state

To go far you must begin near, and the nearest step is the most important one.

—THINK ON THESE THINGS, 1964

of mind had changed, I could see that there was no feeling, but clarity.

EB: When you say the state of mind had changed, do you mean both of your states of mind?

DB: I don't know, I assume that he was similar since we were in close communication. I said that I had no feeling, and he said, "Yes, that's right," which surprised me, because I had previously thought that anything intense must have a lot of feeling, and then when I went out, I had a sense of some presence in the sky, but I generally discount such things…saying that it's my imagination.

EB: Was that a physical sense?

DB: Yes.

EB: You actually could see some…?

DB: Feel. Not see anything there, but feel something there, something universal.

EB: Had you ever felt anything of that nature before?

DB: I had hints of that, but my whole background was such as to say, I didn't tell my parents or anybody, they would have said, "You're just imagining that."

EB: Did you feel that there was any relationship between the intensity of your discussion and what was happening?

DB: Yes, I probably felt that they were related. In fact I might have explained it by saying I was projecting the universality into the sky, as I might have done as a child.

EB: When was your next meeting?

DB: I didn't see a lot of him, but we had discussions every year in London when he came in June, and when I went to Saanen in Switzerland. We began to have discussions in which at least for a while I could feel that was some change of consciousness, but by the time I got back to England, it went away. When you go back into ordinary life.

EB: What would you say are the salient characteristics or qualities of his teaching that differentiate it from that of others?

DB: Well, first of all, the total concern with all phases of life and consciousness, and secondly the question of something beyond consciousness, which began to emerge in our discussions in Saanen.

EB: Did Krishnamurti ever describe any particular influence on his teaching? He says today that he doesn't read books of a religious or philosophic nature, but in his earlier years he may have come into contact with that.

DB: Well he didn't describe it to me, but I've heard people say that he read the "Cloud of Unknowing," which was influential, and probably other books. My feeling is that he must also have been familiar with what the Theosophists were saying. The other things he's read or heard may have awakened him to some extent.

EB: Did you ever feel that he was drawing you away from your scientific interests?

DB: No, because I was going on with my scientific interests, at that time I wanted to understand this whole question of the observer and observed scientifically, and the question of dealing with the universe as a totality. So it didn't really draw me away from the scientific work. I became more and more interested in the question of the nature of thought, which is crucial in everything, including science, since it was the only instrument you had. When I was in London with Krishnaji, I did discuss what to do about scientific research, and I remember he said, "Begin from the unknown. Try beginning from the unknown." I could see that the question of getting free of the known was the crucial question in science, as well as in everything. For example if you take scientific discoveries—I'll take a very simple case. You may have heard of Archimedes and his discoveries. He was given the problem of measuring the volume of a crown of irregular size in order to see whether it was gold or not by weighing it, and it was too irregular to be measured and he was very puzzled, and then suddenly when he was in his bath he saw the water displaced by his body, and he realized that no matter what the shape, the water displaced is equal to the volume of the body, right? And therefore he could measure the volume of the crown. He went out shouting "Eureka!" if you recall. Now, you consider the nature of what went on. The basic barrier to seeing was that people thought of things in different compartments, one was volume by measurement, and two, water being displaced would have nothing to do with that, right?

EB: Exactly.

DB: To allow those to be connected, the mind would have to dissolve those rigid compartments. Once the connection was made, anybody using ordinary reasoning could have done the rest, any schoolboy of reasonable intelligence. The same happened with Newton. Obviously Archimedes as well as Newton and Einstein were in states of intense energy when they were working, and what happens is that the moment of insight is the dissolving of the barrier in thought. It is insight into the nature of thought, not into the problem. All insight is the same. It is always insight into thought. Not its content but its actual physical nature, which makes the barrier. And that is what I think Krishnamurti was saying, that insight transforms the whole structure of thought and makes the consciousness different. Now for scientists that may happen for a moment, and then they get interested in the result, working it out, but Krishnamurti is emphasizing insight as the essence of life itself. Without coming to a conclusion. Don't worry too much about the results, however important they may be. Insight, fresh insight is continually needed. That insight is continually dissolving the rigid compartments of thought. And that is the transformation of consciousness. Our consciousness is now rigid and brittle because it's held in fixed patterns of thought due to our conditioning about ourselves, and we get attached to those thoughts, they feel more comfortable.

EB: Krishnamurti always seems to be able to make the distinction between using thought as a tool and then putting it aside when the tool was no longer needed for a specific reason. Putting it aside leaves space for further inquiry.

DB: Yes, one could feel this space was present in our discussion.

EB: What would you say are the most characteristic features of Krishnamurti's teaching?

True education is to learn how to think, not what to think. If you know how to think, if you really have that capacity, then you are a free human being—free of dogmas, superstitions, ceremonies—and therefore you can find out what religion is.

—THINK ON THESE THINGS, 1964

It is only a religious mind, a mind that is enquiring into itself, that is aware of its own movements, its own activity, which is the beginning of self-knowledge—it is only such a mind that is a revolutionary mind. And a revolutionary mind is a mutating mind is the religious mind.

—LONDON, FIRST PUBLIC TALK, MAY 2, 1961

DB: I think there are several features you could say are characteristic. The emphasis on thought as the source of our trouble. Krishnamurti says that thought is a material process, he's always said that. Most people tend to regard it as other than that, and I don't see that emphasized anywhere. Now it's very important to see that thought is a material process, in other words, thought can be observed as any matter can be observed. When we are observing inwardly we are observing not the content of thought, not the idea, not the feeling, but the material process itself. If something is wrong with thought it's because erroneous things have been controlled in memory which then control you, and the memory has to be changed physically. You see with a tape you could wipe out the memory with a magnet, but you would wipe out the necessary memories along with the unnecessary ones.

EB: Krishnamurti seems to indicate that a certain *tabula rasa* can be achieved through clear perception.

DB: That's right, but it's necessarily happening intelligently, so that you do not wipe out the necessary memories, but you'll wipe out the memories which give rise to the importance of the self. He says that there's an energy beyond matter, which is truth, and that truth acts with the force of necessity. It actually works on the material basis of thought and consciousness and changes that into an orderly form. So it ceases to create disorder. Then thought will only work where it's needed and leaves the mind empty for something deeper.

EB: People often raise the point that they lack sufficient energy to continue this investigation in their daily lives. How would you respond to that?

DB: That's probably because there's not an understanding of the nature of energy. Let's connect it with another objection people raise. They see it at certain times, but it goes away.

EB: That's a frequent complaint.

DB: The way I see that is this: You have to see what is essential and universal, and that will transform the mind. The universal belongs to everybody, as well as covering everything, every possible form. It's the general consciousness of mankind. We come now to energy, this whole process of the ego is continually wasting energy, getting you low and confusing you.

EB: In other words, the individual's perception of themselves as a separate being, is a waste of energy.

DB: Yes, because if you see yourself as a particular being you will continually try to protect that being. Your energies will be dissipated.

EB: Earlier you were saying that since thought is a material process, it's necessary to observe the process of thought rather than it's contents. How is one to do that? How is one to make that shift and observe the material process when it appears as if the only thing that consciousness is aware of is content?

DB: Well, there are several points. Before we get to that, another important difference of Krishnamurti is his emphasis on actual life— on being aware of everything—and also his refusal to accept authority, which is really extremely important. There were Buddhists who said, Krishnamurti's talking much the same as the Buddhists, but he says, why do you begin with the Buddha, why not begin with what is here now? That was very important, he refuses to take seriously the comparison with what other people have said. Now to come back to what you were saying, about observation of the material process. You have to see what can be observed about thought aside from the pictures and feelings and its meaning. Whatever you think appears in consciousness as a show. That's the way thought works to display its content, as a show of imagination. Therefore if you think the observer is separate from the observed, it's going to appear in consciousness as two different entities. The point is that the words will seem to be coming from the observer who knows, who sees, and therefore they are the truth, they are a description of the truth. That's the illusion. The way a magician works is exactly the same, you see. Every magician's work depends on distracting your attention so that you do not see how things are connected. Suddenly something appears by magic out of nothing. You do not see how it depends on what he actually did.

EB: You miss that missing link...

DB: By missing the link you change the meaning completely.

EB: So what appears to be magic is actually not realizing the connection of all of these links.

DB: Yes, and that kind of magic takes place in consciousness, the observer and the observed see things appear and the observer appears to be unlinked to the observed. Therefore it comes out as if from nothing. And if it came from nothing it would be truth. Something that suddenly appears in consciousness out of nothing is taken as real and true. If you see the link to thought then you see it as not all that deep.

EB: You're saying then that thought is more shallow than we believe it to be.

DB: Yes, in fact it's extremely shallow. You see most of our consciousness is very, very shallow.

EB: And what we see as our most profound insights are really rather superficial observations.

DB: Yes, or not even observations. Many of them are just delusions, a great deal of what we think about ourselves is just an illusion. The analogy that is often made in Indian literature is if you have a rope that you think is a snake, your heart's beating, your mind is confused, and the minute you see that it's not a snake everything changes. The mere perception is enough to change the state of mind, and the perception that, for example, the observer and the observed are not independent, will mean that the things which the observer is thinking are not regarded as truth anymore. They lose that power. Now if you see the whole....you could say the whole energy of the brain is aroused and directed by the show which thought makes of it's content, it's like a map. There is a show in which this whole content is regarded as truth, as necessary. Then the entire brain is going to restart up around this show. Everything is going to be arranged to try to make a better show. Now the minute you see it's only a show, this all stops. Now the brain quiets down and it's in another state. It's no longer trapped and therefore it can do something entirely different. But to do that it's necessary not merely to say so but to see it in the way we've been suggesting.

I thought of another case where you can see the power of perception. It was this case of Helen Keller—you may have heard of her, she was blind, deaf, and dumb. When she couldn't communicate she was rather like a wild animal. They found this teacher, Ann Sullivan. What she did was to play a game, as it were, to put the child's hand in contact with something, that was her only sense, and scratch the word on her hand. First it was clearly nothing but a game—she didn't understand what was going on. Then, Helen Keller recalls that one morning she was exposed to water in a glass and the name was scratched, and in the afternoon to water in a pump, and the name

If the end is freedom the beginning must be free, for the end and the beginning are one. There can be intelligence and self-knowledge only when there is freedom at the outset and freedom is denied by the acceptance of authority.

—EDUCATION AND
THE SIGNIFICANCE
OF LIFE, 1953

was scratched, and suddenly she had an insight, a shattering insight, and it was that everything has a name. If water was one thing in all its different forms, this one name "water" could be communicated to the other person who used the same name. From there on she began to use language, and in a few days she learned words, in a few days she was making sentences, and her whole life was transformed. She was no longer this violent wild person, but entirely different. So you can see that this perception transformed everything. Once she had the perception there was no turning back. It was not to say she had the perception and then forgot about it and had to have it again. And I think Krishnamurti is implying that to see that the observer is the observed, would be a perception enormously beyond what she had. It would have a far more revolutionary effect.

EB: You feel then that the concept of the observer and the observed is a key one in Krishnamurti's teachings.

DB: Yes, in fact they are identical.

EB: I wonder if you would recapitulate some of the other key factors in his teaching?

DB: Well, the question of time, psychological time being merely produced by thought. You see time is just the same thing as the observer and the observed. The ending of the observer and the observed is identical with the ending of psychological time and therefore a timeless state comes.

EB: And with the perception of the observer and the observed as one, all of the phenomena of suffering, the human difficulties that we all go through are ended.

DB: That's right, because they all originate in ignorance of the true nature of this question. Then the emphasis on compassion arises. Passion for all, not merely passion for those who are suffering. That is part of the passion which goes beyond suffering.

EB: Authority is certainly another major factor in his teaching.

DB: Yes, you can see now why authority is so important. One of the points you have to add is the enormous power of the mind to deceive itself, which he recognized. Authority is one of the major forms of self-deception. There is authority in the mind, not authority in other matters, they are not necessarily self-deception. If somebody comes out as an authority on truth, the danger is that you say that you had begun to doubt certain things yourself, but now you take what he says as true. Because you want it to be so. It's basically that truth must be for me what I need it to be. I feel uneasy, frightened, worried, and so on, and so the authority—the religious authority—comes along and says, "God will take care of you as long as you are good and you believe," and so on. Therefore I want to believe and therefore I say that that's the truth. I was on the point of having to question all this and along comes the authority who makes it unnecessary. You have to ask why you accept authority. You see, the authority gives you no proof whatsoever, so why do you accept it? Because you want to, you need to, right? I must have comfort, consolation and safety. And here comes this impressive figure, very nice looking, perhaps clothed in certain ways with certain ceremonies, and very nice music and consoling thoughts and a good manner, and he says, "You're alright, everything's going to be all right. You just have to believe."

EB: One of the major characteristics of authority is that it has great power, and that power displays itself, as you said, in ritual and ceremony. Just as a worldly power, a king, would show himself through his trappings through his crown, etc.

DB: That's right. But you see, it's an empty show. The whole point is that authority builds an empty show of power around itself. A display, as you called it. There's nothing behind it whatsoever, except our belief that it's there.

EB: Have you been able to observe in Krishnamurti's writings any breaking point where his teaching deviated or went in a completely different direction?

DB: No, I can't see any fundamental change.

EB: Even as a young man, this teaching was implicit within everything he said.

DB: Yes, yes.

EB: And there was no learning from other models?

DB: No. I think it comes from a source beyond the brain which is, in principle, open to everybody.[72]

We have to bring about a psychological transformation in our relationship with the society in which we live. Therefore, there is no escape from it into the Himalayas, into becoming a monk or a nun, and taking up social service, and all the rest of such juvenile business. We have to live in this world, we have to bring about a radical transformation in our relationship with each other; not in some distant future, but now.

—BOMBAY, FEBRUARY 14, 1965

That period in the United States during the 1950s known as the McCarthy era was to have its impact on many diverse people. Just as David Bohm fell under the shadow of alleged "anti-Americanism," so another man of conscience, in a very different field, fell under its pall.

Howard Fast, distinguished novelist and playwright, is the author of *Citizen Tom Paine* and *Spartacus*. Up to the present time he continues to write a succession of thought-provoking, best-selling books and plays.

HOWARD FAST

NOVELIST AND PLAYWRIGHT, NEW YORK

EB: Mr. Fast, as a writer, is there any relationship between Krishnamurti's insight into the psychological condition and the writer's process itself?

HF: Oh, certainly, certainly. The influence of the Krishnamurti type of thinking on a writer is very important. The problem the writer always faces is to get inside the mind of another, to define character, to understand character, to understand why people do the things they do, why the most evil, the most worthless criminal does what he does and not simply to condemn it, but to understand it. And this need for understanding the illusions of people, the deceptions within which people live, this is very much a part of Krishnamurti's teaching.

EB: What was it about Krishnamurti's work that first attracted you?

HF: I came to Krishnamurti through Zen many years ago. When I first began Zen meditation, it was a response to my sense of a world that was crumbling around me and a desperate need to find some truth in a pool of insanity. I found a Zen teacher who was kind enough to take me on and in the beginning of my training, as with so many people who undertake Zen, I began to read, and read everything I could find on Zen. Eventually, I came to a book about Zen by a Belgian physicist who constantly spoke of Zen teaching and Krishnamurti teaching in the same breath as the same thing. He would say, "as in Zen teaching or as in Krishnamurti teaching." Now this was my first introduction to both the name and the teaching of Krishnamurti. Having seen this in the book, off I went to find something by the Krishnamurti he was referring to, and I found a lot of books and I read them with great excitement and great interest. The initial interest was of being so delighted with a man who cut to the core of things, who brooked no nonsense and who swept away illusion and was so absolutely definitive, specific and provocative in his teaching, in his arguments.

EB: What do you think Krishnamurti's primary contribution has been?

HF: I've been trying to think of what one might call Krishnamurti's main contribution. Again, I think it's his ability to separate illusion from truth. His constant saying, "Now listen to me. I'm telling you something of great importance. Pay attention. Listen."

In that first act of asking for attention, he differentiates himself. He says, immediately, "You, like everyone else in the world, are not listening. Now listen to me." And getting the attention, he then picks up the illusion that is referred to and shatters it. If for instance, someone is to say, "I believe totally in the X religion." And Krishnamurti will say, "What is there in the X religion? What is possible there? What is truthful there? What makes sense there? Why do you believe in this? Have you looked at it? Have you tried to understand it?" And this is very different from any other teaching today, very different.

EB: Did Krishnamurti see any answers to the questions of today, and the timeless questions facing us all?

HF: Krishnamurti's assertion over and over again is that the only real solution for the troubles and the tragedies of our time is an inner solution. And I would agree with this as a dream, as an ideal, but to change a human being, to change the thinking of a human being and to change the mind of a human being is possible with a handful of people, but not, to my belief, with masses of people, ever. And so long as masses of people remain unchanged, as far as their inner thinking is concerned, social work must continue. And there, I think, was the one area in which Krishnamurti was not as effective as he should have been. But, this applies not only to Krishnamurti, but to many others, what I might call, both mystical and materialistic ways of teaching and of thinking. They tend to believe that the only hope is a change in the man, that he must become the new man, a different man. We haven't got time for that. We've got atom bombs and every other horrible device of killing and work must be done now with those who have not had interior change. Work must be done to convince people that they must stop this endless war and this endless stupidity.

EB: Some see Krishnamurti as a very pragmatic teacher, others assert that he was a true mystic. How do you regard him?

HF: Krishnamurti, who asserts himself as a very stringent materialist, is also a mystic. There is no question about it, and true mysticism is materialistic. It is not a belief with no foundations. It's a belief that is proved by the changes in the mystically influenced man. Now in this sense, speaking of mystical paths, Krishnamurti thinking, Buddhist thinking, certain other mystical investigations, these are people who thousands of years ago, came up with theories about the nature of the universe. And today, after all these years, our scientists, our physical scientists, particularly those involved in nuclear mechanics, are coming to the same conclusions. In some of Krishnamurti's most fascinating dialogues with the physicist David Bohm, he reaches for the similarities between the mystical belief and the scientific belief. The physicist arrives at the position where there is nothing but energy, and all that we see of solid matter is an illusion. We begin to touch on some of Krishnamurti's preachments against the endless desire for things that has wrapped up so much of the human race today.

EB: Who do you think was the audience that Krishnamurti actually reached?

HF: The number of people who became, in a sense, wedded to his ideas always surprised me. When I went to hear Krishnamurti at Ojai, there was a huge crowd there. But I said to myself, "This is reasonable out here. This is his base of operation." I was charmed then, the first time, by the fact that the car park contained everything from ancient little Volkswagen "Bugs" to Rolls Royces and other very expensive cars. But on the other hand, when I heard that he was going to lecture in New

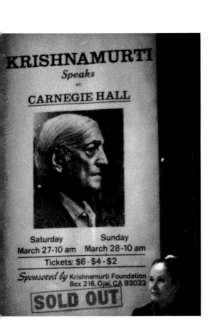

"WHEN I HEARD THAT HE WAS GOING TO LECTURE IN NEW YORK, I WENT TO HEAR HIM IN CARNEGIE HALL, AND WAS AMAZED THAT EVERY SEAT WAS FILLED AND THERE WAS EVEN STANDING ROOM THERE. THE SECOND TIME IN NEW YORK, THE SAME THING."

—HOWARD FAST

York, I went to hear him in Carnegie Hall, and was amazed that every seat was filled and there was even standing room there. The second time in New York, the same thing. Now, I had no sense of the size of this following because the following that appears in a hall to hear a speaker is only a fraction of a following that has been unable to come to that hall and hear the speaker.

So evidently, Krishnamurti's influence is very wide. And in relation to Zen, it was initially suggested to me and then thinking through and reading Krishnamurti, listening to him, I would agree with the proposition that if there is an ideology of Zen Buddhism being preached today, it is the ideology that Krishnamurti preached. Now, in Zen, there is no preaching. They say that the sitting alone, the work on cleaning one's mind, and by the work on sensing one's own existence is sufficient to change people.

Of all the Zen sayings, the one that I find most interesting is the saying: "If you see the Buddha, kill him. Destroy him."

This is a very profound statement, that if you take a man and venerate him as a god, then in that veneration all possibility of reality, of satori, of enlightenment will disappear. And so if you see Buddha, you're seeing an illusion. Get rid of it quickly. There is no Buddha, he died many, many centuries ago and he must never be venerated in that fashion.

"I WAS CHARMED THEN, THE FIRST TIME, BY THE FACT THAT THE CAR PARK CONTAINED EVERYTHING FROM ANCIENT LITTLE VOLKSWAGEN 'BUGS' TO ROLLS ROYCES."

—HOWARD FAST

EB: What do you think has been the effect, if any, of all of these years that Krishnamurti has been speaking?

HF: When I reflect on the fact that Krishnamurti said that his only reason for existence was to set man free, and I'm asked sometimes, did he do that? Well in some cases he did, and in some cases he didn't. He certainly planted seeds, and no one has any way of knowing where these seeds will go. If ten people or a hundred people or a thousand people perceived the central focus of his teaching and were able to clear their minds and to probe questions clearly and explain them and teach others what Krishnamurti taught them then certainly he has been a very important part of the process that sets men free. I think he sensed that time was very short. Either we must begin to think sensibly about things, or we are destroyed.

There is a man who teaches us to think because if we don't think properly, we would no longer exist. So, one has to say that here's a man who can in some way influence the world. How much, I don't know, but perhaps a great deal, perhaps not so much. But there will be influence there. And I always come back to my own proposition that it's better to light that one little candle than to curse the dark.[73]

Very few people have traveled as extensively as Krishnamurti did. In each country his visits, although relatively brief, perhaps several months in each region, sent down long roots and firmly took hold among those he came in contact with. He never was one of a casual list of acquaintances of those around him, but rather, was a unique and memorable focus in the lives of each.

One whose life was deeply touched was the young medical student Asha Singh, later Asha Lee after marriage to R.E. Mark Lee, now Executive Director of the Krishnamurti Foundation of America. Asha recalls a unique incident in her relationship with Krishnamurti.

ASHA LEE, M.D.

PEDIATRICIAN, OJAI, CALIFORNIA

AL: I took my mother to hear and see Krishnamurti for the first time in New Delhi when I was still a medical student. When I heard him I had a strong feeling and understanding of the truth Krishnamurti was talking about. The simplicity of it, the beauty of it touched me.

EB: What year was that, Asha?

AL: That would be 1964. That's when I started going to hear him. I never missed any of his talks. I would do my hospital work and then go to hear him at Constitution club. I went to the back door of the Pandal and slipped in, because I'd get there just before he would start to talk. I'd stay at the back, hear him, and right away leave and catch a bus to go home.

When I was traveling down south in Andhra Pradesh in 1965, I visited the school at Rishi Valley. That trip was almost a pilgrimage because I'd been hearing Krishnamurti, and then going to his place…the valley was so beautiful, untouched. There was a school in the middle of the valley with a few villages and the mountains around it, very much like Ojai; rocky and the valley nesting with hills all around. I spent a week or ten days in the valley and it was quiet and beautiful. Then I came back and did my post-graduation before going to England where I did pediatrics work. On my return to India I got married and went and lived in Rishi Valley; that was March of 1969. In November, Krishnaji came, and it was a very beautiful period for me.

"THERE WAS A SCHOOL IN THE MIDDLE OF THE [RISHI] VALLEY WITH A FEW VILLAGES AND THE MOUNTAINS AROUND IT, VERY MUCH LIKE OJAI; ROCKY AND THE VALLEY NESTING WITH HILLS ALL AROUND."
—ASHA LEE

EB: When you returned to Rishi Valley you went with the object that you were going to be living here?

AL: Yes, I was going to be living there. I became the school doctor and very soon the villagers around there discovered that I was a doctor and so they started coming for treatment. I opened a clinic for the villagers as well as for the students and staff.

The school had many gardens so I was delighted to do the flowers in his apartment when Krishnaji arrived. Early in the morning at four, or late in the afternoon after the sun had gone down I would walk through the gardens and cut the flowers so they would be fresh. If I cut them at night, I would put them in buckets of water to keep until the morning. My object was to go to his apartment before Krishnaji would wake up and delight him with fresh flowers. I would tiptoe up the steps with these buckets of flowers, collect the vases of old flowers from the rooms of the apartment and bring them to a doorway of the west facing veranda. There was enough early morning light so I wouldn't have to turn on a light. I would sit in the doorway and arrange the flowers. I would set them all around in different parts of the rooms, and then return to our cottage, which was next door.

E B: Did Krishnamurti know that you were doing this?

A L: I had also gone later to leave letter paper and pencils there and had taken juice up to the apartment. Well, what happened after two or three days was that when I walked in they were all having breakfast and the Principal, Dr. Balasundaram said, "Come in and join us for breakfast." I did, and he told Krishnaji, "This is Asha, and she is the one who is doing the flowers and brings the juice in the mornings." So he realized that it was me doing the flowers.

I don't know whether the incident I am going to tell you about was before or after that breakfast. One of those mornings when I was arranging the flowers I heard, as if from the bedroom (which was at the back of the big room where I was arranging the flowers) I heard sounds as if someone was getting up, so I became very quiet. Realizing that that was Krishnaji's bedroom, and maybe he was getting up and wouldn't know I was there, I didn't want to startle or disturb him, so I became very quiet and stopped what I was doing. Then I heard the wooden slippers that he wore in India; the Kharow which has a little knob that goes between the big toe and the rest of the toes. When you walk with those wooden slippers, you can hear the wood clapping on the floor. I heard the clap of his steps going towards the bathroom. I said to myself, "Yes, now he'll go back to bed." But then he walked on and went through the next room, which was like a reception room where he had meetings and discussions. He went through that room and then came across the veranda in front of the living room on the eastern side of the apartment where I sat with the flowers all around me. I shrank from the lighted area into the shadowed part of the doorway so that I wouldn't startle him. I sat quietly as he passed on his way to the dining room.

What I saw was amazing because it wasn't the figure of Krishnaji who passed by. It was an unusually tall luminescent figure that passed. He looked like the figure of the Buddha, with the same kind of stature. This figure went towards the kitchen and then came back again in a few moments. This time, as he passed the living room door, he stopped and turned and smiled, as if saying, "I know you're there." I just sat there absolutely still. I couldn't understand this at all. There was no fear, it was extraordinary. It was something very beautiful.

E B: It was Krishnamurti?

A L: Well, it was Krishnamurti, because that was his bedroom. He had come from there, he walked through his bathroom, across the veranda to the dining room, kitchen, and then back again. There was no one else in that apartment.

EB: Could you describe in what way he appeared to be different?

AL: Krishnaji is a very slender, delicate, small-statured person. This figure was at least twice his height and bigger. It was as if there was a light within the body. The face was very peaceful and compassionate and there seemed to be something over the head. Because I have seen paintings from Ajanta and Ellora and other places it reminded me of the Buddha with that head and figure. I sat there very still for some time, then I picked up my things very quickly and quietly went down the stairs. I was shaking all the way. I told my husband, Mark, what I had seen and I never told anyone else about it because it was something so sacred that I didn't want to belittle it by talking about it. The only other person I did tell, until now, was Krishnaji before he died. I went to see him. I requested to see him privately, as I did every year. It was a very poignant question in my mind. I said, "Krishnaji, I

want to ask you about something that I saw. I'm not a superstitious kind of person, I don't usually see visions, even if I see something or if I hear something in the dark I go and check it out; I'm related to fact and reality." I explained to him how I was in his apartment in those early years, soon after I had gotten married and gone to Rishi Valley, and how I was sitting over there and what I had seen. He sat with his hands folded and his head bowed. After I had finished he looked up and said, "You saw something. Why do you question it?" I said, "I'm not questioning it because I did see it, but I'm just trying to understand it. I thought maybe talking with you would explain it." He said, "You saw it, there is no other explanation." We sat very quietly while he held my hand and then I came away.

That occurrence in the first year that I was at Rishi Valley established in me a relationship with Krishnaji. There was something beyond the ordinary that was present that morning. When I attended his talks I felt there was the presence of something extraordinary and I am sure many other people felt it as well.

EB: Was it more of a sensation, or a feeling that you had, or did you actually see or perceive anything different about his stature or his appearance?

A L : I never saw what I saw in Rishi Valley again, but often I would feel as if there was the presence of something that wasn't of my level, there was something extraordinary that would come in.

E B : Have you ever had anything else of that kind before or after?

A L : No, because I was not relating to temples, or sitting and singing and chanting. I was relating to my studies, I was very reality-based. That's why I wanted to talk to Krishnaji because I couldn't relate it to my reality base.

E B : But he didn't actually explain it.

A L : He didn't explain it, he just said that you've seen something, and if you see something, why do you need to question what you see, that it is a reality as well.

E B : Was there any relationship between what you saw and Krishnamurti's teachings?

A L : To me, his teachings represent truth, a very basic truth that is related to life and the world, the rhythm of it, a timelessness. Maybe something of that timelessness was touched, and that's what I saw.[74]

Krishnamurti continued to be questioned on all facets of the human condition. The following question was of a kind that was frequently asked.

QUESTION: I AM FULL OF HATE. WILL YOU PLEASE TEACH ME HOW TO LOVE?

No one can teach you how to love. If people could be taught how to love, the world problem would be very simple, would it not? If we could learn how to love from a book as we learn mathematics, this would be a marvelous world; there would be no hate, no exploitation, no wars, no division of rich and poor, and we would all be really friendly with each other. But love is not so easily come by. It is easy to hate, and hate brings people together after a fashion; it creates all kinds of fantasies, it brings about various types of co-operation, as in war. But love is much more difficult. You cannot learn how to love, but what you can do is to observe hate and put it gently aside. Don't battle against hate, don't say how terrible it is to hate people, but see hate for what it is and let it drop away; brush it aside, it is not important. What is important is not to let hate take root in your mind. Do you understand? Your mind is like rich soil, and if given sufficient time any problem that comes along takes root like a weed, and then you have the trouble of pulling it out; but if you do not give the problem sufficient time to take root, then it has no place to grow and it will wither away. If you encourage hate, give it time to take root, to grow, to mature, it becomes an enormous problem. But if each time hate arises you let it go by, then you will find that your mind becomes very sensitive without being sentimental; therefore it will know love.

The mind can pursue sensations, desires, but it cannot pursue love. Love must come to the mind. And, when once love is there, it has no division as sensuous and divine: it is love. That is the extraordinary thing about love: it is the only quality that brings a total comprehension of the whole of existence.[75]

—*THINK ON THESE THINGS, 1964*

As was said earlier in this book, Krishnamurti was meticulous in all aspects of his life, including the physical side. Perhaps knowing that his body was frail and not a strong one, he devoted time each day to the practice of yoga. It was in this connection that he came to know Desikachar, then a young yoga teacher, now the world renowned yoga master.

T. K. V. DESIKACHAR

YOGA MASTER, MADRAS, INDIA

I first became aware of Krishnaji in a letter my uncle B.K.S. Iyengar (renowned yoga teacher) wrote to my father from Switzerland. For my uncle, it was a great event when Krishnaji attended his Asana Demonstration in Saanen. My father showed me the letter, but the information had little impact on me.

Eventually, however, events brought me very close to Krishnaji. We were to meet year after year, travel together, share thoughts, and chat about mutual friends and all despite, or perhaps because of, the very traditional student teacher relationship which I maintained with my father the great yoga master and philosopher T. Krishnamacharya.

How this came about I will share with you.

In December of 1965, Alain Naudé, the Secretary to J. Krishnamurti, called on my father at our small flat in Gopalauram, Madras. He had a message from Krishnaji. It was a request for my father to visit his residence and demonstrate to Krishnaji how asanas and pranayams (yoga postures and breath control) should be practiced. My father readily agreed. On the appointed day, Alain Naudé came to take him to Vasanta Vihar. My father asked my brother, Shribhashyam, and me to join him.

"HE TAUGHT SO MUCH BY HIS EXAMPLE...CLEANLINESS, PUNCTUALITY, DIGNITY OF LABOR, RESPECT FOR OTHERS, HUMILITY BEFORE THE TEACHER WHATEVER HIS STATURE OR AGE, KEENNESS TO LEARN THOROUGHLY, CONSIDERATION FOR OTHER CULTURES."

—T.K.V. DESIKACHAR

When we arrived, Krishnaji came out with folded hands and thanked my father profusely for the visit. My first recollection of Krishnaji is of a gentle, elderly person with a long, flowing shirt and very straight back. He took Krishnamacharya's hand and led us into his room. Soon he expressed his wish to see how we practiced yoga.

On my father's instruction, my brother and I began the demonstration of yoga postures. After some thirty minutes of observation, Krishnaji enthusiastically requested of my father, "Sir, I want to learn asanas from you, but you should not be disturbed. Can you send one of your sons?" I translated this request to my father. My father assured Krishnaji that he would arrange something soon.

This first visit in December of 1965 started an association with Krishnaji which was terminated only by his recent death.

The following day when Alain Naudé again called, my father directed me to go to Krishnaji, insisting I should show the greatest respect.

When I went to his residence, Vasanta Vihar, there he was on the porch with open arms to welcome me. As he led me to his room, he enquired affectionately about my father as if they had known one another for ages. Before beginning our first lesson I expressed a desire to see Krishnaji's yoga practice. He was ready in no time. In spite of his sixty-nine years, the postures he demonstrated were of the most advanced nature—all the variations of headstand, shoulder stand, hand balance, and many difficult back arches. And although his frame was small and the postures varied and stupefying, his chest was as tight as a barrel. I also

You are the teacher

and the taught and

the teaching.

—1977

noticed that his breath was restricted and panting, his hands trembled, his neck was like granite, and his eyes sometimes rolled with tears. Yet his enthusiasm never flagged.

I explained to Krishnaji that he must practice postures and breathing exercises that could reduce these problems, and certainly not ones that would increase them. He simply accepted my advice and assured me that he was there to learn whatever I would teach. He also gave me more information about his health. It was obvious that he needed special attention and clear, too, that I needed guidance in these matters. I took leave, confessing that I would ask my father for direction. Krishnaji was pleased. We agreed to meet the following day.

I discussed Krishnaji's yoga practice and health problems with my father. He felt that Krishnaji should do very simple postures and breathing regimens. He gave me clear instructions, some of which were so unique to my experience that I was taken aback. For example, he wanted me to teach Krishnaji a pose with his legs raised against the wall. Here he should remain doing deep breathing. No more head stand! His neck stiffness was to be corrected by the most simple of head movements. I faithfully carried out my father's instructions. Krishnaji was so keen to learn that I saw him every day, some days more than once. I was amazed at his remarkable ability to adjust to this new instruction, so contrary was it to the instruction which he had previously received and practiced. In a few weeks, there was no trace of previous training.

His practice was so regular and punctual that it amazed me. Every day he

would be on the porch, right on the dot, to receive me. His place of practice was immaculate. Everything was in its place, right down to his pencil and magazine. He was always eager to understand the significance of what was taught him. Thanks to his probing questions, I was forced to learn more and more about yoga from my teacher. He often would ask me, "What is Yoga? What is Yoga?" And the only answer that seemed to have satisfied him was when I defined it as Shanti. *["Peace" is the equivalent English word.]*

His attitude towards me was exactly as a student towards his teacher. He would not sit before I did. He would lead me into his room. He would never let me help him to arrange the carpet for his practice. It was not easy for me, in my twenty-seventh year, to let this happen—especially when the student was sixty-nine and J. Krishnamurti—but I had no choice.

His health began to show signs of improvement. When he left Madras for the school at Rishi Valley, he invited me to join him. Later he invited me to Saanen, Switzerland. He insisted that I must go there to continue our classes and to teach some of his friends. I assured him that I must first consult with my teacher in Madras and would respond.

Back in Madras my father advised me to accept the invitation. But I felt that first my uncle, Shri B.K.S. Iyengar, who for many years had taught both Krishnaji and other friends of Krishnaji's in Saanen, must approve this arrangement. I wrote to Krishnaji accordingly.

Krishnaji met with my uncle in Bombay and I soon received a positive letter. So while hesitant, I was left with no choice but to accept Krishnaji's invitation.

In June 1966, I went to Saanen, where I stayed with Krishnaji in Chalet Tannegg. In a few weeks, my uncle arrived to give his classes. He also stayed in the chalet.

Here I was, teaching Krishnaji, while in the same chalet my uncle was teaching his students. And it was here just the previous year that it was he teaching Krishnaji. The potential for tension was real, yet Krishnaji did everything possible to make me at ease in spite of the delicate situation. Thanks to his care my first visit to Europe came off well and nothing happened to strain my relationship with my uncle, with whom I am still on the best of terms.

Krishnaji introduced me to so many distinguished visitors. He showed me some of the best places in Switzerland. He himself would drive his Mercedes and talk about the special features of the car. In all the conversations I found that he was so well informed about different parts of the world and various customs of the West.

In fact, my first lessons on western table manners came from him: "Don't rest the elbows on the table. Use the left hand for the fork. Don't spread your elbows. Don't take your mouth to the plate. Wait for the second helping." He also introduced me to the value of eating fruit first, why salads must precede cooked food, what nuts were best, how to crack Brazil nuts. He was so meticulous about different household chores. He used to clean the bathroom himself. I used to see him, many times, cleaning the bathroom, and he would say, "One should leave it as clean as it was before it was used." His bits of advice when dealing with people and situations were unequivocal:

"Don't be another monkey."

"Be yourself."

"Watch the other fool" [when driving a car].

He insisted on taking me to the best places when we dined out. What taste! What concern for the guest. He had his secretary at my disposal for anything I needed during my visit.

Often he would take me for walks. On these walks he would urge me to study, to learn everything my father had to teach. He even offered me a scholarship so that necessity would not keep me from this study, and that was when he himself had financial problems. One day he told me, "Sir, if necessary, I will sell my shirt and send you money, but please study; you must."

The following year, when Krishnaji returned to Madras, I phoned Vasanta Vihar for an appointment. The gentleman who received my call did not know me. He replied curtly, "You cannot see Krishnaji. Maybe after a few weeks, not now." I responded, "Sir, it is not so much that it is I who seek to see Krishnaji. It is perhaps Krishnaji who would see me." He was surprised, "What is your name?" I gave him my name. He tersely told me, "Wait." In a few seconds he came back. "Excuse me. Krishnaji is on his way to speak to you." When Krishnaji arrived he *was so apologetic, even though I made no mention of this interchange.*

Krishnaji expressed a wish to see my father. He came to our small flat in Mandaveli. He sat on the bare floor facing my father. Even though my father is not conversant in English, he made sure that my father got the following message: "Sir, please teach your son Desikachar everything you know."

Every year, for nearly ten years, I gave lessons to Krishnaji—sometimes in England, sometimes in Switzerland, often in Madras. Every time I saw him he was a "fresh" student ready to learn something new. I always had the privilege of visiting him whenever I wished. However, after our formal lessons ceased, I did not see him for several years because I did not want to disturb him.

In 1984, we met after a break of two years. I was surprised when he challenged me, "Why have we not met these years? Maybe you have become a big shot."

In January 1985 we met again. He invited me for lunch. I suggested that it was I who should invite him. "Maybe I can offer a meal of Vedic Chant?" He was quick in response, "Sir, do it. Do it now." I suggested bringing a small group to make it more interesting.

We did the chant. He sat attentively through ninety minutes, sometimes chanting with us. At the end of the session, he asked for a specific piece, it was a prayer to Krishna, from Mukun-da Mala.

Last January 1986 I met with him a few days before his sudden departure to the United States. He was his same old self. He enquired about my family. He wanted me to take his respects to my father. Spontaneously I made a totally uncharacteristic request, "Sir, I ask for your blessings." He replied, "No, sir, we are friends."

That was the last message he gave me.

Krishnaji never accepted the role of "guru," but those like me who had the opportunity to teach him something, know he was the perfect example of the student. I wonder whether he wanted us to go and do likewise before even seeking a teacher? It is said, "The teacher appears only to the earnest student."

I don't pretend to know what Krishnaji taught by the word, but he taught so much by his example…cleanliness, punctuality, dignity of labor, respect for others, humility before the teacher whatever his stature or age, keenness to learn thoroughly, consideration for other cultures.

Often it is said that he was not aware of the common man's problems. But his concern for the Indians, the poor Indians, who are exploited by everyone, was overflowing. He was sad when religion exploited the poor. He used to share all those feelings of sadness which was evident in his eyes.

Krishnaji is no more. I, for one, can say he never showed less concern for me than for those who were associated with his following. He was always warning, "Sir, don't become a guru, don't exploit, don't become rich."

Thank you Krishnaji. I will remember you and your advice.

⌐

To see is to act. And if one does not see very clearly, naturally all action becomes confused. And we go to somebody else to tell us what to do, because we cannot see for ourselves what to do…. Nobody can help another to see clearly….Therefore, your responsibility in listening becomes very significant because you have to find out if it is possible to change radically so that we live a totally different kind of life.

—MADRAS, 1965

Alan Rowlands is a distinguished pianist and has been a piano teacher for many years at Brockwood Park School. He tells of the beginning of his association with the school and also of the lighter side of Krishnamurti.

ALAN ROWLANDS

CONCERT PIANIST AND TEACHER, LONDON, ENGLAND

"I WALKED OUT [OF KRISHNAMURTI'S TALK] ALMOST IN A DAZE, WITHOUT TALKING TO ANYBODY, FOR I THINK I REALIZED EVEN THEN THAT THAT HOUR WAS PROBABLY ONE OF THE MOST IMPORTANT EXPERIENCES OF MY LIFE."

—ALAN ROWLANDS

BROCKWOOD PARK EDUCATION CENTER MEETING (ABOVE) AND KITCHEN GARDEN, HAMPSHIRE, ENGLAND (BELOW).

I had never heard Krishnamurti, but something made me go to his talk. It was in Friends' House, Euston Road (May 10, 1966), and I found no sign outside to explain who Krishnamurti was, or what was going to happen. Inside I found a hall full of peculiarly silent people and a single chair on the platform with a microphone in front of it. I thought probably a chairman would come on to introduce him, but that didn't happen. At exactly seven o'clock a small man came on to the platform, sat down and began to speak, and at eight o'clock he went off again.

I walked out almost in a daze, without talking to anybody, for I think I realized even then that that hour was probably one of the most important experiences of my life. From the moment he started speaking, I felt personally addressed and the talk seemed directed at exactly the state of mind I was in at that time. He gave an extraordinary impression of authority (in the sense of someone who knew what he was talking about) and the whole experience carried a strange feeling of completeness, which I didn't want to touch.

(I remember I had been to hear Billy Graham the same week. There was a tremendous build-up—introductory speakers, bands, choirs, and then the great man himself. He wrung our hearts, but when he invited people to walk forward for Christ, I walked the other way. And then the total contrast of that quiet talk in the Euston Road!)

The next year, 1967, I heard about the Saanen gathering through a newspaper advertisement and went. Dorothy Simmons was there, but I didn't meet her until the Wimbledon talks of 1969, when all who were interested in Brockwood were invited to go and talk to her at a table in the foyer. This I did, rather nervously. Dorothy was very open, and invited me to visit Brockwood Park and help to get the place ready, which I did regularly that year, meeting Krishnaji for the first time when he arrived in May.

Later that year she asked me if I would do some piano teaching on a visiting basis. I started in September 1970 and have been doing it ever since—now twenty-three years! We first had a borrowed piano in the main sitting-room until, through the College, I managed to get the present Brockwood grand (1904) for £200.

In those early days of 1969, when Alan Hooker was doing the cooking, we all ate round the big table in the kitchen. Krishnaji would sometimes become conversational during or after a meal.

He liked telling jokes sometimes and I thought one of the best was of the Three Wise Men visiting the Holy Child at Bethlehem. After making his obeisances, one of them straightened up and hit his head on a beam. "Jesus Christ!" he exclaimed. "Oh, that's a nice name," said Mary. "We were thinking of calling him Fred."

K was shy by nature and mentioned this in an interview I had with him in 1970. I had been trying to lay out some problems that were bothering me, but he wouldn't discuss any of them in detail and just said, "Can't you let all this drop away?" A little later he himself introduced the topic of shyness (which I had not mentioned) and spoke of the experience of going into a room full of people and how one could let them do the talking—they were just like oneself, confused and looking for the answer. He said, "Let the other parts of yourself tell their story." This reference to others as "the other parts of yourself" made a profound impression on me.

Other things he said on that occasion which have remained with me are, "just watch," "see what happens," and "you can't change those clouds."

Some of the meetings with staff in those days were very intense. At one he put the question, "What is the most important thing in your life?" with great urgency. We tried to answer in various ways, both idealistic and actual, but nothing satisfied him. Least of all would he tolerate anything he had said before, but he kept on putting the question. Finally, after about an hour, he said, "I wonder if it would help if I told you what it is for me?" He seemed to hesitate, and then said, "To be nothing, to be absolutely nothing."

Alan Hooker was living in Columbus, Ohio and traveling frequently as a Theosophical lecturer when he came in touch with Krishnamurti's writings in 1945. That was the beginning of a commitment which lasted until Alan's death in 1993.

After moving to Ojai in the late 1940s he was asked to look after feeding and housing people for the Ojai camps. He also continued cooking at Saanen and Brockwood for many years.

Some time earlier he and his wife, Helen, had opened a garden restaurant, The Ranch House, in Ojai, California, which featured an unusual cuisine of fresh vegetables and herbs. He added poultry, fish and meats to the menu, as at that time there were not enough vegetarians to support the restaurant. Alan Hooker has been called "The Godfather of California cuisine."

"I NEVER FELT I KNEW THE MAN; BECAUSE, TO ME THERE WAS THE QUALITY OF NOTHING BEING THERE...."

—ALAN HOOKER

ALAN HOOKER

RESTAURANTEUR, OJAI, CALIFORNIA

Although I used to help prepare meals for Krishnamurti—and this went on many, many months and many years—I never felt I knew the man; because, to me there was the quality of nothing being there; there was no person that I could meet as you meet other people with their habits and their likes and dislikes. Here was a man who seemed to be completely free of all that as far as I could see and there was no one to meet, but it was a privilege to sit at the table and listen to him talk with people who would come. In my life, I can't imagine anything quite so marvelous as those privileged luncheons with him.

I think the most important contribution that Krishnamurti made to the thinking person on this planet is that he has caused us to investigate the nature of belief, because most religions are founded on belief and he explodes the whole thing as merely a process of thinking. He seems to be one of the first people who has said this outside of, perhaps, Buddha and it's rather startling and shocking and disconcerting to people who are rooted in belief.

Earlier in this book, Ingram Smith wrote of an event which took place in Colombo, Sri Lanka. Here is another anecdote which took place in Sydney:

In 1955 at Spencer English's house in Sydney, Australia six of us were seated at dinner with Krishnaji. As we were finishing the meal a violent storm erupted, there was lots of lightening—a real November, late spring turbulence in the southern hemisphere. We stopped talking to watch. Krishnamurti pushed back his chair, and without a word walked out onto the open patio and began to dance in the rain, joyously leaping in the midst of that tremendous lightening and thunder storm. How beautiful to watch a man dancing spontaneously, wildly, and gracefully in the midst of nature's violence!

Understanding is now, not tomorrow. When you are interested in something, you do it instantaneously, there is immediate understanding, immediate transformation. If you do not change now, you will never change because the change that takes place tomorrow is merely a modification, it is not transformation. Transformation can only take place immediately; the revolution is now, not tomorrow.

—BOMBAY TALK, 1948

When we are aware of "what is," we want to transform it, and there begins sorrow. Because with the ending of sorrow is the beginning of wisdom, and the ending of sorrow is the understanding of "what is."

—OJAI TALK, 1966

Krishnamurti had seen Rajagopal only periodically over the last several years, but still, reconciliation seemed impossible. Requests for financial statements were refused. Krishnamurti asked to be reinstated on the board of Krishnamurti Writings, Inc., or KWInc. as it was called. He felt that he should have some access and control over his own writings as well as knowledge of financial matters. He had been carefully kept in the dark in all of these things. It was, in part, his own fault as he had shown little interest in the business or administrative side of the work. Krishnamurti was aware, however, that large sums of money had been given to support his work, but had no knowledge of how much or where this money actually was.

The growing strength of the Saanen, Switzerland gatherings was seen as a supposed threat to the work that was nominally headquartered in Ojai, California. However, in July 1964, $50,000 was reluctantly given to purchase land on which the Saanen gatherings were held, with the understanding that the land revert to KWInc. upon Krishnamurti's death.

The redoubtable Doris Pratt wrote Rajagopal suggesting that the Saanen Committee pay all of Krishnamurti's travel expenses, etc., while in Europe and that KWInc. cover expenses connected with travel to India and the United States. Krishnamurti never has had any money of his own except for the yearly £500 left to him in 1913 by the American, Mary Dodge.

As the situation reached a crisis point, Krishnamurti knew he had an obligation to those whose funds were given to support his work. Ethically, he felt responsible to them.

In July 1968 he broke completely with his long-time associate and severed his relationship with Krishnamurti Writings, Inc. He revoked the 1955 document, which gave over his copyrights, and also denied permission to have Rajagopal draw any new contracts.

A public statement was made on July 7, 1968 to thousands at the Saanen gathering.

Krishnamurti wishes it to be known that he has completely

disassociated himself from Krishnamurti Writings, Inc. of Ojai,

California. He hopes that as a result of this public announcement

those who wish to be associated with his work and teachings will give

their support only to the new international Krishnamurti Foundation

Trust, England, whose activities will include a school. The deed

which establishes the Foundation insures that Krishnamurti's

intentions will be respected.

—SAANEN TALK, 1968

The new entity, the Krishnamurti Foundation Trust, Ltd., which saw to the publication of books, as well as foreign translations of those books and managed his speaking engagements etc. A network of European Committees was also formed which helped with the distribution of books in their own countries.

In the following year, 1969, the Krishnamurti Foundation of America was constituted and in 1970 the Krishnamurti Foundation of India. Sometime later a lawsuit was reluctantly begun to reclaim donated funds and the Ojai lands. Erna Lilliefelt, who had first heard Krishnamurti speak in India in 1952, joined the Foundation. She and her husband Theodor were original Trustors of the Krishnamurti Foundation of America. Erna retired from her work for the Foundation in 1994 after almost thirty years of service. She speaks of the formative days of the their work.

E R N A   L I L L I E F E L T

BUSINESSWOMAN, OJAI, CALIFORNIA AND ORIGINAL TRUSTEE
OF THE KRISHNAMURTI FOUNDATION OF AMERICA

"THE PURPOSE OF THE
FOUNDATION WAS TO
DISSEMINATE THE
KRISHNAMURTI TEACHINGS.
THERE HAD BEEN A NEW
ORGANIZATION, STARTED IN
ENGLAND SOME MONTHS
PREVIOUSLY....THE PURPOSE
WAS TO...LET PEOPLE KNOW
WHERE KRISHNAMURTI WOULD
BE SPEAKING AND TO ORGANIZE
THE TALKS IN THE UNITED
STATES."

—ERNA LILLIEFELT

EB: When Rajagopal removed himself, who took over to help arrange the talks?

E L : There was a branch organization there operated by Doris Pratt and Mary Cadogan. Doris Pratt, in those days, organized talks in England and then I think the talks developed in Saanen with the help of Mrs. Scaravelli, who had a chalet in Gstaad. When Krishnamurti visited there, people suggested he give some talks, and that's how the Saanen talks started. In India the talks were organized by Indian friends.

EB: How did Krishnamurti manage financially during that period?

E L : People helped him. English friends asked for funds from donors to pay for his trips and others also helped.

EB: How would you describe the formation of the current Krishnamurti Foundation of America?

E L : I wrote a document on that called the *KFA History*. It is in the archives and available at the KFA (Krishnamurti Foundation of America) library. Before we actually filed the lawsuit there were two or three years during which we tried to come to some settlement agreement. As soon as Krishnamurti arrived in Malibu in 1968 he asked Theo and me to meet him. He felt it was important to start a new organization and get going in the U.S. again. So the KFA was founded.

EB: When you started the KFA, who were the trustees?

E L : There were four trustors, each of whom put up $500 to start the trust. They were Theo Lilliefelt, Ruth Tettemer, Mary Zimbalist, and Krishnamurti. The original trustees were the same people plus Alain Naudé and myself—Erna Lilliefelt.

EB: What were your intentions as you set up this foundation?

E L : The purpose of the foundation was to disseminate the Krishnamurti teachings. There had been a new organization, started in England some months previously, that was the Krishnamurti Foundation Trust, Ltd. The purpose was to build up a mailing list and let people know where Krishnamurti would be speaking and to organize the talks in the United States, all of which we did. He had no place to speak in Ojai at that point because the Oak Grove was closed to him, so he spoke in Santa Monica, in San Francisco, and in New York. It grew from there.

EB: During that whole period the law suit continued?

EL: Yes, the activities with regard to the claims against Krishnamurti Writings, Inc. and Rajagopal continued until 1975, when we settled through the courts. At that time we were able to get back the property, the Oak Grove and the property at Meiners Oaks, which enabled the Oak Grove School to start. We also recovered the property at Arya Vihara where Krishnamurti could stay again and could come to Ojai.

EB: Over those years you had an opportunity to see Krishnamurti under all kinds of circumstances. What was your reaction, to Krishnamurti the man and the teaching?

EL: I never separated the two: the man and the teaching. They were his teachings. When he spoke, he spoke the teachings. When he wasn't speaking, our contacts with him when he was here dealt with the work of the Foundation and the School, our plans and what we were going to do. We didn't have philosophical discussions unless he had small group meetings especially arranged for that.

EB: You saw people around Krishnamurti, attending the talks over the years. He had an affect on people and he must have been aware of it, how did he react to that?

EL: He wasn't a man that reacted, if you know what I mean.

EB: One saw in India and elsewhere an intense adulation, but he would tend, to my observation, to put it off.

EL: That's what I mean by not reacting. I think that was somewhat difficult for him, I don't think he responded positively to adulation and that sort of thing. I feel that people who responded in that manner missed the point of his talks.

EB: Did Krishnamurti feel that he had a mission?

EL: Whether "mission" is the word or not, the term teachings was his own term and I think that he obviously had an educational mission if you want to use that word. He had something to say that I think was helpful to human beings and I think that had a great effect on people.

EB: What would you say is Krishnamurti's legacy?

EL: I think what he said then is just as effective now because it's so true, it's so real. He never varied in what he said, he may have said the same thing in many many different ways but it was always the same message. He evolved it, he expanded it, went on with it, but it wasn't different.

EB: How did Krishnamurti affect your own life?

"I NEVER SEPARATED THE TWO: THE MAN AND THE TEACHING. THEY WERE HIS TEACHINGS. WHEN HE SPOKE, HE SPOKE THE TEACHINGS."

—ERNA LILLIEFELT

EL: It was as if suddenly there was a door closed and another door opened. I can't say any more than that. But I never felt dependant on him in any way. It's true that we got involved in the law suit but that was for a specific reason. When I left India after I'd heard him for the first time I didn't know if I'd ever hear him again. It never occurred to me that I would follow him around and go to other talks. I felt that now I had stopped searching and was on my own. He gave me something that enabled me to face life on my own without looking to anybody for psychological advice, for counsel or comfort or answers.

EB: What is the heart of his teaching? When you look back at his denial of authority going back to 1929, to stand on your own has been a constant theme.

EL: I think that's his great message. How we can live as individuals without psychological dependence. It's such an exciting message.

EB: Would you say that your move from Catholicism to Theosophy, which you spoke of earlier, was part of the same movement? You moved away from those forms, after hearing what Krishnamurti had to say. Could the 1929 statement free people from any kind of religious dependency?

EL: Yes from dogmatic religious or psychological dependency.

EB: K was interested in starting a new organization, yet he constantly spoke against organizations, what is the difference?

EL: The Krishnamurti Foundation is not a spiritual organization. It was founded just to make what he was saying available, to make it possible for him to speak. To organize a talk in New York or Boston; it had nothing to do with the spiritual aspect of it. What he said may be considered spiritual depending on how you define that word.

EB: Did Krishnamurti regard himself as a religious figure?

EL: That's hard for me to say. You'd have to define religion or religious figure. I don't think I can answer that for him. He could not possibly have done what he has done without this tremendous energy, to speak what he felt apparently was a message for the benefit of people, to have them see something rather than to be blinded by their conditioning and the things they had heard for generations.

EB: When you speak about Krishnamurti's energy, which was quite noticeable, did he ever describe what the source of that energy was?

E L : I don't think I can say that he ever described it. It was there. He talks about it a great deal in his writings, this energy being there and there's no doubt at times that he felt it was something other than himself. I don't want to get into a mystical discussion, but there's no doubt that that energy came to him or was with him almost constantly.

EB: Do you think that Krishnamurti had a particular feeling about Ojai?

E L : I think he did have a special feeling because it went back so far. But I always felt Krishnamurti was a very impersonal person; he didn't have the same sentimental reactions to people or places. I think he had great compassion and sensitivity but I wouldn't say there was anything sentimental about him.[76]

Krishnamurti remained aloof from the atmosphere of legal charges and counter-charges. If questions were put to him he would respond as needed, but there was never any emotional involvement or personal animosity.

However, the Krishnamurti Foundation Trust in England felt it necessary to issue a clarifying statement to its readership in its *Bulletin #3*, summer 1969 issue. It reads as follows:

Many people have written expressing concern over Krishnamurti's disassociation from Krishnamurti Writings, Inc., and asking why this has happened. Krishnamurti feels that the public should be informed, because they have for the past forty years supported his work and made substantial contributions to Krishnamurti Writings, Inc., on his account.

For the past ten years Krishnamurti has repeatedly asked Mr. Rajagopal, the President of Krishnamurti Writings, Inc., to inform and consult him about its policy and affairs. Mr. Rajagopal has consistently refused to do so and denied Krishnamurti access to his own manuscripts and archives in the Krishnamurti

Writings, Inc. In addition Krishnamurti recently learned that through the years changes were made in Krishnamurti Writings, Inc. excluding him from all say in its affairs. Krishnamurti tried many times to settle matters amicably with Mr. Rajagopal and members of the Board of KWInc., but to no avail.

He very much regrets that it has been necessary to appeal for funds all over again, but the money given to Krishnamurti Writings, Inc. for his work is at present tied up in that organization and is not at his disposal.

Every precaution has been taken in the formation of Krishnamurti Foundation Trust and the Krishnamurti Foundation of America to insure that a similar problem will not occur in the future.[77]

There were some aspects of Krishnamurti's life that he rarely spoke about. However, on a few occasions he told of healing powers.

Giddu Narayanan had been a teacher for many years at the Rishi Valley School, later becoming its principal. He has now moved on to the Valley School at Bangalore, in a similar capacity, where he remains today.

GIDDU NARAYANAN

EDUCATOR, THE VALLEY SCHOOL, BANGALORE, INDIA

EB: You told a story in which Krishnamurti recounted what was called a miracle. Would you tell us about that?

GN: Years ago I was walking with Krishnaji on the beach at Madras. This was around 1959. As we walked along, I asked him about miracles and what he thought of it. He said, "I will tell you an anecdote." He said a husband had come and wanted Krishnaji to help his wife. Her leg was in serious condition after a fracture and there was some kind of flesh growing between two joints and it couldn't be operated on and there was a need for amputation of the leg at the knee. So Krishna said, "What can I do? If you want, you can bring your wife." So next day the wife was brought in the office room and she was carried on a stretcher and as she was coming along, Krishnaji came out of his room and the lady saw Krishnaji and their eyes met and she got up and walked away. This is the anecdote. Krishnaji turned around to me and said, "Old boy, I thought they were pulling my leg." So I kept quiet. I thought probably it was a joke. Then he said, after a pause, "Next day, in the morning, the daughter came along with a garland and said, "Do you know what you have done to my mother? It's a miracle." There was a great sense of humor in this. So I asked Krishnaji, "Is it because the woman had faith in you?" He said, "No, this was not the reason." "Then, how did it happen?" I asked. He said, "Somewhere, something clicks." So I asked him again, "What is it that clicks?" He said, "Energy—energy passes." So that was the end of the conversation. Krishnaji was very modest about us talking about his healing powers. But he made a very interesting comment. he said, "Healing the body is a simple matter. A good doctor can do it. But healing the mind is far more profound and greater. To heal the mind of sorrow and fear and

"KRISHNAJI WAS VERY MODEST ABOUT TALKING ABOUT HIS HEALING POWERS....HE SAID, 'HEALING THE BODY IS A SIMPLE MATTER. A GOOD DOCTOR CAN DO IT. BUT HEALING THE MIND IS FAR MORE PROFOUND AND GREATER. TO HEAL THE MIND OF SORROW AND FEAR AND LONELINESS, REQUIRES GREAT ATTENTION AND DEPTH.'"

—GIDDU NARAYANAN

loneliness, requires great attention and depth." So, Krishnaji didn't want his friend to talk about his healing powers because that was not his function. His main mission, if it could be called a mission, was to heal the mind. And this comes out very clearly because the main purpose of his teaching is to set man unconditionally free.

EB: You said that Krishnaji communicated more through silence, perhaps, than through words. How do you explain that?

GN: Krishnaji was a very great exponent of dialogue, through words and refinement of communication, but one had to know him, personally, to understand the nature of quietness, because if you went for a walk with him, it was very difficult for you to ask any questions. You experienced a quality of silence, beauty and compassion, and it's difficult to isolate one from the other; inquiry, silence and observation go together and you could see the embodiment of these qualities in Krishnamurti in the way he spoke and the way he lived.[78]

D URING THE 1970S, Krishnamurti returned again to India after an absence of eighteen months and embarked on the usual round of talks, dialogues and conferences. Because of a legal dispute as to the ownership of Vasanta Vihar at Madras resulting from the Rajagopal case, he was unable to stay there, as he had in past years. Ongoing discussions with the Assistant Attorney General of California and the other party still had not seen a resolution. Rajagopal was not interested in settlement.

In March 1970, Krishnamurti spoke at the Santa Monica Civic Auditorium which holds three-thousand people and hundreds had to be turned away. There were always some who left part way through the talks, offended by some particularly challenging observation on nationalism, religion or the many other things we hold dear. This would happen inevitably in whatever country he was in, whether in India with its deeply rooted and traditional ways, or Europe at the international Saanen gatherings or in the United States, where a rising tide of fundamentalism brought irritable, peckish responses to some of the talks.

One orientation that seemed to be above these narrow interpretations was the psychotherapeutic group so much in vogue in the fifties, sixties and seventies.

David Shainberg was a distinguished member of this psychotherapeutic group. Dean of the Specialty Training Program in Psychoanalytic Medicine at the Postgraduate Center for Mental Health in New York, author of *The Transforming Self* and numerous professional papers, he engaged in many extended dialogues with Krishnamurti, some of which were video taped. *The Transformation of Man* series with Krishnamurti, Professor David Bohm and Dr. Shainberg has been especially noted.

In this article written for the summer bulletin of the Krishnamurti Foundation, he writes of this important meeting.

In yourself lies the whole world, and if you know how to look and learn, then the door is there and the key is in your hand. Nobody on earth can give you either that key or the door to open except yourself.

—*YOU ARE THE WORLD,* 1972

DAVID SHAINBERG, M.D.

PSYCHIATRIST, NEW YORK CITY

KRISHNAMURTI
"CHALLENGED ANOTHER
BASIC PSYCHOANALYTIC
ASSUMPTION BY ASSERTING
THAT IT IS UNNECESSARY
THROUGH TIME TO DISCLOSE
THE DEEP LAYERS OF THE
UNCONSCIOUS."

—DAVID SHAINBERG

On April 29 and 30, 1975, Krishnamurti met in New York with twenty-five psychotherapists. The group represented a variety of theoretical orientations, including those of Freud, Horney, Sullivan, and Rogers. There were four social workers, four psychologists, and seventeen psychiatrists. There were several directors of psychoanalytic training institutes, a director of a hospital department of psychiatry, many professors, and several people who have contributed extensively to psychoanalytic knowledge.

This group assembled to explore the relationships and implications of Krishnamurti's teaching for their daily work. Each person knew well the difficulty involved in helping another human being. From the moment the discussion began the atmosphere of the dialogue was intense, deeply serious and respectful.

Appropriately, the first issue raised was: What is the root of fear? A useful distinction immediately emerged: there is a biological concern in which we know about fires, snakes, etc. Some called this the domain of "practical fear." Krishnamurti pointed out that this is not psychological fear, but is an "intelligence of self-preservation." Psychological fear is different. Krishnamurti stressed that psychological fear is caused by thinking. Becoming, he said, with its fear of not becoming, is the root of all fear. "If there were no thinking, there would be no fear." One psychiatrist responded. "If there were no thinking, you would not be human." But Krishnamurti urged the discussion toward considering the possibility of no thinking as being truly human. There was initial difficulty in understanding this, but the group began to get at the heart of the dilemma as Krishnamurti emphasized the need to go to the root of fear, not to its branches. Fear and its branches always arise when, instead of immediate action, there is thinking as becoming.

Psychotherapists customarily focus on the thoughts of their patients or, if not on the thoughts, on becoming and being. The therapist tries to help the patient become less fearful, more mature, more adept in society. So it was something of a shock for many of the participants in this dialogue to consider that thought and becoming were the root of mental disease. But to many it was more than shocking, often even deeply confusing, when Krishnamurti pointed out that being itself was the deepest root of fear. Few understood, but all were wondering. Krishnamurti asked how is it possible to prevent disease altogether.

From there the group moved to a central difference: psychotherapists, and of course the whole world, are accustomed to think in terms of process. This implies that it takes time to change, time for any transformation to occur. One man, for example, said that Krishnamurti's point about the transforming of consciousness

Concern yourself

with the root of sorrow

and not with the cry

of pain.

seemed to imply a process. Patients, it was argued, get better "over time" as a result of participation in a dialogue we call therapy. It can be observed that these patients have less fear as the result of a change in their knowledge about themselves and about the world. How, the therapists wondered, is it possible to throw out the idea of process when they see this betterment over time happen so often? Krishnamurti wondered if such people did not actually pick up another dependency to alleviate their fears. He asked: Is it possible to be totally free of fear and not simply to have less fear (as was suggested is the usual result of psychotherapy)?

This kind of question came up in another form in a discussion about development, a concept which attracts the interest of most therapists. Central to psychoanalytic theories is the idea that the child develops in time and that diseases of the mind emerge in faulty accomplishment of various developmental tasks over the course of a process. Similarly, the therapist observes a process in the patient who gradually resolves his various fears. As the therapy progresses there are changes; different fears emerge into the foreground. The patient is gradually able to extend his life and live more "productively" and more "freely." Krishnamurti agreed that the organism as such has undergone development. But the organism is different from the "me." This me is a product of thought as an avoidance of immediate action. The me or self, which therapists focus on, is a feature of the process of becoming and is the disease itself with its incessant need to be.

This also raised questions about the kind of change seen in patients who the therapist considers improved. Though they may get "better" at adapting to this corrupt world, does that mean they are able to love or are free of fear? Krishnamurti asked if there is an action which is not of the me or of time. Does that have anything to do with knowledge and learning? And is love in any way related to knowledge?

The issue of process came up in another way when one therapist noted: "We see a lot of patients who feel like they are nothing. That is, they are, as you suggest, feeling empty of the me and of the content of consciousness." Krishnamurti observed that the problem with such people is that they are really feeling they want to be something. Another doctor felt this was more of a problem than Krishnamurti had implied. He insisted that this state of feeling nothing was because these patients were afraid. It was not the result of overcoming fear. It was a state before feeling, experiencing, or contact with life. This doctor and others felt it was necessary for the patient to go through a process of experiencing a me, a self, before he could let go of the me.

Krishnamurti kept pointing out that no process is necessary in order to be aware of the nature of thought and becoming, or of the formation of ideals, and that the interval between what is and the inventions of thought is to be instantaneously finished with. He challenged another basic psychoanalytic assumption by asserting that it is unnecessary through time to disclose the deep layers of the unconscious. The therapists felt that a process of such revealing was necessary, but Krishnamurti said complete attention to the moment of action is all-inclusive action and is sufficient. It was clear that therapists felt that patients were not capable of attending to the moment, and that they needed preparation in order to gradually realize the limits of thought, including help in going through a process of accentuating the self.

Through the dialogue the recurrent theme was how to find an action which is beyond time and thought. It was disturbing for many to hear that it was impossible to act consciously without fragmenting, and that truth had nothing *whatever to do with reality which is the product of thought. Implicit in the discussion and often emerging in explicit bursts was the question: How can psychotherapists help their patients if they are not whole themselves? Of course everyone in the room was aware of his own fragmentation and this confronted everyone with questions of what kind of helping they were doing.*

To explore this, Krishnamurti emphasized that there is no psychological security. The action of thinking and becoming is the action of insecurity. The only security is the full realization there is no psychological security. In the realization of this, thought and becoming come to an end. This discussion challenged the analytic process in which most participants engaged daily. Krishnamurti observed that analysis as thought was a paralysis of action. It goes from one part to the next part, endlessly incomplete. Acting from conclusion to conclusion produces endless fragmentation and is itself a process of fragmentation; it is all an action of thought. It can never move to freedom.

Most of the psychotherapists who attended the two-day conference were deeply moved by the discussion. In general they had great difficulty understanding that no process was necessary. This challenged the psychoanalytic assumptions of growth and development. To be nothing and to live directly in the moment intrigued and interested many who appreciated that the endless analysis through thought was not helping their patients. Many reported they were stirred, and moved to question; some said they felt more tranquil after the work with Krishnamurti. One man said, "It was like a breath of fresh air." But it is clear that further dialogue is necessary to comprehend the process of thought.[79]

At the other end of the spectrum was iconoclast Henry Miller. His candid, autobiographical books shocked generations of readers, but in Krishnamurti he found the intellectual freedom he himself so ardently espoused.

HENRY MILLER

AUTHOR, PARIS, FRANCE AND BIG SUR, CALIFORNIA

I have never met Krishnamurti, though there is no man living whom I would consider it a greater privilege to meet than he... [His] language is naked, revelatory and inspiring. It pierces the clouds of philosophy which confound our thought and restores the springs of action. It levels the tottering superstructures of the verbal gymnasts and clears the ground of rubbish. Instead of an obstacle race of a rat trap it makes of daily life a joyous pursuit...His career, unique in the history of spiritual leaders, reminds one of the famous Gilgamesh epic. Hailed in his youth as the coming Savior, Krishnamurti renounced the role that was prepared for him, spurned all disciples, rejected all mentors and preceptors. He initiated no new faith or dogma, questioned everything, cultivated doubt (especially in moments of exaltation), and, by dint of heroic struggle and perseverance, freed himself of illusion and enchantment of pride, vanity, and every subtle form of dominion over others. He went to the very source of life for sustenance and inspiration. To resist the wiles and snares of those who sought to enslave and exploit him demanded eternal vigilance. He liberated his soul, so to say, from the underworld and the overworld, thus opening to it "the paradise of heroes"...I know of no living man whose thought is more inspiring.[80]

The highest function of education

is to bring about an integrated individual

who is capable of dealing with life as a whole.

—EDUCATION AND THE SIGNIFICANCE OF LIFE, 1953

A SIGNIFICANT EVENT OF THE 1970S was the establishment of the Oak Grove School in Ojai, California. Its first years were in cramped quarters in Arya Vihara, Krishnamurti's old home. Later, after settlement of the Rajagopal lawsuit, building began on 140 untouched acres adjacent to the Oak Grove, where Krishnamurti had spoken since May 21, 1928. For some time he had talked of starting a school in the United States. Trustees of the Foundation were somewhat dismayed at the prospect, as when discussions first began, the lawsuit still continued and it was felt that everyone had their hands full.

Mark Lee, now the deeply-committed Executive Director of the Krishnamurti Foundation had been a teacher at Rishi Valley and other schools for some time. He was the most suitable candidate to head the then tiny, now flourishing Oak Grove School. With a handful of children at the beginning the school has grown into a widely respected educational institute for children from nursery through the high school years.

R. E. MARK LEE

EXECUTIVE DIRECTOR, KRISHNAMURTI FOUNDATION OF AMERICA, OJAI

"KRISHNAMURTI WANTED A
'TIMELESS' SCHOOL, ONE
THAT WOULD LAST HUNDREDS
OF YEARS. HE WENT SO FAR
AS TO SUGGEST THAT THE
SCHOOL BUILDINGS THEM-
SELVES NOT REFLECT THE
LATEST ARCHITECTURAL STYLES."

—R. E. MARK LEE

"The purpose of educating children is to let goodness flower in them and to help them see that knowledge is one small corner of a vast field." With the help of friends and educators, Krishnamurti created half a dozen schools with just this intent in mind. Unlike the boarding schools established in England and India, the school he founded in Ojai, California, was conceived as a day school where parents could take an active part in educating their children, so that there would be no division between school and home. Having come to the United States in the 1920s, Krishnamurti knew the American people well. He was attracted to them for their great energy and generosity, and felt them fortunate in their lack of heavy tradition, but saw that their culture was in serious decline.

In December 1974, at Krishnamurti's invitation, I came to Ojai with my wife, Asha, and our one-year old daughter, Nandini, to undertake the opening of the Oak Grove School. The Krishnamurti Foundation of America had just

secured the title to a rambling, white-board and batten, California ranch house known as Arya Vihara—the place where Krishnamurti most often stayed in America from 1920 until his death in 1986. Asha and I immediately set about restoring the property so that it could serve, at least temporarily, as the school itself. Right from the beginning, there was no difference between our family life and the work of the school, which was carried on seven days a week, twenty-four hours a day.

By September 1975, we had a modest school with three faculty members and three students. It grew remarkably over the next three years to fifteen students and five faculty. Within two years, we were overseeing the construction of a marvelous school facility: shingled, skylit classrooms adjacent to the oak grove where Krishnamurti spoke every year.

Krishnamurti loved being in Ojai. The beauty of the valley rejuvenated him as every evening he walked its paths and trails with long strides, his large eyes observant of everything and everyone. Arriving each January, after an exhausting schedule of talks and meetings in India, England and Switzerland, he reveled in the peace, the quiet and the privacy Ojai affords. Yet the fire to create a new mind and a new generation grounded in a truly religious spirit was always raging within Krishnamurti. It was a passion that never abated.

Almost immediately upon returning to Ojai each year, he would plunge into the business of the school, holding dialogues and meetings with the faculty, the trustees and parents. The faculty wanted Krishnamurti's advice on curriculum and educational matters, but his response—that "the academic life and the spiritual life are one"—kept our relationship with him on the highest and most universal of terms. It was obvious that his deepest concern was that the faculty have clarity within themselves, so that questions related to classroom work could be intelligently answered by those actually performing the work. Krishnamurti saw his own job as bringing us to a discovery of the religious grounding of the school.

Repeatedly he asked us: "What is the purpose of education?" "Do teachers have the feeling of unlimited energy?" Our only concern should be learning— whether we were creating an environment for learning, whether this learning was actually happening in ourselves.

Krishnamurti wanted a "timeless" school, one that would last hundreds of years. He went so far as to suggest that the school buildings themselves not

reflect the latest architectural styles. What was astounding was the way he so unsparingly scrutinized the educational strictures held by even the most progressive minds in the faculty; we were to be neither "experimental" or avant-garde. During the mid-1970s, environmental studies were much in vogue and everyone talked of returning to nature and a simpler life. Krishnamurti said to me, "It may be a totally wrong approach to take a child for a walk and point out nature to him. It is only words. Rather, quicken the brain by teaching the art of listening and looking. Sensory awareness is lost as knowledge is gathered. Knowledge should come from sensory awareness." His admonitions to "prevent the child from developing the ability to concentrate," and that "all knowledge is a hindrance," challenged parents and faculty to the very root of their thinking.

At every turn, we examined popular culture and the elements of prevailing educational theory. Sensing the mentality of the young Americans we had gathered to teach in the school, Krishnamurti often warned us of the dangers of "cooperation," "togetherness" and, most dangerous of all, a "community" built around a group-mind in pursuit of an ideal. He helped us to see that these were all divisive approaches, and that only a religious mind could break the wrong direction taken by mankind long ago. Asked year after year of the same people, his questions were like rocks steadily sinking into well water, sounding within us, all the time. It is difficult to convey the effect of this intense inquiry into the nature of education and our commitment to the school other than to say that time stopped. Years went by, unaccountably.

Yet deeply and irreversibly, passionate inquiry was changing our small band of the intrepid. Slowly we realized that the purpose of the school was to develop the art of listening and learning. It was only then that the persistent conundrum of Krishnamurti's trashing of knowledge while at the same time saying that a school must be academically "tops" unraveled. "The quiet brain is the most active brain," Krishnamurti told us. "If your brain records, you have not listened." Statements as radical and profound as this are either dismissed as obscure or provoke a quantum leap—an insight without time—into the very nature of learning.

As we worked day after day to establish the school and its credibility, Krishnamurti helped make us sensitive to the hazard of developing an educational catechism based on his teachings. He confronted us whenever we took refuge in fixed points. His affection for us was obvious and he never gave up on anyone. He did not get involved in our private lives, but we knew he was deeply concerned about our understanding of ourselves and whether we were learning—or "flowering," as he called it. If he sensed someone had great energy, which he felt flowed if one was not self-absorbed, or was "an empty vessel," then he worked with that person—"cooked" them, in his words—in discussions, at meals, and on walks.

The probing was so extraordinary that it fired those open to learn, yet the attrition rate was high during the first ten years. We looked at why teachers wear out and lose focus, and found that if staff or faculty came only for the job *or the association with Krishnamurti, they would usually burn out or leave disappointed. The psychological morbidity rate was high because the challenges were so great. There was among us a spirit of agonizing adventure and we worked hard to make the school worthy of Krishnamurti's association with it, but at every turn we faced our self-created limitations. The interstices of personalities, professional training, and unseen motivations could not be hidden during the four months Krishnamurti was in Ojai each year.*

In retrospect I now see that we were pioneers without direction; we carried the frontier with us. The curriculum was developed in hundreds of hours of meetings, the result of which was that the educational requirements of the State of California were carefully upheld while at the same time everything was honed to the creative intent of the school. The Oak Grove School established a solid reputation for excellence in academic circles. It matured with the staff and faculty, as they deepened in self-understanding and professionalism.

The Oak Grove School is a place of learning in the greatest sense of the word.

I am confident it will have a long life and not become an institution. It has no history or traditions to weigh it down.

Throughout my participation with the school, as a parent, teacher and its director, I felt blessed and found that enormous energy naturally came with this unusual, intense life. Krishnamurti once told me that if a person lived the teachings, that person would be "protected." I asked him what he meant and he replied, "Sir, find out for yourself." I have been finding out ever since. I have come to see that energy brings insight, insight brings awareness, and— perhaps—this awareness is what protects. There is more to it than that, but while finding out, the mind is made fundamentally different.[81]

Love is not the product of thought; love, like humility, is not something to be cultivated. You cannot cultivate humility, it is only the vain man who cultivates humility; and when he is "cultivating," that is, progressing towards humility, he is being vain—like a man who practices non-violence, in the meantime he is being violent.

So, surely love is that state of mind when time, when the "observer" and the "observed" are not. You know, when we say we love another—and I hope you do—then there is an intensity, a communication, a communion, at the same time, at the same level, and that communion, that state of love, is not the product of thought or of time.[82]

—*TALKS WITH AMERICAN STUDENTS, 1970*

When we remove the division between the "me" and the "you," the "we" and the "they," what happens? Only then and not before, can one perhaps use the word "love." And love is that most extraordinary thing that takes place when there is no "me" with its circle or wall.

—*YOU ARE THE WORLD, 1979, 1989*

The Brockwood Park Educational Center in England had always focused on somewhat older students, ranging in age from fourteen years through the span of high school and college. The young American student at Brockwood, Julie Desnick had much to say about the impact of Krishnamurti on her life. She is now a film student in California.

JULIE DESNICK

AMERICAN STUDENT, BROCKWOOD PARK EDUCATIONAL CENTER

"...WE SEE THIS TREMENDOUS BEAUTY IN WHAT HE'S SAYING. TO ME, IT'S LIKE BUMPING INTO THE SUN, OR SEEING SOME FANTASTIC JEWEL, AND YOU WANT TO GRAB ON TO IT, BUT YOU CAN'T BECAUSE IT DOESN'T WORK THAT WAY."

—JULIE DESNICK

When I was about seventeen a friend of mind told me to read a book of Krishnamurti's and I read about three pages and nearly jumped out of my skin. I was absolutely blown away. I'd read other things and he seemed to go much further. I'd never read anybody else like that. At Brockwood Park I went through a lot of struggles with the teachings, I think a lot of people do in trying to capture them; in looking at them as kind of a salvation; ignoring that you still have to live in this world as what you are. Today I feel just as impressed by them as I did when I first read them. They're still very beautiful, clear and unusual.

To me, Krishnamurti's teachings seem to come from some pure source. About the only thing I could compare it to would be being in nature or Mozart's music or a great poem, like a poem of Keats. They felt effortless. Most teachings seem to be put together by the intellect. They're intellectual concepts. Whereas I really felt that K was speaking from a pure source, a direct contact with something rather than just intellectual theories.

Besides the logic of his teachings which I feel are very rational, I also find that they have tremendous beauty, a kind of poetic beauty. I feel that he lived his life with great integrity and that he had a special presence that was like an intense silence and compassion, like I feel when I'm on a mountaintop, or listen to the most beautiful music. I don't think I've ever met another human being with that kind of feeling.

Krishnamurti's teachings are radical; most people won't even let them in, though I feel that they are affected by them, even though they won't admit it. I've seen people who claim that they have zero appreciation or understanding of his teachings, absolutely melt in his presence; but they are very pure and he doesn't offer any crutches or any comfort, and that's what most people want. On the other hand, those of us that feel that we do understand them better seem to get very frustrated because we see this tremendous beauty in what he's saying. To me, it's like bumping into the sun, or seeing some fantastic jewel, and you want to grab on to it, but you can't because it doesn't work that way.[83]

In the educational spectrum, Professor P. Krishna stands in a special position. As Professor of Physics at Banares Hindu University he held an eminent position, but when he was asked by Krishnamurti to head the school at Rajghat he did not hesitate. The school, on a 250 acre campus is comprised of the Rajghat Besant School, a residential school for children of the middle years, Vasanta College is a pioneer in women's education in India and the Rural Primary School educates four-hundred children of nearby villages.

PROFESSOR P. KRISHNA

RECTOR, RAJGHAT EDUCATION CENTER, VARANASI, INDIA

"I LEARNED FROM HIS TEACHINGS THAT TRUE TRANSFORMATION HAS TO COME FROM WITHIN AND NOT BEGIN OUTSIDE, SO THAT IT IS NOT THE PRACTICE OF VIRTUE THAT IS IMPORTANT, IT IS BEING VIRTUOUS THAT IS IMPORTANT."

—P. KRISHNA

The first time I came across the teachings of Krishnamurti was when I was a college student about sixteen years of age. It was in the form of a small pamphlet which described his talks to young students in India. What attracted me was the directness of his approach, the simplicity of what he was addressing and the fact that it dealt with their everyday life. It was not an abstract, philosophical discourse of the kind one comes across when one talks to a professor of philosophy. I felt greatly interested and as I read on, I found that all kinds of questions that had been coming to my adolescent mind were discussed in that small book. I found an approach which appealed to me as a very intelligent and realistic approach to these questions. Krishnamurti would ask, for example, simple things like, Why do you stand up when the teacher enters the class? Why do you dress the way you dress? Why do you put a tika on your forehead. Why do you do puja? Is respect a form of fear? He questioned everything around you and your everyday life. This created great interest in me because I felt I didn't understand the way I was living. As I read on, I discovered more and more things which appealed to me. For example, I learned from his teachings that true transformation has to come from within and not begin outside, so that it is not the practice of virtue that is important, it is being virtuous that is important. It is not practicing acts of kindness that is important, it is important to be kind from within and that there is a distinction between the two. This was a point which had not occurred to me before, because all religions had asked us to lead a virtuous life and described virtue in terms of acts of virtue. Here was a man who was saying that the practice doesn't do it; that unless you

are kind within, practicing acts of kindness only produces a dichotomy between what you are and what you want to be and this conflict troubles you.

I learned about Krishnamurti from the book and then I met the person and found him very different from the image of an imperturbable saint which my mind had built up. Meeting him triggered a lot of questions in my mind.

Meditation is that light in the mind which lights the way for action; and without that light there is no love.

—*THE ONLY REVOLUTION*, 1970

Secondly, Krishnamurti's teachings shook my faith in reason. "Until I came across him, I believed that if you were very rational and you could reason things very finely, you could achieve anything. After reading him I learned to question whether that is true, because his teachings told me clearly that our mind often works like our personal lawyer, justifying and defending whatever opinion it has identified with. We usually identify with a view that suits us and then the mind finds all kinds of reasons to prove that it is virtuous. It deceives you into thinking that you are doing the right thing whereas, really, you are doing what you want to do.

It became clear to me that merely to sharpen the intellect, to learn more and more about philosophy or read the opinions of different people doesn't do very much. A mere intellectual understanding doesn't change you. A professor of philosophy is not very different from a professor of physics or from any other individual. Indeed, Krishnamurti brings out this point very clearly, that the problem is the same for all human beings, from the poorest man to the biggest business executive, to the philosopher to the religious man. They are all facing the same psychological problems. They are all trying to achieve something and if they are unable to achieve that they get frustrated.

When I met him, I saw for myself that he was not like an ordinary intellectual giving a good lecture or a very learned talk or who could analyze things better than others; but that he was a seer who was really living the teachings himself. That made all the difference to me. One was not now talking to a professor or a philosopher but was actually in the presence of a seer who had seen what he wanted others to see, who said he cannot give his insight to them, that they must find it for themselves. There is no authority in the world that can give insight to you and that made me realize that I must not look to others, I must stand on my own feet and see the truth of it within myself. The basic effect of Krishnamurti's teachings is to open the doors and windows of your mind. If you don't shut them again you keep learning all through life—you live with questions instead of living with answers.

If you are a prisoner, I am not concerned in describing what freedom is. My chief concern is to show what creates the prison and for you to break it down, if you are interested. If you are not, of course that is your own affair.

—OMMEN, HOLLAND, 1933

Angel Patrick Boyar, born in El Paso Texas, now living in California, has recently been released after serving several years in security housing in isolation from the general prison population at Pelican Bay State Prison. While there, and earlier in the general population at San Quentin Prison, he began to educate himself by reading voraciously. Among the works at the prison library which he read was a book by Krishnamurti. He was able to obtain others from the Krishnamurti Foundation of America.

In the isolated and ferocious world that is prison life, Boyar sought to clarify the meaning of his existence in the hostile environment both within and without prison walls.

In a lengthy hand-written manuscript entitled *Nobody, Somebody the Experience of Being Alive: A Desultory Prison Journal*, of which the following is a portion, Boyar describes in great detail the course of his observations during the thirteen years of his adult incarceration. The quotations of Krishnamurti within the writing which follows are entirely the selection of Angel Patrick Boyar.

ANGEL   PATRICK   BOYAR

AUTHOR, FORMER PRISONER

> "MY GREATEST DESIRE IN LIFE WAS TO BE SOMEBODY! I WAS INCESSANTLY HAUNTED WITH THE FEAR OF BEING REGARDED AS A NOBODY."
> —ANGEL PATRICK BOYAR

My greatest desire in life was to be somebody! I was incessantly haunted with the fear of being regarded as a nobody. I was plagued with the ambition to excel beyond my peers and I literally began to work at building what I believed to be an intriguing personality and character that would capture the worlds attention and then I would bask in the glory of being known.

I arrived at San Quentin State Prison in the month of January 1982. I was sentenced to an eight years prison term for voluntary manslaughter. I had made the big house! After a couple of months in San Quentin I came across a few books by Erich Fromm and read them voraciously. From then on I knew that my survival in prison would be dependant upon my intelligence because I was not the physically, aggressive type, nor prone to violence. Plus, I was and still am a man of small physical stature and I needed something to compensate for this disability in an environment teeming with some of the most dangerous and violence-prone criminals in the prison system who would not hesitate to hurt and kill at the slightest provocation.

Every prisoner had his own technique of surviving. My shield of protection was a heavy dose of self-education which later turned out to be the cause of much poisoning influence that led to increasingly disabling inner problems and eventually to what I knew to be psychosis.

Why am I writing! Well, for many reasons, none of which I believe are relevant. I'm probably just trying to write and express what is there, which is really not that easy for me as the "cluttered" mind is always there in the way to block the flow.

Actually what can be said when nothing can really come out of the emptiness we are?

We are ever trying to fill the void with "something"—anything that will help us to escape the reality of existence "as it is." We cannot run away from all that we fear—there is nothing to hold on to—there is no isolated identity— there is just the void and our own security needs that are ever driving us to put a "fix" on everything, as though we could hold on to or cultivate the "feelings" that give us the experience of being alive.

Identity and life are synonymous: To be alive is to be somebody!

"Do you want to be a hero?" After fifteen years those words still echo in my mind and they have turned out to be prophetic.

It was my Dad who asked me did I want to be a hero. But the full significance of those seven words are just now beginning to have their greatest impact as I contemplate their existential connotations.

Dad knew what he was saying when he asked me those prophetic words. He knew why I was running around the neighborhood acting like a vato loco: because I wanted to be a hero!

Like Nostradamus, my Dad prophetically peered into the future like an ancient seer and had seen prophecy fulfilling itself in my life.

Dad did not need to be endowed by inspiration to see the panoramic vision that unfolded before his penetrating gaze…that day I stared into the eyes of my Dad…the only hero whose attention would have given me the life I was vainly and desperately seeking by committing stupid and daring acts of mischief to build a reputation in the barrio in order that I might be recognized as being somebody and thus come to real life by establishing an identity…which I have since learned was and always had been a falsely projected image of a "scared" human being who was frightened of being nothing and nobody; yet para-doxically being compelled by the inescapable thoughts, feelings, belief that the experience of being alive could only come as one became somebody in the eyes and minds of everybody else.

In prison the majority of prisoners are hurting to be somebody—especially those who are associates of established prison gangs.

Image is the most valuable asset and is connected with the belief that becoming known as "somebody" is a power—and there are virtually no rules as to what one can do to create a public image worth being recognized and admired in prison.

It is the prison experience which has taught me that the only thing sacred to man is power. And in prison unless you are somebody you are powerless! Being somebody in prison is belonging to some prison clique where the only guiding principle that governs the activities of the group(s) is Nietzsche's "Superman" philosophy.

These men instinctively know there is no room for weakness in a universe that is expanding, that power is all that man respects; and these prison cliques have, as it were, become feared cabalistic type entities of organized violence having established a reputation of being killers. Their identity is not really who they are but what they have the power to do—take life!

The Mexican Mafia is a respected and notorious prison gang of sanguinary individuals who have long held sway over prisoners in California penal institutions. They are especially paid homage to by the non-organized and weaker Mexican prisoners out of fear and are adulated by those aspiring to be Mafiosos, who regard them as heroes and demigods.

Many Chicanos in prison desire and aspire to become members of the Mexican Mafia because for most of their lives they have had a low sense of self-esteem, a poor self-image and a pseudo-identity as gangsters that has become a stigma ever since the advent of the Pachuco and the zootsuit era; an adverse posterity that the Chicano has been unable to live down.

Being held in contempt and prejudice by the larger Anglo-dominated society and forced to congregate in shabby barrios, refused entry into mainstream society, Chicano youth became alienated, and families which once were held together by paternalistic family values of the old country began to disintegrate as the Jefe could no longer instill respect (having lost his own self-respect) in his children for failing to provide them with an adequate and decent home environment. Having to work long hours at menial jobs for minimum pay the Jefes' authority in the home began to decay. The Jefita could not adequately supervise a house full of children.

With stability gone in the home; inadequate supervision and disregard for basic recognition of growing youth who needed attention to feel loved and cared for, the youth take to the streets and begin hanging around with the homeboys and homegirls, who become a surrogate family in the barrio.

Enter the vato loco in prison. He is lost, lonely, alienated and hurting to be somebody. And the only image he has of himself is the stigmatic stereotype gangster surrounded and admired by gorgeous ladies of the night, owner of valuable possessions, feared by others and respected as being somebody because now he is the epitome of the so-called American Dream, which is really an illusion. For some ephemeral moments he transcends his poor image to bathe in egotistical self-glorification as he contemplates the power he has over those whom he exploits because of his status and membership in the Mexican Mafia.

"So meditation has significance…in this process of meditation there are all kinds of powers that come into being: one becomes clairvoyant…all the occult powers become utterly irrelevant, and when you pursue those you are pursuing something that will ultimately lead to illusion."

—TRUTH AND ACTUALITY, 1978

While in prison I began reading and studying many books on philosophy, spirituality, religion, eastern mysticism, oriental metaphysics, psychology and the occult.

I was thirsty for knowledge, devouring books that I thought would lead me to discovering my true identity, and years later I could see that so-called knowledge had brought me no closer to being totally integrated, as I was still an incomplete and fragmented human being.

For many years I considered myself the victim of the system and believed that there were powerful unseen forces of the universe being wielded by unscrupulous power-motivated men in high places who had somehow tapped into the secrets of the universe and were using those discovered secrets as tools to subjugate and manipulate the masses for purposes of wholesale exploitation in order to remain in power themselves.

While in San Quentin I adopted the conspiratorial view of history and politics and began reading historical and political books on the theme of conspiracy as well as secret societies and subversive movements.

At this time I was also trying to get hold of any books that expounded on brainwashing, mind control and psychological warfare. I desperately wanted to know how I was being manipulated, brainwashed and controlled by those unseen manipulators who I had by now concluded were somehow responsible for my lost identity.

Vigorously, I delved into my books on the theme of conspiracy thinking that at last I was getting closer to the whole truth of what was really going on; how it was happening; why it was taking place and where I fit in in the scheme of things. I was going to learn every detail possible of this struggle for world power and expose this diabolical conspiracy. Along the way I was bound to discover my true identity.

I became arrogant and obnoxious because I considered myself to be in a small circle of people who knew what was really going on in world affairs behind the scenes. At that time I was not fully aware that my own sense of inferiority coupled with my fear of being nothing and nobody caused me to overestimate *myself and put others down; looking upon others who were illiterate and naive with contempt so that I could feel important about myself.*

I didn't want to share my knowledge with anyone because then if they knew what I knew I couldn't stand out as being intelligent and unique when all along I knew that my motive for refusing to share my knowledge with anyone was to have power over them.

As, I see it now, my full motive for withholding knowledge was for identity, power and security.

My brain was like a Christmas tree and I just kept adding all that book knowledge to the brain like decorating a dead Christmas tree pulled up from its life source, and that knowledge to me was like the lights on the tree whose brightness outshined the other dull and mediocre minds around me.

I thought I was deep but I was very shallow because in my vainglory I failed to see that being knowledgeable and intellectual did not provide me with the significant self-help I really needed to bring an end to the spiritual and psychological conflict within me.

I was afraid to accept that I was completely empty within myself that I was nothing and nobody.

Today I know that the only conspiracy going on is me against myself!

I have read many books that have profoundly affected my mind, and naively I thought that each thought-provoking discovery of some hidden knowledge of revealed truth was significantly shifting my consciousness so that I was gradually being liberated from lies, illusions, false knowledge, self-imposed limitations, and I thought that I was making progress in liberating myself by degrees; but I was only further enslaving myself psychologically and exacerbating the confusion going on inside of me; poisoning myself with other people's theories on life.

For years I was desperately seeking the answer in books but I never stopped to realize that all those books were written by people postulating their own theories on life. They were very good at diagnosing the problems of humanity, by pointing the finger at the culprits who were responsible for creating the human condition, yet those pointing the fingers never considered that they themselves were creating the problems of the world:

The problem is not the world, but you in relationship with another, which creates a problem; and that problem extended becomes the world problem.

The above statement is true. This is a fact. Not because Krishnamurti said it but because I can see this is true for myself. It is my "relationship with another, which creates the problem." I never thought of myself as being the problem. It was always the other fellow!

The world would be a better place to live in as soon as others came to their senses and accepted the truth as I knew it to be; as soon as everybody started seeing reality my way and started living according to my reality, then a new world order of sane human beings would emerge.

The schism in man, the proverbial dichotomy of life against death, good against evil, the spirit against the flesh; it is we, you, I, who perpetuate this conflict because we believe it is necessary to give us the experience of being alive.

I witnessed a dramatic transformation when I ceased all effort to change myself:

It is truth that frees, not your effort to be free.

For many years it was known that the psychological "I" was only an image, a projection of the me. It was an impostor, a pretender to the throne who had usurped the heart of no boundaries and it now had a stake in preserving its non-existent identity. It convinced itself that it was the real John Doe and all along it was playing a game of truth or consequences with itself.

To know is to be ignorant, not to know is the beginning of wisdom.

All along I thought that by the accumulation of knowledge I was becoming more wise, but I had momentary insights that revealed that as I gained more knowledge of the world that this knowledge was my own state of ignorance. The more that I came to know, the more that I could see how ignorant I really was.

Each time I thought I had moved and made progress in the gaining of knowledge, but when I checked to see the distance I had come, I found myself standing in the same spot.

Indeed, even if I contained all of the knowledge of the world and the universe, I would still be an ignoramus because all that knowledge would not even be a microscopic drop in the bucket of the eternal moment.

Nobody can put you psychologically into prison. You are already there.

—*COMMENTARIES ON LIVING*, VOLUME I, 1956

I was paroled from San Quentin prison on March 17, 1986. I remember the night before I was paroled that I was not feeling anxious to get out. After approximately six years of incarceration I thought that I should be excited about getting out, that I should be agitated with the feeling of emotional elation because I was about to be set free. I expected that I would take on the proper feelings as I stepped out the front gate of the prison and into the so-called free world.

Morning arrived. Still no proper feelings for the momentous occasion of being on the verge of becoming a free man. I was processed for release at R&R. I removed my state issued prison clothing and changed into my dress outs. I was issued my two hundred dollars gate money, and then we were off—being escorted to freedom!

Passing through the garden chapel plaza I saw a few buddies whose smiling facial expressions indicated feelings of peacefulness and inner joy. They waved good-bye to me and I managed a smile and a reciprocal wave of the hand. Then I became aware I am still on the prison grounds—and there is still some distance I had to go to get from "here," to freedom over "there," past the front entry gates of the prison. Finally I arrived, but when I crossed the final threshold to freedom, nothing!

I was still in prison! The mind was pretending to be free. I knew that this freedom was an illusion. There was no experience of being free, I did not come alive.

So, freedom had nothing to do with being on the other side of the prison walls. Psychologically, I was still in prison; enslaved by passions and desires and surrounded by the Chinese wall of images and ideas that were the real barriers that shut freedom out.

I N   O J A I ,   D U R I N G   T H O S E   S P R I N G   M O N T H S   before the annual Oak Grove talks were given, each day was a delight and a special delight was lunch! There, into the long afternoon, those who happened to be around shared moving, stimulating, gripping, humorous times. Politics, the Vietnam War, Watergate, all of the events of the day, and more were discussed. Frequently the talk was serious, probing, at other times, the dining room at Arya Vihara rang with laughter.

Michael Krohnen, in addition to being an excellent chef who prepared delicious vegetarian food for Krishnamurti and his guests, had a special charge to inform Krishnamurti of the news of the day. He recalls Krishnamurti's delightful sense of humor.

M I C H A E L   K R O H N E N

CHEF, KREFELD, GERMANY

"KRISHNAMURTI'S JOKES, REVEALED THE NATURE OF HUMAN THOUGHT....IT WAS MORE THAN A COINCIDENCE THAT ONE OF KRISHNAMURTI'S MOST CELEBRATED SPEECHES, WHICH FORMALLY DISBANDED THE WORLDWIDE ORGANIZATION SET UP FOR HIM STARTED WITH A JOKE."
—MICHAEL KRONEN

It was after years of daily contact with Krishnamurti that I came to fully discover and appreciate the endearing aspects of his personality. He extended genuine care and affection to those around him. His friendship for me, and many others, was honest and without pretense and conveyed a wonderful sense of freedom and joy.

What I most dearly loved about him was his laughter and his sense of humor, which encompassed the whole spectrum of human living. At the lunch table in Ojai where I most regularly got to meet him, he would often display his infectious laughter, recounting jokes from his considerable repertoire of witty stories and anecdotes. Even during his public speaking in front of thousands and during the most probing dialogues with scientists and academicians, he managed to intro-duce light-hearted humor, shedding light on the ironies and absurdities of life.

But he didn't stop there. He was also more than willing to laugh at himself and the ludicrous situations in which he sometimes found himself. Publicly and privately, he'd jokingly refer to himself as "the poor chap on the platform," or "the old boy," and enjoyed telling amusing stories from his unusual life. All of them were charming anecdotes of his daily life which poked gentle fun not only at others but also at himself. Once at lunch, during the time of the public talks at Ojai, we had been discussing the excessive worship and adoration which he often found himself subject to. Suddenly Krishnamurti broke into joyous, liberating laughter, exclaiming, "It's all so crazy, it's all so utterly absurd."

I was sitting next to him and readily joined his uninhibited laughter, although it was not entirely clear to me what exactly he was referring to by "it." After our exhilaration had quieted down a bit, I asked him, "What do you mean, sir, by "it all?" You mean the talks and all this?" And I made a general gesture toward the other guests at the table, including the whole situation at hand. Tears of laughter were still in his eyes as he turned to look at me. "Yes, sir, all of that, and the whole circus about him," he replied with a puckish smile, pointing at himself. Everyone at the table, about sixteen of us, shared another round of exuberant laughter, in which was mingled the sheer joy of living.

At the 1970 San Diego public talks, he answered a question about his definition of humor by saying, "I suppose it means really to laugh at oneself. We have so many tears in our hearts, so much misery....just to look at ourselves with laughter, to observe with clarity, with seriousness and yet with laughter, if one can." [84]

Only months before his death in 1986, he remarked, "Laughter is part of seriousness, right? If you don't know how to laugh and look at the sun and the trees and the dappled light and everything, well, you're half (dead), you're not quite a human being. If you are merely churchy serious—on Sundays only— then it's not serious. I mean laughter, a smile, that sense of humor, and to enjoy good jokes, not vulgar jokes, really good jokes." [85]

I perceived his refined sense of humor as the joyous aspect of the extraordinary intelligence which he manifested. It imbued his person and talks with a warm human side without which one could easily be intimidated by the lofty, or even majestic, quality of what he said and its sometimes austere presentation. Having provided a most incisive insight into the prevailing human situation on a global scale, with its appalling fear and suffering, he would unexpectedly tell a brief amusing story, or one of his jokes. It was a healing touch through which, all at once, everything was set right again, was made whole by the liberating power of shared laughter—as if all of us suddenly became aware of a great cosmic joke.

KRISHNAMURTI ENJOYING A MOMENT WITH A STUDENT AT RISHI VALLEY SCHOOL.

The jokes which he so exquisitely delighted in recounting were predominantly of a "religious" or political nature, i.e., they dealt with the themes of heaven and hell, God and the devil, the Pope, St. Peter and Jesus, yogis and gurus, and politicians. Krishnamurti would probably have objected to an analysis of his jokes, or any attempt to impart a deeper meaning to them. Of course, they were "only" jokes, nothing more—but a joke, its presentation and appreciation also manifests a state of mind. Krishnamurti's jokes, I think, revealed the nature of human thought, its absurd and incongruous superstitions, its proclivity to create belief systems, dogmas, and spiritual authorities, and its devious ways of establishing and defending a center with its "self-interest." they playfully and sympathetically dealt with the ludicrous and ironies in our age-old traditions and everyday lives.

I think that it was more than a coincidence that one of Krishnamurti's most celebrated speeches, which formally disbanded the worldwide organization set up for him as the world teacher, started with a joke, a circumstance overlooked by

his biographers. The speech, given by Krishnamurti at the Ommen Camp in the Netherlands, in August 1929, dissolved the "Order of the Star," and is better known for its poignant phrase "Truth is a pathless land." In fact, Krishnamurti repeated the joke told on that occasion many times throughout his life, slightly modifying it as he went along. One of the last times that he recounted it in public, he revealed that he himself had "thought it out (and)...invented it about forty or fifty years ago." [86] It was probably the only joke which he himself had made up. All the others he had either been told by someone or read. Surprisingly, some of the major themes of his life and teaching are contained in this short joke: man's search for the sacred, truth, and religious organizations.

Here it is in its original 1929 version: You may remember the story of how the devil and a friend of his were walking down the street when they saw ahead of them a man stoop down and pick up something from the ground, look at it, and put it away in his pocket. The friend said to the devil, "What did that man pick up?" "He picked up a piece of truth," said the devil. "That is a very bad business for you, then," said his friend. "Oh, not at all," the devil replied, "I am going to let him organize it." [87]

His inimitable sense of humor and affectionate, joyous laughter enhanced Krishnamurti's humanity and completed his wholeness. At the same time, he was careful to note the other, licentious side of all-too-easy laughter. During the very last talk ever at the Oak Grove in Ojai, he admonished the crowd in front of him, "Please, don't laugh, this is much too serious. Not that we shouldn't have humor. It's good to laugh, but laughter may be the means of avoiding facts. So one has to be aware of that. Not that we shouldn't have humor: laugh with all your being at a good joke." [88]

Humor, joy, goodness and intelligence were fused in him in wholeness, the full flower of humanity. He was a great human being, and his teaching is the perfume which remains with us.

We are like two friends sitting in the park on a lovely day talking about life, talking about our problems, investigating the very nature of our existence, and asking ourselves seriously why life has become such a great problem, why, though intellectually we are very sophisticated, yet our daily life is such a grind, without any meaning, except survival—which again is rather doubtful. Why has life, everyday existence, become such a torture? We may go to church, follow some leader, political or religious, but the daily life is always a turmoil, though there are certain periods which are occasionally joyful, happy, there is always a cloud of darkness about our life. And these two friends, as we are, you and the speaker, are talking over together in a friendly manner, perhaps with affection, with care, with concern, whether it is at all possible to live our daily life without a single problem. Although we are highly educated, have certain careers and specializations yet we have these unresolved struggles, the pain and suffering, and sometimes joy and a feeling of not being totally selfish....And as two friends sitting in the park on a bench...in the dappling light, the sun coming through the leaves, the ducks on the canal and the beauty of the earth, let us talk this over together. Let us talk it over together as two friends who have had a long serious life with all its trouble, the troubles of sex, loneliness, despair, depression, anxiety, uncertainty, a sense of meaninglessness—and at the end of it always death.[89]

Krishnamurti had a particular love for nature. This love was shared by Alan Kishbaugh who, over the past twenty years, has been active in Krishnamurti's work. They had many interests in common.

ALAN   KISHBAUGH

AUTHOR, ENVIRONMENTALIST, LOS ANGELES, CALIFORNIA

"KRISHNAMURTI LOVED NATURE. NATURE, HE STATED, IS SOMETHING OUTSIDE OF THE MIND, UNTOUCHED BY IT. HE PREFERRED SPEAKING OUTDOORS UNDER A CANOPY OF TREES WHERE HE COULD HEAR THE BIRDS, FEEL THE BREEZES, AND SEE THE PLAY OF LIGHT THROUGH THE LEAVES."

—ALAN KISHBAUGH

I feel very privileged to have had twenty years with Krishnamurti. There was such a quality of caring in him, of affection toward all living beings, that just being near him one felt included in an unseen and all-encompassing protection.

His affection for people manifested in his seeing more in them than they often saw in themselves. K brought out the best in people and they were often surprised to realize the depth of their own being in his presence. What developed from that inner-recognition, that generosity of spirit, was a tremendous affection. Here was someone wanting you to be what you could be, who was extending a hand to you to be just that.

Our relationship felt like that of two close brothers, or of good friends with mutual respect for one another. We used to go shopping together in London, or to the movies in Los Angeles. He was a wonderful companion.

K appreciated excellence and had an eye for detail, qualities that are apparent in his teachings. His talks were carefully and responsibly crafted with precise language aimed at minimizing ambiguity. He chose his words to avoid faddish usage and multiple connotations. He paid close attention to word origins and consulted several dictionaries which extensively detailed root meanings.

The teachings are about order and right behavior. He sometimes defined sanity as "...everything in its right place." In order, there is a natural unfolding of beauty. In K's appreciation of well-made objects, such as clothes, cars, and watches there is the logical, outward reflection of the same principles that pervade all of the teaching—order, beauty and intelligence. These same principles and values—so painstakingly applied to well-made material objects—are also in the inner world, and fundamental to sanity and right behavior.

Krishnamurti loved nature. Nature, he stated, is something outside of the mind, untouched by it. He preferred speaking outdoors under a canopy of trees where he could hear the birds, feel the breezes, and see the play of light through the leaves.

We took many walks together in Switzerland, England and Ojai. He was a keen observer of animal behavior and wildlife and while walking, we would often swap stories of animals we had encountered.

In the sixties the hippie movement spurred a great deal of questioning of all of society's values. People were searching for new directions and there appeared to be a break with the past and an opening to the new. Initially, it looked like a real revolution was occurring, along with a fundamental change in the mechanism of perception. But the gap that had formed—between ending the old and staying open to the ever-forming new—began to be filled with Asian philosophy, drugs, and all manner of "fixed" notions.

So, instead of seeing the depth of one's conditioning, and staying open to that observation, as K talks about it, there was yet another movement away from what is, to a re-conditioning. People went from being true revolutionaries—

newly and continuously perceiving themselves in action—to not being revolutionary at all. It was like being in a prison, opening the cell door and declaring oneself free, only to walk next door and enter a new cell. The view was different, but the prison of conditioning still remained.

Krishnamurti speaks about true revolution as the moment in which we see the depth of our conditioning. Once seen, it startles the organism long enough to perceive something beyond one's habitual patterns. When there is no movement toward either the old or the new, then one has the possibility of being free to act from no fixed position of accumulated concepts, beliefs, and perceptions.

Other disciplines such as Zen, Yoga, or Buddhism speak of liberation. But Krishnamurti, aware of the ancient meaning and long-usage of "liberation," chose instead to talk of freedom. Freedom is central to K's work and what differentiates it from liberation is the concept of personal responsibility. K talks about freedom at the core of one's being, whereas "liberation" is wrapped in the notion of being free from something.

Other approaches speak of attainment through will, self-mastery, balance or harmony of the various parts of ourselves, physical, emotional, and mental. But again, there's a sense of "freedom-from" in this concept of attainment and liberation. Certainly the Buddhist doctrine of Liberation means much more than that, but still absent is the notion of freedom as something you can't work directly for—a gift that comes with seeing the depth of our conditioning. That gift of freedom, whether it's cosmic or otherwise, defies definition. Hardest of all is the recognition that seeing requires no other "action" than seeing. There is no need to be, or act. Doing, becoming, attaining are all projections of our conditioning.

The teachings encompass three areas. First, there's the body of everything that K said, recorded, filmed, taped, and wrote wherein he set the tone and parameters of what he deemed important.

Then, there is the teaching that develops internally when people begin to listen and watch how they are in the world. As they proceed from the truth of what they see in themselves, and their conditioning, how they are in the world and not separate from it, the teaching begins to live.

"What will you do when I am gone?" Krishnamurti often said to those charged with the work of the foundations. In other words, "if the work is only "mine," and not yours, how will it live?"

It is at this point, as the teachings become ours, that a third phase comes into being. In accepting responsibility for seeing one's life, not in judgement, but how it actually is, and how we are all connected to the rest of humanity—in that, lies the possibility of living a sane, intelligent, non-destructive life. In such a life, as Krishnamurti so eloquently and gracefully has shown us, there is affection for all living beings.[90]

The international aspect of the circle around Krishnamurti was stirring. Actually, it had been present since the early Theosophical days, that being a noticeable feature of the movement. His constant travels brought him the friendship of many from around the world. Noticeable among them was Jean-Michel Maroger, who has continued to be deeply involved in the Krishnamurti Foundation Trust in England.

JEAN-MICHEL MAROGER

SHIPPING CONSULTANT, PONTLEVOY, FRANCE

"THE FIRST TIME I SAW
KRISHNAMURTI IN THE TENT, I
HAD A SHOCK. SOMETHING
MAGIC, ALMOST IRRATIONAL,
HIT ME. IT WAS BEYOND THE
WORDS I WAS HEARING....I
FELT THAT WHAT WAS BEING
SAID WAS ESSENTIAL."
—J.M. MAROGER

I have no natural inclination for spirituality. Rather, I was somewhat drawn into that field through parental influence, my parents having themselves become interested in such matters when I was in my early teens.

A long incurable illness took my father in 1965 after a period of grace which lasted some twenty years. Medical science had long ago given up curing him and this period of grace was attributed to prayer. After his death, my mother expanded her investigations and eventually came upon Krishnamurti, but I remember having first taken her enthusiasm rather cooly.

It was my first contact with the teacher in 1975 that awoke my interest. My mother had invited the family to Saanen to attend K's talks. The first time I saw him in the tent, I had a shock. Something magic, almost irrational, hit me. It was beyond the words I was hearing, which at first did not particularly stir me up, although unconsciously I felt that what was being said was essential. I remember leaving the tent at the same time as him, running after him and taking his hand in gratitude.

We went through the whole series of talks, and upon our return in Paris (where my family lived at the time), I attended a meeting with some of my mother's friends who had also been to Saanen and was amazed by the distorted way in which they referred to what they had been listening to. This is what induced me to dub the tapes of the talks I had brought back from Saanen, hoping this would convince these people that they were wrong and help them grasp what K had actually said.

The following year, my mother suggested that we attend the Brockwood talks. I took my dubbed tapes along and showed them to the first responsible person I met there, which happened to be Mary Zimbalist. Her knowledge of French helped her realize the importance such a work could have in spreading the teachings, and this is how my involvement with Brockwood started.

My first close encounter with K was not that easy: despite the fact that I was in my forties, I remember being terribly shy, almost to the state of paralysis, and for some time I remained unable to hold a sound conversation with him. K probably felt that and since he was usually at his best when challenged, it took me many months before I was able to engage in a serious talk with him. I recall a specific occurrence when walking through the tent after the end of one of the first talks I attended at Brockwood I came across Krishnamurti who was standing in a corner, apparently waiting for someone. This is the chance of my life to get to him, I thought! But when I came close to him I was unable to utter a word, and most reluctantly walked away (I learned much later that Dorothy Simmons had asked him to return to the tent after the talk to somehow "play the host," as she put it, which he accepted but he seemed so miserable in that role that no one apparently dared disturb him!).

However, self-knowledge was making its way and when I eventually realized that it was the image I had of Krishnamurti was opposed to the image I unconsciously wanted him to have of me that caused the shyness, the whole thing dropped. This was my first realization of the power of understanding oneself at depth.

As my involvement with the work grew, I got to visit Brockwood more and more often, the more so as my second daughter became a student of the school. In 1979, hearing that K wanted to spend a holiday in France I dared invite him to come to our country house in the Loire Valley—where we had permanently moved to—with Mary Zimbalist. They both accepted, and this was an exhilarating experience which was prepared with great secrecy, since we wanted to make sure that our guests would have an undisturbed rest. I believed his stay here was both a success and a God sent opportunity to get to know the man away from the environment we were used to see him in.

I then realized to what extent Krishnamurti was an exceptional person, the utter simplicity of the man coupled with an extraordinary sense of awareness of the smallest details of existence and an unfathomable attention to another human being once the latter was prepared to engage in a serious talk with him. This last quality probably explains why K could very quickly grab the core of a human problem presented to him and find the exact words which would bring the person to see clearly in him or herself.

His love for nature, for animals (he showed such affection for our German Shepherd that he insisted in taking him along for excursions in the car, and once I was distressed to see the dog licking K's face while they were both sitting on the back seat!), the way he always yielded to another person's casual desires in the organization of daily life were part of the features one could not miss noticing in him.

A few years later, my family and I accidentally had another opportunity to get physically close to Krishnamurti. This was in Saanen when my younger daughter, Diane—who has a rare bone illness—broke her leg and could not be transported home. It happened nearly at the end of the talks and we could not find accommodation in the full holiday season. Without our having asked for anything K arranged for us to stay at Chalet Tannegg in the flat below his own which was unoccupied although rented by an old friend of his. We stayed there at least three weeks, and almost every day K came downstairs and spent some time with Diane. Occasionally, I sat close to them in silence and I must say that several times I felt something beyond description which I imagine as being related to what he called the "otherness" in his diary (the Note Book*). At other times, one could hear them both have the laugh of their life—but I was never able to obtain from Diane a recount of what had caused such laughter.*

Much more could be said about Krishnamurti. However, I believe that in his own view what imports most is the impact of his teachings on our lives. For my part, it has been tremendous and is still growing as I mature in an expanding awareness.

Alas, total insight has not been my lot, at least so far, but revealing insights into topics such as fear, competition, ambition, success, etc. are the immense gifts I have received through Krishnamurti's teachings.

Does the great privilege of having been close to Krishnamurti or of being involved in the work connected to his teachings give us an edge in getting a deep grasp of these teachings? Judging from my own experience and from what I have

*observed around me I feel tempted to say that unless one is deadly careful not to
fall into the trap of self-delusion, it is likely not to make much of a difference.
More than once did Krishnamurti draw our attention to this danger, and heaven
knows how right he was. I feel this is probably the greatest lesson I have learned
from all these years: nothing should ever be considered as permanently acquired
in the field of self-knowledge, and because of this one should never stop
questioning oneself at all levels, upon every opportunity life presents us with.*[91]

One who was totally captivated by Krishnamurti's message and was
especially close was Friedrich Grohe, a businessman who owned a large
manufacturing firm. Krishnamurti called him his *ange gardien* or guardian
angel. It was Friedrich who made possible the beautiful study center at
Brockwood Park in England.

FRIEDRICH GROHE

RETIRED GERMAN BUSINESS MAN, NOW LIVING IN SWITZERLAND

"ANOTHER STRIKING ASPECT
OF BEING IN HIS COMPANY
WAS THAT MY PERCEPTION OF
THE BEAUTY OF NATURE WAS
MORE INTENSE."

—FRIEDRICH GROHE

It was in 1980 that I first read a book by Krishnamurti, The Impossible
Question. *Even though I found that Krishnamurti cannot be read like a novel, I
could not put it down. He appeared to be saying the opposite of what one had
learned and experienced. One seemed to have vaguely felt before what he
expressed there in clear, simple and overwhelming language.*

*Although I knew in 1981 that Krishnamurti used to give a series of public
talks each year at Saanen, Switzerland, I had no desire to attend them as I was
quite content just studying his books. In fact, I lost interest in philosophy,
psychology, literature, art, and the like, which had once captivated me, because
I suddenly felt: "This is it!" Other people's books simply became superfluous.*

*This was a time of great change for me. Besides other things, I was about to
retire from business life. Previously, I had not had much time to face essential
questions, but now, all at once, K made it clear to me how important it was to
concern oneself with central issues like death and love, pleasure and pain,
freedom, desire and fear. The more I explored the teachings, the more fascinating
they became.*

*I attended the talks at Saanen, Switzerland for the first time in 1983.
Sitting on the steps which led into the giant tent where about two-thousand
people had gathered, I would listen to K Here, under the awning, I was
protected from the heat and could still enjoy a fresh breeze. As I usually walked
all the way from Rougemont, which takes about one and a half hours, and
would arrive just before the talks started, I could use the side entrance and did
not have to sit amidst the crowd. Right in front of the podium from where
Krishnamurti spoke, people were squatting and pushing against each other;
every square inch of sitting space was highly valued. At Saanen and Brockwood,
people would queue all night long in front of the tent to be the first in when it
was opened. In the United States and India, it was usually a bit more relaxed.*

*This first summer was so hot that on my hike back to Rougemont I bathed in
the Fenilbach River which would normally have been too ice-cold to have done
so. In the tent, it was possible to buy books by K translated into various
languages, and I had been glad to fill my rucksack with them.*

It was overpowering to listen to him. He emanated so much energy that I felt

I simply could not sit directly across from him. He spoke simply and clearly, with few gestures and no rhetoric. While listening to him, I would forget about food and drink and would not even take note of the heat.

My personal contact with him developed very quickly. To meet the man personally had such an impact that from then on I went to all the talks in Brockwood, India, Ojai, and Washington till the last talks in Madras in December/January 1986, just before his death.

This necessitated intensive traveling, more than half of the year I was out of Switzerland. My contact with family and friends decreased considerably. Those were the outer changes.

Essentially my life had already started changing. It seems that it was time to meet a man like Krishnamurti. My full time business life I had already left behind. My consuming mountain climbing activities had been considerably cut back since a close friend and mountain guide had died in a climbing accident. My longtime passion of collecting paintings had already lost its appeal. When K visited my house at Lake Geneva, as he stepped inside he covered his eyes for a

second with an exclamation of startled surprise. He seemed to be struck by the powerful ambiance of all the paintings. This was just the final step. I also had already stopped eating meat, but here as in many other areas K accelerated a development which was already on the way. When he said during a gathering "We eat dead animals," something became absolutely clear to me and I stopped eating meat once and for all. But perhaps the most impactful statement I recall him making in one of his talks was: "Love has no cause." These words were like a revelation to me.

Another striking aspect of being in his company was that my perception of the beauty of nature was more intense. On some occasions, I would accompany him on his regular afternoon walks. Usually some close friends would go with him on such walks, but he would talk very little on these outings. He had an intense relationship with the things of nature. He maintained that the roots of trees had a sound, but we don't hear it anymore. Once, when walking across the Brockwood meadows behind the "Grove," I was about to pass between a group of five tall pine trees. He caught me by the arm and said: No, around them! We must not disturb them.

"ONCE, WHEN WALKING ACROSS THE BROCKWOOD MEADOWS BEHIND THE 'GROVE,' I WAS ABOUT TO PASS BETWEEN A GROUP OF FIVE TALL PINE TREES. HE CAUGHT ME BY THE ARM AND SAID: NO, AROUND THEM! WE MUST NOT DISTURB THEM."

—FRIEDRICH GROHE

An event which took place in India also showed this intimate relationship he had with living things. There was a plantation of big mango trees at Rajghat which did not yield any fruit. Therefore, it was planned to cut them down. K recounted with a twinkle in his eye how one day he walked among the trees and said to them: Listen, if you do not bear any fruit, they are going to cut you down. They bore fruit the next year.

Krishnamurti called me his brother, his ange gardien. *In 1984 in Schoenried he embraced me and suggested I should live with him. I knew what he meant by that. He had asked several people before to live with him very closely so that he could work with them, saying that they then would change. But I was not ready for this total change. I could not imagine then letting go of everything. Would I be ready to do it now, ten years later? I don't know.*

At the end of his life K said that nobody had understood what he had to say. With reference to one of the jokes he used to tell, "Everyone has to die—perhaps even myself" I could say: "Nobody has understood him—perhaps not even myself."

When we use the word "attention" there is a difference between concentration and attention. Concentration is exclusion. I concentrate, that is, I bring all my thinking to a certain point and therefore it is excluding, building a barrier so that it can focus its whole concentration on that. Whereas attention is something entirely different from concentration. In attention there is no exclusion, no resistance, and no effort, and therefore no frontier, no limits.

—*A WHOLLY DIFFERENT WAY OF LIVING*, LONDON 1991

In February 1974 an unusual opportunity for dialogue arose. In San Diego, California, Krishnamurti and Dr. Alan W. Anderson embarked on an in-depth series of twenty hours of video-taped dialogues, covering fear, desire, meditation and the sacred mind and many other themes that Krishnamurti regularly addressed. It is perhaps the most definitive sequence of thematic dialogues Krishnamurti has held. The series has since become the book, *A Wholly Different Way of Living*. Dr. Anderson who has been honored with a distinguished teaching award is a published poet.

A L A N   W .   A N D E R S O N

PROFESSOR EMERITUS OF RELIGIOUS STUDIES, SAN DIEGO STATE UNIVERSITY

"FROM THE MOMENT WE BEGAN OUR CONVERSATIONS I WAS STRUCK BY HIS QUALITY OF ATTENTION. THERE WAS NOTHING CONTRIVED ABOUT IT NOR WAS IT BASED ON A MUSCULAR EFFORT OF THE WILL TO ATTEND. IT MIGHT BE LIKENED, ON A DIFFERENT LEVEL, TO THE DYNAMIC OF BALANCE AS WHEN ONE RIDES A BICYCLE, DRIVES A CAR OR SIMPLY WALKS."

—ALAN ANDERSON

Great teachers are rare. This statement is a commonplace and, as a truism, it hardly draws notice. However, such usual inattention in no way alters the fact that the obvious conceals the most salient significances. Sages over millennia have stressed this to virtually no avail. The pre-Socratic thinker, Heraclitus, wrote that nature loves to hide and that unless one expects the unexpected he will not find it for it is difficult and hard to come by. In the same vein the seminal Spanish thinker, Ortega y Gasset, contemplated this theme with his statement that masks surround us.

It is one of the characteristics of our human species that we can entertain these remarks cerebrally and even dilate upon them intellectually, yet without meeting them viscerally or being touched by them emotionally. Such a bloodless relation to the obvious has through technology given us great material power over our physical environment. Unhappily, it has done nothing to generate or to advance self-inquiry. Without self-inquiry human nature cannot reach its essential promise which is to become free of self-misunderstanding.

As a species we deform ourselves when we apply a sheerly abstract measure for our conduct whether from memory, dogma, ideology, self-image or a collapse into another's authority. Imagination itself, which since the Romantic era continues to enjoy the wildest praise, is no less an abstract guide. Unlike nature, imagination is not its own rule. This want of inherent self-correction is imagination's Achilles' heel. The overweening confidence in imagination is depth psychology's chief liability and until it shifts its center of gravity it will go on failing the promise touted for it in the early days of Freud and Jung. Important as it is to recognize a thing's constant tendency or essence (whether represented mathematically or literarily) this intellectual abstraction cannot stand in for the thing's existence which is fraught with incalculable changes in the give and take of its career.

A philosophical grasp of this distinction between essence and existence is still an abstraction unless with Socrates one regarded philosophy as concerned in

wisdom. Unfortunately, academic philosophy in our time shows little if any interest in the wisdom tradition as such and on that account many gifted students shy away from it who otherwise might contribute with distinction to this discipline.

These matters held my attention for many years before I met Krishnamurti. I was privileged to be invited to share twenty dialogues with him, eighteen of which comprise the book, A Wholly Different Way of Living. *These video-tapes and transcriptions pursue the theme of the transformation of man independent of knowledge and time. He made a profound impression upon me and was the single most decisive influence of any living teacher I had personally encountered. His approach to self-inquiry was lucid, unwavering and correcting. I owe him a debt impossible to repay.*

From the moment we began our conversations I was struck by his quality of attention. There was nothing contrived about it nor was it based on a muscular effort of the will to attend. It might be likened, on a different level, to the dynamic of balance as when one rides a bicycle, drives a car or simply walks. Unless there is a disturbance in the inner ear or other impediment, normal walking is unselfconscious yet not unconscious. Beyond strength and skill, it entails knack, which is a gift. Since most of us walk there doesn't seem to be much, if anything, of a gift about it. Yet, without knack our walking would be unspontaneous, graceless, sheerly mechanical and wooden-puppet-like. Krishnamurti's listening was knackful. It had the simplicity and openness of a child with the alertness of a warrior. It combined the harmlessness of the dove with the wisdom of the serpent.

This way of being taught me much about education and teaching. It brought home to me why so many gifted students are lost to higher education—their chief complaint being that it all seems unreal, there being no relation shown between thinking one's life and living it.

I know of no other way of meeting this objection than through inviting the student to look at his or her conflict of motives through a pure act of attention, not as positive effort but as a negative one; negative, that is, since "in attention there is no exclusion, no resistance, and no effort—and therefore no frontier, no limits." Negative again, in that a pure act of attention does not open out upon a positive understanding. Rather it discovers the astonishing sufficiency within just not misunderstanding. Suddenly the distance between the striver and the goal no longer obtains for no time elapses between the act of attention and the healing already taking place. Here, timeliness is exact.

This negation is not undertaken in order to attain to something better. Krishnamurti puts it precisely: "Negation is to deny what is false [while] not knowing what is truth. [It is] to see the false in the false and to see the truth in the false, and it is the truth that denies the false. You see what is false, and the very seeing of what is false is the truth."

During our conversations over the span of those eighteen dialogues, another feature of attention as negation (in the above sense) began to disclose itself to me. The dialogues were entirely unrehearsed yet proceeded as from an order intrinsic to them. Many persons who saw and heard them from beginning to end have remarked this to me and in some cases the remark generated a dialogue between us that moved in like fashion provided that an uncontrived act of attention prevailed..

Literally, process is a going forward. Going forward means movement from a source. A complete process entails a beginning, a middle and an end and these structural nodes are susceptible to derangement if not held together by an ordering principle. As noted above, this principle is present with an uncontrived act of attention. Uncontrivance means that there is no preconceived set-up imposed upon the act of attention.

As the dialogues progressed it became clearer to me from Krishnamurti's statements that, as he put it, "the first step is the last step." It is this first step that at the outset either subverts the process or calls its flowering into being. Further, this first step cannot be one step among the others that follow. Rather, it is the one step that must inform all steps if the process is to remain sound throughout or, to put it remedially, if healing and health are to prevail. In that sense we never get beyond square one, nor is there any need to.

This first step is the seeing of the false in the false and this seeing of the false is the truth. How different this is from the egoic notion that one can look on truth, goodness and beauty, bare. In the strict sense there is no I here who makes a pure act of attention upon an object over there. Thus there is no contradiction between subject and object—the contradiction that has since time out of mind generated endlessly tiresome debates over how we know that we know and the conundrum of free will. Life lived genuinely meditatively, i.e., with an abiding pure act of attention is not embarrassed by such questions since even upon entertaining them it is lived free from a conflict of motives.

It is some twenty years since Krishnamurti and I conversed together and after the conclusion of our dialogues it was not my good fortune to see him again but our discussions continue to abide with me in spirit as freshly as they did two decades ago.

In pondering these things since then, one question in particular has grown in importance for me. What resource have we for making as well as abiding in an uncontrived act of attention? This question has the most poignant significance for anyone who asks, "What is the relation between thought which is goal oriented and life lived meditatively or without a why?"

During one of our dialogues called "Hearing and Seeing" Krishnamurti made the remarkable statement that hearing is not letting anything interfere with seeing. This remark renewed my passion for Socrates' claim that he had a demon within that always told him what not to do and this divine voice attended him constantly. I have thought to give this resource the name, primal intuition. By intuition here I do not mean one of Jung's four functions of the psyche, a function chiefly concerned in insight. Primal intuition, on the contrary, has no content and acts simply as a warning. Primal intuition lies below the threshold of personality and the psychic self. It is not coopted by archetypes nor is it subject to the suasions of will and feeling. However, when these latter are ineptly related to primal intuition, as the voice that tells one what not to do, this voice becomes muffled or even quite unheard. It seems that wild creatures receive it purely—especially those that continue to survive our human atrocities upon their domains. Perhaps it is allied with what the Hindus call Atman, the Buddhists, Suchness, and Christians, the Holy Spirit.

I believe this resource enables the serious self-enquirer to keep unconfused the natural function of goal oriented linear, calculative thinking and life lived meditatively, a way of being that is satisfied by its own exercise, a living without a why. Calculative thinking which is bent on a goal that lies outside the means taken to reach it is necessarily time-bound. Some have misunderstood Krishnamurti as denigrating thought of this order. This has caused them to look askance upon, even reject technology. This is a misreading. It is not technology, thought and knowledge that Krishnamurti inveighs against but their misuses.

Calculative and meditative thinking are opposed only in thought which has not yet penetrated to their reciprocal operation. A pure act of attention is not

"AS THE DIALOGUES PROGRESSED IT BECAME CLEARER TO ME FROM KRISHNAMURTI'S STATEMENTS THAT, AS HE PUT IT, 'THE FIRST STEP IS THE LAST STEP.' IT IS THIS FIRST STEP THAT AT THE OUTSET EITHER SUBVERTS THE PROCESS OR CALLS ITS FLOWERING INTO BEING....IT IS THE ONE STEP THAT MUST INFORM ALL STEPS IF THE PROCESS IS TO REMAIN SOUND THROUGHOUT."

—ALAN ANDERSON

prejudiced by any practical undertakings. On the contrary, without the meditative attitude that is open to primal intuition, practice of any kind is hostage to any number of fixations and aberrated notions. Imagination, for all its essential service to creativity, all too easily subserves the vagaries of chaotic emotion.

The sound relation between calculative and meditative thinking is not a coincidence of opposites but their co-operation. In this relation thought and existence reciprocate, the work of the world gets done while one lives without a why. Lao Tzu and Krishnamurti seem at one in Lao Tzu's line: "Tao does nothing, yet nothing is left undone."

I am deeply grateful for the instruction I received through my conversations with Krishnamurti for they remain an inexhaustible font of inspiration, suggestion and nourishment. They open out upon the boundless.[92]

Krishnamurti had an enduring relationship with the Spanish-speaking world. Although he was never able to spend as much time in those countries as he would have wished, still the bonds were there, sustained over the decades.

For years the Fundación Krishnamurti Latinoamericana was headquartered in Puerto Rico under the able leadership of Enrique Biascoechea and later Alfonso Colon. When it was decided to move the central office to Spain, Juan Colell was there to help. Steeped in the teachings, he had for years traveled around the world to hear Krishnamurti speak.

JUAN COLELL

PHARMACIST, BARCELONA, SPAIN

If you look at your problems and worries as you are observing the flowers now, your problems will be over.

Sometimes in life things happen without apparent meaning. That was the case for me in 1965 when my mother asked me if I wanted to come with her to attend the Saanen gatherings. I accepted the invitation without knowing exactly what that meant. During the talks it was easy to make friends and immediately a mutual friendship arose between Mr. Enrique Biascoechea from Puerto Rico and myself. Mr. Biascoechea was the first president of the Fundación, a position that he held until his death.

Enrique and his wife Isabel had a close friendship with Krishnaji and frequently the latter used to invite them to have lunch with him. On one of these occasions I drove them in my car from Gstaad to Chalet Tannegg where Krishnaji was waiting for us in front of the main door, Mr. Biascoechea introduced me to him saying: "This is my friend Juan; a young boy from Barcelona, Spain." Krishnaji looked at me smiling and said in perfect Catalán (a spoken language in a small area of North-eastern Spain and South-eastern France) taking us by surprise: "Barcelona és bona si la bossa sona." More or less that means: Barcelona is fine if the money bag makes a noise.

It is difficult to say that my life underwent a change because it depends on the references we make but it is not exaggerated to say that many deep challenges or incidents happened during Krishnaji's talks or when talking with him, that undoubtedly affected my life.

I remember one of these happenings some years later when a friend and I went to see Krishnaji. We went with a lot of questions and great inward turmoil. Krishnaji welcomed us in a simple room and we sat around the table bedecked with a little vase in the middle of it containing a bunch of flowers. It took a long time to bring out all our worries, meanwhile Krishnaji was looking at the flowers. Later on when we had finished our demented psychological talk, Krishnaji still remained looking at the flowers saying nothing. A little relieved but awaiting anxiously for some illuminating words, we joined with him in looking at the blooms. For a while, we stayed together with a certain harmony observing the flowers attentively. I cannot remember how long it took, until Krishnaji without removing his eyes from the bouquet said: "Sirs, if you look at your problems and worries as you are observing the flowers now, your problems will be over." That was the end of our meeting but even now these words are still living in my brain.

I am not able to see what my life would be without knowing the teachings. That does not mean that I understand profoundly the meaning of life and that I live every minute with no single shadow of conditioning, but it is also true that the contribution of Krishnaji and the teachings to my life, the logical sense of the words that this friend of all humanity said, has had some effect inside of me. In the same way, as the water is not the flower but contributes to its beauty, the teachings push me to grow in goodness.

"THE MAN WHO IS REALLY SERIOUS, WITH THE URGE TO FIND OUT WHAT TRUTH IS, HAS NO STYLE AT ALL. HE LIVES ONLY IN WHAT IS."

—BRUCE LEE

In his studies of both philosophy and the martial arts, Robert Colet came to a deeper understanding of the well spring behind certain aspects of *Jeet Kune Do* (the martial arts style of Bruce Lee). A martial artist himself he was interested to discover the relationship between Krishnamurti and Bruce Lee. The following article appeared in *Inside Kung-fu*.

R O B E R T   C O L E T

AUTHOR, KRISHNAMURTI: THE SPIRITUAL FORCE BEHIND BRUCE LEE

"You cannot look through an ideology, through a screen of words, through hopes and fears," so says Krishnamurti. Applying this to the martial arts, Bruce Lee finds, "You cannot express and be alive through static put-together form, through stylized movement." So began Lee's profound revolution of the martial arts. Empty-hand combat would never again be the same.

Bruce Lee found in the teachings of Krishnamurti the foundation of Jeet Kune Do. Remember: we are talking about Lee's philosophy and its relationship to the martial arts. We are not taking into consideration the combat aspects of JKD. There has already been plenty written on that aspect of the art. Rather, we are concerned with the "mental" or "spiritual" side of JKD, which is how the style differs so dramatically from its counterparts. The foundation of traditional martial arts are kata (forms), where the practitioner uses singular movement to simulate a fighting technique. He imitates the kata until they become second nature. JKD differs from styles because of the "absence of stereotyped techniques." as Lee succinctly put it.

Lee wanted "more." Traditional philosophy as an aid to martial arts development and as an avenue for spiritual growth were not enough. And this is where Krishnamurti came in.

Philosophy as a complement to the martial arts dates to the sixteenth-century, when the need lessened for fighting skills. Philosophy (Zen) transformed the martial arts from combat-to-the-death tactics to spiritual growth. A practitioner of the martial arts thus gained not only fighting techniques but also character and enrichment.

Taking the sayings of Krishnamurti—just as Lee must have done—one can apply them to the martial arts through Lee's words. Of course, this is not to say the teachings of Krishnamurti were the only source of Lee's philosophy. Lee also consulted the teachings of Zen and Taoism, among others. However, it is evident Krishnamurti played a significant role in the formation of JKD.

The following quotes are taken from Krishnamurti's Freedom from the Known, *unless otherwise stated. The right side [indented] shows how Lee applied Krishnamurti's words to the martial arts in the Tao of Jeet Kune Do.*

KRISHNAMURTI
BRUCE LEE

You cannot look through an ideology, through a screen of words, through hopes and fears.

You cannot express and be alive through static put-together form, through stylized movement.

We are those books, we are those ideas, so heavily conditioned are we by them.

We are those kata, we are those classical blocks and thrusts, so heavily conditioned are we by them.

As long as I am looking at life from a particular point of view or from a particular experience I have cherished, or from some particular knowledge I have gathered, which is my background, which is the "me," I cannot see totally…I can see the totality of something only when thought does not interfere.

You cannot see a street fight in its totality, observing it from the viewpoint of a boxer, a kung-fu man, a karateka, a wrestler, a judo man and so forth. You can see clearly only when style does not interfere.

Truth is not something dictated by your pleasure or pain, or by your conditioning as a Hindu or whatever religion you belong to.

Fighting is not something dictated by your conditioning as a kung-fu man, a karate man, a judo man or what not.

We accept a standard of behavior as part of our tradition as Hindus or Christians or whatever we happen to be. We look to someone to tell us what is right or wrong behavior, what is right or wrong thought, and in following this pattern our conduct and our thinking become mechanical, our responses automatic.

The secondhand artist blindly following his sensei or sifu accepts his pattern. As a result, his action and, more importantly, his thinking become mechanical. His responses become automatic, according to set patterns, making him narrow and limited.

The man who is really serious, with the urge to find out what truth is, what love is, has not concept at all. He lives only in what is.

The man who is really serious, with the urge to find out what truth is, has no style at all. He lives only in what is.

These examples are not a definitive comparative analysis of the two men, but what can be easily observed is the enormous impact Krishnamurti had on Lee. He became riveted by Krishnamurti's teachings and their application to the martial arts. He discovered that style was limited; it was merely a routine, a mindless repetition of set patterns, a form of conditions which offered no self-knowledge or freedom. For Lee, style was merely propaganda.

Through the teachings of Krishnamurti, Lee sought a fuller self-expression through the martial arts. From the time he took up Wing Chun at age fourteen, Lee grew, improved, and flourished in what was to become his first love. But still he wanted more. He was constantly "creatively discontented" with the state of martial art. He realized the limitations in every martial art, including wing chun. He shattered these limitations, challenged tradition and broke uncharted ground.

He had to tell the wold of his discovery. So he went to Hong Kong and made several movies. Then came his enduring masterpiece, Enter The Dragon.

His mission was complete. He revolutionized "consciousness" of the martial arts. Through motion pictures he made the world and the martial arts community witness his discovery. He brought upon himself and the world a new vision.

And then he left as quickly as he appeared. But by then he had completed his process and yearned for peace. It came suddenly—too suddenly—but nevertheless, he fulfilled his mission.

Just like itself, the martial arts go on, forever searching for fuller expression.[93]

THE PILGRIMS PATH TO SARNATH IS THE PLACE WHERE THE BUDDHA WALKED AND GAVE HIS FIRST TALK TO HIS DISCIPLES AFTER HIS ENLIGHTENMENT.

K RISHNAMURTI'S YEARLY STAYS IN INDIA attracted more than their share of philosophers and religious figures. With the Tibetan diaspora of the 1950s, many of those fleeing from the Chinese incursion settled in India. In addition to Dharmsala, the main center in the north and headquarters of the Dalai Lama, Sarnath was a potent focus of Buddhism. A short distance from the Krishnamurti Rajghat school on the banks of the Ganges, the pilgrims path to Sarnath was the place where the Buddha walked and gave his first talk to his disciples after his enlightenment. In that auspicious spot lives Professor S. Rinpoche, who had many long talks and discussions with Krishnamurti.

PROFESSOR S. RINPOCHE

DIRECTOR, CENTRAL INSTITUTE OF HIGHER TIBETAN STUDIES, SARNATH, VARANASI, INDIA

I have had the great fortune of having listened to Krishnaji and discussed with him many a philosophical matter. In the beginning, I always tried to understand him with my Buddhist background. While doing so, I had a feeling of uneasiness. I thought that perhaps that was not the correct way to understand him. I felt that I must listen to Krishnaji with all emptiness, the state devoid of thought, without any presupposition or conditioning. But my mind was so conditioned with the Buddhist teaching that I placed him into Buddha's position and that was not the correct way to understand him.

I discussed this matter with Krishnaji himself in depth and then I realized that between the Buddha and Krishnaji, there was a basic difference of approach. The Buddha always spoke at two levels, the relative and the absolute. Krishnaji never spoke at the relative level; he always spoke at the level of the absolute. The relative truth goes with the process of thought and the Buddha adopted that as one of his methods to help people take a deeper inquiry. Apparently, Krishnaji's approach is that this method is a longer journey; it would take a longer way and people should therefore get away from the relative truth in a spontaneous manner and get into the absoluteness, the absolute truth. When the Buddha speaks of the absolute, I personally do not find any difference with Krishnaji's teachings or Krishnaji's teachings with the Buddha's teaching of prajna-paramita *or the absolute truth.*

Another difference between them is in preparation of the people, the listeners. Krishnamurti is silent or doesn't speak of preparation, whereas the Buddha dealt quite a lot with the preparation of the person, it being a prerequisite for them to reach the level of transformation. Both the Buddha and Krishnaji have similar positions; at the moment of transformation or transmutation there is no time, there is no graduation. It must be spontaneous and immediate; whether this side or that side, perception is perception. There is no slow growth or graduation. The Buddha dealt with the preparation of the person aspiring by reaching up to that level with certain graduations and methods. But Krishnaji never accepted these things. He perhaps took for granted that everyone was capable of transforming himself without involving the preparative measures.

Thought is a basic instrument of our life; but for perception, thought has no role at all to play. All kinds of thought have to be negated, according to the

"THE BUDDHA ALWAYS SPOKE AT TWO LEVELS, THE RELATIVE AND THE ABSOLUTE. KRISHNAJI NEVER SPOKE AT THE RELATIVE LEVEL; HE ALWAYS SPOKE AT THE LEVEL OF THE ABSOLUTE."

—S. RINPOCHE

Buddha as well as according to Krishnaji. But among Buddhist people thought has been accepted as one of the means or methods during preparation. As I said earlier, Krishnaji doesn't accept or doesn't talk about preparation.

The basic point to be emphasized is to become free from every kind of conditioning, imposition or presupposition. In order to be free from all kinds of thought, the words of the teacher would be one of the major hindrances. Therefore, Krishnaji specifically emphasized denying any teacher-taught-relationship in the ordinary sense and he encouraged people to participate in inquiry, in search. Their own minds are to be actively used for searching. The attitude of dependency is the most dangerous hindrance to the development of a person to perceive reality.

Both the Buddha and Krishnamurti employed the method of negating things—negation, because reality as perceived by them is incommunicable through language, through words, or through any other means of communication. The only way left for them is to negate all possible conceptions of thought or imagination. In this way the person comes closer to reality after negating everything, then the way of seeing reality becomes more pointed, there is a possibility of seeing reality as it is.[94]

It is only a mind that looks at a tree or the stars or the sparkling waters of a river with complete self abandonment that knows what beauty is, and when we are actually seeing we are in a state of love.

—*FREEDOM FROM THE KNOWN, 1969*

Professor Hillary Rodrigues is deeply versed in Indian religious culture and philosophy and although Krishnamurti's teaching is not an offspring of Hinduism—despite his Indian name and nationality—Rodrigues found reading him was "extraordinary," as he says. His doctoral thesis was entitled *Insight and the Religious Mind: An Analysis of Krishnamurti's Thought.*

HILLARY PETER RODRIGUES, PH.D

PROFESSOR OF RELIGIOUS STUDIES, UNIVERSITY OF LETHBRIDGE, ALBERTA, CANADA

It was with some reluctance that I picked up my first Krishnamurti book in 1973. I had been scouring bookstores for literature to satiate my growing interest in classical Eastern philosophy and the exploration of consciousness, but, unlike many of my generation, was determined not to succumb to the exotic appeal of a contemporary Eastern guru. Krishnamurti's obviously Indian name had triggered my reactions. I had already realized, by this time, that satisfactory and enduring answers to my burning questions about the mystery of existence were not likely to be found in a book, or in the words of some great sage, however inspirational. Meaning was something I would have to find for myself although I really did not know where to look or how to proceed. So it was with a certain disenchantment with myself for hoping for a glimmer of light in yet another book, partially with an amplified critical faculty, ready to discard anything that smacked of nonsense, but also with a sincere thirst for truth, that I first read Krishnamurti.

The experience was nothing short of extraordinary. Unlike the other works I had been reading, where the language was cloaked in mystery, or where the ideas were culturally and historically remote, here was a man who spoke about the world as I saw it in the depths of my heart. His language was my language, his concerns my concerns, his observations my observations. But where he differed was in his courage to speak of truth as he saw and lived it, and in the profound distance he had travelled in his journey with it. Through the example of his own passion, Krishnamurti gave me the courage to continue a self-reliant inquiry into truth without capitulating to the temporary and detrimental solace offered by faith, hope, and ideologically-based community. I travelled extensively, and in the years that ensued this spirit of inquiry led to insights into thought and the processes of consciousness which radically changed my life and which, to this day, I can still mark as its most significant events. Some years later, still with the euphoria of those transformative events, to my good fortune and quite by chance, I heard Krishnamurti speak in the Oak Grove at Ojai.

This time the encounter was tempering. I saw that it was possible to continue to live vulnerably within the new landscape I now inhabited, allowing myself to be revealed and shaped by the unfolding processes of consciousness. Here, before me, was a man who had matured through the action of the creative movement of the real, unimpeded by the limitations of thought. What struck me most of all was his utter ordinariness. It was this which was extraordinary, for Krishnamurti was above all a human being, naked and vulnerable, unadorned and unconcealed, fearlessly unattached to anything even the peculiarities of his own nature.

While engaged in graduate studies in religion, I again found myself inclined to examine Krishnamurti's teachings in depth, although this time from a scholarly perspective. While enthusiastically supported in this endeavor by many respected mentors, I encountered opposition from a small faction of intellectually gifted but small-minded scholars who felt that work on Krishnamurti was at best unimportant, if not quite irrelevant. To my great satisfaction, and in vindication of the confidence shown in me by my thesis supervisors, Insight and Religious Mind *became the first analytical study of Krishnamurti's teachings to be accepted for publication by an academic press in the West. Such studies open the door to serious scholarly work on Krishnamurti's thought enabling him to take his rightful place among the most renowned educators, philosophers, and religious figures of this century.*

Krishnamurti's life, as well as his teachings, are crucially important to scholars in the field of religious studies since he is widely regarded as a contemporary religious person of the highest distinction. What is particularly noteworthy is that Krishnamurti belongs to no established religious order, and intentionally left without establishing one. Instead, Krishnamurti points to an essentially religious way of life which is open to everyone, but which can only be lived without reliance on any authority whatsoever. It is an approach which frees the individual to a direct and anonymous relationship with the source and substance of creation. As a result of his life and teachings, Krishnamurti has expanded the meaning of religion to encompass a way of life which is fundamentally mystical. However, unlike conventional mysticism which is often forcibly confined to the language and symbolism of a particular cultural milieu, Krishnamurti's approach is utterly and necessarily divorced from the context of tradition.

The surging interest in Krishnamurti suggests the capacity of his teachings to prove remarkably meaningful in areas where conventional religions appear to

"WHAT IS PARTICULARLY NOTEWORTHY IS THAT KRISHNAMURTI BELONGS TO NO ESTABLISHED RELIGIOUS ORDER, AND INTENTIONALLY LEFT WITHOUT ESTABLISHING ONE. INSTEAD, KRISHNAMURTI POINTS TO AN ESSENTIALLY RELIGIOUS WAY OF LIFE WHICH IS OPEN TO EVERYONE, BUT WHICH CAN ONLY BE LIVED WITHOUT RELIANCE ON ANY AUTHORITY WHATSOEVER."

—HILLARY RODRIGUES

be seriously failing. A close and ongoing examination of his thought and impact is certain to yield fruitful insights into social processes and the human condition.

Miles away in California a young film-maker was touched by the talks he heard and books he read. At the request of the Krishnamurti Foundation of America, he later video-taped many of Krishnamurti's talks and discussions and brought a high standard of excellence to the quality of the work. Mendizza is also the director of two feature-length documentary films, *Krishnamurti: The Challenge of Change*, released in 1984, and *Krishnamurti: With A Silent Mind*, released in 1989, both films have toured in the United States, Canada, Europe and India.

MICHAEL MENDIZZA

FILMMAKER, LOS ANGELES, CALIFORNIA

"WE TRAVELED AGAIN TO
ENGLAND AND TO INDIA
INTERVIEWING THOSE
WHO WERE TOUCHED BY
KRISHNAMURTI'S LIFE AND BY
HIS LIGHT. I SEARCHED THE
ARCHIVES AND HIS PERSONAL
WRITINGS HOPING TO REVEAL
SOME ESSENCE."

—MICHAEL MENDIZZA

I came first as a seeker. A set of tapes arrived unsolicited and I listened each night for over a year. They were compelling. They were new, important and they confused me. Then I found a book and it led to Ojai. He was still alive and would soon be speaking under the oak trees.

It was spring and the mountains sparkled. Older men with canes, ladies with sun hats sitting in well marked chairs, middle aged professors and young hippies all huddled together, listening, struggling. It must have been 1975 or 1976. I was alone, eager, and sat as close as I could.

I came again the next year and he was there, sitting in that special chair, under the trees, intense, passionate, almost desperate. The following year, as I walked into the grove, three video cameras poked above the audience. As the talk began a mysterious vastness came and when it had passed I approached the woman who had given the announcements. I offered my services as a young film-maker. It was six months before we met to discuss the importance of documenting the last years of Krishnamurti's life. This is how it all began.

The following spring I was invited to lunch. This was to be my first real meeting, the closest I had ever been. We all sat around a long table. Relaxed, light and very human he listened, told stories and made us laugh, not at all the speaker I had seen in the grove. Though I grew to love him deeply, I never felt familiar. I called him Sir, which seemed close enough for me.

A few weeks later, with camera in hand, I was on a plane headed for British Columbia. He was visiting a school there. Soon I was in Switzerland filming the public talks. Then in the Netherlands visiting people and places that were so much a part of his youth. England was next and then on to India. I found in India that most people were like those I had met in America and in Europe, each understood a little.

I was still a seeker, following the sun as it pushed away the darkness. I had a thousand questions and each seemed important, but none, I found, was deep enough or real enough to trouble him. Yet I wanted to understand, not just a little but the truth of it. While in India I wrote in my journal: "To understand in this way, each thought must be large enough to hold the entire universe." Then

I set down my pen and as the sun set behind the ancient hills of the Rishi Valley, a sudden clarity arose and I caught a glimpse of what I believe he must have meant by "freedom from the known." With that my search came to an end.

For five years the woman, the one who shared my passion and who believed in me, worked on that picture. When it was done Krishnamurti sat near the front and watched like a child, as glimpses of his life flickered on the screen. It was important that he approve and he did. None of us knew then that the next two years would be his last.

A few weeks before Krishnamurti's death a second film was begun. People from around the world had come to say good-bye. Those who were willing sat before my camera and described the moments they had shared with this man who lay dying near by. We traveled again to England and to India interviewing those who were touched by his life and by his light. I searched the archives and his personal writings hoping to reveal some essence. What was it all about? Years passed. The work became a meditation, a mantra. The process gave new shape to my life and what I would do with my life.

A year after his death I was walking the grounds of Brockwood and that special presence—his presence—surrounded me. Then another feeling emerged. Several months earlier my son, then only seven or eight months old, lay sleeping. My wife was away and he awoke, frightened to be alone. I came, lifted him and he looked at me. Then completely secure, he drifted off to sleep again. As this child relaxed in my arms that familiar feeling radiated from within him. It passed through me and filled the room. It was vast. It was affection beyond description, hovering.

While walking in the English countryside I understood something about the man and his life. Without giving it a name he was there in the boundless affection radiating from an innocent child. The teachings are but road signs pointing to something alive, vital and expansive. When he spoke the words he used lay upon this boundless sea of affection. It surrounded me like the trees and the mountains he loved so much. It was immediate and spread in all directions, reaching out before it poured over the horizon.

He once said, and I feel it is true…when we stand completely alone, and in that stillness become a light to ourselves, there we will find Krishnamurti.

The love of trees is, or should be, a part of our nature, like breathing. They are part of the earth like us, full of beauty with the strange aloofness. They are so still, full of leaves, rich and full of light, casting long shadows and wild with joy when there is a storm. Every leaf, even at the very top, is dancing in the slight breeze, and the shadows are welcoming in the strong sun. As you sit with you back against the trunk, if you are very quiet, you establish a lasting relationship with nature. Most people have lost that relationship; they look at all the mountains, valleys, the streams and the thousand trees as they pass by in their cars or walk up the hills chattering, but they are too absorbed in their own problems to look and be quiet. The smoke is going up in a single column across the valley, and below a lorry goes by, heavy with logs of recently-cut trees, their bark still on them. A group of boys and girls passes by chattering and shattering the stillness of the wood.

UNPUBLISHED DIARY, AUGUST 7, 1981

T HE YEARS WERE WEARING DOWN FOR KRISHNAMURTI. The constant travel in different climates and time zones inevitably took its toll, yet the 1980s saw activity that was as intense as ever. As we have seen, one of the great joys of Krishnamurti's life and a great release from the intensity of talking was to be in nature. Trees, plants and animals had been close kin to him for all of his life. Many stories are told of his relationship with bears, tigers, monkeys and birds.

Alasdair Coyne had an opportunity to work with Krishnamurti in the garden of Pine Cottage and was able to be with him when he was not the "speaker."

ALASDAIR COYNE

LANDSCAPE GARDENER, ENVIRONMENTALIST, OJAI, CALIFORNIA

At university in Scotland I was studying philosophy and related subjects and I came across the writings of Krishnamurti. For a year or so I wasn't aware of any foundation or of any school or center, or in fact that the man was still alive. By

chance, I came across the information that there was a center at Brockwood Park and I went there to attend a gathering, probably in September 1974. I camped out in the rain with everybody else and was enthralled with the place and with the speaker. I applied several months later for a position as an apprentice gardener with no experience. I was accepted in the spring of the following year. I was attracted to the place mainly because of Krishnamurti and I suppose those aspects of his teachings which attracted many people. Such as, no down pat answers to questions and throwing you back on yourself to find answers to the deeper things that concern you as an individual. I also went there being interested in becoming a gardener which has since become my life-long work, although I wouldn't have known it then. I worked there for two and a half years before coming to live in

"HE WOULD LIKE TO HAVE BEEN A GARDENER IF HE HAD NOT BEEN A SPEAKER."
—ALASDAIR COYNE

ABOVE: KRISHNAMURTI AT CASTLE EERDE IN HOLLAND, 1921. OPPOSITE PAGE: KRISHNAMURTI PLANTING TREES IN OJAI.

Ojai, where I was hired to plant and maintain the garden around the newly-enlarged Pine Cottage.

Krishnaji was very interested in the garden at Pine Cottage. He would take time off from his other responsibilities to come and walk around the garden, show an interest in the plants and want to know how things were doing, or what plant would fill in this gap. For me, that brought him down to a much more human level than that at which I had previously seen him. We developed a warm, caring relationship where there was a common concern with the look of the grounds and an excitement with something new coming into bloom. Every year when he would come back to the U.S., usually in the spring, he would always want to walk around the whole garden, we took a look together at what had changed, what might have not done so well, what was doing well, what we could improve, always where we could plant more roses. Roses were his favorite flower; he loved the fragrance of them and a red rose was his favorite color. Over the years I got to know Krishnaji much more as a man concerned with the plants.

In spite of the public impression of Krishnaji as a person who would speak in front of thousands of people during the year, inside he was a very shy person. When I would be up around Pine Cottage, working in the garden, if there were other people around he wouldn't come out and look at the garden. It was on days when nothing was happening and it was quite quiet and there was nobody else around the orchard or in the grounds, that he would put on his hat and gloves and come out and walk around the garden and grab me and take me around to the far side of the house and show me this or that or ask me something. I even handed him a rake a couple of times.

Krishnaji said publicly several times, and I recall also hearing it privately in the grounds at Pine Cottage, that if he hadn't been a speaker he would have liked to have been a gardener. He would have been a good gardener. I know that he would gesture towards the orange trees around Pine Cottage and say that he had planted all of them; probably back in the 1940s. He would look at a plant and wonder what it needed to make it happier. He deeply appreciated the plants and flowers, things with a scent, things with a particular color, things that attracted humming birds, all of these were important to him.

It has only recently occurred to me (in 1994) that one common garden request from Krishnaji has become one of my most valuable landscaping principles. Whenever he'd see seedlings germinating around the garden, he'd say, "Leave it, leave it." He didn't have the kind of mind that says, "This is growing in the pathway; we must hoe it up." And so the pathway around Pine Cottage became landscaped by self-sown seedlings. And very nicely so, though naturally we left somewhere to walk, too. In the last few years I've been designing landscaping areas to emphasize the use of plants which sow seedlings fairly readily—because these seedlings can fill in an area and eventually expand it, without any irrigation, soil amendment or cost, which is quite a bonus in this arid climate.

Krishnaji treated me very much as an equal when we were out in the garden—or even just discussing the garden. If I would try to hold the door open for him he'd say, "No, no, no. You first," and hold it open for me instead. It was an equal relationship, it wasn't one of employer-employee. He was interested in

"HE WOULD GESTURE TOWARDS THE ORANGE TREES AROUND PINE COTTAGE AND SAY THAT HE HAD PLANTED ALL OF THEM; PROBABLY BACK IN THE 1940S. HE WOULD LOOK AT A PLANT AND WONDER WHAT IT NEEDED TO MAKE IT HAPPIER."

—ALASDAIR COYNE

what I could tell him about a particular garden question and he was interested in learning the reasons why some things were growing poorly and how to help plants that looked like they needed assistance.

My last meeting with Krishnaji was about a week before he died. He was in the living room of Pine Cottage, wrapped up warmly in a blanket and not looking very well. Naturally he had wanted to say hello. He knew I was around the house—he'd probably seen me go past the windows and I was asked to come in for a few minutes. In spite of all the business he had to do with the Foundations in many countries, he wanted to talk to the gardener for a minute. He asked some questions about how the plants were doing. He'd seen from inside the house the new rose bed that we'd planted for him, and I don't know if he ever got to see it close up outside. He wanted to know what we could plant on a little area to the east of the house that had some bare spots. It was touching that in his final days he wanted to know what would be continuing on afterwards. He wanted to have an idea of how it would look, even though he wouldn't be there to see it; then he said, "Come see me again," and that was the last time I saw him.

I don't believe, as many have, that Krishnaji was more than a human being. I feel that every individual has a validity in their own right and I don't think Krishnaji had any more than any other person. On the other hand, some people are more wonderful and have done great things with their lives and I appreciated the privilege of getting to know Krishnaji as the gardener when he wasn't the speaker. Many people got to know the speaker, got to see the speaker and listen to him talk. I felt privileged to have gotten to know the man when all of those things were not going on. I'm not saying there were two different people, the ordinary human being and the speaker,—but I enjoyed knowing the human side of him.

Krishnaji was very fond of the scenic beauty of Ojai; he would gesture up to the hills and describe how he had been all over them in his youth. He'd been up and down Topa Topa, along Chief Peak and probably behind the ranges there, exploring on his own or with others. This inspired me to work for ecological preservation—which has since become a major focus for my life.

Krishnaji loved being close to wildlife. He spoke of following a bobcat for several miles in the foothills behind Ojai—close but unseen. In India, he spoke to the monkeys. He wanted to touch a tiger from the car window, in a forest preserve.

Perhaps my favorite comment from Krishnaji the speaker, however, is when he said something like this to a public gathering—"You'd all be much better off to be out in nature somewhere. You can learn much more from nature than from the speaker."

Coming down on a different, equally stony path, there was a small open space, green and fresh. As one came up around a bend, there was a huge, dark black bear with four of its cubs, the size of large cats. The mother pushed them up a tree and as they were furiously climbing up it one could hear the noise of their claws on the bark. They stopped after reaching a certain height. The mother was barring the way, firm on four furry legs, facing one. We looked at each other without any movement, she challenging and the other not accepting it. We stood there, unafraid, and presently the man turned his back and went on his way. One never realized the danger of the situation. It dawned upon one only when the incident was related to the forest ranger. He was furious, pointing out that the bear could have mauled one to pieces, especially when she had her cubs. But the huge bear with its small cubs, the floating snow-capped mountain, the vast stillness, wiped away all fear and danger.

UNPUBLISHED DIARY, AUGUST 7, 1981

Deepak Chopra is well known as the best-selling author of *Ageless Body, Timeless Mind* and many other books and tapes which relate to inner and outer healing. He is Executive Director of the Sharp Institute for Human Potential and Mind Body Medicine.

DEEPAK CHOPRA, M.D.

AUTHOR, *AGELESS BODY, TIMELESS MIND*, SAN DIEGO, CALIFORNIA

"IN MY OWN LIFE
KRISHNAMURTI INFLUENCED
ME PROFOUNDLY AND
HELPED ME PERSONALLY
BREAK THROUGH THE
CONFINES OF MY OWN SELF-
IMPOSED RESTRICTIONS TO
MY FREEDOM."

—DEEPAK CHOPRA

My first encounter with Krishnamurti was in the mid 1980s. He was giving a lecture at the Felt Forum in Madison Square Garden. It was a cold wintery morning, there was sleet and snow and a thousand people were waiting outside. I was one of them. Krishnamurti spoke for two hours. He was direct, profound and ruthlessly honest. When I walked out the sleet and snow had stopped and there was bright sunshine. For some reason I was feeling that the sun was bright and warm because I was feeling bright and warm inside.

I never met Krishnamurti personally although I have been close to many who were close to him and I see the remarkable effect this man had on their lives.

In my own life Krishnamurti influenced me profoundly and helped me personally break through the confines of my own self-imposed restrictions to my freedom.

In Washington D.C., Lois Hobson was head of the South African office of Africare, a training program for young Africans studying in the United States until their return to their own countries in Africa. Currently living in Johannesburg, she is pursuing similar work independently.

LOIS M. HOBSON

MANAGEMENT CONSULTANT, JOHANNESBURG, SOUTH AFRICA

I think I was one of those children who grew up an old woman long before my time. From a very early age I was quite conscious of being alive and wondering, "Why was I born?"—not as cynicism, but out of a deep sense of wonderment about it all. This level of inquiry was not just childish curiosity, but something much deeper which persisted in my consciousness throughout my life. Religion played a part in my younger years, slowly dissolving over the decades into a spiritual search rather than a secular choice.

As I entered my fourth decade, this spiritual search had become a priority in my everyday life. I read just about all the popular and esoteric literature having to do with humankind's spiritual journey, even traveling to India to experience the mystical teachings of one renowned guru. I suppose at this point in my life, my own maturity, together with the unrelenting question about the "why" of my birth into this world, had unknowingly prepared me for the clear, concise, and shattering teachings of J. Krishnamurti.

My first encounter with K's teachings was through one of his books The Awakening of Intelligence, *which had rested in my bookcase for well over a year before I picked it up to read. I read every chapter with the blissful satisfaction of a gastronome dining on a culinary feast. In the midst of imbibing*

the dialogue between K and David Bohm on the nature of thought and the "I,"
something extraordinary happened which I am at pains to express today. The best
I can say is that a crumbling took place inside—a shattering of something
which over the next several months played out in my dreams. I finished the book
some time later and immediately sought to find out if this person, this J.
Krishnamurti, was still alive so that I could meet him. My search, which had
stretched out well over forty years, ended that day with the reading of The
Awakening of Intelligence *and the introduction from that period on to the*
teachings of J. Krishnamurti

I did have the good fortune to meet K and to spend some limited time in his
company. I read every word of his teachings that I could obtain, taking them in
as if my very life depended on it. What I began to find in my life was a new
inner freedom, a capacity to observe myself, to experience my own baggage, to
savor more objectively my relationships, and to watch and feel the emotional
rollercoaster of my own self. The answer to "Why was I born?" became "I" do not
know—and with that came freedom. The search is over. The journey continues.[95]

Sarjit Siddoo and her sister Jugdis Siddoo, both medical doctors with a dedicated and longtime involvement with Krishnamurti's work, spend part of the year in Canada, where they support a Krishnamurti Educational and Conference Center. The rest of the year they are in the Punjab in India, where they founded and run a hospital in their mother's native village. The Village Hospital was opened in 1957 by Indira Gandhi and was attended by many dignitaries including the Canadian High Commissioner.

Their work in Canada takes them from Vancouver to Victoria Island where their Conference Center is located.

"KRISHNAJI ASKED MY SISTER
AND ME TO SPREAD THE
TEACHINGS ACROSS CANADA
LIKE A PRAIRIE FIRE."
—SARJIT SIDDOO

SARJIT SIDDOO M.D.

FOUNDER, THE VILLAGE HOSPITAL, PUNJAB, INDIA AND KRISHNAMURTI
EDUCATIONAL CENTER, VICTORIA ISLAND, CANADA

EB: Over the last several years what kind of interest
have you found in Canada? People are apparently
reading Krishnamurti's books. Have you noticed an
outpouring of interest?

SS: Definitely. When we first started one hardly saw any
Krishnamurti books in bookstores, and now you can
go into even the most conservative bookshops and K
is there on the shelves. Now almost every library has
at least some K books.

Some years ago, Krishnaji asked my sister Jugdis and
me to spread the teachings across Canada. Since then
there has been an upsurge in interest. Many academics as well as lay
people are asking for more information about K Our biggest problem
is that Canada is a vast country stretching from the Atlantic to Pacific
Oceans, and yet proportionately Canada has a very small population.
One of our greatest concerns has been how to centralize the teachings
in Canada and make them available to a maximum number of people.
Recently we have been greatly

JUGDIS (SECOND FROM LEFT)
AND SARJIT SIDDOO WITH
KRISHNAMURTI AND FRIENDS.

encouraged to find people coming to the Center on Victoria Island from as far away as Nova Scotia.

EB: You've had the opportunity over these last twenty some years to be in quite close contact with Krishnamurti. Have you any observations about Krishnamurti the man, as well as the teachings?

SS: I think his teachings are extraordinary, just as I feel the man himself was extraordinary. For many years, my sister and I were looking for a "guru." We had read many scriptures of various religions, including what we were brought up in, which was the Sikh religion, as well as the Christian, Hindu and Buddhist religions. I used to wonder if enlightened people really existed on earth at this time? Our primary search in India was to see if saints existed now. If truth *is* then why couldn't we find someone now?

It was about that time that I had given up and was becoming cynical about the whole thing. Coming into contact with Krishnaji changed that. It definitely changed the course of our lives. I was having personal difficulties at that time and I found that, after Mother and Father passed away, I was confronted with other things in life which perhaps I was not ready to face. At such times I would read Krishnamurti. He said that when you read his books with total attention, that in itself was a meditation.

EB: What was most significant to you in the teaching?

SS: Perhaps the most significant thing was that he forced you to look for salvation not out there but within yourself, which he referred to as the "Inner Revolution." It is true that throughout the ages man has looked for change out there, whether political, religious, social or economic. People want to find a teacher who is going to instantly transport them into Nirvana. K pointed out that there is no easy way to enlightenment, it's hard work. That, I feel, is the most significant thing he pointed out—look inward not outward.

It is easy to understand all of this intellectually, but the application is a Himalayan task. When you are in a crisis, reading K, one realizes that intense sorrow, for instance, is not really for the departed one but for oneself who is left behind.

Krishnamurti has made a very great contribution to the world especially in this century. He speaks to us in 20th-century language. Other spiritual giants have talked in their own era, but through interpretation, the real message gets diluted and is often biased according to the interpreter. With K one does not have to interpret. Everything is available in his exact words—in books, audio tapes and videos.

EB: What do you think the future of his work is going to be?

SS: Well, I think it's something that will emerge. There will be a latent period of hard work behind the scenes so to speak. Then, if there is unity and love among all the foundations, a tremendous energy can be created and this energy will then take care of the future.[96]

Van Morrison needs no introduction to the music loving public. His songs are legendary and have attracted a world-wide following. His intense and personal lyrics probe the heart of today's generation and reflect his own inner search.

VAN MORRISON

SINGER, SONGWRITER, AND MUSICIAN, LONDON, ENGLAND

Although I came across and read Krishnamurti's books in the early 1970s, I only heard him speak once, at Masonic Hall in San Francisco.

As far back as I can remember I have been influenced by religious and philosophic works and I had a big change in my state of mind just prior to discovering Krishnamurti's books. His philosophy corresponded to what I myself was going through on an inward level.

I feel the meaning of Krishnamurti for our time is that one has to think for oneself and not be swayed by any outside religions or spiritual authorities.

Some time ago I wrote "In the Garden" from my album No Guru, No Method, No Teacher. *Part of the lyrics are:*

> *And then one day you*
> *came back home*
> *You were a creature all in rapture*
> *You had the key to your*
> *soul and you did open that*
> *day you came back to the garden*

The song concludes with:

> *In the garden, in the*
> *garden, wet with rain*
> *No Guru, no method, no teacher*
> *Just you and I and nature*
> *And the father in the garden*

With the expansion of the scope of modern medicine, Dr. Larry Dossey has been a leading practitioner of "alternative medicine". His most recent book, *Healing Words,* explores other avenues of medical possibilities. Dr. Dossey is co-chair, Panel on Mind/Body Interventions, Office of Alternative Medicine, National Institute of Health.

LARRY DOSSEY M.D.

AUTHOR, SPACE, TIME AND MEDICINE, SANTA FE, NEW MEXICO

"KRISHNAMURTI'S WRITINGS
CHANGED MY LIFE, AS THEY
HAVE INFLUENCED THE LIVES
OF THOUSANDS OF OTHERS
WORLDWIDE. HIS BOOKS
SHOULD BE REGARDED AS
WHAT THEY REALLY ARE:
SACRED LITERATURE."

—LARRY DOSSEY

In this post-literate age, it is commonly said, that books are too rational, intellectual, and "left-brained" to make much of a difference in one's spiritual progress. Nonsense! Krishnamurti's writings changed my life, as they have influenced the lives of thousands of others worldwide. His books should be regarded as what they really are: sacred literature.

G.K. Chesterton once said, "Christianity has not been tried and found wanting, it has been found difficult, and not tried." The same could be said, by and large, of Krishnamurti's teachings. Many say they are too difficult because they contain no pat formulas. But what of it? Transformation has never been easy; it has never been something automatically attainable at a weekend seminar. Krishnamurti knew this, of course, and I honor his refusal to trivialize or popularize the majesty of his teachings.

"Is the universe friendly?" Einstein once asked. To which we could reply: "It must be; it gave us Krishnamurti."

Another in the vast network of friends and co-workers in their own countries is Shigatoshi Takahashi. In every field of endeavor something of Krishnamurti's message found a home. In the life of a businessman it also found its mark.

The story is told that as Krishnamurti made his last trip from Madras to Los Angeles, stopping briefly at the Tokyo airport, he was met by Takahashi. A round-trip ticket had been purchased, and after flying on the same plane with Krishnamurti to Los Angeles, Takahashi, never leaving the airport, returned immediately to Tokyo.

SHIGATOSHI TAKAHASHI

BUSINESSMAN, TOKYO, JAPAN

EB: What has Krishnamurti taught you about how to run your business?

ST: Before I came across Krishnamurti's teaching, my business was to make effort, to compete with others, to compare with others, to have a target, to have the will to realize something, to make some kind of plan, but after I understood Krishnamurti's teaching, all of those things I found quite unnecessary, because they are all based upon your self-centered activity, your self-centered consciousness, which gave you confusion in handling your business. If you can be free, entirely, of it, then you can engage in that business deal most smoothly with the result as satisfactory as possible. That is my present way of operating business. I am now enjoying my business much more than before.

EB: If you are not competitive and aggressive, won't you be taken advantage of?

ST: I considered it that way in the beginning and I felt very uneasy of what the result might be but once you forget your self-centered activity and carry on your business free of it, the result will be completely different.

EB: Did people respond differently to you?

ST: Naturally. Because I changed, why can't they change? So when I changed myself, I found out they changed too, and the result was completely contrary to what I had feared.

EB: What religious disciplines have you studied and how is Krishnamurti different from those other disciplines?

ST: In my case, I had been studying Buddhism, and in Buddhism they are asking us various things. For instance, to make meditation, that means Zen, to make fasting, and in some cases they ask us to make an entire copy of a long sutra. In my own case, I copied all the words of a long sutra of the name of Hokekyo with a Japanese brush pen. It took me about one year and a half writing at least for one hour every morning. They also asked us to recite in the morning some kind of sutra, or to tour from one temple to the other totalling eighty-eight temples. But Krishnamurti did not ask us to do anything other than observe things as they are, to perceive things as they are, and apply it to your daily life.

EB: There is a great tradition of meditation in Japan. How does that differ with what Krishnamurti has to say?

ST: In Buddhism it is usually understood that during meditation you sit in a corner quietly for hours in the morning or in the evening, or even at midnight. During that time you have to concentrate your whole mind, on something, on some subject. But in the case of Krishnamurti, he does not ask us anything like that. Instead, he tells us, you can meditate twenty-four hours continuously and you can apply your meditation to everything in your daily life, in your daily action by which you can see things as they actually are. That is his meditation. That is my understanding of the way of his meditation, the meaning of his meditation.

EB: You heard K speak; you read his books. Has that changed your life?

ST: His teaching changed me a lot. Beforehand, I was a man of hot temper; I was a man of self-conceitedness, I was a man of very strong egotism. But after I came across his teaching and after I studied his teaching, I became a man of not so much arrogance, and so much self-centeredness. Now I can be compassionate with whomever is relating with me.

EB: Can you describe the time when you first met with Krishnamurti face-to-face and what impact that had on your understanding of his teachings?

ST: When I saw Krishnamurti face-to-face, I wanted to ask him this question and that question and I expected his answer to this question and that question respectively, but when I actually saw him, I instantly found those things were quite unnecessary because, all of a sudden, I realized that I was covered and surrounded, enshrouded by the strong wave of his love and this wave of love, when it fell on me, made me desire nothing more than to shake hands with him which made me feel the warmth of his unparalleled compassion.[97]

"ALL OF A SUDDEN, I REALIZED THAT I WAS COVERED AND SURROUNDED, ENSHROUDED BY THE STRONG WAVE OF HIS LOVE."

—SHIGATOSHI TAKAHASHI

Meditation can take place when you are sitting in a bus or walking in the woods full of light and shadows, or listening to the singing of birds or looking at the face of your wife or child.

—FREEDOM FROM THE KNOWN, 1969

A unique individual who came into Krishnamurti's life at a time when her presence was much needed was Mary Zimbalist. Over a long period of time, as she followed Krishnamurti's talks from Ojai to Saanen and India, Mary found that she was able to be of assistance, at first driving him about and later, assuming such functions as taking care of correspondence, making appointments, accompanying him on travels, etc. As she said, "Being useful when things were needed for a person for whom you had great regard and wanted to help in any way you could."

From the mid-1960s she has devoted her life to helping Krishnamurti and furthering his work in every way.

Later, Krishnamurti was to be her house guest when he was in the United States, staying at her home in Malibu and then in the expanded and extensively remodeled "Pine Cottage" in Ojai. This supportive arrangement was to last for the rest of Krishnamurti's life.

MARY ZIMBALIST

PERSONAL ASSISTANT TO KRISHNAMURTI

"TALKING WAS HIS JOB, HIS RESPONSIBILITY, AND EVEN WHEN HE WAS ILL HE WOULD, IF HE COULD, FULFILL THAT. I DON'T THINK MANY PEOPLE REALIZE HOW VERY HARD HE WORKED."

—MARY ZIMBALIST

EB: You became quite close to Krishnamurti. You were doing many things for him; did you detect any difference between the man and his teaching at that time?

MZ: Absolutely none. One of the many extraordinary things about him was that there was never any shadow in Krishnamurti. He really was what you saw, what you sensed, and infinitely more, but nothing was ever in contradiction. I don't know if many people realized it, I'm sure you do, but he was also a very human person. He loved to laugh, he liked funny jokes, he looked at television and went to the movies. He liked Westerns, as is well-known, and sometimes when the mayhem on the screen had me ducking and closing my eyes, he would say, "Look at those mountains!" meaning the scenery of Monument Valley. While people were being slaughtered in the foreground, he was lost in the desert scenery. At some time he had asked me things about movies and I must have told him that it wasn't really blood on the screen, so when I would quail he would reassure me by saying, "It's all right, it's just tomato juice." He had this very endearing and almost childlike quality about many things and yet there was also this limitless extraordinary man.

EB: What were his other interests? Was he interested in art, in literature, politics, nature?

MZ: He was keenly sensitive to the beauty of language. Apart from his well-known enjoyment of detective stories—thrillers, he called them—and which he read for relaxation, he read mostly poetry and used to read the Old Testament, not for religious reasons but for the language. In art he always spoke of marvelous architecture—the Acropolis, the Gothic cathedrals, and he found something almost sacred in the beauty of the Winged Victory and the great Maheshamurti statue at Elephanta. As to politics, he followed the news, often on television, and in the weekly magazines. Also he would talk to people, question then. He was well-informed, more than you might think.

EB: Would you say that he fitted in any particular category, politically-speaking? Would it be liberal or more conservative? Did he express those kinds of views?

MZ: He wasn't sophisticated in matters of politics, but he didn't tolerate the pettiness of divisions of people, the fighting between countries, political groups, divisive beliefs. He would be most dismissive or impatient of such things in general conversation, but he was always enquiring.

He liked to listen to music in the morning while he had breakfast. After giving him his tray I used to ask what he would like to hear and almost invariably he would reply, "You choose." So I tried to guess what he would enjoy. Most of all he loved Beethoven. Then Mozart, Bach, Haydn, and sometimes he would take a fancy to a particular performer. I think he liked Richter which I played often.

EB: Sviatoslav?

MZ: Yes, and the great Italian pianist, Michelangeli. I once asked him which of those two he preferred; he thought for a moment and said, "One is like snow and one is like sunlight"

EB: Most people tend to view Krishnamurti as more, I won't say intellectual, but the fact that he liked Beethoven was certainly more romantic.

MZ: Beethoven was his favorite. But what moved him deeply was chanting—the Sanskrit chants in which he joined most wonderfully and also Gregorian chant.

EB: It is also known that he had a special affinity to nature, that it was beyond just our environmental concerns—a really deep link to nature.

MZ: He reacted more to nature than to visual art. He felt looking at a tree or a mountain was more moving than a Leonardo painting. He didn't dismiss it but he said the beauty of nature, of a tree, is beyond anything that man can create.

EB: Which puts artists in their place, doesn't it? A chastening experience. He had, and this is also well-known, a rather mechanical aptitude which is somewhat at variance with the other aspects of his life.

MZ: He used to say he had once taken a car apart when he was quite young, and then put it together again. And he took great care of his watch, checking it carefully in Geneva so that it was correct to the second.

He liked that. Once I asked him what he would do in India if he were not what he was? How would he earn a living? He said, "Oh, beg around."

EB: It's rather interesting to think what would have happened to Krishnamurti had he not had a European English education. He might have been "begging around" in India.

"ONE OF THE MANY EXTRAORDINARY THINGS ABOUT HIM WAS THAT THERE WAS NEVER ANY SHADOW IN KRISHNAMURTI. HE REALLY WAS WHAT YOU SAW, WHAT YOU SENSED, AND INFINITELY MORE, BUT NOTHING WAS EVER IN CONTRADICTION."
—MARY ZIMBALIST

MZ: He said that he would probably be dead because he was very unhealthy as a child. His brother had tuberculosis, as we know, and Krishnamurti had scars on his lungs. His must have been an arrested case and only because his health was looked at very carefully did he think he was alive.

EB: Now another question about his interests: Krishnamurti was not a good student when he was a young man. How did that translate into his interest in education for children and for adults, with the founding of the schools and centers?

MZ: As you know, a central part of his teaching is the role of knowledge—both the good of knowledge and the limitation of knowledge. We need knowledge even to speak, but the mind mustn't be confined by knowledge, it must have the ability to go further. He was endlessly explaining the limitation of thought, which is so fundamental to his teachings. He used to feel that to help young people who are more pliable, less conditioned, to understand the role of knowledge was very important. I remember one of the first summers in Gstaad he used to lunch with some friends who had a photograph of him as a child with his little brother, Nitya. He stared at it a long time as though it were of someone else and said he had no memory of it at all, but when I asked him what was going through his mind when he looked at it, he said, "If we could understand why that boy was not conditioned, why in spite of all the adulation and the fuss that went on around him, it left no mark on him, perhaps we cold help other children to be less conditioned." I think that was why he wanted to bring about a different kind of education in which there is an understanding of the function of thinking, and also understanding the potential of the brain not simply to reflect what it had been taught or what it had already experienced. That, I think was the reason behind his creating schools. After starting the Brockwood Park School in England, he thought of beginning with younger children, in the Oak Grove School in Ojai, to see if they would be less conditioned. I'm afraid that one came to feel, eventually, that children are conditioned practically from the crib, that was what he was trying to see—if you could free children from the grip of conditioning.

EB: Do you think that he ever felt that the schools were a success? Did they help the children?

MZ: I think what he wanted in all this was something unlimited, so he never would say, "This is good," he would point out what was wrong and go into how to make it right. Approbation was not given as such, but it didn't mean he was carping. He would see an insufficiency or where there was need for something else and try to open that door, but there was never a moment when he said, "That's a good job." I don't think he ever thought in those terms. Excellence was, I think, the quality he looked for and it wasn't defined.

EB: Was he disappointed if things didn't live up to expectations?

MZ: Oh, he would point it out in no uncertain terms. When things went wrong he would really chastise people, not in a personal, hurtful way, but saying, "Look what you're doing."

HE STARED AT A PHOTO-
GRAPH OF HIMSELF AS A
CHILD WITH HIS BROTHER,
NITYA "AS THOUGH IT WERE
OF SOMEONE ELSE AND SAID
'HE HAD NO MEMORY OF IT
AT ALL, IF WE COULD
UNDERSTAND WHY THAT BOY
WAS NOT CONDITIONED,
WHY, IN SPITE OF ALL THE
ADULATION AND THE FUSS
THAT WENT ON AROUND HIM,
IT LEFT NO MARK ON HIM,
PERHAPS WE COLD HELP
OTHER CHILDREN TO BE LESS
CONDITIONED.'"

—MARY ZIMBALIST

EB: Krishnamurti's language changed greatly over the years, he seemed to speak with increasing clarity and a scalpel-touch somehow to words.

MZ: Yes, he was precise about his choice of words. Often before talks he would ask me to look up dictionary meanings, most often for the derivation of the word. He didn't prepare the talks the way most people would, but he often had some direction in mind.

EB: He didn't make notes?

MZ: Never in my time. In fact, many times in the car driving to the talks, he said, "What am I going to talk about?" I never answered, but almost invariably a great and extraordinary talk would take place.

EB: How did you weigh that in the balance of your own early experience of hearing him talk and being overwhelmed by the words that would come out, against someone who asked "What shall I talk about?."

MZ: It would come. He didn't like to listen to his own tapes. When it was over, it was finished. He wanted to come to things afresh and when he started taking written questions he didn't want to see them ahead of time. People dropped them in boxes and he would have me collect them and I would sort them by subject. Questions about fear—always the most numerous—and nationalism, jealousy, greed, gurus, all these different topics and I typed them onto the paper he took with him. He didn't plan what he would say, but he would choose a question, read it out to the audience, explore it as if he were looking through a celestial microscope, and this marvelous reflection would come out in his language.

EB: When you were driving him to a talk did he ever resist talking, did he ever say "I'm so tired" or "I really don't want to do this today?"

MZ: No. Talking was his job, his responsibility, and even when he was ill he would, if he could, fulfill that. I don't think many people realize how very hard he worked. For over seventy years his life was spent giving talks, writing, seeing people privately, holding discussions with teachers, students, very erudite people, and the continual traveling. It was gruelling constant work. Only when he was physically unable to do so did it let up. And even then there were times when he was seriously ill with fever for two days before the talks, but on the day of the talk he would be astonishingly able to speak. On such days he would be ready and everything would be exact. He would be up early, the car would be in front before the time to leave. If I were driving, when I heard him coming I would have the engine started, the door open and in Saanen, for instance, the tent was reached exactly at the moment for him to walk in and climb onto the platform. He didn't want to pause or, heaven forbid, be late!

EB: Mary, you've heard it said that some being was speaking through Krishnamurti; this was particularly prevalent in the early days. Did you ever have the sense of some entity speaking through Krishnamurti?

MZ: No, I have never had such notions. To me that is nonsense because Krishnamurti could speak at any moment as he spoke on the platform.

"HE SPOKE VERY OFTEN
ABOUT OTHERNESS, THE
IMMEASURABLE, ALL THE
MARVELOUS WORDS HE USED
ABOUT IT, AND THIS THAT HE
CALLED MEDITATION WOULD
COME TO HIM, USUALLY IN
THE NIGHT."

—MARY ZIMBALIST

If at the lunch table conversation became serious, he would talk with the same depth and perception. In interviews, private or public, he spoke that way. This was the man himself, not some spirit talking through him. But often on the platform one could feel in him a tremendous energy and it seemed that it was out of that energy and ability to go to the heart of things that he spoke. This may be speculation, but one felt it intensely. I felt it. It was out of his intelligence, his own perception.

EB: And yet he seemed to have a connection with what he described as "the other," what was the line if any, between the other and his speaking, or for that matter, his life?

MZ: He never spoke of a line, but he spoke very often about otherness, the immeasurable—all the marvelous words he used about it—and this, that he called meditation would come to him, usually in the night.

EB: Would he be sleeping and then wake up?

MZ: I don't know, because he would only talk a little about it, but he would often say, "I had an extraordinary meditation last night," and sometimes when alone with him or on a walk—particularly on a walk when he liked to be silent and look at nature—one felt he was very far away. Something was happening or present. It was almost palpable at times.

EB: You yourself would have a sense of the otherness?

MZ: I would feel some invisible force.

EB: It's rather like when you listen to the radio you are able to tune in and get a concert or the news or whatever. Apparently, K was able to tune into this energy which surrounds all of us.

MZ: In a way. Again this may be just my imagination, but it is as though there is something that is nameless but can be called intelligence or truth or beauty—any of those things—but most of us are blind and do not sense it.

EB: Was it something that he could do deliberately?

MZ: He said meditation cannot be done deliberately, it has to come to you.

EB: Did he describe his sense of meditation? Of course he has written and spoken about it in his talks, but did he talk with you about meditation?

MZ: He talked about being quiet, being very quiet and not letting thought have its way in your mind. Not letting all the train of association that generally streams through our heads; not to stop it by will, but not to pursue it. It goes by and you watch it and you let it pass. You learn from it. So when we talked about these things it would often be in terms of being quiet, of just watching the mind, not doing anything about it, not pushing or stopping it. He had many descriptions of meditation, they are in almost all his writings. An essential was a quiet mind. He could have that quiet, even once on a flight to somewhere this meditative state came to him.

EB: But as he described in his writings, never something that he deliberately sat quietly to do.

MZ: You cannot induce it, he said. When he was so ill at the end, still that extraordinary thing continued to come to him through all the pain and suffering. He said, "Something else controls what will happen to me. When the body can no longer do the things necessary to speak, the life will end." And that is what happened.

EB: Does that imply there is something else?

MZ: Something else. Not that he was just an instrument of that, but that the expression of that other was his task; from that he spoke, and when physically he could no longer talk his life would end.

EB: He felt that the reason for his life was to be able to give these teachings?

MZ: Yes, that was his life. A personal life existed but that other was the reality.

EB: His last days must have been quite overwhelming for you.

MZ: He had spoken of his death for some time. He knew he was dying, he wanted to do his job to the end, and he did. He was entirely rational, his mind was not touched by the illness, the pain or the medication, and as his body grew weaker, his way of talking became infinitely painful to hear because his voice was so weak, but he was Krishnamurti to the very end in the fullest sense of all he ever was.

EB: You have described Krishnamurti as a fountain giving forth his teaching; what was the wellspring, where did it come from?

MZ: I cannot say. All I could say would be my imagining, and that has no value. I can try to put it into words, but it is only my speculation. It is as though there are abstract realities—intelligence, beauty, love—qualities that he spoke of. They are not the product of the human mind. One could use the word God too as long as it is not an imagined God in one's own image. Different words can be used but they are aspects of one infinite life force. I think this was reality for Krishnamurti, and if you want, a well-spring.

EB: It has been suggested that Krishnamurti might represent an evolutionary step in humanity, a prototype of something new. Is that a possibility?

MZ: I don't know about a prototype, but to me his life was proof that a human being is capable of extraordinary intelligence and perception, and a way of living that is very different from most human life. It was real in him, it was not something I imagined. Doubtless some will say I am projecting onto him some ideal. But for me it was incontrovertibly evident that this man was what he was talking about and he lived that way. In all the years I was with him I never saw anything that denied that or was inconsistent with a life lived that way. There were no contradictions. At many, many times there was undeniably a sense of something I can only call sacred.

EB: Mary, obviously Krishnamurti has had a tremendous impact on your life; how would you describe that impact?

MZ: I don't know how to characterize it. I'm not being trivial when I say that I don't know why I was lucky enough to be able to be with him as I was. If there was something that was looking out for him in life, people who came along, I suppose, were instruments of that. I don't mean

> "HE HAD SPOKEN OF HIS DEATH FOR SOME TIME. HE KNEW HE WAS DYING, HE WANTED TO DO HIS JOB TO THE END, AND HE DID. HE WAS ENTIRELY RATIONAL, HIS MIND WAS NOT TOUCHED BY THE ILLNESS, THE PAIN OR THE MEDICATION."
>
> —MARY ZIMBALIST

OPPOSITE: INTRODUCTION
OF THE SPEAKER BY EVELYNE
BLAU IN THE OAK GROVE,
1984.

that I was sent from heaven to do something for him, I simply was at hand and it came about, and the good of it was overwhelming for me, but I can't measure or describe it. I was privileged, I was blessed beyond any words to be able to be around him and in small ways be just useful in a human sense, doing things that needed to be done.

EB: What would you say was Krishnamurti's impact on the world?

MZ: I feel that his impact on the world is almost in a very seed-like state. I feel that perhaps in years to come, in one hundred years, history will look back and see this as an extraordinary time when Krishnamurti was alive on this earth. If you look back at human history, how many people knew the Buddha was there at the time, or for many centuries afterward, but what was said and spoken has grown and entered the lives of millions and millions two thousand years later. I feel that Krishnamurti is of that order and we must do what we can to make his teaching known because it is and will be something vast for humanity. I feel our responsibility now is to keep the accurate record of what he said and taught. For those of us who knew him that is our most essential responsibility: to preserve and protect the authenticity of his teaching so that it is there for centuries, as he gave it, uninterpreted by others. But there is another even deeper responsibility for those who have known and listened to him: The ultimate one is to reflect his teachings in our lives, in our relations to others, to whatever life brings. It is to live the reality, not just the words of his teaching.[98]

Mary Lutyens whose mother, Lady Emily Lutyens, befriended Krishnamurti when he came to England for the first time in 1911, was introduced earlier in this book. She has written profusely on Krishnamurti in her detailed and excellent biographies which cover his entire life span.

MARY LUTYENS

AUTHOR, LONDON, ENGLAND

"PEOPLE ASKED HIM LATE IN HIS LIFE, 'WHY DO YOU GO ON TALKING AT YOUR AGE, TRAVELING ROUND THE WORLD, TALKING, TALKING?' HE THOUGHT FOR A MOMENT AND THEN SAID, QUITE SIMPLY, 'OUT OF AFFECTION.'"

—MARY LUTYENS

One aspect of Krishnamurti to be considered was his deeply affectionate nature. Affection was part of his teaching. When people asked him late in his life, "Why do you go on talking at your age, traveling round the world, talking, talking?" he thought for a moment and then said, quite simply, "Out of affection." "Then why don't you stay in one place and let them come to you?" "Because most of them have not got the money to travel." He had seen something very beautiful and, being so affectionate, he wanted to share it. He said, "I offer them something and if they don't want it, it doesn't matter at all. I'm not pressing them to listen to me."

He saw love in a different way from how most of us see it. He could only say what love was by finding what it was not. Love wasn't jealousy, love wasn't possessiveness, love wasn't this, wasn't that. Only when you eliminated all the things that love wasn't might you discover what this extraordinary flame was that everybody wants and everybody is searching for. Because, in a way, what they want, perhaps, is not truth but love.

Meditation is that light in the mind which

lights the way for action, and without that

light there is no love.

—*THE ONLY REVOLUTION, 1970*

1985 was a full year for Krishnamurti as all the years had been. Following his stay in India with its usual round of talks he returned again to Ojai. There, he came under the care of a new doctor, Gary Deutsch, M.D. of nearby Santa Paula. It was good to have expert care so close at hand, as well as someone he had great confidence in.

GARY M. DEUTSCH, M.D.

KRISHNAMURTI'S ATTENDING PHYSICIAN, SANTA PAULA, CALIFORNIA,

NOTES FROM A MEDICAL JOURNAL

MARCH 21, 1985

I first met Jiddu Krishnamurti in my Santa Paula office as I had previously done hundreds of times with other patients. However, I was soon to learn that this encounter would be like no other physician-patient experience I had had. A small, elderly, dark-skinned man, appearing younger than stated age of eighty-nine would be his standard medical description. After speaking to him, it became quite evident that this was no ordinary patient.

I had been "screened" to be Krishnamurti's physician by his guardian and friend, Mary Zimbalist. I had seen her the month before to be established as a new patient. Little did I realize that as I was examining her, she was "examining" me. I must have passed, as later that month Krishnaji became my newest celebrity patient. What struck me first was how gentle this man was. I knew nothing of his teachings or writings and even less of his world fame. This changed immediately as I was compelled to learn about the man and his work. I was also impressed by the extremely good condition of Krishnaji's body when I did his physical exam. For a man of eighty-nine years, he had remarkable skin, hair and teeth. I attributed this to his vegetarian diet, meticulous self-care, vigorous exercise and controlled nervous system, minimizing internal stresses. He walked daily, utilizing deep breathing exercises.

APRIL 25, 1985

Krishnaji had just returned from New York after having addressed the United Nations. His diabetes had not been well-controlled and his diabetic medications were adjusted in my office. He looked quite healthy and spent most of his visit talking about New York, taxicab drivers, and automobiles. He had a particular interest in the automobiles and how they worked, the makes, the models and the mechanical engines. He asked me what car I drove and I told him a 1982 Volvo. He nodded with satisfaction.

MAY 1985

I had done some reading about Krishnaji, and my wife and I had attended the May 1985 Oak Grove talks in Ojai. Little did I know at that time that this would be his last talk in the Grove. I found his school and serene Oak Grove setting to be quite tranquil and conducive to thoughts which dated back to the 1970s. My wife Deborah and I discussed his talk in the car on the way home.

We had both thought his style was thought-provoking and intuitive but many of his thoughts and teachings did not seem practical to us as a young physician and wife raising three children in the turbulent eighties. I surmised that one had to pick and choose from Krishnamurti's vast teachings to meet ones' needs and lifestyle. The fact that we were talking about this was a start.

April saw Krishnamurti in New York, where he spoke at the United Nations and received a silver peace medal. On to Washington, D.C. where a Congressional reception hosted by Senator Claibourne Pell was given. On April 20, Krishnamurti spoke twice at the Kennedy Center to over-flowing, attentive audiences. Later, across the vast expanse of the Dulles airport it was amazing to see Krishnamurti unexpectedly, looking out of the huge window at incoming and outgoing planes, for all the world like an elegant, alert and solemn child.

Following the round of talks at Ojai, Saanen, and Brockwood there was a noticeable drop in his energy. The walks became shorter and by the time he returned to India again he was extremely frail and had all his meals in bed. Dr. Parchure, his long-time friend and medical advisor who often traveled with him when he was not in Ojai, was alarmed at his loss of weight—ninety-seven pounds.

At Madras it was quite apparent that he could no longer continue speaking. At his next-to-last talk, on January 1, 1986, he spoke, in part, of death.

We are trying to find out what it means to die, while living—not committing suicide; I am not talking about that kind of nonsense. I want to find out for myself what it means to die, which means, can I be totally free from everything that man has created, including myself?

What does it mean to die? To give up everything. Death cuts you off with a very sharp razor from your attachments, from your gods, from your superstitions, from your desire for comfort, next life and so on and on. I am going to find out what death means because it is as important as living. So how can I find out, actually, not theoretically, what it means to die? I actually want to find out, as you want to find out. What does it mean to die? Put that question to yourself. While we are young, or when you are very old, this question is always there. It means to be totally free, to be totally unattached to everything that man has put together, or what you have put together—totally free. No attachments, no gods, no future, no past. See the beauty of it, the greatness of it, the extraordinary strength of it—while living to be dying. You understand what that means? While you are living, every moment you are dying, so that throughout life you are not attached to anything. That is what death means.

So living is dying. You understand? Living means that every day you are abandoning everything that you are attached to. Can you do this? A very simple fact but it has tremendous implications. So that each day is a new day. Each day you are dying and incarnating. There is tremendous vitality, energy there because there is nothing you are afraid of. There is nothing that can hurt Being hurt doesn't exist.

All the things that man has put together have to be totally abandoned. That's what it means to die. So can you do it? Will you try it? Will you experiment with it? Not for just a day, every day. Your brains are not trained for this. Your brains have been conditioned so heavily, by your education, by your tradition, by your books, by your professors. It requires finding out what love is. Love and death go together. Death says, be free, non-attached, you can carry nothing with you. And love says, love says—there is no word for it. Love can exist only when there is freedom, not from your wife, from a new girl, or a new husband, but the feeling, the enormous strength, the vitality, the energy of complete freedom.[99]

—MADRAS, JANUARY 1, 1986

DEUTSCH MEDICAL JOURNAL (CONTINUED)

DECEMBER 30, 1985

I [Dr. Deutsch] received a call from Mary stating that Krishnaji was very ill in India and would be arriving in Ojai on January 13, 1986. I made arrangements to see him in my office on that day.

JANUARY 13, 1986

K had been ill for six months in India during which time he had lost approximately ten pounds. He felt a little better since he had been home but was obviously exhausted and had difficulty keeping his food down. On examination, he appeared to be different, in that his color was not good and he did not have that robust voice that he had previously had. Lab tests were ordered and his liver functions were extremely elevated, indicating that this was a more serious condition.

JANUARY 22, 1986

I convinced Krishnamurti that he needed to be in the hospital for intravenous feedings and decompression of his stomach with a tube as he continued to have fevers, vomit and was unable to eat. He consented to going to Santa Paula Hospital, which was my primary facility. He was admitted to the Intensive Care Unit because he could have the best nursing and was quite ill. At first it was difficult taking care of him in a hospital setting because he was no ordinary patient. He had world-wide celebrity status but I had to treat him like any other patient with the proper diagnostic testing as well as trying to make him as comfortable as possible. We accommodated him in the Intensive Care Unit with provisions for both Mary and Scott Forbes (of Brockwood Park) to be at his bedside twenty-four hours a day. I was warmed by the obvious devotion and extreme love these two people had for this man. For the next six weeks there was always one of them at his side. I called in multiple consultants including a surgeon, oncologist, urologist, radiologist as I did not want to overlook any possibilities. It became obvious with diagnostic testing that Krishnamurti had a pancreatic obstruction from a primary carcinoma. His blood test which was diagnostic for this was extremely elevated and further investigation was not necessary. This test was a new, investigative tumor marker and had just come on

I saw of an evening,

over a city of vast

habitation, a bird

swiftly flying towards

its distant home.

—*STAR BULLETIN,*
AUGUST, 1930

the market. Unfortunately it was extremely high and there was no question to the diagnosis of pancreatic carcinoma. This was an ominous diagnosis as there was no medical or surgical treatment. However, I was glad that we would need no further invasive procedures done as he tolerated the hospital extremely poorly. I felt obligated to protect him from any further investigative testing and made arrangements for him to be transferred home as quickly as possible with home medical care. On January 30, 1986 he was transferred to his Ojai home to come full-circle to where he started his teachings in the United States. He told me before he left the hospital that he wanted to die at home and not in a hospital setting. He asked me to keep him as comfortable as possible and I promised him that I would do this. He spoke of his body in the third person and did not want it to suffer any pain.

During Krishnamurti's last days, friends and foundation members gathered from around the world to come together in Ojai—three months short of Krishnamurti's ninety-first birthday. Over seventy of those years spent in talks and dialogues, there was still much to be said. Organizational matters needed to be sorted out, and relations between the foundations clarified. It was in this period that some of the trustees present were interviewed for the 1989 film, *Krishnamurti: With a Silent Mind.* Many of those interviews appear in this book. Among those present was Asit Chandmal, who had known Krishnamurti since childhood. Asit is the author of the beautiful photographic book, One Thousand Moons: Krishnamurti At 85.

ASIT CHANDMAL

AUTHOR AND COMPUTER MANAGEMENT CONSULTANT, BOMBAY, INDIA

EB: What has been your sense of Krishnamurti in these latter days of his life? Have you noticed any change in him?

AC: If you're speaking of the last few days, he has clearly told all of us that the body is dying. Are you asking about that?

EB: Yes.

AC: I was in Singapore at the end of December 1985 and I got a call saying Krishnaji was very ill in Madras so I flew there immediately on the night of December 31 and I met him on the morning of January 1. He was lying in bed but he appeared to be as alert as he has ever been. He was eating breakfast and we spoke of many things, as we had done in the past, and aside from the fact that he was eating breakfast in bed, there was no difference in his manner, his movements, the energy in his voice. He addressed a large gathering that same evening, about six-thousand people, and spoke with extraordinary energy for one-and-a-half hours, as usual without notes. He had told me in the morning that he was dying, that perhaps he had a few more weeks to live and at that time we didn't know he had cancer and I don't think he did either, but in the evening talk he spoke about death and fear and not having fear about death. That had a tremendous impact on me because of his conversation about his personal death and the next day, when I met him, he started asking me questions about computers and since my daughter was with me and she is very interested in genetics, he sat up in bed and we got into a very interesting discussion on what would happen, in Krishnaji's words, when the computer and genetics met, when the two technologies got together, what would happen to the human mind? He was his old self, full of energy, a strong voice, a great insight into the topic he was discussing and exploring.

Two days later he gave his last talk. He told the audience that the body is ninety years old and it can't go on, so it was the last talk and once again, he spoke with great energy and I don't think there was anyone in the crowd who would have suspected that this man was dying of cancer and the end was so near because of the manner of his speech was exactly as it has been five years ago, ten years, thirty years ago.

He left for California on the night of January 10, and on that evening he went for his usual walk on the beach at Adyar, where he was discovered, and at the end of the walk, he did something I have never seen him do before. Everyone else went into the house. He stayed behind on the beach and he looked at the sea and the sky quietly. He stood for a few seconds, facing the sea and the sky in one direction, then he turned in another direction and he did that in four different directions, and then quietly he went into the house. That was a way, I felt, of saying goodbye.

That evening I got the same flight with him from Madras to Singapore. I got off at Singapore and he had to get off the plane to catch the connecting flight to go on to Los Angeles via Tokyo. In Singapore, a couple of weeks later, I got a call saying Krishnaji is very seriously ill; he was in the hospital; he was in intensive care. On February 1 I went to see him in his bedroom at Pine Cottage, because by that time he had been discharged from the hospital, and when I met him in the morning I was utterly shocked at his condition. He could hardly raise his hand to shake mine. He didn't recognize me. His attention span was less than two seconds because his eyes couldn't keep open. It wasn't only with me because my aunt and my cousin were there too, and the same thing happened with them. We were in a state of great shock to see him like that when a month earlier he had been the old Krishnamurti, talking to six-thousand people and going for walks and engaging in serious discussion. When I went to see him the next day an astonishing thing happened. He smiled and he held my hand and I felt a strong pulse beating and suddenly, in his old voice, a strong voice, he said, "Sir, where is your anchor?" I said, "In you, Sir." And he replied, instantly, "I'm going." And then he said, "If you have touched that, you must be anchored in it, otherwise you will go to pieces." And then he smiled and he said, "You are a nice chap but you are wasting your life." And then he closed his eyes. The amazing clarity and energy would seem to rise in him when I thought he would not even live that day. It was quite extraordinary and I felt that there were certain powers or energies that he could summon up when he needed to. That is the last real memory I have of him, except for one more talk, when he invited some of us around his bed. He said, "There must be no hierarchies. There must be no apostles. No one must set himself up as an interpreter or an authority and you must all stick together and be with each other and work together. The teachings are important and not the teacher." And then he said, "I am very tired." [100]

EVELYNE BLAU

DIARY ENTRIES

JANUARY 27, 1986

In a day of radiant sunshine I leave for Santa Paula Hospital. It is about twelve noon. Driving over the hills, through winding passes, it is a day of exultant gladness—nature sings in praise. On such a day one thinks there is no death—all is beauty.

The hospital sits on the brow of a hill overlooking Santa Paula, which is larger than expected from this overview. The environment is pleasant, clean and friendly, all that a small and small town facility should be. On the way in, I pass what appears to be a large truck and rig but is actually the vehicle for a portable Cat Scan, which rotates between several small facilities in the area. This is where K had his test.

Mary Zimbalist is sitting in a waiting room at the back of the hospital near the intensive care unit. I wait with her there expecting news of the test. Dr. Parchure comes in to tell us the test is over and that K is back in his room. Mary goes in to him and then comes out to say that K would like to see me. I am surprised at my own reaction, a gasp of happiness to be able to see him.

Entering the unit with its nurses, charts and monitors one goes to K's room. He is in bed and looks incredibly tiny and birdlike. He grasps my hand in his slender one and holds it to his cheek. We exchanged words but now I cannot remember what we said. The burst of joy on seeing him erased the words from my mind. As he put his hand back under the blanket I could see the intravenous tube in his upper chest, near the shoulder. The area looked bruised and dark. He had several days growth of beard and his hair lay softly about him. The eyes were alert and clear but he closed them several times in tiredness.

This little figure inspires such love, and he embodies love even as he lies there, frail and ill. The short time that I was there was timeless in its dimension. How I wish I had said how much I loved him, perhaps he felt it although it was unspoken. How difficult to separate this man from his teaching. I wonder what those who do not know him but love the teachings feel? Is the teaching clearer because it is unclouded by that personal love? Actually I never realized how much I loved him—I recognized feelings of respect, awe, admiration and affection in my response, but now it is clear that it is all of those, permeated by love. I know everyone else feels the same way too. Coming to this recognition of love I see that it does not ask anything, even a deeper understanding of the teaching. It just wants to be. It is.

I have come to have greater and greater respect for Dr. Parchure. As we drove back to Ojai I questioned him closely as to K's condition. His responses were clear, detailed and sobering. He has a keen mind, great dedication, and clarity of expression. I came away feeling that a balanced view had been expressed. Although it is not encouraging, still, one awaits developments calmly.

The drive back to the hospital again at 5:00 p.m. is quiet, all the better to view the setting sun reflected on the mountains. They appear to be illuminated from within, a golden pink suffuses the air and folds softly on the ridged hills. Apparently the famous "pink moment" of Ojai extends to Santa Paula. It has been a rare day—a day of beauty.

Earlier in this book, Dr. Hedda Bolgar spoke of being present in 1929 as Krishnamurti dissolved the world-wide organization that had been formed around him. She turned later to thoughts of his impending death:

Some time ago I started to think about the fact that he must be close to death and I remember talking about it and having this strange feeling of loss, of sadness, of chill, that he was going to die and that his physical death, for some reason that I couldn't quite understand at the moment, would mean such a tremendous loss to me and therefore probably even more so to a lot of other people. And then I began to think about what was so special about him, what was the greatness in him or the special quality, the absence of which would leave such an empty space and I began to remember what he looked like, what he sounded like, what it felt like to be around him. What I came up with was that here was an incredibly whole person, somebody who was incorruptible, who was strong, who could not be tricked, trapped, bribed, flattered, moved in any way to deviate from what he knew what was, at least, his truth and what had become his answer to most of the questions human beings seem to ask. He was beautiful, and his beauty had nothing to do with conventional features or body, but there was the tragedy that one always felt about him, and all the sadness of his life and I always felt he didn't have a moment in his life when he wasn't really suffering, but with all that, there was an incredible serenity which somehow got across without any words, without any reassurance, without any of the usual words in which serenity is expressed. He was a whole human being with an integrity that really radiated and with his death, this would be gone and in a sense I also hoped that nobody would try to prolong his life by starting up replacements for him. [101]

Since earliest childhood, Radhika Jayakar—Radhika Herzberger following her marriage to Hans Herzberger, Canadian Professor of Philosophy—had a close relationship with Krishnamurti. Her mother, Pupul Jayakar, had a friendship of many years' standing with Krishnamurti; Radhika inevitably was drawn into that circle at an early age. Her doctorate in Sanskrit and Buddhist Studies suits her admirably for the position she now holds at Rishi Valley Educational Center as Director of Studies.

RADHIKA HERZBERGER, PH.D

DIRECTOR OF STUDIES, RISHI VALLEY EDUCATIONAL CENTER

...Critical stages of my life have been marked by encounters with Krishnaji, both in his presence and in his absence, because I associate Krishnaji, not only

259

The mind that has put its house in order, has understood the nature of knowledge. Such a mind is completely silent. And that silence has no cause. You see, "silence" can be illusory; it can be put together by a thought that is determined to be silent. You have the silence between the two whistles of a train, the silence between two notes, between two noises, between two sounds, between two thoughts—but that kind of silence is still within the realm of cognition. But when the mind is completely silent, it is not even aware that it is silent. If it were, it would merely be playing tricks. The mind that has put its house in order is silent. That silence has no cause and, therefore, has no end. Only that which has a cause can end. That silence—which has no ending —is absolutely necessary, because it is only in that silence that there is no movement of thought. It is only in that silence that that which is sacred, that which is nameless, and that which is not measurable by thought, is. And that which is, is the most sacred. That is meditation.

—PUBLIC TALK, MADRAS, NOVEMBER 29, 1981

with his personality, but with a certain feeling that he communicated and that he left us with, it's like a jewel. He liked to use that analogy of a jewel—a transparent jewel which can filter one's personality and reflect it, in some sense, act like a magnifying glass. So by looking at oneself, one can change oneself.

Krishnaji once asked me, if one had discovered something new, original, why should one want to use somebody else's words to describe it, and that question made me reflect on the vocabulary he had used and the way he had talked. Now, reflecting on that question, I realize that one uses older, traditional vocabulary, to reinforce one's ideas and one realizes that is not what Krishnamurti was trying to do, unlike other teachers who use traditional vocabulary and somehow get the aura of a sanctified past into their sphere of talk. There was another level at which Krishnaji's relationship to people interested his friends, as he called them, it was not one of the guru, it was not coercive—he was your friend, one who walked with you and—in public talks, usually at the beginning of the first talk—he would say how we must learn to walk together like two friends going on a long journey and when one walked with him, when one was close to him, one really got the feeling of somebody walking very close to you, walking by the side of your mind, next to your thoughts, and it was that feeling which was free and easy and affectionate that marked his presence. I have seen other gurus. I have heard them talk. One gets the sense of the exercise of power—a feeling of some secrets that they have and that if only you came within the purview of their aura, became their disciple, they would give you something which they alone have access to. Krishnaji had none of that, his relationship to you was never one of power. In fact, he declared over and over again, "I have nothing to give," and when he said that, he was giving of himself abundantly. But one could not feel that aura, latch onto that unless one was prepared to change, and that act of change was something that the human being has to do for oneself. And so, he was a friend, not a guru, despite the fact that a tremendous radiance emanated from him. He gave that freely, not to his disciples, not to those who submitted to him, but to anyone who came to him.

If there is a cornerstone to Krishnamurti's teachings, it is that one was really the master of one's life, one's destiny. That stemmed from the fact that he considered the key to living the ability to look at facts as they are; not to indulge in self-pity, not to look for causes, not to blame others. It is from this conviction that honesty and facing facts—and that no one can help you face facts—comes the idea that one must be, as he put it, a lamp unto oneself and not rely on anything. There is no refuge, neither in God nor in other human beings. Man is not the refuge for man. One is one's own refuge; one's own teacher and one's own disciple. That gives one both courage and a certain independence and no self-pity. He always thought that self-pity was the door to hell.

During Krishnaji's last visit to India, at Rajghat, I had my most intense sense of the sacred. It was as if sanctity hung like a curtain over the Ganges conveying what I felt was a sense of intense tenderness, plus a clarity of vision, so that my mind was very still and alert and I could see far and wide around me and my heart melted constantly. I felt very tender, and it was this combination of clarity and tenderness that I associate with sanctity. He was dying and his body was weak, but it was as if sanctity oozed out of him, radiated out of him and filled the world in Banares. I have not felt that intensely ever since. His body shrank and his radiance emanated out.[102]

William Quinn spoke earlier in the book of Krishnamurti's life during the 1940s. Here he sumarizes his feelings.

I think of him as being the flowering of humanity. He was the most important person to appear in this world for centuries, and a great part of his beauty consisted in his humanity. I would like to see this emphasized, because there are so many people around the world who wish to romanticize, or even deify, him. This encourages a sense of an inseparable gulf between us and Krishnamurti, whereas I think the significance of his life is that it is a brilliant mirror showing us what is latent in us all, what it means to be fully mature, and not stillborn, human beings.

BLAU DIARY ENTRIES (CONTINUED)

JANUARY 28, 1986

The drive to the hospital is a welcome immersion in glory. Grasses of an intense green roll out over the upper Ojai. In the orchards where the trees are still bare, golden mustard dots the green carpet. The mountains rising up above the valley are austere, burned by the recent fire, but with great dignity and somber beauty. As you drive down the winding road that drops to Santa Paula, the oil seeping from underground sources lies black on the earth. Pooling here and there, or running in little rivulets.

Having reached the bottom of the hill you turn right and climb again to reach the Santa Paula Memorial Hospital. Leaving the car parked to face the view of the valley, you enter the hospital.

Erna and Theo Lilliefelt are in the waiting room along with Mark Lee and Mary Cadogan. Dr. Parchure has spent the night there. Scott Forbes is in almost constant attendance and Mary Zimbalist is practically living at the hospital. K has not yet been taken in for the biopsy. As we wait we are told of the dreadful explosion of the space shuttle Challenger *soon after take-off. We watch the horror unfold on television even as we are to be told the wrenching news of the outcome of K's tests.*

We cluster in the station of the intensive care unit as attending physician Dr. Deutsch spells out some details of the tests.

The biopsy could not be completed due to K's pain upon the needle striking a hard mass in the liver. There is therefore indirect evidence to suggest that the problem lies there and the mass is malignant rather than a possible inflammation, as had been hoped. Blood tests indicate cancerous cells.

K is to return home Thursday or Friday and will continue to be fed intravenously, as the possibility of dehydration and malnutrition are far greater risks than the possibility of infection from the tubes.

We leave the intensive care area and retire to the waiting room. Discussion follows as to what statements should be given out. I recognize my bent for secrecy in attempting to phrase things in a more guarded way. Others feel the entire truth should be told and the statement formulated by Dr. Parchure and others is the outcome. I concur with the eventual statement and we all leave.

" IN THE ORCHARDS WHERE THE TREES ARE STILL BARE, GOLDEN MUSTARD DOTS THE GREEN CARPET. THE MOUNTAINS RISING UP ABOVE THE VALLEY ARE AUSTERE, BURNED BY THE RECENT FIRE, BUT WITH GREAT DIGNITY AND SOMBER BEAUTY."

—EVELYNE BLAU

T. PARCHURE, M.D.

KRISHNAMURTI'S PERSONAL PHYSICIAN

JANUARY 28, 1986

After all possible tests there is indirect evidence to suggest that there are cancerous deposits in the liver. Krishnamurti's life-span is short.

He will be discharged from the hospital (Thursday or Friday) to be treated at home and to be made as comfortable as possible.

⟶

BLAU DIARY ENTRIES (CONTINUED)

JANUARY 29, 1986

The morning clouded, with a light wind stirring the trees. The smell of dampness and sense of an approaching weather front. By afternoon the rain begins, lightly at first and later in good earnest. By evening there is a steady downpour, much needed for the thirsty hills, and somehow more in keeping with the somber events of the day.

At 3:30 I go to Erna's [Lilliefelt] for tea. She and Mary Cadogan have worked on an obituary—a draft. It seems good—only some minor corrections.

There is so much to go over—we spend hours talking. The Bulletin—again. Mary Cadogan reads notes that she has made. The Pathless Land statement is to be included. Mary Lutyens will write a short remembrance. After dinner at Arya Vihara I go back to the cottage. Erna, who had not been at dinner had been to the hospital to pick up Dr. Parchure. She had seen K at the hospital and had a devastating report.

Another test had proven that there is cancer of the pancreas. We had thought that this was clear before—mistakenly. The mass in the liver is secondary. The cancer has metastasized. K is in great pain. He will be coming home tomorrow (Thursday) at 10:00 a.m. [Apparently he has asked to see everyone together. When that will be we cannot know but it should be early next week when Pupul, Radhika, and Asit arrive on Sunday.] I am to pick up Dorothy Simmons, Jane Hammond—who will stay with me—and Mary Lutyens and her husband, Joseph Links, at the airport on Friday.

There is nothing more to say. An overwhelming sense of loss. We are bereft. His dear and noble presence has lifted us all up—made us greater than we are. His teaching is a searchlight that illuminates the recesses of the brain and brings light and clarity to the mind. I feel blessed to have had the privilege of being in his presence and to have received the teaching. We can only hope to live it.

JANUARY 30, 1986

I questioned whether K would return from the hospital today. The weather is stormy and heavy rain is falling—three inches during the night.

Arriving at the office at about 10:30 to be on hard in case of need. So far still going forward with plan of film tour of The Challenge of Change *in Seattle and Canada. This work must continue despite everything, perhaps it is needed more than ever. I walk to Pine Cottage to see if I can be of help. Mary Zimbalist welcomes me warmly and we go into K's room to see if bed is properly prepared. Two nurses are there and all is in readiness. Mark Lee had been helping to set up the bed. Shortly after the ambulance pulls up two attendants jump out and remove a gurney. Plastic sheets are brought to cover K and protect him from the rain. I stand at the doorway but do not come closer, as too many does not seem right. Scott, Mark, Dr. Parchure, and Mary hold umbrellas against the pelting rain. By now it is a great downpour. The little body looks so tiny swathed in plastic, hardly anything there at all. K is taken in by his entrance (the old part of Pine Cottage) and made comfortable. Dr. Parchure comes out and tells me K has had a good night—has slept for over eight hours. Surely he will be more comfortable at home than in the hospital—that in itself is the best therapy.*

Shortly after, the storm seems to break and a sudden welling of sun floods the room with gold. The sky is now broken with clouds drifting and pulling apart. Light rain still falls occasionally but this storm appears to be moving on. The trees shine newly washed.

DEUTSCH MEDICAL JOURNAL (CONTINUED)

JANUARY 31, 1986

My first of many house calls. Krishnaji was extremely sleepy after the transfer. I realized now that I would need to make frequent house calls on Krishnaji. It was seventeen miles from Santa Paula to Ojai and then another twenty miles back to my home in Ventura. Fortunately this was in a loop and I was able to make this stop on my way home from work. However, I realized that I would be seeing less of my family over the next several weeks to months. My pregnant wife and three sons had always been understanding having lived with a physician for many years, however, this would put them to the true test. I knew I would have to juggle my practice, family and home visits in a way that none would be neglected. But, as always, my family life would be the part that would strain the most.

FEBRUARY 1, 1986

K slept extremely well after being medicated. I started him on vitamin supplementations in hopes of improving his energy level and he actually seemed to wake up enough to have a conference with two Indian trustees. He was extremely lucid during his talk and at that time, he asked me to keep the procedures at a minimum, avoiding medications unless they were absolutely necessary.

FEBRUARY 2, 1986

K was quite energetic and alert today. He slept most of the night without any artificial sedatives. He appeared to be well hydrated with his IV and I felt that he must have opened up his biliary obstruction. Mentally he improved and was encouraged to make some recordings. He sat up and used his tape recorder. He told me he was quite content with himself after the visits from his Indian friends.

FEBRUARY 4, 1986

K went outside yesterday with his walker and assistance. He meditated for thirty minutes. He had two hours of meetings this morning with trustees and visitors. We talked about his early life and his desire not to live if he is unable to continue to give his talks and travel. However, he states that since he was not having pain at this time and he was feeling stronger, he wanted to go on. He asked that I continue to treat him. We carried him to the living room to visit with people and to rest in the great room.

FEBRUARY 6, 1986

K was very weak today after having had a long session in the living room with many visitors. There was a lot of weeping and people were quite emotional. Krishnaji's home had a magnificent living room, which was in actuality a "great" room. This was a two-story open-beam ceiling with indirect lighting, all in white. The wooden ceiling and walls were all white with large shuttered windows. The floor was of white Italian tiles and the furniture was all lightly colored. There was a floor-to-ceiling fireplace with magnificent bookshelves and stereo system. Immediately when I went into this room I felt as if I had entered some type of a sacred temple. It was obvious that Krishnaji felt most comfortable in this room in front of the fireplace listening to classical music. He told me "he could not go on this way like a zombie." I told him that we can give him morphine for his discomfort.

FEBRUARY 8, 1986

K was getting weaker each day, unable to lift his arms now, but his mind remained remarkably clear. He told me stories of the current state of world affairs, war, overpopulation. He was glad that he had finished his mission and that now he only wanted to fade away without pain. He stated he does not want to be kept alive artificially but would only like to go peacefully. He then told me that he would leave the decision to me on further IV therapy. I specifically asked him about taking his own life and he stated that he does not want to die "artificially" but qualified this by stating he does not want to suffer. After this extremely intense discussion, he then started telling me jokes. I was impressed by the fact that he could lighten a situation with his sense of humor.

FEBRUARY 9, 1986

K continues to weaken. We take him to the living room by wheelchair and this seemed to heighten his spirits. He enjoyed Beethoven's Ninth Symphony in front of the fireplace. We have a discussion about his early childhood days as a Brahmin.

FEBRUARY 11, 1986

K stays in the living room now for eight to nine hours per day looking at the fire, lying on the couch. He spoke less often now and Mary stated that his thought process is not as sharp as before. After seeing K today I felt that he was much weaker and he asked not to speak as often. He seemed to be listening and staring while others speak. He told a joke about actors which amazed me that he still had a strong sense of humor. We have an interesting talk about homeopathic medicine and quack cancer cures. K kept repeating "this is all a grain of salt." I did ask him specifically about cancer cures and he told me that he would never want chemotherapy or any other type of treatment now. I made arrangements for him to have full-time R.N.s living in his home. At this point, I felt the end of this magnificent man's life was near and wanted to comfort him totally.

FEBRUARY 12, 1986

We had a lengthy discussion with K regarding further medical treatment. He stated he wants to die and I felt that he had a clear state of mind. He stated he wants no further intervention. He will, however, allow us to keep the status quo with major concern regarding his comfort.

FEBRUARY 14, 1986

K had more pain during the evening. Today he told me many stories about animals. Once when he was meditating in India, a monkey sat down beside him and offered him his hand. He said it was the most beautiful hand he had ever felt. He spoke of trailing a Bengal tiger in Nepal. It was the most awesome, magnificent animal he had ever seen. I then asked him if he meditated while lying in bed and he said, "Yes," telling me the origin of the word "meditate." The word comes from the Greek "to measure." When one meditates he should not measure or compare to a higher life or standard. This thinking exerts energy, and meditating is for saving energy, not for consuming it. He then spoke of Ansel Adams, Yosemite, and the beautiful mountains he had climbed. His favorites were the Himalayas. As we spoke there is a rainstorm occurring in Ojai and I suggested that we have electrical generators brought to the house to provide an auxiliary power source for his IVs and heaters.

FEBRUARY 15, 1986

K had a good night's sleep with medication. He awoke with a fever of 102°. I asked him a few days ago if he enjoyed going to the movies, and to my shock he told me that he liked Clint Eastwood westerns. I was quite surprised, with all the shooting and violence, but he told me he enjoyed looking at the background scenery. He told me he does not like the romance or the sadistic character of the movie. So today I brought him my video collection of Clint Eastwood movies and he watched two hours of The Outlaw Josie Wales. *He stared with open eyes, enjoying it but seemed to tire at the end and wanted to sleep. Today he is quite weak, shivering for a few minutes with his fever. He was given cool compresses. We had previously spoken of Yosemite, so I had also brought him some slides of the giant redwoods and waterfalls which I had from my last vacation. He seemed to enjoy these pictures and slept the rest of the morning. Before I left he presented me with a beautiful handmade Indian silk scarf which he had previously worn around his neck. He spoke of Pupul, who was in charge of the entire weaving industry in India. I spoke to her and Asit, her nephew, about his prognosis. She is leaving for India in the morning. I assured her that he would be kept comfortable. She asked me "how long" and I answered "a few days, but less is possible." She seemed satisfied with the care given to him and with my response. Asit then presented me with his recently-published photography book with a beautiful handwritten inscription thanking me for my care.*

FEBRUARY 16, 1986

The pain began early in the morning. By noon he had required a substantial amount of medication. By late in the afternoon K had drifted off intermittently into a sleep. When the pain was most intense, K seemed to be the most lucid. He stated he did not want to go on like this. I felt that he would not survive another day of pain and I was quite concerned about his suffering, as I had promised him he would feel no more pain. I was frustrated in that I wanted to be at his side, but I felt that I had neglected my family since I was spending so much time at K's bedside. It was Washington's Birthday and this was the first holiday weekend that I had had for quite a while. My wife was six months pregnant with three young boys and I felt the need to be with her as well. However, she was quite understanding and at 9:30 that Sunday evening I drove to Ojai because I felt that this was most likely Krishnamurti's last day with us. When I arrived K was in a deep coma despite turning off his pain medication. K quieted and his respiration seemed to slow down. I was amazed at how strong Krishnamurti was and I attributed this to his extremely well-kept body. At this point, I felt he was feeling no pain although his respiration and pulse were slowing. I sent Patrick, the R.N,. to the kitchen to get Mary, as I knew that she would want to be at his bedside at the very end. He stopped breathing at six minutes past midnight and his final pulse beat was detected at ten minutes and fifteen seconds in the early morning hours of February 17, 1986. I gently closed his eyes. Before I left Scott [Forbes] thanked me and said something that I will always remember: "Krishnaji took a special liking to you, as if to make you his last student."

FEBRUARY 17, 1986

Krishnaji was a great teacher and in the end I learned much from him. The longer I knew him he became less my patient and more my friend. I will never forget this experience, both as a physician and as his friend. After his death, I felt a desire to know this man in a deeper sense. I felt fortunate to have known him and will continue to educate myself through his writings.

ADDENDUM

OVERLEAF: THE LAST TALK, MADRAS, INDIA, JANUARY 4, 1986.

It is now eight years after Krishnamurti's death. As I sit reading my notes from his medical chart, I reflect on the experience of having known this wonderful man and his followers. Since his death, I have been to his library several times and have read and re-read his teachings. I continue to see Mary as a patient and a friend as she keeps me abreast of the happenings in the Krishnamurti Foundation. By putting this in writing, I am fortunate enough to recollect the feelings I had during this brief period of time and am eternally grateful for the privilege of having known and cared for such a gentle yet profound individual. His memory and teachings will be in my mind and heart forever. Having known him, I am a better person.

THANK YOU SIR!

Whoever you were, whatever you were:
Thank you for having touched my life -
Much rarer, more unique, more splendid
Than Haley's Comet,
More like the sun, the moon and all the stars
Rolled into one,
One glorious event.

Perhaps I cannot claim and say:
Yes, I have been changed,
Been transformed at the root,
The well-spring of my being,
Of my consciousness.

But thank you for having touched my life
With your presence,
With your smile, your laughter,
With your friendship
Which was but sheer love and compassion,
Thank you for having touched my life!

And the Teachings:
Majestic, impersonal, star-bright,
A beacon for all humanity
For many, many years to come:
Thank you, sir!

—MICHAEL KROHNEN
CAZOULS D'HERAULT, FRANCE

In a seemingly irrational world often felt to be random and devoid of meaning we may ask if there is any significance to one solitary life.

Amid the turmoil of these past ten decades, unprecedented in ferocity in the history of humanity, the life of Krishnamurti shows us that there can be intelligence, compassion, great love and sanity in a world awry.

Krishnamurti's work did not end with his death in 1986. It reaches out to the years ahead. Those who are willing to explore, to question, and to observe themselves will find a companion in Krishnamurti. His numberless books, audio, and videotapes and films invite study and reflection though always bearing in mind that he pointed out that "You are the teacher, the taught and the teaching," and "You are the book of life." With that reminder, one can say that Krishnamurti continues to stand at our side, a friend in our continuing dialogue. Never theoretical or abstract, but always related to "what is," he continually questioned, pushing the boundaries of thought. If there was one dictum in his life it was that he was *not* an authority. To make him into that would be to distort his entire teaching. From his declaration of independence in 1929 until his death, he sang the song of freedom. Others may have tried to make him an authority, in a "spiritual" sense, but he refused the mantle, shrugged it off.

There may be elements in this book, as recounted by witnesses to extraordinary events, that may seem incomprehensible, confounding to our linear, rational thinking. But let us not linger too long with this part of the story—it is unknowable. Let us move on: the present moment awaits.

—EVELYNE BLAU, 1995

NOTES

1. There are seventeen talks and books where the phrase "The first step is the last step" is cited. Apparently the first time Krishnamurti used it was on February 20, 1955 in his second public talk, Bombay, India.

2. Theosophical Society archives, Adyar, Madras.

3. Ibid.

4. The author is indebted to Krishnamurti biographers Mary Lutyens and Pupul Jayakar for these accounts.

5. From the film script: *Krishnamurti: The Challenge of Change*, Michael Mendizza, director and Evelyne Blau, producer, Ojai, California: Krishnamurti Foundation of American, 1984.

6. Besant, Annie, lecture at Queen's Hall, London, 1911.

7. The search for the coming world teacher was already in place, as the young Hubert van Hook had previously been singled out. His displacement by Krishnamurti must have been a vast disappointment to him.

8. Krishnamurti, J., account taped in Ojai, California, January 9, 1972, in the presence of trustees of the Krishnamurti Foundation of America.

9. Conversation: Russell Balfour Clarke and Evelyne Blau. Adyar, India, 1979.

10. Clarke, Russell Balfour. *The Boyhood of Krishnamurti*, Bombay: Chetana, 1977.

11. Lutyens, Mary. *The Years of Awakening*, New York: Farrar, Straus & Giroux, Inc., 1975.

12. Krishnamurti, J., account taped in Ojai, California, January 9, 1972.

13. Letter: Krishnamurti to Annie Besant, January 12, 1910, Adyar Archives.

14. Interview: Russell Balfour Clarke and Evelyne Blau, Adyar, India, 1979.

15. Leadbeater, C.W. *The Masters and the Path*, Adyar, Madras: Theosophical Publishing Company, 1925.

16. Krishnamurti, J. *At the Feet of the Master*, in preface by Annie Besant, Adyar, Madras: Theosophical Publishing Company, 1910.

17. *The Adyar Bulletin*, December 1911.

18. Ibid., June, 1912.

19. Lutyens, Emily. *Candles in the Sun*, Philadelphia: J.B. Lippencott, 1957.

20. Krishnamurti, J., account taped in Ojai, California, January 9, 1972.

21. Letter: C.W. Leadbeater to Fabrizio Ruspoli, Adyar Archives, Madras, December 31, 1911.

22. Krishnamurti, J., address at the First International Conference of the Order of the Star in the East, 19 Tavistock Square, London, The Herald of the Star, October 25, 1913.

23. Conversation: Russell Balfour Clarke and Evelyne Blau, Adyar, Madras, 1978.

24. Krishnamurti, J., account taped in Ojai, California, January 9,1972.

25. Illustration and passage from *Star leaflet*, Hollywood, California: Order of the Star in the East, 1923.

26. Letter: Jiddu Nityananda to Annie Besant, Krishnamurti Foundation of America Archives, Ojai, California, September 1922.

27. See also the accounts in Pupul Jayakar's *Krishnamurti: A Biography*, San Francisco: Harper and Row, 1986 and Mary Lutyens' *Krishnamurti: The Years of Awakening*, New York: Farrar, Straus & Giroux, Inc., 1975.

28. Krishnamurti Foundation of America archives., Ojai, California, August 17, 1922.

29. Lecture: Annie Besant, Ommen Star Camp, August 11, 1925, reprinted in The Herald of the Star, September 1925.

30. Krishnamurti Foundation of America archives. Ojai, California

31. Clarke, Russell Balfour. *The Boyhood of Krishnamurti*, Bombay: Chetana, 1977.

32. Besterman, Theodore. *Mrs. Annie Besant: A Modern Prophet*; London: Kegan Paul, Trench, Trubner & Co. Ltd.; 1934.

33. Interview: Phillip van Pallandt and Evelyne Blau, De Weezenladen Hospital, Zwolle, the Netherlands, September 9, 1978.

34. Order of the Star in the East conference, Hotel Sherman, Chicago, 1927.

35. Conversation: Helen Nearing and Evelyne Blau, Murietta Hot Springs,
     California, 1989.

36. Conversation: Sidney Field and Evelyne Blau, Los Angeles, April 7, 1987.

37. Larsen, Stephen. From *A Fire in the Mind: The Life of Joseph Campbell*, Copyright
     © 1991 by Stephen and Robin Larsen. Used by permission of Doubleday, a division
     of Bantam Doubleday Dell Publishing Group, Inc.

38. Reprinted in *The Star Bulletin*, Ommen, Holland: Star Publishing Trust, April 1928.

39. Conversation: Jiddu Krishnamurti and Leopold Stokowski, *The Star Bulletin*, Eerde,
     Ommen: Star Publishing Trust, May 1929.

40. National Organizers Meeting, Ommen, Holland, 1928.

41. Interview for the film *Krishnamurti: With a Silent Mind*, New York: Mystic Fire Video,
     1989.

42. To those familiar with Krishnamurti's work, Mary Lutyens needs no introduction.
     A distinguished biographer of Krishnamurti, she has added greatly to the store of
     knowledge about a man she has known since the age of three. Through her writings,
     much insight can be gained into a remarkable life.

43. Besant, Annie and Theodore Besterman. London: Kegan Paul, Trench, Trubner &
     Co., Ltd, 1934.

44. Conversation: Beatrice Wood and Evelyne Blau, Ojai, California, October 30, 1993.

45. Conversation: Harry Wolfe and Evelyne Blau, Los Angeles, California,
     February 18, 1985.

46. Newsletter Number 3, Ommen, Holland: Star Publishing Trust, July 1934.

47. Jeffers, Robinson. *Rock and Hawk, A Selection of Shorter Poems*, Robert Haas, ed.,
     New York: Random House, 1987.

48. Landau, Rom. God Is My Adventure, London: Ivor Nicholson and Watson Ltd.,
     1935.

49. Krishnamurti Foundation Archives, ed., *Collected Works of J. Krishnamurti: Volume II*,
     Dubuque, Iowa: Kendall Hunt, 1991, p. 154–155, from the First Talk, Montevideo,
     Uruguay, June 21, 1935.

50. Ibid., p. 132. from Questions and Answers, Rio de Janeiro, Brazil, April 17, 1935.

51. Ibid., p. 139. from Questions and Answers, Santiago, Chile, September 7, 1935.

52. Loos, Anita. *Fate Keeps on Happening*, New York: Dodd Mead, 1984.

53. Krishnamurti, J. *The First and Last Freedom*, introduction by Aldous Huxley,
     New York: Harper and Row, 1954.

54. Conversation: Lex Muller and Evelyne Blau, Enschede University, the Netherlands,
     September 8, 1978.

55. Letter from Phillip van Pallandt, Eerde, Ommen, Holland, June 10, 1945.

56. Conversation: Sidney Field and Evelyne Blau, Los Angeles, California,
     April 7, 1987.

57. Interview for the film *Krishnamurti: With a Silent Mind*. Further conversation, 1994.

58. Interview for the film *Krishnamurti: With a Silent Mind*.

59. Chari, Ahalya. *Krishnamurti at Rajghat*, India: Krishnamurti Foundation,
     India, 1993.

60. For a fuller account see *Krishnamurti: A Biography* by Pupul Jayakar,
     New York: Harper and Row, 1986.

61. Conversation: Pupul Jayakar and Evelyne Blau, Rishi Valley, India,
     December 8, 1978.

62. From an address to the women of India at the annual meeting of the Women's Indian
     Association, Madras, India, 1928.

63. Krishnamurti, J., *Commentaries On Living*, Third Series, London: Victor Gollancz
     Ltd., pp. 32–33, 1960.

64. Interview for the film *Krishnamurti: With A Silent Mind*.

65. Ibid.

66. Ibid.

67. Smith, Ingram. *Truth Is A Pathless Land, A Journey with Krishnamurti*, Wheaton,
     Illinois: Quest Books, Theosophical Publishing House, 1989.

68. Interview for the film *Krishnamurti:With A Silent Mind*.

69. Ibid.

70. Ibid.

71. Albert, David Z. "Bohm's Alternative to Quantum Mechanics," *Scientific American*, Vol. 270, No. 5, May 1994.

72. Conversation: David Bohm and Evelyne Blau, Brockwood Park, September 2, 1978.

73. Interview for the film *Krishnamurti:With A Silent Mind*.

74. Conversation: Asha Lee and Evelyne Blau, Ojai, California, December 6, 1987.

75. Krishnamurti, J. *Think On These Things*, New York: Harper and Row, 1964, pp. 62–63.

76. Conversation: Erna Lilliefelt and Evelyne Blau, Ojai, California, June 12, 1992.

77. *Bulletin #3*, Ojai, California: Krishnamurti Foundation of America, Summer 1969.

78. Conversation: Giddu Narayanan and Evelyne Blau, Rishi Valley, India.

79. Shainberg, David, *Bulletin #26*, Ojai, California: Krishnamurti Foundation of America, Summer 1975.

80. Miller, Henry. *The Books in My Life*, London: Village Press, 1974.

81. Lee, R.E. Mark. "Do Teachers Have the Feeling of Unlimited Energy?" (written especially for *Krishnamurti: 100 Years*), 1994.

82. Krishnamurti, J. *Talks with American Students*, Boulder, Colorado: Shamballa, 1970, pp. 178–180.

83. Interview for the film *Krishnamurti:With A Silent Mind*.

84. Second public talk, San Diego, California, April 6, 1970.

85. *The Role of A Flower*, England: Krishnamurti Foundation Trust, 30-minute television program, 1985.

86. Brockwood Park, Question and Answer meeting, August 28, 1984. England, Krishnamurti Foundation Trust, 1984.

87. *The Star Bulletin*, September 1929, p. 28. Also compare the intriguing version presented in the book *Krishnamurti to Himself*, pp. 86–87. Entry dated Saturday, April 23, 1983.

88. Ojai, California, Fourth talk, May 19, 1985.

89. Krishnamurti, J. *The Network of Thought*, New York: Harper and Row, 1982, p. 99.

90. Kishbaugh, Alan. "Krishnamurti and the Gift of Freedom," (written especially for *Krishnamurti: 100 Years*), 1994.

91. Maroger, Jean Michel. "Krishnamurti, A Fundamental Discovery," (written especially for *Krishnamurti: 100 Years*), Pontlevoy, France, 1994.

92. Anderson, Alan W. "On Krishnamurti's Teaching: An Ongoing Personal Response," (written especially for *Krishnamurti: 100 Years*), La Jolla, California, 1994.

93. Colet, Robert. "Krishnamurti: The Spiritual Force Behind Bruce Lee," *Inside Kung Fu*, Burbank, California: C.F.W. Enterprises, 1986.

94. Interview for the film *Krishnamurti:With A Silent Mind*.

95. Hobson, Lois M. *Seek and Ye Shall Find: An Encounter with J. Krishnamurti*, written especially for this book, 1994.

96. Conversation: Sarjit Siddoo and Evelyne Blau, Vancouver, Canada, February 18, 1986.

97. Interview for the film *Krishnamurti:With A Silent Mind*.

98. Conversation: Mary Zimbalist and Evelyne Blau, Ojai, California, April 24, 1992.

99. Krishnamurti's next-to-last talk, Madras, India, January 1, 1986.

100. Interview for the film *Krishnamurti:With A Silent Mind*.

101. Ibid.

102. Ibid.

103. Deutsch, Gary M. "My Thoughts on Krishnaji: Notes from a Medical Journal," 1985-1986.

SELECT BIBLIOGRAPHY

BOOKS BY KRISHNAMURTI

- *At the Feet of the Master*. Adyar, Madras, India: Theosophical Publishing House, 1910.
- *Herald of the Star*, Quarterly (later Monthly). London: 1913-1927.
- *The Server*. Hollywood: Krotona, 1920-1927.
- *Life in Freedom*. New York: Horace Liveright, 1928.
- *International Star Bulletin*. Zwolle: Star Publishing Trust, 1928-1931.
- *Star Bulletin*. Ommen, Holland: Star Publishing Trust, 1932-1933.
- *Education and the Significance of Life*. New York: Harper & Row, 1953.
- *The First and Last Freedom*. New York: Harper & Row, 1954.
- *Commentaries on Living*, three volumes. New York: Harper & Row, 1956, 1959, 1960.
- *Think on These Things*. New York: Harper & Row, 1964.
- *Freedom from the Known*. New York: Harper & Row, 1969.
- *The Only Revolution*. New York: Harper & Row, 1970.
- *The Urgency of Change*. New York: Harper & Row, 1970.
- *The Flight of the Eagle*. New York: Harper & Row, 1971.
- *The Impossible Question*. New York: Harper & Row, 1972.
- *You Are the World*. New York: Harper & Row, 1972.
- *The Awakening of Intelligence*. New York: Harper & Row, 1973.
- *Beyond Violence*. New York: Harper & Row, 1973.
- *Krishnamurti's Notebook*. New York: Harper & Row, 1976.
- *Truth and Actuality*. New York: Harper & Row, 1978.
- *The Network of Thought*. New York: Harper & Row, 1982.
- *The Ending of Time*. Co-authored with David Bohm. San Francisco: Harper & Row, 1985.
- *The Collected Works of J. Krishnamurti*, seventeen volumes 1933-1967. Dubuque, Iowa: Kendall-Hunt Publishing Co., 1991.
- *A Wholly Different Way of Living*. London: Victor Gollancz, Ltd., 1991.

BOOKS OF POETRY BY KRISHNAMURTI

- *Come Away*. New York: Boni & Liveright, 1927.
- *The Search*. New York: Boni & Liveright, 1927.
- *The Immortal Friend*. New York: Boni & Liveright, 1928.
- *The Song of Life*. New York: Horace Liveright Inc., 1931.

BOOKS BY OTHER AUTHORS

- Arundale, George. *Thoughts on At the Feet of the Master*. Adyar, Madras, India: Theosophical Publishing House, 1919.
- Besant, Annie. *Annie Besant: An Autobiography*. London: T. Fisher Unwin, Ltd., 1893.
- ———. *The Immediate Future: Annie Besant 1911 Lectures*, Queens Hall, London. Chicago: Rajput Press, 1911.
- Besterman, Theodore. *Mrs. Annie Besant: A Modern Prophet*. London: Kegan Paul Trench, Trubner & Co. Ltd., 1934.
- Blavatsky, H. P. *The Secret Doctrine*. London: Theosophical Publishing Company, 1888.
- Bragdon, Claude. *More Lives than One*. New York: Alfred A. Knopf, 1938.
- Chandmal, Asit. *1000 Moons: Krishnamurti at 85*. New York: Abrams, 1985.

- Chari, Ahalya. *Krishnamurti at Rajghat*. Madras: Krishnamurti Foundation India, 1993.
- Clarke, Russell Balfour. *The Boyhood of J. Krishnamurti*. Bombay: Chetana, 1977.
- Field, Sidney. *Krishnamurti: The Reluctant Messiah*. New York: Paragon House, 1989.
- Holroyd, Stuart. *Krishnamurti: The Man, the Mystery, and the Message*. Shaftsbury, Dorset: Element, 1991.
- ————. *The Quest of the Quiet Mind: The Philosophy of Krishnamurti*. Wellingborough, Northamptonshire: The Aquarian Press, 1980.
- Jayakar, Pupul. *Indira Gandhi*. New Delhi: Viking India, 1992.
- ————. *Krishnamurti: A Biography*. New York: Harper & Row, 1986.
- Landau, Rom. *God Is My Adventure*. London: Ivor, Watson, Nicholson, 1935.
- Leadbeater, C. W. *The Lives of Alcyone*, Volumes I & II. Adyar, Madras, India: Theosophical Publishing House, 1924.
- ————. *The Masters and the Path*. Adyar, Madras, India: Theosophical Publishing House, 1925.
- Lee, Bruce. *The Tao of Jeet Kune Do*. Santa Clarita, California: Ohara Publications, Inc., 1975.
- Lutyens, Emily. *Candles in the Sun*. Philadelphia: J. B. Lippencott, 1957.
- Lutyens, Mary. *Krishnamurti: The Open Door*. London: John Murray, 1988.
- ————. *Krishnamurti: The Years of Awakening*. New York: Farrar, Straus & Giroux, 1975.
- ————. *Krishnamurti: The Years of Fulfillment*. New York: Farrar, Straus & Giroux, 1983.
- ————. *The Life and Death of Krishnamurti*. London: John Murray, 1990.
- Meade, Marion. *Mme Blavatsky: The Woman Behind the Myth*. New York: G.P. Putnam's Sons, 1980.
- Murphet, Howard. *Hammer on the Mountain: The Life of Henry Steel Olcott*. Wheaton, Illinois: Theosophical Publishing House, 1972.
- ————. *When Daylight Comes: A Biography of Helena Petrovna Blavatsky*. Wheaton, Illinois: Quest Books, 1972.
- Nearing, Helen. *Loving and Leaving the Good Life*. Vermont: Chelsea Green Publishing Co., 1992.
- Nethercot, Arthur H. *The First Five Lives of Annie Besant*. Chicago: University of Chicago Press, 1963.
- ————. *The Last Four Lives of Annie Besant*. Chicago: University of Chicago Press, 1963.
- Pavri, P. *The Coming World Teacher*. Adyar, Madras, India: Indian Star Headquarters, 1923.
- Taylor, Anne. *Annie Besant*. Oxford, England: Oxford University Press, 1992.
- Wachtmeister, Constance. *Reminiscences of H. P. Blavatsky*. Wheaton, Illinois: Theosophical Publishing House, 1976.
- Weeraperuma, S. *A Bibliography of the Life and Teachings of J. Krishnamurti*. Leiden: E.J. Brill, 1974.
- Williams, Gertrude Marvin. *The Passionate Pilgrim*. New York: McCann, 1931.
- ———— *Priestess of the Occult*. New York: Alfred A. Knopf, 1946.

INDEX

Abandonment, death as, 255

Acosta, Julio, 59

Adams, Ansel, 266

Affection, 154, 249

Aggression, 239

Aloneness
human fear of, 82–83
as human situation, 98

Analytic method, Krishnamurti's teachings correlated with, 81

Anderson, Alan W., 218–21

Androcles and the Lion (Shaw), 104, 105

Anthroposophy, 20

Archimedes, 163

Arcos, Tomas Povedano de, 59

Art
authority and, 70
of listening and learning, 196
mediums of expression in, 67
nature vs., 243
standard or criterion for beauty in, 69–70

Arundale, George, 21, 23, 36, 37, 41, 91

Attention
concentration compared with, 218
as negation, 219

At the Feet of the Master (Krishnamurti), 18, 59, 60, 146, 147

Authority
art and, 70
dependence on others for spiritual, 86–87
as form of self-deception, 167–68
people's search for spiritual, 79–80
of religion, 107
spiritual, 141
truth and, 53
See also Organizations

Awakening of Intelligence, The (Krishnamurti), 233, 234

Awareness
ego-process, 139–40, 165
Krishnamurti's use of term, 119
mind and, 110
repetitive thoughts and diminished, 116
sensory, 141, 196
See also God; Knowledge; Truth

Bach, Johann Sebastian, 243

Bal Anand school, 147

Balasundaram (school principal), 173

Barrymore, John, 58

Beatniks, 122

Beauty, 61
in art, 69–70

Beethoven, Ludwig van, 243, 265

Besant, Annie, 6, 7, 8, 11, 17, 18, 19, 20, 21, 23, 25, 26, 29, 32, 36, 37, 41, 42, 44, 47, 50, 54, 76, 82, 83, 91, 91, 96, 106, 127, 129, 130, 146
first meeting with Krishnamurti, 14
Krishnamurti's relationship with, 55
political activities, 78–79

Besant, Frank, 7

Besterman, Theodore, 92

Bhave, Vinoba, 144

Bhoodan movement, 144

Biascoechea, Enrique, 221

Biascoechea, Isabel, 221

Blau, Evelyne, 258–59, 262, 263–64

Blavatsky, Helena Petrovna, 6–7, 8, 44, 91, 146

Bohm, David, 157–68, 170, 190, 234

Bohm, Sarel, 159

Bohr, Nils, 158

Bolgar, Hedda, 78–83, 259

Books, 238

Bourdelle, Antoine, 64, 66

Boyar, Angel Patrick, 202–7

Brockwood Park Education Center, 155, 180, 198

Buchenwald Concentration Camp, 113

Buddha, 58, 81, 135, 139, 141, 165, 171, 174, 225

Buddhism, 8, 213, 225–26, 239

Burton, Jack, 44

Cadogan, Mary, 147, 149–52, 184, 262, 263

Campbell, Joseph, 64–65

Castle Eerde, 43, 64, 65

Catholic Church, 59, 106

Central Hindu College, 8

Challenge of Change, The (film), 264

Chandmal, Asit, 256–58, 263, 266

Chaplin, Charlie, 109–10

Chari, Ahalya, 122, 127–29

Chesterton, G. K., 238

Chicanos, 204–5

Children
education of, 194
psychological development, 81, 192

Chopra, Deepak, 233

Christianity, 7, 8, 238

Churchill, Winston, 112
Citizen Tom Paine (Fast), 169
Clarke, Russell Balfour, 10, 11–14,
    17, 23, 42
Colell, Juan, 221–22
Colet, Robert, 222–24
Collective consciousness, of
    humanity, 142–43
Collectivity, freedom and happiness
    and, 68
Come Away (Krishnamurti), 61
Commentaries on Living
    (Krishnamurti), 159
Compassion, 71, 142
Competitiveness, 239
Concentration, attention compared
    with, 218
Consciousness
    distinct entities within, 165
    stream of, 158
Conspiracy thinking, 205
"Contra Krishnamurti" (Catholic
    Church pamphlet), 106
Cordes, John, 52
Cosmology, 159
Costa Rica, 59
Coyne, Alasdair, 230–32
"Creative reality", 110
Creativity, 69. *See also* Art
"Credo" (Jeffers), 105

Death
    as abandonment, 255
    meaning of, 254
de la Warr (Lady), 23
de Manziarly (Madame), 36
Desikachar, Shribhashyam, 176
Desikacher, T. K. V., 176–79
Desnick, Julie, 198
Deutsch, Deborah, 253
Deutsch, Gary M., 253–56, 262,
    264–67
Development, children's
    psychological, 81, 192
Dialectics, of thought, 160
Disciples, 76, 86
Djwal Kul (master), 12
Dodge, Mary, 182
Dogma, rejection of, 92
Dossey, Larry, 238
Drug use, 123

Eastwood, Clint, 266
Eddy family, 6
Education
    art of listening and learning, 196
    of children, 194
    freedom and, 128
    function of, 194
    good of knowledge vs. limitation
        of knowledge, 244

thinking and, 164
*Education and the Significance of
    Life* (Krishnamurti), 147,
    152
Eerde Castle, 112–13
Ego-process, 139–40
    energy waste and, 165
Einstein, Albert, 157, 158, 159,
    163, 238
Emotion, 141–42
Energy
    as discrete units, 157–58
    ego-process and waste of, 165
    life as, 154
Enter the Dragon (film), 224
Essence, existence and, 218–19
Europe
    conditions prior to World
        War II, 111
    post World War I conditions in,
        78
Evil, resistance to, 118
Existence, essence and, 218–19

Fabian Society, 7, 78
Fast, Howard, 169–71
FBI, 115
Fear, 124
    freedom from, 93
    root of, 191
Federal Bureau of Investigation
    (FBI), 115
Field, Sidney, 57–61, 115
Fifty Years of My Life
    (Krishnamurti), 5, 13, 15
First and Last Freedom, The
    (Krishnamurti), 147, 152
Flagg, James Montgomery, 27
Followers, 76
    Krishnamurti's rejection of
        necessity to have, 86
Forbes, Scott, 264, 267
Foundation for New Education,
    152
Franco, Francisco, 108
Freedom
    centrality to Krishnamurti, 213
    education and, 128
    from fear, 93
    happiness and collectivity and,
        68
    Krishnamurti's desire for, 86
    liberation compared with, 213
    prison and, 207
    psychological, 126
Freud, Sigmund, 125, 191
Friendship, 87
Fromm, Erich, 124, 203

Gandhi, Indira, 130
Gandhi, Mohandas K., 129, 139

Garbo, Greta, 109–10
God
    desire to know of existence of,
        108
    meaning of, 92
    as unknown, 160
    war and, 118
    See also Awareness; Knowledge;
        Religion; Truth
Goddard, Paulette, 109–10
God Is My Adventure (Landau),
    106
Graham, Billy, 180
Gray, Mary, 29
"Great White Lodge", 8
Gregory, Angela, 64
Grohe, Friedrich, 216–17
Gurdjief, G.I., 159

Hammond, Jane, 263
Happiness, freedom and collectivity
    and, 68
Happy Valley Association, 129
Hate, 175
Haydn, Franz Joseph, 243
Healing Words (Dossey), 238
Heard, Gerald, 109
Hearing, seeing and, 220
Hegel, Georg Wilhelm Friedrich,
    160
Heraclitus, 218
Herald of the Star, The
    (magazine), 19, 21, 23
Herzberger, Hans, 259
Herzberger, Radhika, 263
    259–61
Hinduism, 8
Hippies, 122, 212–13
Hitler, Adolf, 108, 111, 118
Hobson, Lois, 233–34
Holland. See Netherlands;
    Ommen, Netherlands
Hooker, Alan, 180, 181
Horney, Karen, 124, 191
House Un-American Activities
    Committee (HUAC),
    157
Humanity
    collective consciousness of,
        142–43
    destiny as undivided whole,
        140–41
Humor, 209–10
Huxley, Aldous, 96, 109, 110,
    115, 123, 129, 147
Huxley, Maria, 109
Huxley, Matthew, 109

Identity, life and, 203
Ideology, 222, 223
    pacifism as, 118

Ignorance, knowledge as discovery
    of, 207
Image, 143, 156, 204
Imagination
    overweening confidence in, 218
    thought as show of, 165
Immortal Friend, The
    (Krishnamurti), 61
Immortality, search for security and
    desire for, 107
Impossible Question, The
    (Krishnamurti), 216
Independence, human problems
    concerning, 82–83
India
    exploitation in, 102
    factionalism in, 139
    independence, 129
    liberation movement in, 79, 129
    material conditions in, 108
    plight of women in, 128
    women and poverty in, 132
Información, La (newspaper), 59
Ingleman, John, 105
Initiation
    Krishnamurti repudiates ritual
        of, 37
    into Theosophical Society, 17
Insight, thought and, 163
Insight and the Religious Mind: An
    Analysis of Krishnamurti's
    Thought (Rodrigues), 226,
    227
Inspiration, intelligence and, 67–69
Intelligence
    inspiration and, 67–69
    See also Knowledge; Truth
"In the Garden" (Van Morrison),
    237
Intuition, 68, 69
    primal, 220
Isherwood, Christopher, 109–10
Isis Unveiled (Blavatsky), 7
Iyengar, B. K. S., 176

James, William, 158
Jayakar, Pupul, 122, 130–37, 147,
    259, 263, 266
Jealousy, 94–95
Jeet Kune Do (martial art form),
    222–23
Jeffers, Robinson, 105
Jesus Christ, 65, 71, 81
Jews, 149
    during World War II, 111, 112,
    113
Jiddu, Krishnamurti. See
    Krishnamurti, Jiddu
Jiddu, Narayaniah (Krishnamurti's
    father), 3, 4, 12, 14, 17, 20,
    23

retirement of, 6
Jiddu, Nityananda (Krishnamurti's
        brother), 3, 22, 25, 26, 37,
        47, 48, 51, 52, 54, 57, 64,
        83, 93, 94, 118
    death of, 37
    deterioration of health, 36
    develops tuberculosis, 29
    first visit to England, 20–21
    Krishnamurti's reflections on
        death of, 38–39
    Krishnamurti's relationship
        with, 54–55
    Leadbeater first meets, 10
    relationship with Krishnamurti
        following death of mother, 4
    strain of travel affects health,
        35
Jiddu, Sadanand (Krishnamurti's
        brother), 3
Jiddu, Sanjeevama (Krishnamurti's
        mother), 3
    death of, 4
Jinarajadasa, C., 36, 92
Jokes, 209–10
Jubilee Convention, 41–42
Jung, Carl, 220

Keats, John, 198
Keller, Helen, 166–67
Keyserling (count), 18
KFA History (Lilliefelt), 184
Kingdom of Happiness, The
        (Krishnamurti), 64
Kishbaugh, Alan, 212–13
Knothe, Helen. See Nearing, Helen
        Knothe
Knowledge
    as discovery of ignorance, 207
    of God, 108
    instantaneousness of, 103
    and limitation of thought, 244
    mind and awareness and, 110
    in present, 182
    science as, 116
    search for, 56
    self-knowledge, 156, 164, 215
    sharing of, 206
    silence of mind and, 260
    See also Awareness; Truth
Korean War, 122
Krishna (god), 3, 134
Krishna, P., 199–202
Krishnamacharya, T., 176
Krishnamurti, Jiddu
    affection for people, 212
    applies to university, 26
    arrival at Adyar, 41
    audience of, 170–71
    on authority and truth, 53
    on beauty, 61

Krishnamurti, Jiddu (cont.)
    birth, 3
    Buddhism and, 225
    at Castle Eerde, 43–47
    changes during life, 142
    companionship with, 120
    on compassion, 71
    compassion for poor, 128–29
    on concentration, 218
    concern over brother's health,
        36, 37
    courage and risks taken by, 92
    on death, 254
    death of, 267
    death of brother, 37, 47
    death of mother, 4
    desire for freedom, 86
    dialectical nature of thought of,
        160
    difficulties in school, 10
    on discovery of truth, 70
    dissolves Order of the Star in the
        East, 85–87
    earliest blessings and devotions
        to, 22
    ends Krishnamurti Writings,
        Inc. relationship, 182, 183
    estrangement from Theosophical
        Society, 55
    as exponent of dialogue, 190
    extraordinariness of, 44–45, 236
    family of. See listings of
        members under surname
        Jiddu
    first California visit, 29–32
    first initiation, 17
    first literary endeavor, 4
    first meeting with Besant, 14
    first visit to England, 20–21
    on followers, 86
    greatness as teacher, 80–81
    has transforming experience,
        32–35
    health of, 147, 178, 253, 255–
        56, 257, 258, 262, 263–67
    importance of teachings, 108
    independence as preoccupation
        of, 83
    independence of thought and
        character, 82
    innocent nature of, 120
    interest in politics, 243
    on jealousy, 94–95
    at Jubilee Convention, 41
    on knowledge, 260
    language style of, 92, 150, 227,
        245, 261
    last talk given by, 257
    Leadbeater first meets, 10
    legacy of, 185, 249, 270
    literary output, 61

Krishnamurti, Jiddu (cont.)
  on love and hate, 175
  love of detective stories, 99
  love of music, 243
  love of nature, 212, 215, 229,
      243
  made into cult figure, 20
  on meaning of God, 92
  meditation, 119–20, 201, 205,
      241, 246, 250
  as mystic, 170
  Oak Grove School and, 194–97
  as object of curiosity, 29
  on organizations and societies,
      47–48
  as pacifist, 115, 118
  passion for automobiles, 45, 46
  on peace, 118
  perceptions of mind, 124
  personality of, 60, 150–51, 208,
      259
  personal relationships, 131–32
  physical beauty, 97
  playful side of, 132–34
  poetry, 61
  position on social action, 144–45
  presence of, 154–55
  prisoner's commentary on,
      202–7
  "process, the", 35, 51-52, 122
  questioning nature of, 83, 99, 199
  questions Theosophical ideas, 25
  radio talk banned in
      New Zealand, 104–5
  Rajghat Besant School and,
      127–29
  recounts miracle, 189–90
  reflections on death of brother,
      38–39
  relationship with Besant, 55
  relationship with brother, 54–55
  relationship with Nityananda
      following death of mother, 4
  and resistance to evil, 118
  return to Ojai, 36
  romantic relationship, 50
  sacred thread ceremony, 4
  on science as knowledge, 116
  on search for God, 108
  on search for knowledge, 56
  on search for security and desire
      for immortality, 107
  second visit to England, 37
  on self-transformation and
      transformation of world, 106
  sense of humor, 208, 209–10
  sensory awareness, 141, 196
  sexuality ideas, 120–21
  shyness of, 50, 180–81
  sickliness in childhood, 3–4

Krishnamurti, Jiddu (cont.)
  simple manners and humor of,
      27
  on social transformation, 100
  speculations on own death, 153
  on stagnation in life, 76
  start of mission, 29
  on teaching and disciples, 76
  teaching style, 169–70
  on true friendship, 87
  on truth, 85–86
  varied interests of, 242–43
  on war and strife, 115
  on women and men, 137
  as world teacher, 27, 46
  on world teacher, 71, 86, 93
  yoga practice, 176–79
Krishnamurti: The Challenge of
    Change (film), 228
Krishnamurti: The Reluctant
    Messiah (Field), 59
Krishnamurti: With a Silent Mind
    (film), 228, 256
Krishnamurti at Rajghat (Chari),
    127
Krishnamurti Foundation of
    America, 184, 194, 202
Krishnamurti Foundation of India,
    91, 184
Krishnamurti Foundation Trust,
    183, 184, 187
Krishnamurti's Notebook
    (Krishnamurti), 136, 215
Krishnamurti Writings, Inc., 152,
    182, 183, 187, 189
Krohnen, Michael, 208–10, 269
Kundalini, 52
Kuthumi (master), 12, 146
KW Inc. See Krishnamurti
    Writings, Inc.

Landau, Rom, 106
Language, Krishnamurti's style of
    use of, 92, 150, 227, 245,
    261
Larsen, Robin, 64
Larsen, Stephen, 64
Laughter, 209
Leadbeater, Charles Webster, 8,
    10, 12, 17, 18, 20, 22, 23,
    35, 36, 41, 42, 47, 54, 79,
    91, 106, 146
Lee, Asha, 172–75, 194
Lee, Bruce, 222–24
Lee, R. E. Mark, 172, 194–97,
    264
Liberation
  definition of, 121
  freedom compared with, 213
  happiness and, 68
  love and, 121

will and symbol system and, 110
Life
    death and, 254
    as energy, 154
    function of, 70
    identity and, 203
    insight as essence of, 163
    manner of living, 148
    self as master of own, 261
    stagnation in, 76
    transcendent spontaneity of, 110
Light of Asia, The (play), 94
Lilliefelt, Erna, 184–86, 262, 263
Lilliefelt, Theodor, 184, 262
Lincoln, Abraham, 6
Links, Joseph, 263
Lives of Alcyone (Leadbeater), 17
Logan, Robert, 96
Logan, Sarah, 96
Loneliness, human fear of, 82–83
Loos, Anita, 109–10
Love, 110, 249
    cultivation of, 197
    hate and, 175
    liberation and, 121
    observer and observed and, 197
    peace as way to, 118
    psychoanalysis and, 125
    removal of "me" from, 198
    thought and destruction of, 148
Lutyens, Edward, 21
Lutyens, Emily, 21, 23, 36, 37, 41,
    50, 51, 55, 60, 76, 249
Lutyens, Mary, 91, 249, 263,
    273n42
Lytton, Bulwer, 21

McCarthy, Joseph, 122, 157, 168
Macduff, Robert, 112
McFarlane (FBI agent), 115
Maroger, Diane, 215
Maroger, Jean-Michel, 214–16
Martial arts, 222–24
Matter, discreteness of, 157
Meditation, 201, 205, 241, 246,
    250
    Buddhist practices, 239
    meaning to Krishnamurti,
        119–20
    mind and awareness and, 110
Mehta, Nandini, 134, 147
Mendizza, Michael, 228–29
Messiah, people's search for,
    79–80
Mexican Mafia, 204
Michelangeli (pianist), 243
Miller, Henry, 193
Mind
    "creative reality" and, 110
    knowledge and silence of, 260

Krishnamurti's perceptions of,
    124
perception and state of, 166
See also Awareness; Knowledge;
    Thought
Miracles, Krishnamurti recounts,
    189–90
Mohammed (prophet), 81
Mozart, Amadeus, 198, 243
Muller, Lex, 111
Music, Krishnamurti's love of, 243
Mussolini, Benito, 108
Mysticism, 120, 170

Narayanan, Giddu, 189–90
Nationalism, 91, 149
Nature
    art vs., 243
    Krishnamurti's love of, 212,
        215, 229, 243
Naudé, Alain, 176, 184
Naziism, 112–13
Nearing, Helen Knothe, 48–56,
    64, 65
Nearing, Scott, 48
Negation
    attention as, 219
    perception and seeing and, 226
Netherlands
    during World War II, 112–13
    See also Ommen, Netherlands
Newton, Isaac, 163
New York Herald, The, 41
New York Times, The, 41
New Zealand, Krishnamurti's radio
    talk banned in, 104–5
Ninth Symphony (Beethoven), 265
*Nobody, Somebody, the Experience
    of Being Alive: A Desultory
    Prison Journal* (Boyar), 202
No Guru, No Method, No Teacher
    (Van Morrison), 237
Non-verbal sensitivity, 143
Nonviolence, as ideology, 118
Nostradamus, 204

Oak Grove School, 185, 194–97
Object, contradiction between
    subject and, 220
Observation
    love and, 197
    thought and consciousness and,
        165–66
    transformation and, 158
Occult hierarchies, 41
Ojai, California, 95, 121–22, 129
    cuisine at, 181
    first visit to, 29–32
    Oak Grove School at, 194–97
    return to, 36
Olcott, Henry Steel, 6–7, 91

Ommen, Netherlands, 36, 43,
44–47, 48, 60, 65, 78, 82,
83, 95
during World War II, 111
One Thousand Moons:
Krishnamurti at 85
(Chandmal), 256
Oppenheimer, J. Robert, 157
Order of the Star in the East, 19,
22, 23, 27, 29, 43, 56, 58–
59, 71, 80, 81, 82, 96–97,
149, 210
dissolution of, 85–87
Organizations
deterioration into spiritual
crutches, 86
futility of efficacy of, 87
Krishnamurti's dislike of, 47–48
systemized thought and, 93
See also Authority
Ortega y Gasset, José, 218
Otherness, 246
Ouspensky, P. D., 159
Outlaw Josie Wales, The (film),
266

Pacifism
as ideology, 118
Krishnamurti's belief in, 115
Parchure, T., 254, 258, 262, 263,
264
Pathless Land, The (Krishnamurti),
263
Patwardhan, Achyut, 139–40, 144
Patwardhan, Pama, 140, 144–45
Patwardhan, Sunanda, 140–43, 144
Peace, as way of truth and love,
118
Pearce, Gordon, 146
Pearl Harbor attack, 115
Perception
negation and, 226
state of mind affecting, 166
Philosophy, martial arts and, 222
Physics, quantum, 157–68
Poetry, 61
Pole, Reginald, 94
Poles, during World War II, 113
Political action, Krishnamurti's
position on, 144–45
Politics, Krishnamurti's interest
in, 243
Porter, Mima, 94
Poverty
compassion for poor, 128–29
in India, 132
Pratt, Doris, 147–48, 150, 152,
159, 182, 184
Primal intuition, 220
Prison, prisoner's commentary on
Krishnamurti, 202–7

"Process, The", 35, 51–52, 122
Process (in general)
as movement forward, 219–20
thought and, 192
Prokoviev, Sergey (composer), 116
Psyche, 220
Psychoanalysis, 81, 124–26,
191–93
Psychological development, of
children, 81, 192
Psychotherapy, patients'
improvement, 191–92
Purity, as uncontaminated
perception, 119–20

Quantum physics, 157–68
Quinn, William, 116–23, 262

Rajagopal, 36, 37, 42, 47, 64, 93,
94, 95, 96, 104, 105, 115,
121, 147, 152, 182, 184,
185, 187, 190
Rajghat Besant School, 127–29
Ramakrishna Vedanta, 149
Rao, Rama, 36
Rao, Sanjeeva, 127, 130, 131
Rao, Shiva, 37
Relationships
actions affecting, 100
society and transformation of,
168
Religion, 227
immortality promised by, 107
role of religious figures, 81–82
as systemized forms of thought,
93
true religion, 92
See also God
Resistance, to evil, 118
Review of Reviews (journal), 7
Revolution
as moment of seeing
conditioning, 213
salvation as inner, 236
thought and, 140
Richter, Sviatoslav (pianist), 243
Rinpoche, S., 225–26
Rioch, David, 124
Rioch, Margaret, 124
Rodrigues, Hillary Peter, 226–28
Rogers, Carl, 191
Roman Catholic Church, 59, 106
Rowlands, Alan, 180–81
Russell, Bertrand, 109–10

Saanen gatherings, 153, 182
Sacred thread ceremony, 4
St. John of the Cross, 120
Salvation, as inner revolution, 236

Sanity
    definition of, 212
    human independence and,
        82–83
Savior, people's search for, 79–80
Scaravelli, Vanda, 108, 184
Science
    as knowledge, 116
    mysticism and, 170
    quantum physics, 157–68
    tentative character of
        formulation of, 117
    World War II and, 116–17
Search, The (Krishnamurti), 61
"Secret Brotherhood", 8
Secret Doctrine, The (Blavatsky),
        7, 44
Security
    desire for immortality and search
        for, 107
    psychological, 193
Seeing
    clarity in, 179
    hearing and, 220
Self-deception, authority as form
        of, 167–68
Self-involvement, 125
Self-knowledge, 156, 164, 215
Senses
    awareness, 196
    importance of role of, 141
Sentiment, 141–42
Sexuality, chastity vs. practice,
        120–21
Shainberg, David, 124, 190–93
Shaw, George Bernard, 7, 94, 104
Shrowthulu, Kumara, 3
Siddoo, Jugdis, 234
Siddoo, Sarjit, 234–36
Silence, of mind, 260
Simmons, Dorothy, 147, 153–55,
        180, 214, 263
Smith, Ingram, 146, 181–82
Social action, Krishnamurti's
        position on, 144–45
Social work, 131, 132
Society
    inner solution for troubles of,
        170
    transformation of, 100
    and transformation of
        relationships, 168
Socrates, 218
Song of Life, The (Krishnamurti),
        61
Sorrow, transformation and, 182
Spanish Revolution (1936–39), 108
Spartacus (Fast), 169
Spirit, unfolding of energies, 123
Stagnation, in life, 76

Star Camp, Ommen, Netherlands,
        36, 43, 44–47, 48, 60, 65,
        78, 82, 83, 95
    World War II use of, 111
Star Congress, 41–42
Star Publishing Trust, 91
Stead, W. T., 7
Steiner, Rudolph, 20
Stowkowski, Leopold, 67–70
Strife, 115
Subject, contradiction between
        object and, 220
Sullivan, Ann, 166
Sullivan, Harry Stack, 124, 191
Sviatoslav (musician), 243

Takahashi, Shigatoshi, 238–39
Talmadge, Norma, 58
Teaching
    of masses vs. disciples, 76
    See also Education; World
        teacher
Telang (representative), 22
Tettemer, Ruth, 184
"Thank You Sir!" (Krohnen), 269
Theosophical Society, 6–7, 8, 19,
        25, 26, 36, 44, 46, 59, 65,
        82, 146
    belief in past lives, 17
    brothers' first contact with, 10
    conflict within, 91–92
    Krishnamurti's estrangement
        from, 55
    Krishnamurti's initiation into, 17
Theosophy, 23, 149, 162, 186
    roots of, 6–7
Thought
    Buddhist constructs, 225–26
    calculative and meditative
        compared, 221
    and destruction of love, 148
    dialectics of, 160
    education and, 164
    insight and, 163
    intrinsic limitation of, 139–40
    knowledge and limitation of,
        244
    as material process, 164
    organizations and systemization
        of, 93
    process and, 192
    revolution and, 140
    and seeing of totality, 223
    as show of imagination, 165
    time and, 167
    See also Awareness; Knowledge;
        Mind
Tibet, 225
Time, thought and, 167
Times of India, The, 41
Tinoco, Federico, 59

Tolstoy, Leo, 94
Transformation
   beginning of sorrow and, 182
   immediacy of, 182
   inner solution for troubles of
      society, 170
   role of observation in, 158
   of self and world, 100
   self-transformation and
      transformation of world, 106
Transformation of Man, The (video
   series), 190
Transforming Self, The
   (Shainberg), 190
Trees, love of, 229
Truth
   authority and, 53
   authority and belief and, 168
   codification of, 26, 47–48
   discovery of, 70
   followers and, 86
   and force of necessity, 164
   instantaneousness of, 103
   and knowledge of God, 108
   as pathless land, 85
   peace as way to, 118
   relativeness vs. absoluteness of,
      69
   repetition and, 92
   and seeing of false, 220
   as unknown, 160
   See also Awareness; Knowledge;
      Mind

Understanding
   in present, 182
   See also Awareness; Knowledge;
      Mind; Thought; Truth
Universe, as indivisible, 158
Upanayanama (sacred thread
   ceremony), 4

van Hook, Hubert, 272n7
van Manen, Johann, 8, 10, 12
Van Morrison (musician), 237
Van Pallandt, Phillip, 43, 44–47,
   48, 50, 112–13
Vasanta Vihar, 91, 176
Violence, 118

Wadia (Theosophical lecturer), 44,
   48
Walton (Liberal Catholic vicar), 32
Warrington, A. P., 29, 32, 33
Washington Psychoanalytic Society,
   124
Watts, Alan, 123
Webb, Sidney, 7
Wedgewood, James Ingall, 37, 92
Wedgewood, Josiah, 92
Weinniger, Benjamin, 124–26

Wholly Different Way of Living, A
   (Krishnamurti), 218, 219
Williams, Rosalind, 32, 36, 37, 64,
   95, 96, 105, 121, 129
Wing Chun (martial art form), 224
Wisdom
   mind and awareness and, 110
   See also Awareness; Knowledge;
      Truth
Wolfe, Harry, 101–3
Women
   and men compared, 137
   plight in India of, 128
   sensuality and dress, 97–98
   status in India, 132
Wood, Beatrice, 94–103
Wood, Ernest, 10
World
   actions affecting, 100
   individual reflected in, 141
   self-transformation and changing
      of, 106
World teacher, 27, 36, 42, 46, 71,
   82, 86, 272n7
   idea germinates, 8
   interdenominational nature of,
      79
   meaning and value attached to
      term, 93
   See also Education
World War I, 25, 78
World War II, 111
   individual responsibility for,
      118–19
   Krishnamurti's life in Ojai
      during, 122
   Krishnamurti's pacifism during,
      115
   Netherlands during, 112–13
   science and, 116–17
Writing, problems and process in,
   169

Yoga, 110, 147, 149, 176–79
Youth
   Chicano, 204–5
   drug use, 123
   Krishnamurti's interest in, 58
   1960s movement of, 122,
      212–13

Zen, 169, 171, 239
Zimbalist, Mary, 184, 214, 215,
   242–49, 253, 258, 262,
   264, 267